Leonidas Le Cenci Hamilton

Hamilton's Mexican handbook

A complete description of the republic of Mexico

Leonidas Le Cenci Hamilton

Hamilton's Mexican handbook
A complete description of the republic of Mexico

ISBN/EAN: 9783337210908

Printed in Europe, USA, Canada, Australia, Japan

Cover: Foto ©ninafisch / pixelio.de

More available books at **www.hansebooks.com**

GEN'L PORFIRIO DIAZ, Ex-President of the Republic.

HAMILTON'S
MEXICAN HANDBOOK;

A COMPLETE DESCRIPTION

of the

REPUBLIC OF MEXICO,

**Its Mineral and Agricultural Resources, Cities
and Towns of every State, Factories, Trade, Imports
and Exports, how legally to acquire property in
Mexico, how to transact business under
Mexican laws, Railroads and
travelling in the Republic,
Tariff Regulations,
Duties, &c.,&c.**

and a Commercial Directory of the

PRINCIPAL BUSINESS MEN OF MEXICO;

Combining practical information for ready reference by the

Merchant, Miner, Real Estate Investor, Railroad Builder,

Mining Engineer and Locator, Traveller and Settler.

BY

LEONIDAS LE CENCI HAMILTON, M.A.

**Author of the "Border States of Mexico," "Hamilton's
Mexican Law," &c.**

ILLUSTRATED.

London :
SAMPSON LOW, MARSTON, SEARLE, AND RIVINGTON,
CROWN BUILDINGS, 188, FLEET STREET.
1884.

LONDON :
GILBERT AND RIVINGTON, LIMITED,
ST. JOHN'S SQUARE.

INTRODUCTION.

The favorable reception accorded the publication of the "Border States of Mexico," some four editions having been sold since its first publication in San Francisco in 1851, has induced us to enlarge and revise the work until it has assumed the form herewith presented. We have endeavored to make the volume useful for reference and information, and entirely impartial, and have had access to Mexican official records and documents, besides many works extant on Mexico in the English and Spanish languages, which we have utilized in collecting the data presented. The details have been carefully collected in many instances from inaccessible reports of mining experts and travellers, and we have sought to give only the facts as we find them without unnecessary embellishment or fanciful description. The principal object of the work has been to give reliable data to those who desire information on the business opportunities of Mexico, whether for investment in real estate, mines, railroads, or any other enterprise, as well as the opportunities for trade. With the good opportunities offered by Mexico, we have also attempted to point out the unfavorable features in order to give the facts, and allowing every one to use their own judgment. While Mexico offers great inducements to foreign capital for legitimate enterprises, it is to be deplored that her great mining industries should be injured by unworthy enterprises fostered by unscrupulous adventurers, and bad and extravagant management of inexperienced mining men. This will at last be ended and her incalculable resources in minerals and agricultural productions will be developed by energetic and prudent capitalists.

1

A thorough acquaintance with Mexico and its people is what the business man wants, and no book of travel can supply the data necessary. The information must be complete in detail, giving a description of the republic, its resources, its productions, exports and imports, its business rules applicable to foreigners, its tariff regulations, a list of its principal business men, and the exact status of its trade ; the description of its cities and towns, and number of their inhabitants, its factories and various industrial establishments; and lastly, a description of its great mineral wealth, which has given the great country of the Moctezumas the foremost rank among the silver-producing regions of the world. While we have not ignored the information necessary for the tourist and traveller, we have attempted to give to the public a book intended for the business man, containing practical business information.

Respectfully submitted,

LEONIDAS LE CENCI HAMILTON.

LONDON, MARCH, 1884.

CONTENTS.

GEN'L MANUEL GONZALEZ, President.

GENERAL DESCRIPTION

OF THE

REPUBLIC OF MEXICO.

Physical Features.

The Mexican Republic is a land of marvels for the scientist, and, with its grand gorges, deep *barrancas*, lofty mountain peaks, beautiful valleys, elevated *mesas*, and ancient cities nestling among unrivaled scenery, will always be an object of interest to the traveler. Within its 1,224,996 square miles of territory, the shores of which are washed by two oceans, may be found a greater variety of scenery, climate, productions in agriculture, and minerals than in any equal area. Its series of mountain chains and elevated plateaus, extending from the northwest to the southeast the entire length of the Republic, have yielded immense mineral wealth, and contain within them deposits of all the known metals. These two great ranges of mountains, one on the eastern and the other on the western boundary, form a continuous chain with the great *mesas* in the center, and slope gradually down toward the Pacific Ocean on one side and the Mexican Gulf on the other, interrupted by plateaus, on which towns are to be found on the lakes, rivers, and amidst luxuriant vegetation. The varying altitudes produce a diversity of climate, ranging from the cold through the temperate to the torrid, and a wonderful variety of fruits and flowers of every description, from the European apple and rose to the Cuban guava and cactus, beside other species unknown to any other country.

Political Divisions and Population.

The present population of the Republic, as near as can be estimated from the work of Antonio Garcia Cubas of the city of Mexico, is somewhere in the neighborhood of

9,525,000, in round numbers, taking into account an increase since 1876: divided among the different states, as follows :

Sonora	125,000	Oaxaca	680,000
Coahuila	115,000	Chiapas	200,000
Chihuahua	190,000	Durango	185,000
New Leon	200,000	Zacatecas	420,000
Tamaulipas	180,000	Aguas Calientes	100,000
Vera Cruz	550,000	San Luis Potosi	555,000
Tobasco	100,000	Guanajuato	900,000
Campeachy	95,000	Queretaro	170,000
Yucatan	350,000	Hidalgo	430,000
Sinaloa	200,000	Mexico	750,000
Jalisco	980,000	Morelos	150,000
Colima	75,000	Puebla	750,000
Michoacan	620,000	Tlaxcala	130,000
Guerrero	350,000		
Total			9,500,000

With the territory of Lower California, which Antonio Garcia Cubas, in his geography of Mexico, places at 23,195, in 1874, the population of the whole republic may be estimated at about 9,525,000, allowing an increase in Lower California, up to 1880, or about six years, of about 2,000 more.

National and State Governments.

Under the present Constitution of the Republic, adopted February 5th, 1857, the Government was organized with three branches: Legislative, Executive, and Judicial—Congress, President and Cabinet, and Supreme and Circuit and District Courts.

The supreme legislative power is vested in the Congress of the Union, composed of a Senate and Chamber of Deputies. The members are elected by secret ballot, deposited by Electors chosen by the people. One Elector is chosen for every five hundred inhabitants, and one for every fraction thereof, in each Congressional district. The Senators are elected at the same time as the Deputies—two for each State and one for the Federal District and Territory of Lower California respectively. A Deputy is chosen for each 40,000 inhabitants and one for every fraction over 20,000. Substitute Senators and Deputies are chosen at the same time and in the same manner. In order to be eligible for the officer of Senator it is requisite to be a Mexican citizen in the full exercise

MUNICIPAL PALACE.

of his rights, thirty years of age at the opening of the session, resident of the State or Territory he represents, and not to be an ecclesiastic. The Deputies must be of the age of twenty-five years and possessed of the other qualifications demanded from Senators. Each Chamber of Congress decides with regard to the election of its members, and determines any doubts that may occur regarding the same. Over one-half the total number constitutes a quorum in the Chamber of Deputies. The quorum of the Senate consists of two-thirds of the members elected. Two ordinary sessions are held each year. The first commences on the 16th of September and terminates on the 15th of December; the second commences of the 1st day of April and ends on the last day of May.

The President is elected by secret ballot by Electors, in the same manner as Senators and Deputies, taking his seat on the 1st of December, for the period of four years, and he is ineligible to a re-election to a second term without another intervening. To be eligible to this office he must be a native citizen, thirty-five years of age at time of election, and *not to belong to the ecclesiastical state*, and a resident of the Repulic. The Cabinet is appointed by the President, and consists of Secretaries of Foreign Relations, Treasury, War and Navy. Interior and Public Works. Eligibility to these offices require the candidate to be a native citizen and twenty-five years of age. The President and Cabinet constitute the Executive branch of the Government.

The Judicial power is vested in a Supreme Court and Circuit and District Courts. The Supreme Court is composed of eleven Judges Proprietary, four Supernumeraries, one Attorney-General and one Solicitor-General. The term of office is for six years. This body is also chosen by Electors. To be eligible it is necessary to be a native citizen, "instructed in the science of law in the opinion of the Electors," and over thirty-five years of age. The Judicial Circuits are eight in number, presided over by Circuit Judges, appointed by the Executive at the request of the Supreme Court. These Circuit Courts convene at the following cities: Mexico, Mazatlan, Celaya, Durango, Guadalajara, Monterey, Merida, and Puebla. There are thirty-one District Judges, distributed as follows: Two in Mexico, two in Tamaulipas, and one in each of the other States and Territory, appointed in the same manner as the Circuit Judges. The District-Attorneys of each District and Circuit are appointed by the Executive, also.

The State Governments are divided into three parts—the

Executive (Governor), Legislature, and Judiciary." The The Governor and Legislature are elected by the people and the Judiciary is appointed. The State Judiciary consists of a Supreme Tribunal and Courts of the First Instance and Municipal Courts; the latter are presided over in some cities by Prefects and Sub-Prefects, and in others by Alcaldes and Justices of the Peace.

In relation to religious belief, Article 123 reads as follows: "It belongs exclusively to the Federal power to exercise in matters of religious belief and discipline the intervention which may be prescribed by the laws." The Constitution, laws of Congress, and treaties are, by the Constitution, declared to be the supreme law of all the Union.

It will thus be seen that much of the Mexican Constitution is modeled after our Federal Constitution, and even, in some instances, contains improvements on the same.

Nominally all religions are tolerated in the Republic, although the Roman Catholic predominates for the most part. In the large cities some of the Protestant denominations have obtained a foothold. On the overthrow of the Church party all the real estate held by the Church was confiscated, and by the Constitution of 1857 this class of property was forbidden to ecclesiastical corporations. Each State of the Federation is declared sovereign, and all the powers not expressly delegated to the General Government by the Constitution was reserved to the States, respectively. The Federal district and Lower California are, however subject to the General Government, and controled entirely by Federal laws. The Codes originally adopted by the Federal Congress for the Federal District and Lower California have since, with some slight modifications, been adopted by most of the several States, and the laws may therefore be said to be uniform in their main features throughout the Republic.

The Republic was declared independent February 24t 1821; established as an Empire, under Iturbide, in 1822, an proclaimed a Republic December 2d, 1822, by Santa Anna. Iturbide abdicated March 20th, 1823. The Republic contains 27 States, 1 Territory, and 1 Federal District. The present Constitution was adopted February 5th, 1857.

Education.

The principle of obligatory education is now in force in the greater part of the states of the republic, penalties having been decreed for those who contravene the law, and rewards for those who voluntarily observe the same. Primary instruction in the schools of the republic consists of the following branches: Reading, writing, Spanish grammar, arithmetic, tables of weights and measures, morality, and good manners; and moreover, in the girls' schools, needlework and other useful labors. In some of the states the study of geography, national history, and drawing are also obligatory; whilst, in the schools that are not supported by the government, a knowledge of algebra and geometry is taught, with the elements of general and natural history, ornamental and lineal drawing, and the French language. The number of primary schools in the whole of the republic reaches 8,103. Of the number referred to, according to the work of Señor Diaz Covarrubias, 603 are supported by the state governments, 5,240 by the municipal authorities, 378 by private corporations or individuals, 117 by the Catholic clergy, besides 1,581 private establishments that are not gratuitous, and 184 not classified. These schools are attended by scholars of both sexes. Secondary instruction, as well as professional education, are under the charge of the state, with subjection to the programmes established by the law, which prescribes as a mandate the liberty of education and professions.

In the republic there are 105 establishments of secondary and professional instruction. These embrace preparatory schools, civil colleges of jurisprudence, schools of medicine and pharmacy,(no one can practice medicine or keep a drug-store without a diploma from the government) schools for engineers, naval schools, commercial schools, academies of arts and sciences, agricultural schools, academies of fine arts, conservatories of music and oratory, military colleges, conciliatory seminaries supported by the Catholic clergy, blind school, deaf and dumb school, and secondary schools for girls. In these latter, mathematics, cosmography, geography, domestic medicine, history and chronology, book-keeping, domestic economy, and duties of women in society, natural, figured, and ornamented drawing, manual labors, horticulture and gardening, music, the French and Italian languages—certainly, a young lady who graduates in these schools may be said to be accomplished, and our female seminaries might find some suggestions in a finished education. The whole number of educational establishments is 8,208, with 364,809 pupils. Besides these are eight model schools; 285,509 males and 79,300 females receive instruction, and this does not include the education under private tutors. There are 20 public libraries in the state, containing, in the whole, 286,000 volumes; and private libraries, containing from 1,000 to 8,000 works, are innumerable; and there are some with as many as 20,000, and collections of manuscripts and books upon history and travels, literature, law, biography, eloquence, encyclopedias, classic authors, mathematics, physical sciences, and antiquities, relating to America, Asia, Egypt and Nubia.

The most remarkable museums of the Republic are those of antiquities in Mexico, Campeche, Puebla and Merida; those of paintings in Mexico, Oaxaca and Puebla; those of natural history in Guadalajara and Mexico. The National Museum of Mexico, to which is annexed that of Natural History, contains a rich collection of Mexican antiquities, hieroglyphics, manuscripts, arms, utensils, idols, jewels, and every species of ornaments.

The Museum of Natural History at the Mining College, now the School of Engineers, is composed of two cabinets. In the first, there is a well classified collection of geological specimens, and another of zoology, which contains a large assortment.

In the second, are found two collections of minerals from Europe and Mexico, arranged according to the chemical mineralogical system of Berzelius.

The Academy of San Carlos, named in honor of Carlos the Third, of Spain, is one of the most notable institutions of the City of Mexico. It contains several galleries, where numerous original and valuable old Spanish and Italian paintings are to be seen. Among others, are works of Leonardo de Vinci, Murillo, Vernet, Coglietti, Canova, Van Dyck, Cortona, Perugino, Ingres, Decaen, Reni Marko, and other works of Podesti and Silvagni, and several of the Flemish and Dutch schools. In the other saloons are to be seen the paintings of some of the most proficient students of the Academy; also, many remarkable paintings of ancient Mexican artists, as Cobreza, Aguilero, the Juarez family, Ybarra, Arteaga, Vallejo, Echave, and others.

In the republic there exist 73 institutions dedicated to

INTERIOR OF THE CATHEDRAL OF MEXICO.

the cultivation of arts and sciences, of which 29 are scientific, 21 literary, 20 artistical, and three of a mixed character.

Resources of Mexico.

There are now being established, in the greater part of the states of Mexico, cotton, woolen, silk, earthenware, glass, and paper factories, which will add to her present prosperity. If all this great territory were populated, even in proportion to Guanajato and its territory, the census of the republic would reach 58,000,000 to 60,000,000, instead of only 9,000,000 to 10,000,000. This scarcity of population is the one great cause of the undevelopment of the vast agricultural resources of Mexico; and when they are fully developed, they will constitute an element of enormous wealth.

Within the territory of the republic, there are more than 5700 haciendas, (landed estates) and 13,800 farms, (ranchos) and not a few other locations, of immense extent. The value assigned to landed property, based simply on its valuation for taxes, is $161,397,311. The real value may be said to be double that amount, or about $323,000,000. The maize which is grown all over the territory, the wheat in the upper table-lands, the rice in the warm and damp sections, the coffee, vanilla, tobacco, sugar, and cotton in the hot countries, and many other articles, among which may be mentioned the "agave Mexicano," with its abundant returns, constitute the principal branches of national agriculture, and the annual products may be safely estimated at $100,000,000. If colonies were settled in this vast territory, employing their activity and intelligence in making such rich and extensive lands productive, under the influence of the varieties of climate, the benefits derived to Mexico are almost incalculable.

The rich and varied mineral productions of the republic have placed its mines in the niche of fame; and were it not for the scarcity of population before mentioned, they would produce a revenue that has never been dreamed of, in the imaginations of their Spanish conquerors.

The mines of Guanajato, which have been the most worked, and yielded enormously, still present immense wealth, with no signs of their being exhausted. The soil of Guerrero has been pronounced, by a Spanish mineralogist as one extensive crust of silver and gold. This seems like exaggeration, yet it has in a measure proved to be true in the immense deposits there found. In Sinaloa the water have submerged rich treasures, some of which have been rediscovered.

The states of Zacatecas, Sonora, Chihuahua, Durango, San Luis Potosi, Hidalgo, Mexico, and Michoacan contain within their mountain ranges veins of gold and silver in inexhaustible riches. Although the best portion of the mineral district lies in the northern states of the republic, yet throughout its whole territory metaliferous deposits are found. Silver and gold are mostly worked, while the other metals and mineral substances, such as copper, iron, zinc, lead, magistral, antimony, arsenic, cobalt, amianthus, and copperas are almost neglected. The mountain of Popocatapetl is said to be one vast pile of sulphur. Salt mines are found at Peñon Blanco, in San Luis Potosi, Tamaulipas, south of the Isthmus of Tehuantepec, and in the islands of the Gulf of California. The Lake of Texcoco and its adjacent lands possess an extensive supply of carbonate of soda. In every state there exist quarries of white and colored marble. The alabaster of Tecali, in the state of Puebla, has attracted great attention, and the extensive coal-fields, platina, and quicksilver mines all add to the wealth of this great territory. Precious stones are not unknown; the opal with as varied and beautiful hues as those of Hungary, the turquoise, garnet, topaz, agate, and amethyst besides, are found extensively in many places. Building stone of a great variety is plentiful, from which magnificent structures may be built. Aside from the amount of ores that are worked outside of the republic on account of the law permitting free exportation of mineral ores, the annual coinage in gold, silver, and copper is on an average of $20,500,000, and the whole amount of coinage since the establishment of the mints up to 1875 being $3,001,237,281.62. In the colonial period (1537 to 1821): Silver, $2,082,260,657.44; gold, $68,778,-411; copper, $542,893.37—total, $2,151,581,961.81. Since the independence, or establishment of the republic (1822 to 1875): Silver, $797,055,080.71; gold, $47,327,383.11; copper, $5,272,855.93 — total, $849,655,319.84. Total silver, $2,879,315,738.21; gold, $116,105,794.11; copper, $5,815,-740.30. Grand total, $3,001,237,281.62.

Within the last five years, since the investment of additional foreign capital, the amount additional, on the average of twenty and one-half millions a year as the lowest estimate, would reach $102,500,000 more, which would make the sum total in 1880, $3,103,737,281.62 as the amount coined by the republic of Mexico.

To show the increase of production, from the records of the mints, we herewith give the amount coined up to 1865, to compare with the amount coined in 1875, from official records, the first being taken from "El Minero Mexicano" of December 2nd, 1880, and the second or latter from Cubas' valuable work, which he claims to have obtained from the records at the mints.

Amount of Money Coined in the Republic of Mexico from 1772 to 1865.

In the Mints of	Silver.	Gold.	Total.
Mexico	$2,163,836,764	$77,753,472	$2,241,590,237
Catorce	1,321,545	....	1,321,545
Chihuahua	15,626,400	1,286,095	16,912,495
Culiacan	12,795,505	4,735,286	17,530,791
Durango	35,294,581	3,139,889	38,434,470
Guadalajara	28,288,333	754,487	29,042,820
Guanajuato	164,591,216	15,094,529	179,685,745
San Luis Potosi	48,745,584	....	48,745,584
Oaxaca	910,927	236,120	1,147,046
Zacatecas	204,234,941	550,008	204,784,949
Guadalupe y Calvo	2,063,958	2,311,104	4,375,062
Sombrerete	1,551,249	....	1,551,249
Tlalpam	959,116	203,534	1,162,650
1865 —Total	$2,680,220,119	$106,064,534	$2,786,284,654

```
1875—Total amount coined from 1772....................$3,001,237,281 62
1865—   "      "     deducted............................. 2,786,284,654 00

        Increase in 10 years.............................  $214,952,627 62
              (or about $21,495,262.76 cents annually.)
```

The average annual production of the mines of Sonora, from 1835 to 1842, was given by Francisco Velasco at a rough estimate of $1,500,000 annually, or $10,500,000 during the period of seven years. In 1828, Don Juan M. Riesago estimated the annual production at $2,000,000.

The laws originally demanded that all bullion should be brought to Mexico to be coined, and the cost of carrying was so great that the rich mines in these border States became almost neglected by capitalists, and the poorer ones nearest to Mexico City were mostly worked. This resulted in the smuggling of bullion out of the mines in the northern states of the republic, and no record could be kept at the mints, of those mines—in fact, there are no reliable records that give any account of the exports of bullion either from Mazatlan or Guaymas, although some records exist covering the last few years; while it is well known that the mines in those States have been extensively worked in certain localities for over a century.

Lower California.

This embraces a territory or peninsula, washed on its western shores by the Pacific Ocean, and east by the Gulf of California. Its area is over 60,000 square miles. Its capital is La Paz, which is the principal town. The whole of the center is traversed by a volcanic range of mountains of the Sierra Nevada. It is bounded on the north by California and north-east by the Colorado River, dividing it from Sonora.

The soil is generally not productive, though, at the base of the mountains and in small valleys, where the decomposition of lava has been going on for ages, it possesses an incredible fecundity. The formation of the whole State is volcanic, and the coast subject to storms. The scarcity of rivers bars much of its prosperity.

The productions are maize, manioc, wheat, beans, etc.; grapes, from which wine of a very rich flavor is produced; oranges, limes, lemons, citrons, prunes, dates, figs, pineapples, bananas, plantains, and other tropical fruits; stock of various kinds graze in the valleys, consisting of horses, sheep, cattle, goats and hogs. Fish, in its waters, abound to a great extent, such as halibut, salmon, turbot, skate, pilchard, large oysters, thornback, mackerel, cod, lobsters, etc., and pearl oysters.

The pearl fishery is much pursued at La Paz. In this region, a gold mine has been worked to some extent. There are about 20 towns in the state, six bays on the east coast and ten on the west, twelve islands in the gulf, and eight west of the coast.

The territory of Lower California is divided into eight municipalities—La Paz, San José de Comondu, Mulege, Santo Tomas, San Antonio, Todos Santos, Santiago, San José del Cabo. Population, 25,000.

La Paz, the capital, has about 3,000 inhabitants

This territory is about to be colonized, as we learn from the "Diario Official" that a contract has been signed by the Acting Secretary of Public Works, in virtue whereof, Messrs. J. Kelly & Co., of Mazatlan, engage themselves to colonize 36,000 hectares of public lands in Lower California.

The Climate of the Table Lands of the Northern Part of Mexico.

The altitude of the table lands of Mexico has a marked effect upon the climate. In the summer the thermometer records a mean temperature of 85 degrees at El Paso, 3800 feet above the sea. It sometimes reaches 105 degrees in July. The constant breezes, however, make the heat more bearable. In December—the middle of the winter season—the mean temperature is about 48 degrees, the mercury falling sometimes to 5 degrees below zero. Snow falls sometimes two feet in depth, and ice forms a solid sheet on the Rio Grande, and the streams are sometimes frozen to a considerable depth, strong enough to bear a heavy mule team and loaded wagon. The frosts are severe, therefore, and grapevines at El Paso and other points have to be protected by burying in the earth from eighteen inches to two feet beneath the surface. The Rio Grande generally freezes so as to make the fording an impossibility during the coldest weather. The whole of the table lands is subject to extremely cold weather, and travelers not only often suffer severely but actually perish from the cold when not carefully protected. In the mining region of Jesus Maria, in Chihuahua, the ice frequently forms to a considerable thickness in the houses. The rainfall reaches from six to fourteen and fifteen inches, and when accompanied by sleet and snow makes traveling anything but pleasant in the face of some of the winter storms that sweep over the elevated plains. Travelers recount some very disagreeable experiences in midwinter traveling. Mr. Ruxton speaks of riding through one of these storms when his blanket, used as a protection against the storm, froze stiff and hard as a board while he he was in the midst of a storm of sleet and rain. His feet were frozen, and he came near perishing. Stopping and squatting upon the ground, having lost his way in the night, he drew his blanket around him as best he could, and remained till near morning in that position, with his blanket over his head. He says that before morning he was completely snowed in, the snow being over his head on a level. From this we should judge that the climate of these table lands may be said to be somewhat similar to the climate of the Mississippi Valley, bordering Illinois, Indiana and Iowa. The statement, therefore, that the climate of Mexico is tropical will not apply to these table lands. In most of the mining regions of this portion of Mexico snow falls and ice forms.

2

All the mines of any value or located in the mountains or cold regions. Durango, Coahuila and part of New Leon and Tamaulipas have about the same climate as in Chihuahua, with a less proportion of snow in New Leon and Tamaulipas. The table lands are healthy, and the air is pure and bracing. The altitude produces every variety of climate on the plateaus until the low lands or plains are reached, when tropical features alone prevail. The low, marshy regions are to be avoided not only on account of the "vomito"— the scourge of those regions—but also the malarial fevers which make such localities dangerous for the settler.

The climate of Chihuahua City is about the same as at El Paso, with perhaps more cold weather, since the altitude is higher, and the mountains adjacent reaching several thousand feet above the level of the plain, and in the winter time are perpetually covered with snow. The peak of Jesus Maria, in the southwestern portion of the State, is 8456 feet above the sea, and La Tarumara 8340. The city of Durango, Humboldt says, is about 6845 feet above the sea, and the Cerro de Mercado, or Iron Mountain, adjacent is 8220 feet, making the climate, consequently, from the altitude and surroundings, cold in the winter season, with considerable snow and ice prevailing.

In the mountainous part of Sinaloa the same may be said, though the altitude of the whole State is much lower, since the highest peaks, viz., La Bayona and Cabeza de Caballo, make only 5614 and 4365 feet respectively above the sea. In New Leon, El de la Silla and Sierra de Gomez are 7800 and 6602 feet respectively above the sea level.

The State of Tamaulipas has the highest mountain peaks of any of the Northern States of Mexico. Los Gallitos is the highest, being 9633 feet, while Oreasitas is 7562 and El Metate 7144 feet above the sea. Sr. Don Perez Hernandez, in his work published in 1862, gives much valuable information, from which we extract the above figures.

Ruxton says. "The City of Mexico is 7470 feet above the sea level, and La Villa de Leon 6020, thus showing that the table land of Mexico does not decline so suddenly as is imagined. Indeed, excepting in the plains of Salamanca and Silao, there is no perceptible difference in the temperature, and, I believe, in reality but little in elevation in the vast region between the capital and Chihuahua. Snow falls here occasionally, and the mercury is sometimes seen below the freezing point. For the greater part of the year, however, the heat is excessive, and a low, intermittent fever prevails."

SONORA.

CHAPTER I

Boundaries and General Description.

The name of Sonora is derived from "Sonot," an Opata Indian name, which means "Señora," an appellation bestowed by the Spanish conquerors upon an Indian woman who treated them with great hospitality, when they visited the settlements of that tribe. The Indians, in attempting to imitate the Spaniards, pronounced the word "Sonora."

The State comprises nine districts: Hermosillo, at which is located the capital; Ures, the former capital; Guaymas, Alamos, Magdalena, Altar, Oposura or Moctezuma and Sahuaripa. The state originally extended its boundaries from the river "de las Cañas" on the south, to the river Gila on the north. The southern boundary extended then from the state of Jalisco on the south to Arizona, and included a part of the same. Yuma, with Tucson and other towns and ranchos south of the river Gila, were originally included in the state. The state was then 1,395 miles in length, but in 1830 it was divided, and the south-eastern boundary fixed 54 miles south of the city of Alamos, on the border of the Mesquite rancho. This constituted the dividing line between the states of Sonora and Sinaloa; the distance from the former capital, Ures, to the southern boundary being 354 miles. The northern boundary extended to the Gila River, until the boundary line between the United States and Mexico was fixed south of the same river.

The length of the state is about 700 miles. Mean breadth from the state of Chihuahua on the east to the Gulf of California on the west is about 300 miles. The exact measurement is not known, as the state has never been completely surveyed. The most narrow breadth between Mesquite and Alamos is about 120 miles. The area in square miles is about 123,466.

The general direction of the state is from north-west to

south-east, along the Gulf of California. Its whole western boundary, from the mouth of the river Colorado on the north, extends along the coast south-east to Sinaloa. It is bounded on the north by Arizona and New Mexico. Along the coast the surface is diversified by valleys, plains, and foot-hills. Some of the plains are 30 to 40 miles, some reaching to 90 miles, in extent. In the neighborhood of the Sierra Madre mountains it is lofty and broken. The surface may be said to possess three distinct features outside of the mountainous district. First, dry plains; second, elevated plateaus, or table lands; and third, agricultural valleys, or bottom lands. The dry plains are located in the north-western part of the state, between the head-waters of the Gulf of California, and the valley of Santa Cruz, bordering upon Arizona in the north. The table lands lie in the north-eastern part of the state, extending from the Santa Cruz valley and the source of the Bapetito River, the main branch of the Yaqui on the west, to the base of the Sierra Madre mountains, which extend along the boundary line between the state and Chihuahua.

From Guaymas to the northern border line, the surface is generally level, diversified here and there by isolated mountains, conical or table-topped, which give grandeur to the landscape, without occupying much arable area. The soil is of great depth and richness, resembling in many localities the famous *brazos* of Texas, but happily exempt from the malarias of the latter.

In the interior, plains and valleys of immense extent are crossed by the traveler, in some instances 200 miles in length. The largest river of the state is the Yaqui, or Buenavista, which is only navigable for flat-boats in high water. The river Mayo may also be mentioned. Both of these rivers empty into the Gulf of California. The source of each is in the copious springs of the Sierra Madre, and they are never dry in the seasons of most drought.

The river Sonora or Arispe passes through Ures and Hermosillo, and loses its waters in the sandy plains of Siete Cerritos, about 21 miles west of Hermosillo. The Horcasitas, or Rayon, a small stream, joins the Sonora about five miles east of Hermosillo. The same stream is also called Opodepe and Cucurpe. The Oposura, Aribechi, Santa Cruz, San José de Pimas, Tecoripa, Altar, and Caborca, are mere creeks, fordable when their waters are high, and almost entirely disappear in dry seasons, some of them entirely sinking in the sands. The Colorado River on the north-west extends along but a small part of the boundary. There are many sand-plains along the coast, as well as large sterile tracts in the interior, and only on the banks of the streams or river bottoms are the lands capable of irrigation. The principal sand-plain extends from the mouth of the Colorado to the Salinas Bay near port La Libertad.

The only port suitable for commerce is that of Guaymas, to which we will call particular attention hereafter. Some trade is also done at La Libertad. In Santa Cruz de Mayo, of the department of Alamos, in the southern part of the state, there is a small bay or roadstead called the port of Santa Cruz.

That portion lying between Mesquite on the south along the base of the Sierra Madre, extending north to the ancient capital city Arispe, is sterile in places, but has never been completely explored by surveying or civil engineers, while the region further north is, in places, very fertile. This territory will demand a more particular description hereafter. The most valuable agricultural lands are situated on the banks of the rivers and creeks, or river bottoms. Irrigation is necessary for almost the entire territory, either natural or artificial. The yield in this case is vastly greater than is produced in countries where the sole dependence is rain. The dry plains are generally level, with a hard surface, and adapted for purposes of wagon-roads and railroads. Experience has shown that artesian well-water may be obtained. The arid spots cannot be cultivated. The table-lands are covered with a short and luxuriant grass, upon which immense herds of cattle have been and may still be raised.

We herewith give the following from the pen of an able Spanish writer, Velasco, who impartially describes the state, in his valuable work on Sonora, which has been translated by Mr. Nye. Page 14:

" The most thickly settled places are upon the banks of the rivers and creeks, while at the interior settlements between Alamos and Hermosillo there is so great a scarcity of water on the roads that the traveler is compelled to carry a supply with him. It is not uncommon to travel eight or even sixteen leagues, (about three miles to the league) without finding a stream or a place where water may be procured by digging. On that part of the coast called Tiburon, to the west of Hermosillo, the distance between watering-places is still greater, and the supply more scanty, and on the old road of Cieneguilla, which is from fifty to sixty leagues in length,

there are but three watering-places, including one well. On
the road from Hermosillo to the port of Guaymas, in the
dry season, no water is to be had for thirty-six leagues, except at La Posa and La Cieneguilla, and it is occasionally so
scarce at these places that foot passengers perish from thirst.
The coast is so dry that the rancheros have sunk wells in
different parts of it, thirty and forty yards in depth, without
finding moisture. The region between Arispe and the Gila,
however, is well watered by numerous creeks, and abounds
in pools and swamps, and the mountains are well supplied
with water, and timber of various kinds, such as cedar, pine,
evergreen oak, ebony, etc.; well stocked with deer and
birds, and containing medicinal herbs of marvelous efficacy,
one of which, called ' colorada,' is used by the Apaches for
the treatment of wounds. The valleys are expansive and
beautiful, abundantly watered, and clothed in verdure during the entire year; and nature has lavished her vegetable
and mineral wealth upon these frontier regions with so prodigal a hand that they may well be called the Paradise of
Sonora. The inscrutable decree of the Almighty has bestowed them upon savages, incapable of appreciating or en-
joying his munificent gift."

Thus we see the region north-east and bordering upon the
State of Chihuahua, outside of the valleys of the Yaqui and
Mayo rivers, is the best portion of the state, and includes
the valleys and foot-hills of the Sierra Madre. In this region there are now many cattle-ranches of large extent, that
may be purchased at very low rates, we should judge, taking our data from the prices prevailing in Sonora. The
mineral belt also extends through this region, including
valuable mines of gold and silver, galena and coal, to which
we will give a more extensive description hereafter, under
the title of " Mining Districts and Mines."

CHAPTER II.

1. Climate.

The climate is varied in the mountain region from extreme heat to the freezing point. In the winter season, the
cold weather commences in the latter part of October, and
reaches the lowest degree, or freezing point, from Novem-

ber to March. Ice sometimes appears in October, but not usually till November or December. In the settlements nearest the mountains the frosts set in earlier than in the interior. In the latter region, three or four years often pass without any frost, especially near the coast. This is true of Hermosillo, Buena Vista, Alamos, and in the valleys of the rivers Yaqui and Mayo. The warm season commences in May, and the heat becomes extreme during the months of June, July, and August.

At Hermosillo, Guaymas, Ures, Buena Vista, and San Antonio de la Huerta, the mercury reaches above one hundred degrees during the months last mentioned. In September refreshing rains fall, and continue during the winter season. A hot wind occasionally visits Hermosillo during the months of June, July, and August, which blows from eleven in the morning till four in the afternoon, during which hours business practically ceases. The inhabitants seek shelter in their houses, and no one ventures forth unless driven by necessity. These hot winds are a terror to the Sonorians, and they remember, with some degree of apprehension, a time in which the wind scorched the skin like the heat of a furnace, and drove the hares, deer, coyotes, and other wild animals to the settlements for refuge, while plants and trees were literally scorched out at the root. This "*viento caliente*," or hot wind, also springs upon Guaymas suddenly sometimes, and blows for twenty-four hours without intermission. On reaching the coast it meets the damp and cooler atmosphere, and by the time it passes about three miles over the gulf, its heat is absorbed, and it vanishes. Water may be kept cool, however, in jars, even during the prevalence of this wind. In the beginning of June the poorer classes abandon the interior of their adobe houses, and sleep in the corridors or court-yards. Others often sleep in the streets before their doors, for the heat is insufferable within their houses.

At Hermosillo and some other towns a southern breeze springs up about eight o'clock, and continues during the night, making the attempt to sleep more bearable; but, if the breeze fails to put in an appearance, the sleepy god is courted in vain. At Arispe, Bacuachi, and Frontreras, the winter lasts longer than the summer; and at Santa Cruz, near the northern boundary of the state, the altitude of the surrounding mountains is such, that the temperature varies from the cool and pleasant to the freezing point. Serious epidemics are unknown; and at Hermosillo the only diseases that prevail, and that to a limited extent, are phthisis and diarrhea. On the rivers Oposura and Sahuaripa, "goitre," or swelled neck, appears on the necks of men, but mostly on the women. The disease is called "*buche*" by the Spaniards. Intermittent fevers often prevail, probably caused by the immoderate use of fruit, in the interior; but they are of short continuance. We may justly affirm that the climate is, on the whole, salubrious, and is really more healthy than that of the adjoining States, or the central part of the republic. The atmosphere is pure and dry, entirely free from malaria, with but one exception, in the neighborhood of Santa Cruz, where the adjacent swamps sometimes induce fever. The interior of the State is entirely free from noxious vapors. The air is pure and healthy, sweeping over the plains and through valleys from the sierras and the sea.

In Guaymas, Matape, Horcositas, Arispe, and Altar, persons are found who have attained to ages ranging over a century. The average duration of life, with the observance of prudence and temperance, ranges from seventy to eighty years, says Velasco. "Owing to the practice of vaccination, small-pox rarely makes its appearance. Venereal diseases are not common, except in the neighborhood of the rivers Yaqui and Mayo, and on the coast. Catarrhs frequently appear in a mild form during the changes of the seasons. One may sleep in the open air with perfect impunity, and experience no inconvenience. The diseases that affect children are diarrhea, intermittent fevers, vomiting, ophthalmia, eruptions of the face, and other difficulties that accompany teething. These diseases, owing to the lack of medical skill, produce a mortality among children that carries off one-fourth from birth up to the period of teething, annually. After this critical period, good health generally attends them to the age of puberty."

2. Soil and Productions.

The soil along the coast, from the valley or delta of the Colorado to the Altar or Magdalena River, is mostly unfit for productions of any kind, and the land south of the Altar River is used for grazing purposes, from the port of La Libertad on the coast, in places where the sand plains are not prevalent, to the Yaqui River. The exceptions are on the Altar or Magdalena Creek or river and its branch the San Ignacio, and the river Sonora. Wherever no streams exist, it may be safely said the soil cannot be cultivated. Very good grazing lands are found occasionally, from La Libertad to Guaymas or in its neighborhood. On the San Ignacio, sweet and sour oranges, lemons, citrons, limes, pomegranates, and peaches are raised. The territory between the San Ignacio and the river Altar, produces cotton of excellent quality. Several large plantations are in this vicinity, one of which is devoted to the raising of this valuable production. Cotton-mills are here erected, owned by the Ortizes of Hermosillo. Also the "guava" is cultivated, and the plantain-tree attains a large size, bearing a heavy burden of fruit.

In and around the territory of Hermosillo large vineyards are located, from which considerable quantities of *"aguadiente"* or brandy and wine are produced. Wheat is also grown in this locality, with beans, lentils, Chili peppers, garlic, onions, and sweet potatoes. The fruits are abundant, and the grape, muskmelons, and watermelons, are raised of excellent quality. Orchards containing figs, apples, peaches, pears, apricots, etc., are found in this neighborhood. Cotton was first experimented upon in 1811, but was soon after abandoned, and was again continued in 1842, and carried on up to the present time at from 12 to 20 miles west of Hermosillo, on the plantations of Tennaje and Palomos, and at Chino Gordo, 12 miles east. Sugar is produced from the cane, on the coast near the Yaqui River, and at San Ignacio and Ceris. The average yield of wheat is 250 to 300 from one bushel sown, upon the haciendas of Messrs. Antisernes, called the Topahui, and upon the haciendas of Hermosillo it rates from 150 to 175 from one. Indian corn and beans are extensively grown at San Antonio, Santa Rosa, on the rivers Sonora and Yaqui and Santa Cruz, and other localities. The bottom lands of the Yaqui, Mayo, and lands bordering upon the Sonora and Santa Cruz rivers, produce wheat, also. On the river Yaqui, beans, lentils, sugar-cane, cotton, flax, indigo plant, coffee, tobacco, and various kinds of fruits, are raised. Sheep and cattle and horses in immense herds are raised, as well as many domestic fowls. The tobacco has a narrow leaf, owing to the lack of proper cultivation.

Extensive salt-pits are also situated near the mouth of the river Yaqui, on the coast. In the same place, and in the mouth of the river Yaqui, are located the great oyster-beds of common and pearl oysters. The distance from Coccori to Cochori is about 90 miles, across the valley of the river Yaqui. The whole of this tract of land is susceptible of a high degree of cultivation. We will give, hereafter, a special description of this region. The soil is here moist and alluvial, capable of raising all the productions of the temperate and tropic zones. The irrigation is produced by annual overflows of the river, and suffices for the production of wheat, maize, and every class of productions yet experimented upon. This section may well be compared to the rich lands of Egypt lying along the banks of the Nile. Immense sugar plantations may be here established, and produce fortunes for the possessor. The best portion of this land has been granted by the republic to a gentleman residing in Mexico. Near Altar, on the Magdalena or Altar river, pomegranates, figs, and grapes are raised, and immense herds of horses and cattle are seen grazing in the vicinity; also extensive ranchos that are exceedingly fertile are here located.

In the northern part of the state, near Santa Cruz, is located a beautiful valley, clothed in verdure the year round. It is well watered by the Santa Cruz River, that takes its rise from a perpetual spring located to the north of the valley. Immense quantities of stock are here raised, and all kinds of grain, especially wheat, which is of excellent quality. It also produces the best red pepper of the state, and its hides find a ready market. The distance from Santa Cruz to Villa de Guadalupe, by way of Oceua, Santa Ana, Santa Marta, San Lorenzo, and Magdalena, is 120 miles. When heavy clothing is necessary at Santa Cruz, other parts of the state are subjected to immense heat. Many swamps are in the vicinity, which produce fevers.

The Presidio of Bacuachi raises cattle, sheep, and horses, and produces good wheat, which is mostly grown, owing to the early frosts. Near the Presidio of Fronteras, the lands produce excellent wheat, maize, etc.; also, delicious peaches, apples, and the famous bergamot pear. A creek runs through this valley, which is used to irrigate the neighboring lands. Wild game is abundant in the neighborhood. The plains adjacent are all fertile and well watered. The climate is cool and healthy, and would be an excellent place to establish a colony. Indeed, the whole of the north-eastern part of the state presents advantages that no other part of the state combines. It is well timbered, has abundance of water, and is one of the richest mineral regions of the state.

To convince one of the remarkable resources of the state, a visit to the Hacienda de la Alameta, fifteen miles from Hermosillo, owned formerly by the Artazernes, will be sufficient to satisfy the most skeptical. On the Alameta are miles of wheat, corn, and sugar-cane, and cotton. On this hacienda is erected a flour-mill of the best description, with abundance of water power, and a sugar-mill and works, a manufactory of blankets—the wool of which, and the dye-stuffs, are grown on the place. A wagon manufactory, carried on for the sole use of the hacienda, is also located in its limits. Tobacco also is produced of excellent quality. Oranges, lemons, pomegranates, and other tropical fruits of delicious flavor are grown in abundance. These places are simply principalities, where a man has all the products of the earth under tribute and at hand. The large cotton-mill near La Labor, at San Miguel, was offered to San Francisco capitalists on liberal terms, but was purchased by the Ortizes of Hermosillo. The cotton is raised at its very door. Indigo, brazil-wood, cochineal, and other dye-stuffs, grow spontaneously on the Yaqui and Mayo rivers; also coffee of the best quality.

The agricultural resources we thus see are rich beyond that of any state in the Republic of Mexico. If the state were well settled by an energetic class of immigrants, the future of this famous state would be of the most flattering character. We anticipate just such an immigration on the completion of the Southern Pacific and Santa Fé Railroads. We shall hereafter give some attention to the railroads of the state.

CHAPTER III.

Guaymas.

The port of Guaymas is situated on the Gulf of California, about sixty miles above the mouth of the river Yaqui, in latitude 27 deg. 22 min. north, and longitude 104 deg. 30 min. west of Cadiz. It is completely sheltered from the sea, and is one of the best harbors on the Pacific. The entrance runs north and south, and is formed by the island of Pajaras on the east, and the islands of San Vicente, Pitayas, and Tierra Firma on the west. There is also another entrance, called Boca Chica, formed by the island of Pajaras on the south, and the beach of Cochin on the north. The length of the bay is from four to five miles. The bottom is muddy, and when vessels remain for some time it is necessary to sight the anchor every fortnight. The depth of water at the island of Pajaras is seven fathoms, which gradually decreases to two, along the side of the mole. The latter, according to the opinion of mariners, is one of the best on the Pacific, excepting that of Callao. The depth of water at the anchorage is three fathoms; and vessels drawing fifteen feet are loaded, discharged, and hove down with facility. There are three landing-places, but no fortifications, although there are several points well suited to the purpose. The tides are irregular and uncertain, being influenced by the winds from the gulf. In time of full and new moon they rise and fall eighteen to twenty inches; and in the autumnal equinox, about four feet. Sailing-vessels are often delayed by calms in passing up the gulf to reach the harbor; but since the era of steamships has arrived, it will have no appreciable effect on the commerce of the port, save only with sailing-vessels. The harbor abounds in various kinds of delicate fish and shell-fish. The latter comprises the shrimp, crab, lobster, oyster, and mussels of different kinds. The town is situated on the north of the bay, and is surrounded by a range of hills of moderate height, which leaves but one single entrance from the land side. There is but one principal street, called "Calle Principal," from the entrance to the Plaza; the others being short and narrow. The soil is dry and rocky. The climate is not severe in winter; but the north and north-west winds blow with great violence, and cause much inconvenience. The summer heat is excessive; the thermometer occasionally rising up to 104 deg. in the shade, and never falling below 90 deg., from June to September; and when the north wind blows during this season from the dry and parched land lying adjacent and north of the city, it is so dry and parching in its effects that it ruins the finer articles of furniture. The health of the place is good. Water, for drinking, is drawn from four public wells on the skirts of the town, which is carried in carts and on the backs of donkeys, in leather bags. There are no trees in Guaymas but a few stunted ones in the Plaza. In the suburbs is a large orange-grove planted by Mr. John A. Robinson of this city, who resided some fifty years in Sonora. The grove is now owned by Mr. N. Graff, of Guaymas. Wood is scarce, and is brought from nine to fifteen miles from the interior; also from the river Yaqui in boats, by the Indians, and constitutes the only fuel; it is sold by the "carga," or load. There are two kinds of carga—the

" burro," or donkey carga of 150 pounds; and "mule" carga
of 300 ; 50 sticks, or billets, as thick as the wrist, are
counted out, 18 inches long, for the " burro " carga, and
sell for 25 cents per carga ; and the same number of twice
that length for the " mule " carga, and a corresponding
price is demanded. The wagons used are the latest improved, although one sees occasionally the awkward cart
coming in from the ranchos with wheels hewed or sawed off
the end of a log. The houses are mostly adobe, with here
and there a substantial brick building. There are about
one-half dozen wholesale importing houses, and quite a number of retail houses. The former import direct from Europe
and the United States. Lumber is scarce, and is brought
from San Francisco and Puget Sound. It sells from thirty
to fifty dollars per thousand. Lumber is admitted free of
duty. There are no banks either in Guaymas or in the State
of Sonora ; and business is carried on with foreigners by ordinary bills of credit, and by drafts on San Francisco, London,
Hamburg, and Paris banks. The principal business firms
are Aguilar & Co., Sandoval & Bulle, Domingo Carrez, G.
B. Fourcade, W. Iberri, Arvillez & Co., J. J. Rodgers, Luis
Jarequi, Ramon Carrizosa, Aguayo Bros., Echiquyen & Esco-
bos, and some others, who do a large wholesale as well as
retail trade.

An agency of Wells Fargo is the only American institu-
tion finding a foothold in Sonora. The American Consul is
also stationed at Guaymas. There are quite a number of
hotels, among which might be mentioned, " Cosmopolitan "
and " Hotel de Guaymas."

There is also a shoe manufactory, a soap factory, an ice
factory, one Roman Catholic church, and public and private
schools. It is not generally known that compulsory education is one of the Mexican institutions. Courts of the first
and second instance, a hospital, and a railroad depot, are
also found in Guaymas, of A. T. & S. F. R. R. The population is about 5,000. The Atchinson, Topeka, and Santa Fé
Railroad, called the Sonora Railway, commences at Ardilla
Island, so called, and runs north, crossing a bridge across a
portion of the bay near the old rancho of Guaymas. The
land is level beyond this point for ten miles, and no grading
is necessary. The completion of this railway will add to the
commercial importance of Guaymas, and it will open up
one of the richest portions of the Republic. Capital is flowing along the line of the railroad, and new towns are being
established with the accustomed energy of pioneer settlements.

East of the town, the country is more adapted to agriculture and grazing. East and south-east, commencing about sixty miles distant, are located the rich bottom lands of the Yaqui River, which supply the town with fowls, sheep, and grain. Flour and meat are brought from the interior; San Antonio and Santa Rosa furnishing corn and beans for the Guaymas market. Hides and bullion, flour, and, in fact, nearly all the exports of the state, are shipped at this point. There are two Justices of the Peace, a judge of the first instance, and a prefect and board of aldermen. The customhouse is very much lacking in store-houses and offices. The future of Guaymas is yet to come, through the energy and industry of foreign capitalists and immigrants. This will remain the port of the state on the gulf, and it will hold its influence upon the commercial relations of Sonora. It will eventually be the most important town in the state. The railroad will soon connect it with San Francisco and the East. Another road is in contemplation, connecting it with Mazatlan in the state of Sinaloa, and from thence to the City of Mexico, which we will notice more particularly hereafter. A new port, La Libertad, above Guaymas, has been opened, giving an immediate outlet to the valuable district of Altar and north-eastern Sonora. A considerable amount of eastern capital has been invested in Guaymas and landed property adjacent. The foundries of San Francisco are turning out engines, mills, and costly machinery for the several mines owned in part here. The steamship lines established between San Francisco and Guaymas and Mazatlan are carrying this machinery to those ports, and from there transported to the interior. A new steamer has lately been built for the gulf trade above Guaymas.

Alamos.

The city of Alamos is situated some 240 miles south-east from the port of Guaymas, on the direct road by way of Buena Vista, on the Yaqui River. The town is situated in a rolling or hilly country, at the base of the Sierra Madre mountains, and is devoted principally to the mines in the vicinity, furnishing supplies to all the surrounding region. The population is about 5,000. We will give a more particular description of the mines in this district hereafter.

There is much business done here with Chihuahua, and the northern part of Sinaloa. The principal business houses are Thomas Robinson Bours, Vincente Ortiz & Hijos, and A. Goycoolea & Co.

Altar.

Altar is a small mining town of about 2,500 inhabitants, and was formerly called Santa Gertrudis del Altar, and it is sometimes now called Guadalupe. It is watered by a small stream called Rio de la Assumpcion, branching from the Altar or Magdalena river. The stream is insufficient for irrigation in the dry season. The town is situated near the banks of the stream upon a plain about 80 miles northeast from the gulf coast, and about 100 miles from La Libertad, which is located southeast on the coast. The plains on the west are dry and sandy, and are a part of the great Colorado desert, which extends down the coast near Lobos, about 50 miles distant in a south-west direction. The discovery of mines of gold and silver in the vicinity of Altar gave it a great impetus at one period in its history. It is mostly built of adobe houses, and contains several retail shops, one church, two justices of the peace, a prefect, and judge of the first instance. The town is garrisoned by a few soldiers, and the streets are irregular. East of the town are situated ranchos exceedingly fertile and abundantly watered. The place is distant from Santa Cruz about 120 miles, which lies in a north-east direction by way of Magdalena and Arispe. Santa Magdalena is about 70 miles distant. The latter town is also called San Ignacio, and is located due east of Altar, in a beautiful valley. The number of inhabitants is about 3,000.

The stage connects at Magdalena with Hermosillo on the south-east and thence to Guaymas, and on the north with Tucson by way of Tombstone and Benson, Arizona.

Hermosillo.

Hermosillo is the largest town in the State and numbers about 12,000 inhabitants. It is situated in a valley about three and a half leagues, or about ten miles in length and five in breadth, sheltered on the north by valleys, hills, and on the west by the range of hills called "Chanate," and on the east by the "Cerro de la Campana"—hill of the bell —so-called because its rocks, when struck together, produce a sound similar to that of a bell. The base of this hill is bathed by a small stream or river called the Sonora, running from east to west, which is sufficient to irrigate the lands between San Juanica and Chanate, cultivated by the inhabitants of the city, and of the pueblo of Ceris, which is in sight to the south; the said lands being in length, from east to west, 12 to 15 miles.

A large aqueduct passes through the middle of the settlement, which serves for irrigating the neighboring lands. Another passes near the river and the Cerro de la Campana, and a third divides the city north and south, furnishing water to the houses and orchards of orange, citron, lime, and fig trees, pomegranates and peach trees in the neighborhood, as well as immense fields of wheat, corn, and other cereals. The average annual quantity of its agricultural products reaches to about 70,000 bushels of wheat and about 300,000 bushels of Indian corn, and an immense quantity of other cereals. Large vineyards of grapes, from which brandy and wine are produced, and plantain trees of enormous growth, mingle with the rich landscape. The wine produced is hard to keep, owing to its tendency to sour, and it is mostly manufactured into brandy or aguadiente. The Tennage and Palomos cotton plantations are located from twelve to twenty miles west of the city, and at the Chino Gordo, about twelve miles east. Sugar-cane has not been very successfully grown in this vicinity; but at San Juanica and Ceris it is raised in small quantities. The capital of the State is located here, and the Legislature meets biennially, the same as under the Constitution of California. The Constitution of the State of Sonora is mostly copied from the old Constitution of California. The streets of the city are kept clean and are well paved. The principal street is called the "Calle Principal," the same as in Guaymas. The public buildings are, the capitol, the mint, the assayer's office, and municipal buildings, including the prison and public school, and one or two churches. The school is held in a building purchased by the city, and consists of two departments, male and female. The number of pupils is about 600. Public examinations are held every six months.

There are several hotels. The principal ones are, the "Iturbide," "Nacional," "Cinco de Mayo," and "Cosmopolitan." All are one-story adobes, with a court in the center, where the guests are obliged to sleep in the summer season. The houses are nearly all one-story adobe buildings, with occasional brick residences and buildings. A new Catholic church is in course of construction. The principal plaza, in front of the church, is the most attractive feature of the city, and is set with orange trees and evergreens and covered with lawn grass, with enticing paths meandering through flower beds, and bordered with orange trees, which afford an excellent shade. It is kept open all the time, and is provided with convenient seats for the leisure-taking Sonorians. An eye-witness pronounces it, in " size, beauty, and arrangement, as excelling any in San Francisco." The whole is surrounded with a very pretty iron fence. In the center is a grand stand, from which music is wafted upon the evening breeze Thursday and Saturday nights, on which occasions it is the favorite resort of the people of the city. The ladies of Sonora are very beautiful, and, indeed, the town is known as the place of beautiful women.

The ladies of Hermosillo of the higher class never go on the street with their faces uncovered. The " mantilla" of rich and gorgeous material is very gracefully thrown over the head, and one portion, with that indescribable drapery for which the Spanish ladies are noted, is carelessly thrown across the lower part of the face, concealing the features, and over the shoulder, while the beautiful eyes, some lustrous black and others of blue, only are revealed to the gaze of the spectator, as they float along with that grace of carriage and modest demeanor for which the Spanish ladies are so celebrated. The latest styles from Paris are ordered, and Worth has many customers throughout the republic. The descendants of the ancient Castilians are to be seen in blondes as well as brunettes ; and although the taste of the people is generally in favor of bright colors, still fashion has been wielding her scepter in Mexico as well as in the United States.

Hermosillo is celebrated, as well as the rest of the state, for the fecundity of its women. It is not unusual to see a family with from 15 to 25 children. As an instance in point, there is a lady residing in Hermosillo weighing 260 pounds, tall and handsome withal, in spite of her corpulence, who is the last of a family of 28 children. This fact is vouched for by a well-known citizen of this city. Another gentleman, an American by birth, and at one time a prominent citizen of Guaymas, but now residing in this city, married a Spanish or Mexican lady, and is the fortunate father of no less than 17 children. The children of Sonora go almost naked, and thrive remarkably well, since the statement of Velasco that there is a great mortality among children, to which we have already referred. The prominent citizens even dress their children only with a shirt, hat, and boots.

The business of the place is confined to the port of Guaymas and the interior of the state. There are about 30 shops and mercantile establishments in the city. The town is the favorite resort for travelers through the state. The principal business men of the place are the Ortizes, Camous, Pesquiera, Ruix & Mascareñas, Carlos Maneti, Alvistiqui & Alatorre, and Antonio Calderon. Most of these business houses import direct from Europe and the United States. The houses of Ortiz and the Camou Bros. are probably as strong financially as any in the republic. The Ortizes, besides owning a large number of haciendas, comprising several hundre 1 thousand acres, stocked with immense herds of cattle and horses and flocks of sheep, and several of the best mining properties of the state, own the large cotton-mill, called "Industria Sonorense," which employs about 300 men and women; also a sugar-mill and tannery. All these mills are located at Los Angeles, on the San Miguel River. The Camou Bros. own several large haciendas, also, with their thousands of cattle and horses, mules, sheep, and large mines. They also own the steam flour-mill, located at the city of Hermosillo, and another at El Molino Rancho. The town of Hermosillo is orderly, and the police regulations good. There is a very good market-place for the sale of meat and vegetables, but no bakeries, such as are seen in the United States, in the city. Water is found in abundance in wells, at the depth of 20 or 30 feet. Wood is plentiful, and brought from the timber, about two or three miles distant. A natural cement stone is within the town limits, that is easily quarried, being soft, until it hardens on exposure. It may be quarried and used for building purposes. There is also a fine clay, used in the manufacture of brick, in the vicinity. There is also a shoe factory and wagon factory, and plenty of carpenter and blacksmith shops, etc., worked by foreigners. Wardrobes and other pieces of furniture are manufactured in the town.

The railroad now being built from Guaymas will add to the business energy of the city, and its future is assured as the most important inland city in the State. There is a club in the city called the "Casion," of about one hundred members, of the principal citizens of the place, located in the former magnificent residence of Gov. Pesquiera; also a theater; and society is of the gayest during the sessions of the Legislature, when balls and receptions are quite frequent. There is no gas in the city; but an attempt is being made to organize a company for that purpose. The streets and houses are lighted by lamps. Señor Falizardo Torres is the superintendent, and Mr. Edward Norman is the cashier of the mint which is located here. This mint and those of Sinaloa, Chihuahua and Durango, are leased to an English company.

Hermosillo is the centre of the richest mining and agricultural district in the State, and is the distributing point for the supply of numerous mines and haciendas surrounding it. The principal merchants are Germans, who are doing a large and prosperous business. A view of this part of the State may be enjoyed from the summit of the Cerro de la Campana, which lies within the city limits.

The Sonora railway runs from Guaymas, on the Gulf of California to this city, and thence northward through the Valley del Baranca, passing the City of Magdalena, and from thence through the Valley of the Santa Cruz to Nogales on the border, and connecting with the Southern Pacific at Benson, Arizona. The distance from Benson to Guaymas is 352 miles, making a run of about 20 hours, or at the present time, of 19 hours and 40 minutes.

Besides the natural growth of travel over the line of this road in the increase of trade, we predict an immense travel by tourists over this line as well as over the Mexican Central. For the benefit of the tourists, we call their attention to the wonderful Aztec ruins lately discovered about four leagues southeast of Magdalena. These ruins consist of a mammoth pyramid, and a mountain palace. The pyramid has a base of 1350 feet, and rises to the height of 750 feet, with a winding roadway from the bottom leading up an easy grade to the top, wide enough for carriages to pass over, which is said to be twenty-three miles in length: the outer walls of the roadway are laid in solid masonry from huge blocks of granite in rubble work, and the circles are as uniform and the grade as regular as they could be made at this date by our best engineers. The wall, however, is only occasionally exposed, being covered by debris and earth, and overgrown with plants and trees, giving the pyramid the appearance of a mountain.

The mountain palace lies to the east of the pyramid, and is honeycombed by hundreds of rooms cut in the solid rock, with hieroglyphics on the walls, and innumerable stone relics are in and about the rooms. The size of the rooms ranges from 6 by 10 to 16 by 18 feet, and are cut even and true, with an entrance at the top. The ceiling is about 8 feet high. The rooms are one above the other, to three or more stories high. Here is a rare chance for some American archæologist.

The increase of the sale of mines promises well for the State, no less than six mines, said to be valuable, ranging in price from \$200,000 upwards, having been sold to New York and Chicago parties in the last six months, and more are coming every day.

"For the gold mine of Los Mulatos, \$1,000,000 has been refused."

The distance from Hermosillo to Ures is about fifty miles, situated north-east, and to Arispe, 150 miles north-east of Ures, and Santa Cruz, about 250 miles ; thence 170 miles to Tucson by way of Magdalena, distant 300 miles, and is about 100 miles by stage from Guaymas.

Ures.

This town was formerly the capital of the State, and is situated in a most beautiful valley, stretching from east to west, the soil of which is exceedingly fertile and suitable for the production of all kinds of fruits, excellent wheat, sugar-cane and cotton of superior quality. The environs are picturesque and pleasing to the eye of the visitor. It is located on the Sonora River, and on the road from Hermosillo and Alameda, a road lined with trees on each side similar to the Alameda between San José and Santa Clara in this State : the road in this instance being bordered with trees on either side for four miles, and presents an elegant drive for the residents of Ures.

The town originally was environed with numerous creeks that threatened it with inundations, when it was removed upon a neighboring plateau. The town is not so large as Hermosillo, yet its neat and elegant gardens of rare and beautiful flowers, lime, orange, and citron groves, make it a gem of a little city. There are some very substantial residences of brick scattered here and there among the adobe houses, and even elegant residences, among which may be mentioned Gov. Pesqueira's residence, handsomely furnished. A large orchard is attached to his residence and grounds, with orange, lime, lemon, peach, and olive trees bearing finely, besides an extensive vineyard.

Since the capital of the State was removed to Hermosillo the population has shrunk from 10,000 to 5,000. There is quite a rivalry between the two cities, and the dispute over the capital is not yet ended. If the Atchison, Topeka and Santa Fè Railroad passes up the Sonora river to El Paso, it will pass through this place. There is a vast agricultural and mining country around and adjacent to the city, and business is quite extensive. There are some heavy commercial firms in the city, among which may be mentioned Lauro Morales, Joaquin Villaes, Cusa & Co., Francisco Hernandez, Manuel Morales & Co. and Francisco C. Aguilar. The climate is much cooler at Ures than at Hermosillo, and one is able to sleep within doors. Among the important haciendas of arable land may be mentioned, Santa Rita, Molino, Guadalupe, Topahui and others. There are no important public buildings except certain small houses purchased during the administration of General Urea to form a palace, a penitentiary or House of Correction. Excellent stone for building is in the neighborhood of the city. The principal hotel is the Gubion, kept by a Frenchman.

The Rancho of Gov. Pesquiera, called Las Delicias, is located about 60 miles distant by way of Canada Andia, El Puertecito, El Molinate, Soqui, San José, La Estancia, La Concha and Baviacora. The last named town was once an important place, with a population of 3,000, and is situated in a pretty little valley one mile from the Sonora River, in one of the most fertile and beautiful districts of the State.

The grounds of the hacienda of Las Delicias is fenced in and laid out with orange and lime groves and flower gardens, containing rare flowers. The hacienda consists of a little over 30,000 acres of arable land, and about one-fifth is first-class agricultural land, devoted to the raising of wheat, Indian corn, potatoes, etc.; the balance is very good grazing land, covered with alfalfa and gramma grass. It is situated in a valley of considerable extent. Gov. Pesquiera has made this hacienda his residence, owing to the existence of rich mines in the vicinity, which are owned by him, and demand his attention in working them.

Among the reptiles that are found in the State may be mentioned the scorpion, whose sting is deadly. Rumor says that they are more deadly in the interior than on the coast.

One citizen near Guaymas was recently bitten by one of these reptiles on the hand. He simply twisted a strong India-rubber band around his wrist to keep the poison from communicating to the rest of the system, and took some ammonia, and the wound soon healed, without any serious result following. Strong spirits are generally used to work off the virus from the system.

Santa Cruz is the most northern town of Sonora, distant about 120 miles from the boundary line of Chihuahua and ten to fifteen from the boundary line of Arizona, and situated on a road direct to Guadalupe or Altar, which passes through Occua, Santa Ana, Santa Marta, San Lorenzo, Santa Magdalena, or San Ignacio, Tenenate, Imuris, and San Lazaro. The population is about 800. The town is located in a beautiful valley, clothed in verdure the entire year, in latitude 32 degrees 15 minutes north, and in a region that is pronounced to be the best agricultural region of the State, outside of the bottom lands of the rivers Yaqui and Mayo. It is also the best timbered of any portion of the northern part of the state, and in other respects presents advantages to the settler. Indeed, the valley of Santa Cruz, with its adjacent districts, where there are several rich and highly-cultivated haciendas and missions, must become the future granary of Arizona. The Santa Cruz River rises in a broad valley, or rather plain, north of the town, and passes the base of a mountain range through an open country, studded with oaks, into an open plain covered with luxuriant grass, without tree or shrub. It then passes between a low range of hills into the valley where the town is located. The river then flows south nine miles to San Lorenzo—a considerable rancho—and then takes a northerly course, winding its way through a beautiful valley, until it is lost across the line into Arizona, in the desert plain or sands some ten or fifteen miles north of Tucson. It is about 150 miles in length. Its width varies from 20 to 100 feet, and during dry seasons portions of it disappear. This valley was traversed by the earliest Spanish explorers in 1535, seduced by the flattering accounts of Cabela de Vaca.

Marco de Niza and Coronado led their deluded adventurers through it in search of the famed cities of Cibola, north of the Gila River; and before 1600, its richness having been made known, it was soon after occupied as missionary ground. Remains of several of these missions still exist. The Mission Church of San Xavier del Bac, erected during the last century, was the finest edifice of the kind in Sonora. Tumacacori, a few miles south of Tubac, was the most extensive. The towns and settlements of the Santa Cruz valley, across the line, in Sonora, are, Santa Cruz and San Lorenzo. The lands of this valley are suitable for stock-raising and all kinds of grain, especially wheat, which is produced of excellent quality.

Bacuachi.

The town or Presidio of Bacuachi is located about 50 miles south-east from Santa Cruz, on the road to Arispe, which is located on the Sonora River. It was at one time rich in cattle, sheep, and horses; but the Apaches swept them away, and the town became almost a heap of ruins. It is located in a very fertile valley, near the base of a range of mountains on the west, on the Sonora River, that rises in a valley north of the town and across the boundary line, in New Mexico. It also lies in a straight line drawn from the boundary line between Arizona and New Mexico, and is distant from the boundary line of the United States about 40 miles within or near the lower part of the prohibited belt. There are gold mines in the neighborhood of marvelous richness. The rich placers on the Sonora not being very distant, great quantities of this precious metal was extracted from the mines in the vicinity, of twenty-two carats fine. The miners were driven off by the Apaches, and the mines were, consequently, abandoned. The gold is coarse, and pieces have been found weighing twenty-five marcs. These mines might be made to yield a magnificent return if they were opened. The future of this mining district is just to open, since the suppression of the Apaches. A colony of miners will here find a rich field; for the whole region is rich in minerals, and but awaits the hands of man to develop their vast resources. This locality has been peculiarly exposed to the incursions of the Apaches, and for that reason, its mineral wealth has been withheld from the prospector. We predict a tremendous immigration to this point and all along the headwaters of the Yaqui River. The climate is cool and healthful, and epidemics or fevers are entirely unknown, while the soil is of the most fertile character, producing wheat, corn, etc., and presents a grazing region unexcelled anywhere; and there is an entire absence of swamps that are found in the Santa Cruz valley, which sometimes induce fevers. There are here two justices of the peace, subject to the sub-prefect of Arispe.

The town of Fronteras is situated in latitude 31 deg. N., north-east of Bacuachi, distant about 35 miles, and 20 miles from the boundary line of New Mexico. The town contains but one street, at the foot of a creek whose waters irrigate the neighboring lands, which produce excellent wheat, maize, etc; also, the delicious peaches for which Sonora is celebrated, apples, and bergamot pears. The town is situated 35 miles north-east of Bacuachi, and the greater part of the road is between dense thickets. This point was the most exposed to the Apaches of any in the State, but is now comparatively safe. The climate is cool and healthy, timber is abundant, and game plentiful. The plains are fertile and well watered. Two justices of the peace are located here.

Bapispe is situated about 18 miles west of the boundary line of Chihuahua, on the banks of a small creek which empties into the river Bapepito. It is isolated from all other towns, and is situated about 40 miles south of the boundary line of the United States at New Mexico, and east of Bacuachi about 90 miles.

The creek passing the town rises in a valley south-east of the town and flows north-west into a plain about 20 miles; then south-west into the Bapepito, near Oputo. A road connects this town with Janos in Chihuahua, about 40 miles distant. This territory of the Bapispe district contains the towns of Guachinera and Baserac, and haciendas Santa Ana and Loreto; it formerly comprised a number of wealthy ranchos, but all have been despoiled by the Apaches. Bapispe possesses excellent grazing lands and abundance of water. The population is about 800. They are engaged principally in the manufacture of soap and leather. About six miles east is located a rich silver mine, that has not been worked much on account of the Apaches.

Arispe is situated south-west of Bacuachi, on the river Sonora, in a valley skirting an immense table-land or plain, and a range of mountains extending north-east and south-west. Extensive silver mines are located south-east in this range of mountains, called the Babiconicora and Banamiche; also, south-west, the San Rosalio mine is located, also of silver, The hacienda of Las Delicias, owned by General Pesquiera, is also situated south-west of Arispe. A road runs from Bacuachi along the river Sonora, in a south-westerly direction, through Bacadobabi, Chinapa, Guipaberachi, Ciniriasanta, Arispe, Bamori, Sinoquipe, Monteport, Bamanitchi, Huepaca, Mochobavi, Aconche Babiacora, Concepcion, Puretecito, San Francisco, and Ures, distant about 100 miles. The same river passes Ures and Hermosillo in the same direction, until it is lost in the sandy plains on the coast, south-west of Hermosillo, and is about 200 miles long.

Moctezuma, or Oposura, is situated on the Soyopa River, in a large plain, that extends from the head-waters of the river Soyopa, which runs almost due south for about 100 miles, and then taking a south-easterly course, empties into the river Yaqui, about 20 miles further. A road runs from Moctezuma, down the Soyopa River to the Yaqui, and thence along the Yaqui to Comoripa and Buenavista. This plain is one of the largest in the state, and over 100 miles in length, and about 40 miles wide at its widest point. In the mountain ranges west of the head-waters of the Bapepito are situated the silver mines of El Pintos, Sesentero, San Pedro, El Rosario, Cinco Señora, El Humacal, and Plomosa. South-west of Soyopa, on this river, is located the Mina Prieta copper mine, and the silver mines of El Paste, and Los Bronces. East of the latter, the La Barranca, and the great gold mine called the San Antonio de la Huerta; the latter two of which are located near the mouth of the Soyopa River.

Sahuaripa is a small town located on a branch of the Bapepito, east of the river of that name, and distant from Bacuachi about one hundred and fifty miles south-east by way of the road through Bapepito and Oputo, crossing the branch of the river; thence south, along the Bapepito, to Cienega, Guainipa, Iascotol, and crossing the Bapepito to Huasavas; thence to Baca de Huachi, crossing again the same river; thence south-east to Nocori, on the river Viejo, which empties into the Bapepito south-west about fifteen miles; thence to Palmar, Casa, San Gabrielle, through the silver mine of San Felipe to Sahuaripa.

This region is well watered, and abundance of timber is found in the mountains. Several large haciendas are also in the neighborhood, along the stream and between the two streams; the stream on the north being the Rio Viejo, which takes its rise in the same neighboring mountains on the east. North-east of Sahuaripa, distant about fifty miles, is located the great gold mines of Cieneguita and the silver mine called the Minas Prietas Viejas, both of which are located at the base of the mountains; the Cieneguita being north of the latter about fifteen miles.

A road runs direct from the town through a rancho to the Minas Prietas Viejas mine. This is a rich mineral region, and will ere long be completely settled.

The region north of these mines has never been completely explored, and has not yet known the tread of the American miner. The second main branch of the river Yaqui, called the Papigochi or Mulatos, runs south of this region, taking a north-easterly course and emptying into the Bapepito about fifty miles south-west of Sahuaripa.

Gold placers are located east of Santa Cruz, about forty miles; and the mine of La Cananea south-east of Santa Cruz thirty miles; and the Santa Teresa silver mines and San Rafael Valle silver mines, forty miles south-west. The

Planchas de Plata silver mines are located west of Santa Cruz about fifty miles. The Altar mine, or mines surrounding Altar, are located in many districts. West of that place the gold mines of La Basura are located about seventy miles, and silver mines north-east of the same mine about ten miles. The Cajitos gold mines are located southwest of Altar about seventy miles; and south-west of La Basura, the placers of gold Micaray, and Alamo de San Feliz, silver, are also located about seventy miles; also, the silver mines of Los Palomos are located on the river Assumpcion, south-west of Altar about ninety miles, and about seventy miles north of La Libertad, on the coast. South of Altar about thirty miles, are located the Alamitos, silver, and La Tollena, gold mines, near. The Mina Grande silver mine is located about eighty miles south of Altar, and Latesote near Cienega, east about ten miles. Caborca gold mines are located near the same river. Rich gold placers are also found west of Altar on the elevated plains about one hundred miles distant; and the Quitovac gold mines, which were once rich, about one hundred and fifty miles north-west of Altar. So that the town may be said to be completely surrounded by mines.

Rivers Yaqui and Mayo.

The river Yaqui, or Buena Vista, rises in the Sierra Madre Maicova, and takes a south-westerly course through Bapispe, Todos Santos, the pueblo of Soyopa, Honavas, Tenichi, San Antonio and Comuripa, to the city of Buena Vista, where it enters the Yaqui settlement and finally empties into the Gulf of California, in front of the pueblo of Rahum. It has many branches, and may be said to drain all the region east of Arispe, Ures and Hermosillo, to the summit of the Sierra Madre range, which divides the states of Sonora and Chihuahua, and north of the river Mayo.

One of its branches called the Bapepito rises in the southeastern portion of Arizona; and another called the Papigochi, or Mulatos, at the base of the Sierra Madre, across the boundary line in south-western Chihuahua. It is the largest river of the state, and is estimated to be four hundred miles in length, from its source to its mouth. Its waters pass through the richest agricultural portion of the state, and through immense placers of gold, and along the base of ledges of silver, copper, galena, and tin ores.

Its rich bottom lands are the most fertile of any in the state,

TROPICAL SCENE IN MEXICO.

and raise in spots now under cultivation, wheat, sugar-cane, corn, cotton, the indigo plant, tobacco, and the various cereals. At and near its mouth, where the soil is not under cultivation, immense cane-brakes of a kind of bamboo extend along its banks for about sixty miles. If brought under control by proper agriculture, its valuable lands could produce immense quantities of all the products that an alluvial soil, well irrigated, will produce. The best portion of the lands are in possession of the Yaqui Indians, with some exceptions, but its lands are so extensive that after reserving sufficient for the Indians, millions of acres of arable lands would remain to be brought under cultivation.

Here is an opportunity for colonization that is unrivaled in the United States or the Republic of Mexico. The land is easily irrigated from the river, and would provide homes for colonization of a large population. In time of high water the river is navigable for small vessels for from fifty to seventy-five miles. Flour-mills are located on its banks, owned by foreigners—the result of foreign capital and energy. At its mouth are located the best oyster-beds on the coast of the gulf. We are assured by parties who have tested the qualities of these oysters, that they are equal to our best Eastern bivalves. San Francisco will soon have the pleasure of testing them on the completion of the Sonora Railway connecting Guaymas with San Francisco. Packed in ice manufactured at Guaymas, they can successfully be exported direct by rail to San Francisco, on the completion of the railroad, thus opening up a new avenue for some enterprising gentleman who will take the initiative. San Franciscans would like to try some of the Yaqui oysters if they are as represented. We understand that Dr. Charles McQuesten of this city, and Rafael Escobosa of Guaymas, are now the *bona fide* owners of these oyster beds, and the extent of their possession comprises one league square in the delta of the Yaqui at the old mouth. The oysters are found in the sloughs which extend from one to two miles inland.

The basin of this river at its widest point is about ninety miles wide. After the rains have ceased, the river is fordable, though still deep until the droughts in April, May and June. Near Soyopa, Buena Vista, and Honavas, are located a greater proportion of the best bottom lands. The salt-pits of the river, located near the coast, supply the interior towns, and are considered the property of the Yaquis. The annual overflow of the river supplies sufficient irrigation for one crop of wheat, maize, beans, lentils, and various kinds of fruit, at the points thus irrigated. Cotton, flax, and coffee, are also successfully raised. We are told by Velasco, the sheep raised upon its nutritious grasses attain the size of a yearling calf, and make excellent mutton. Beef cattle of the best quality are raised. At one time the Mission of Huirivis alone owned 40,000 head. The tobacco raised by the Indians upon the banks of this river is of very good quality; and the plant might, with proper cultivation, be equal to that of Havana. Immigration to this region must be of incalculable value to the state in the increase of its productions.

The river Mayo rises also in the Sierra Madre, and though it is smaller, and its bottom lands more narrow than those of the Yaqui, yet its fertility is the same, and may produce like results proportionate to the extent of its lands that are susceptible of cultivation. The Mayo Indians are located on its banks. The two rivers are separated by a low range of hills or mountains, and the intervening hills are good grazing lands. The pueblos of the Mayos, from the sierra on the east to Conicari on the west, are Macollagui in the sierra, Conicari, Camoa, Tecia, Nabajoa, Cuirimpo, Guitajoa, Echojoa, Santa Cruz, and Masiaca.

The Yaqui settlements extend from Buena Vista to Belen, over a territory of 84 miles in length. A brig might enter the mouth of the river Mayo, and a harbor is located at the port of Loreto, at this point. It was the first settlement of the gulf, and renowned for its pearl fishery, which has produced splendid fortunes. In the gulf, many large whales are sometimes caught, of various kinds; also, sharks of enormous size haunt its coasts, to the great danger of the pearl fishermen, who are Yaqui Indians. They always carry a long, keen knife with them while diving after pearls, to defend themselves. The "manta," or blanket fish, also, is another great enemy of theirs, and very formidable. It has fins like the arms of a man, says a writer, by which it seizes its prey.

The Presidio of Buenavista is located on the Yaqui River, on the main road to Alamos, about 300 miles from Arispe, by way of Hermosillo, and about 260 miles by way of the road of Matape, which runs along the banks of a stream by that name, south of Hermosillo. It is situated upon a small rocky promontory or hill, and is, consequently, very hot. It claims some importance as a military position, and is supposed to present a barrier against the revolt of the Yaquis and Mayo Indians. Its soldiers are poorly supplied and seldom paid.

The recent attempts to survey the lands of the Yaqui and Mayo rivers have been suspended, awaiting a petition from the Legislature of Sonora to the general government to supply a force of 1,000 soldiers to keep the Yaquis in subjection during the survey and location of certain government grants upon those rivers. For this purpose, a return grant by the owners to the general government of a portion of the lands is to be made to cover the expense of maintaining the military in this district.

The lands adjacent to the town are of the fertile character that belongs to the bottom lands of the Yaqui and Mayo rivers. From this point, the Yaqui River is navigable during the greater part of the year, and timber, grain, and other productions can easily be transported to Guaymas. Mines of gold and silver are located at Cumuripa, Cendraditas and San Francisco de Borja, which, when worked, yield abundantly.

The current of the river is rapid at Buenavista and many other points. Ore might be transported from this place and shipped from Guaymas. Along the river, above Buenavista, there are hundreds of veins of gold and silver that could be worked profitably. The placers are located near this place, and are said to be very rich.

The town of San Pedro de la Conquista is situated south of Hermosillo, on the river Sonora, a short distance. Cattle and horses are here raised, and different kinds of grain grown. There have been no mines of any consequence discovered here. The land is well timbered with iron-wood, the mesquite, the huayacan, (a very solid and compact wood) and the huevito. An herb is here found, called the "confituria," which is much esteemed, as possessing medicinal qualities, and is said to be used as a specific for hydrophobia.

The land is fertile, producing wheat and Indian corn or maize, beans, pulse, lentils, Chili peppers, sweet potatoes, etc. Figs are raised in profusion, grapes, peaches, apricots, pomegranates, quinces, sweet and sour oranges, limes, citrons, and the guava.

Wheat is sown from October to December, and sometimes as late as January, and is harvested from May to July. Two crops of beans are raised annually. The first is planted in February or March, and the second in July and August. Two crops of corn are also sometimes raised, the most abundant being gathered in November and December. That gathered in July or August is generally of inferior quality. Grain, flour, and other products are transported to Guaymas and other places, in wagons drawn by mules and oxen.

There are several grist-mills turned by water-power at this place, the best grinding from 25 to 30 cargas (of 300 lbs. each), in 24 hours. Sugar-cane is also raised. The climate is healthy, and the population about 1,200. The town has two justices of the peace, subject to the tribunal of first instance at Hermosillo.

The Indians and Presidios.

The Yaqui and Mayo Indians inhabit the cane-brakes on those rivers, and are depended upon mostly for laborers all through the state. They are not averse to labor, and are employed in every capacity. They possess remarkable natural abilities, and soon learn the trades of blacksmithing, carpentering, etc. They have been known to manufacture fireworks, and are skillful players on the harp and violin. Their character is resolute, and they are very jealous of their lands. They are generally copper-colored and well formed. The women are of medium height and corpulent. In some of the settlements, the women are exceedingly fair and handsome; but these latter are mostly half-breeds. The Yaqui, with few exceptions, has but few wants. A cotton shirt and drawers for the men, and shawl and petticoat for the women, suffices; while the children run naked, with the exception of a cloth around the loins. Their nature is joyous, and they are very fond of music and dancing. They are suspicious, and a supposition of deception serves as well as the reality. They have been known to revolt against the government and commit great atrocities. They are brave, and have been known to fight steadily for hours against the government troops. They shun the society of the whites, and only live near them for the sake of employment. Velasco says, " They will steal, gamble, and drink, and have no generosity or gratitude "—a rather peculiar trait for the Indian—yet they work in the mines, till the soil, build houses, and perform nearly all the labor of Sonora. They alone of all the Indians are skillful pearl-divers ; but so "great is their love of robbery," says Francisco Velasco, an impartial Spanish writer, " that they abandon any occupation, however profitable, for the purpose of stealing cattle and horses from the ranchos in the neighborhood of the river. This they practice even in times of peace."

But Mr. Andrade tells us that this is not so at present. They have greatly improved since the writing of Velasco's book. Their population amounts to 13,500 in the state, according to Cubas.

The Mayos possess the same characteristics as the Yaquis. Being located on the Mayo, they are called Mayos. The Ceris are more allied to savages, are filthy, drunken, and bitterly hostile to the whites. They are located by the government upon the pueblo of San Pedro de la Conquista, where they have lands assigned to them for their support. They are lazy, and dress themselves in either the skins of the pelican or a coarse blanket wrapped around the waist. Some wear nothing but a strip of cloth about the loins, and none wear shoes. They paint their faces in black stripes, and many pierce the cartilages of the nose, and append to it pieces of a green stone resembling glass. The women perform the greater part of the labor, gathering the crops, etc. The men are tall, erect, and generally stout. The women are copper-colored, and wear a petticoat made of the pelican skin, with the feathers, which covers the form from the waist down. They worship the moon, and prostrate themselves, beating their breasts, and kiss the ground on the appearance of the new moon.

The Opatas are more frank and docile, and are friendly towards the whites, many of them serving as soldiers. They are brave to the last extremity, and have been known to withstand an onset of the Apaches outnumbered eight to one. They are just and humane in their dealings, and capable of a high degree of education. They are the bitter foes of the Apaches, showing them no mercy in an encounter.

The Opatas live in several of the towns, where the mixed race predominates, called Opodepe, Cucurpe, Suaque, Acouchi, Babiacora, Arivechi, Santo Tomas, Bacanora, and Nuri in the center; Oposura, Guayavas, Baca de Huachi, Nacori, Mochop, and Oputo in the sierra; Chinapa, Bacuachi, Cuquiurachi, and Cumpas, to the north. The Opatas are able-bodied, and as fleet as the game they pursue. Their haughty character is illustrated by the following, related by Cubas, of a band of them in rebellion : " Persecuted by General Gandara with very superior forces, in consequence of an insurrection, they refused to surrender themselves, even after each one at his post had shot his last arrow, Their captain, with some few who had survived the contest, took refuge on the summit of an almost inaccessible mountain, and there awaited the approach of General Gandara's emissaries, who had intimated their submission. Believing themselves humiliated at the demand for the delivery of their arms, they declared to the envoys of the general their resolution to deliver themselves up to their conquerors, without abandoning their arms. Upon General Gandara's insisting in his demands, and they in their resolution, their conduct decided him to take them prisoners by force, which they avoided by an act worthy of the ancient Spartans, in throwing themselves over the precipice at the moment the general's troops were ascending the heights." The Opatas are most useful citizens, and have on many occasions proved their loyalty to the Mexican Government by resisting the attacks of the Apaches. They seldom go barefooted, every man has a blanket, and every woman a long scarf. They are good carpenters, masons, shoemakers, and house-painters, and manufacture blankets, shawls, coarse cottons, saddles, pack-saddles, bridles, etc., and considerable quantities of soap.

The Papajos are numerous, and located in the western part of the state, subsisting principally on wild fruits, especially the "pitaya," from which they manufacture a delicious syrup, and carry it to the settlements for sale in earthen jars. In the winter they resort to the settlements of La Pimeria to trade, exchanging skins and baskets. This tribe is also the sworn enemy of the Apaches.

The Apaches are divided into the Coyotes or Pinelores, the Tontos, Chiricahuis, Mimbreños, Gilenos, Mescaleros, Sacramantenos, Mogollones, Carrizalleños, Gipanes, Faraones, and Navajoes. They have had no fixed habitation, and reside in the mountains and on the plains, and often make incursions into Sonora, near Altar and Magdalena, and also in the north-east, in the mountains of Chihuahua, near Janos, and in Coahuilla. They are the most savage of all the Indians of Mexico, and are exceedingly fleet, both in traversing the vast plains and in climbing the rugged eminences of the mountains; and, besides, are excellent horsemen. Their arms are mostly the bow and arrow; but some few have fire-arms, and a lance with a flint point. They use a leather quiver, and a shield of leopard's skin, ornamented with feathers and with small mirrors in the center. They are cowardly, and only attack unawares; crafty and treacherous, and scalp their victims. They make use of smoke for telegraphic signals. They are fond of hunting deer and wild boars, "ciballos," or Mexican bulls, black bears, wild goats, and Rocky Mountain sheep. Their dress consists of a strip of linen passing between their thighs, and fastened at the waist, and leggings of deerskin with fringes, ornamented with beads, and garnished with leather strings, and wear pendants and ear-rings, and in their hair they fasten a long false braid, adorned with trinkets, shells, or silver buckles. The women, who are as active as the men in their habits, use very short garments of deer-skin or kid, which they call "tlacalee," with fringes of leather strings, on the edges of which are hung casebels, tassels, and red beads. They wear, also, a kind of jacket called "bietle," made of the entire deer-skin, open in front, ornamented in the same manner. They wear moccasins of deer-skin, the same as the men, which are called "teguas," and are fastened to the leggings. They are all of swarthy complexion, well proportioned, wear long hair, and no beard. Both the men and women have very small feet. The women decorate themselves with ear-rings of shells, or small green and white stones, resembling crystal; and in some instances the men are decorated in like manner. Their huts are simply poles covered with grass or skins, and a small door, admitting a grown person. If the place is wooded, they encamp at the foot of a tree, and cover the branches with grass to protect them from the rain; but generally they live without any protection whatever. Their atrocities are well known, and they have long been a terror to the Sonorians; but the dispersion of Victorio's band subdued them, with the exception of small roving bands, that do not hesitate to attack even the stages, as they did but a short time since, near Mesilla, in New Mexico. Comparative peace may be said to exist, though settlers may do well to keep on the lookout, and travel well armed.

4

DISCOVERY OF GOLD.

In 1799, the first discovery of gold in the western part of the state was made at San Ildefonso de la Cieneguilla, about forty miles south or south-east of Altar, of which many incorrect accounts have been published. This discovery was accidental, and occurred as follows :

"A company of soldiers from Altar, on their way to chastise the Ceris, having gone in a south-east direction, encamped in that neighborhood. One of their number, who was strolling about one hundred yards from the camp, observed that the bed of a small ditch formed by the rain was of a yellowish color, and on further examination, he collected a number of pieces of gold from the size of a lentil to that of a bean. He reported this to the commander of the detachment, who immediately ordered a careful examination of the surrounding country, the result being the discovery of gold in all parts in greater or less quantities. The gold lay upon the surface, scattered like grains of corn. The gambucinos followed its direction to the west to the distance of six or nine miles, where they encountered a natural phenomenon. The beds of all the ravines within a circumference of more than 12 miles was covered with particles of gold, hundreds of these weighing from one to 27 marcs, and presenting the appearance of having passed through a furnace."— *Velasco.*

After the surface gold was exhausted, shafts were sunk and tunnels run through a vein of calcareous stone in some places, and in others through a stratum of red stone, both of which contained gold, and from which large quantities were extracted. The mine was actively worked until 1803, when a second mine was discovered, called San Francisco, 21 miles east of Cieneguilla, which is about 40 miles southeast of Altar. "This mine proved extremely rich, the gold being scattered about on the surface in great abundance, especially in the ravines. In the ravine called San Miguelena, the gold was so abundant that three, four, and even five mares were often collected in five minutes ; the grains being the size of a bean. Large lumps were occasionally discovered. One found by a Yaqui weighed 100 ounces, and another weighed 28 mares. Quitovac, San Antonio, Sonoita, El Zoñe, La Basura, San Perfecto, Las Palomas, El Alamo, El Muerto, and Vado Seco, are gold mines discovered from 1834 to 1844 in the vicinity of Altar."

Mines of Sonora.

The mines of Sonora have been worked from time immemorial. The immense number of old mines that have a history clouded with early traditions prove the ancient character of the mines of Sonora. Some have been known to reach back one hundred years, and others have no data to determine the first period in their history. The number of abandoned mines are considerable, some of which were unquestionably exhausted, while others were abandoned on account of the ignorance of the miners on reaching ores that were refractory or hard to work. Right here it might be well to caution American capitalists against buying holes in the ground, solely because, at one period in their history, they had yielded millions.

Most of the abandoned mines, or quite a large number of them, and of the richest, have been ruined by the class of miners of Mexico called "gambucinos," a poor class who had no capital, and were in search of " bonanzas," or rich spots, working these solely, and filling the drifts and shafts behind them with rejected ores and rubbish, so that, when they finished a mine it was almost entirely ruined. In some instances, they have extracted the pillars of old mines of great value, and the walls have fallen in, thus doing an incalculable injury to the mines of the state. There is an old Spanish proverb that tersely states: "It takes another mine to work a mine."

This is undoubtedly true of every mine abandoned by these miners. We use strong language on account of the destruction following in the wake of the "gambucinos." The warning of Mr. Mowry to capitalists in his valuable work on Arizona and Sonora, we herewith quote, and leave its lesson with our readers. He says : "As it is desirable that, in the investment of foreign capital there should be no error committed at the outset, than which nothing would retard the progress of this new mining field more; all persons new to the country had better leave abandoned mines alone, unless directed to them by persons long resident in the country, whose character and veracity are undoubted, and who, after the investigation of all the facts, current accounts, and traditions, have full confidence in some abandoned mine or other. There are, undoubtedly, many abandoned mines that are well worthy of attention and outlay of capital, but strangers are not likely to know at once which of the many deserted mines it will be prudent to meddle with. Under the present state of things, the safest investments for new comers will be *those mines that have bona fide owners, for, as long as a mine can be worked according to the custom of the country, it is hardly ever abandoned altogether. The owners are fully alive to the value of their possessions*, and as they are already in a more or less independent position, and always in expectation of a sudden fortune, they are not anxious to sell unless induced by a fair offer. *It is not advisable to enter into any arrangement with Mexican miners to furnish capital to open up a mine*, but it is better to buy the whole at once."

The Mexican people are shrewd and full of grandiose language, extravagant in speech, and due caution in taking their description of properties, with some allowance when they are anxious to sell, is of the first importance. It may be well to remember that where an anxiety to sell is apparent, that the purchaser will do well to make haste slowly, and look further for investment. The properties that are being worked, and where a fair examination can be made by reliable mining engineers, are the ones to buy. These are mostly not for sale, but they may be purchased on a liberal offer. Another way to obtain properties of value, is to prospect for new mines, and when a discovery is made, by "denouncement" a title may be obtained under the laws of Mexico that is perfectly valid; and indeed, this is one of the safest means to obtain valuable mines; for the whole state is rich in veins of gold and silver. In the appendix may be found an abstract of the mining laws of Mexico, with directions as to the obtaining of properties in the republic.

As an instance of the unreliability to be placed on representations of the riches of mines that are for sale in Mexico, we give the following data : A company of gentlemen of this city were induced to open up an abandoned mine, called Santa Gertrudis, near Altar, which was represented by the parties interested, to be very rich. The vein first discovered was narrow, but was followed down on the assurance that it would become broader and richer. Extensive plans were entered upon; a stamp mill and engines purchased, ready to

be shipped as soon as the mine was developed sufficiently to
warrant the erection of the works. The vein was followed
for nearly 200 feet, and some $30,000 were expended. The
result was unsatisfactory and the mine was abandoned; the
representations being entirely erroneous, to say the least,
as far as the experiment progressed. Thus, it is easily seen
that experiments in mines in Sonora are as unsatisfactory as
in California; and it is well to be cautioned in advance in
regard to abandoned mines and properties that are found upon the market. We could point out other instances with simi-
results. *The paying mines, as a rule, are not for sale*, though
there are some exceptions, and no greater mistake can be
made than to expect a rich mine in as old a mining state as
Sonora, to be bought for a mere nominal sum. There are
exceptions, but they are rare; a fair offer has to be made to
purchase a valuable mine.

Mining Districts of the State of Sonora, and Location and Description of Mines.

The Alamos mining district is situated some 240 miles
south-east from the port of Guaymas, on the direct road from
that point to El Fuerte in Sinaloa, and on the road also from
Arispe on the north to the same place, and from thence to
Culiacan and Cosala and Mazatlan. This district is particularly rich in silver leads. The principal mines are as follows: The most ancient and richest mine is the Quintera,
several millions having been taken from it since its discovery, over 100 years ago. It is of immense depth, and has
been abandoned, and is worked occasionally by gambucinos,
and is mostly exhausted. There are many old mines of
whose origin we can obtain no data, their origin being known
only by tradition. Among the Promontorio mines in the
small Real of Promontorio, five miles north of Alamos, may
be mentioned the Nuestra Señora de Vabranora, which was
owned and worked by the family of Almados for the last
century. Don José M. Almado reached a deposit of black
ores at a depth of 600 feet with surprising results. The
present owners are an English company, who purchased the
mine from Mr. Robinson of Guaymas. The ores are reduced
at the works situated at Las Mercedes, about two miles east
of Alamos. The Promontorio mines contain the best ores
in the district. The Promontorio mine, from which the
mines were named, especially has produced exceedingly
rich and abundant ores. The Tirite mine, to the south of

and adjoining the Promontorio, is said to be still richer, but its vein is not so wide. It was formerly owned by James Brady of Guaymas, who reopened it by running a tunnel into the heart of the vein. The pillars in the old shaft and drifts were taken out some years ago by Pascual Gomez, and two of them yielded $80,000. The Dios Padre mine, adjoining the Promontorio on the north, was, prior to 1860, owned and worked by Fernando Aduaña, son-in-law of José de Almado. In August, 1860, Mr. Andrew J. Wiley from California purchased the mine, and associated himself with Messrs. W. W. Light, D. Maddox, U. F. Moulton, Skinke, Backus, Beard, Sanborn, Oatman, Robinson, and L. A. Garnet. The mine was reopened by a shaft and yielded very profitably.

The Quintera and Libertad mines are located north of the Dios Padre. The Pulpito, on the same lead, was discovered by a Mexican, who worked it secretly. In January, 1861, Mr. Benjamin Rountree purchased the rights of both parties and associated with himself Messrs. W. W. Light, Johnson, Price, Thos. Finley, Robert S. Stillwell, J. R. Hardenburg, and others, and they proceeded to open up the mine, but found it unprofitable and abandoned it. The Nacharama mine is situated nine miles from Alamos, and is one of the most celebrated in the district, but it was abandoned on account of the influx of water. In 1860 the mine was purchased by Messrs. W. T. Robinson, J. G. Baldwin, Thomas H. Williams, Wm. S. Long, Henry Fouche, and others. The mine had the reputation of being rich at the time of its purchase. The Vista Nacacharama mine was purchased by Messrs. Robinson, Ira Oatman, Goggins, Bowman and Whiteside, and was called the Sacramento Company's mine. The Mina Grande, Europia, Iglesia, and Palomos are well spoken of by tradition. The first two were denounced by Michael Gray in January, 1860, and afterwards sold to John Heard. The Pietras Verdes, 15 miles north of Alamos, and Narvayez, in the Promontorio, are filled with water.

There are three large haciendas for the reduction of metals in the city of Alamos, called La Aurora, La Ubalama, and Las Cabras.

The district or Real of Minas Nuevas is located about two leagues west of Alamos, and contains many rich mines, among them, San José Ubalama, which is situated six miles from Alamos, and was owned by W. J. Hill and E. B. Johnson, who erected machinery at the mine to work it. Tradition spoke of it as exceedingly rich. The Descubridora, Rosario de Talpa, Sambono, and others, are located in this district.

The Rosario de Talpa and the Sambono were once successfully worked by Mr. Robinson of Guaymas, and T. Robinson Bours, formerly of Stockton, but who now resides at Alamos. The San José mine is situated six miles from Alamos, in this district, and was owned by W. J. Hill and E. B. Johnson, in 1861, who placed machinery at the mine to develop its riches, which tradition declared to be fabulous. There are many other mines in the vicinity, as we have only mentioned the principal ones, and the district is unquestionably one of the richest in Sonora.

The mine called Balvaneda, situated in Promontorio, formerly belonged to José Maria Almado. It was formerly rich, and yielded handsomely up to 1861, though the water flowing into it caused such trouble and expense that it was afterward abandoned. La Europita, in the Promontorio, was worked by Don Manuel Salido up to 1861, with good results.

Lead is found in the ores of the Promontorio mines, which may be used for smelting, although most of the ore is reduced by mills. La Europita was once one of the richest mines of the district, and with Quintera, produced an immense amount of silver. These two mines gave to Alamos its greatest celebrity. The former was worked up to 1861.

Although Aduaña is generally included in the district of Alamos, yet it possesses a group of mines that are distinguished from the Promontorio mines. The Aduaña is situated about three miles west of Alamos. In this district, which, with that of the Promontorio, comprises an area of eight leagues, with the face of a small mountain range included on the south, are located many old and new mines over the whole area, which Velasco pronounces, that "without exaggeration, there is not a hand's breadth of the soil which does not contain some vein of the precious metal." La Cotera and Santo Domingo, and Nacacharama and La Libertad in the Aduaña, were all worked up to 1861. Calesa and Los Cangrejos are full of water.

There are five haciendas in Aduaña for the reduction of ore—one in Talajiossa called Zarragoitas, La Espinosa, and the old hacienda of Promontorio; also, two in Minas Nuevas; making eleven in all.

The district of Alamos contributes very largely to the export of silver from Sonora, part of which is exported from the port of Santa Cruz de Mayo, south of Alamos, on the coast, distant about 100 miles, which is said to be one of the favorite points for smuggling bullion out of the state, while the larger proportion is carried to Guaymas.

San Ildefonso de la Cieneguilla.

This district is located in the western part of Sonora and north-west of Hermosillo about 100 miles, and south-east of Altar the same distance. Scarcely any region equals this in its number of veins of gold and silver. Its first mine, called Descubridora, was discovered four years after the first placers, to which we have referred under the heading of "The Discovery of Gold." This mine yielded abundant quantities of silver ores, the yield of the poorest being five to seven and the best 12 to 15 marcs to the "bulto" of three cargas (900 lbs.). Its owner received from it, in less than four years, $2,000,000. Fifty small establishments for crushing ores were erected and in constant operation, from which large profits were realized. The vein was crossed, after the mine had been worked for five years, by a species of hard rock, called "caballo," which was again repeated. This discouraged its owner, and the pillars were removed, which yielded $500,000, and supports of strong timber exchanged for them; but the gambucinos soon left the mine in ruins. Many other mines were discovered in the neighborhood, but none so rich or abundant in ores. Only one exceeded it in the quantity of its ores, viz: the Cerro Colorado, in the Cieneguita district, six leagues to the east of Cieneguilla, on the right of the road to the placers of San Francisco.

From the appendix of the work entitled "Sonora," a translation of Francisco Velasco's great work, by Mr. Wm. F. Nye, published in 1861, we quote the following interesting fact in relation to the Cerro Colorado mine. He says: "The Cerro Colorado mine is situated some eight or nine leagues from the city of Alamos, on the bank of the Mayo River, and derives its name from the reddish color of the mountain in which it is located. It was formerly owned by Castro and Don Manuel Salida, and afterwards by Dr. W. J. Hill, of Alamos, who sold one-half his interest some few months since for $12,000. Messrs. J. S. Garwood, E. D. Wheeler, Michael Gray, and others of San Francisco, were the fortunate purchasers. The last owner of this mine, Don Manuel Salida, took from it more than a million of dollars, and, at the time of his death, gave orders to blow the mine up, which was accordingly carried into effect by his peons.

The writer visited the mine in company with Dr. Hill; but, on account of its dilapidated condition, could not explore it. At a depth of 70 feet is a chamber 20 feet in diameter and 25 feet high, the walls of which, impregnated with virgin silver, glittered like diamonds by the light of a solitary candle. In working the mines of this district, it is not unusual to discover spots of exceeding richness, called by Mexicans 'bonanzas,' and from one of these, from two to three hundred thousand dollars are frequently extracted."

Gold Mining Districts.

The district of San Francisco is located seven leagues to the east of Ildefonso de la Cieneguilla, and was discovered Oct. 4th, 1803, by Teodoro Salazar, who was searching for a mine of which he had received notice. This mine proved extremely rich, the gold being scattered about on the surface in great abundance, especially in the ravines. The ravine called San Miguelena was the richest spot, and the grains were coarse, being about the size of a bean. Large lumps were occasionally found, one of which weighed 100 ounces, and another 28 marcs. In portions of this mineral region the gold was mixed with white quartz, which led to a ledge of very rich gold-bearing quartz. Here a mine was opened by Teodoro Salazar, and he occasionally struck extensive pockets that were very rich. The mine was eventually abandoned, and another found one league distant from San Francisco, not so rich as the former, but yielding very fine gold, of 22 and 23 carats fine. In the Sierra to the south, veins were found near the creek of San Blas, a small town near the northern border of Sinaloa. The water in the creek having failed, this mine was abandoned. The annual yield, on an average, of the mine of San Francisco, Velasco puts at from $4,000,000 to $5,000,000. Quitovac, San Antonio, Sonoita, El Zoñe, La Basura, San Perfecto, Las Palomas, El Alamo, El Muerto, and Vado Seco, were the gold mines discovered from 1833 to 1844. Since that time, many other mines have been found, bearing both gold and silver. The great drawback to the mines of San Francisco, which are so rich in gold, is the scarcity of water, which has been brought from the river Arituava, 21 miles distant, and commanded fabulous prices. If the waters of the river were conducted to the placers, or artesian wells sunk and reservoirs formed, the mines would yield immensely.

The district of Mulatos is located to the north-east of

Alamos, and nearly due west of Jesus Maria in Chihuahua, upon the slope of the Sierra Madre towards the gulf, and is called the Mineral of San José de Mulatos, which was discovered in 1806. Two gold mines were here found, from which were taken several thousand marcs of gold, 24 carats fine. The region is located near the eastern border of the state, in the pass of Mulatos, about 70 leagues, or 210 miles, from Hermosillo. It is said that several millions were extracted from these mines. The gold was first found in a small stream which descends to the river below. Adjoining this ravine and near the placers, three elevated crests were discovered, one of them over one hundred varas in height, which were intersected in all directions by small threads or veins of gold-bearing white earth, or rotten quartz, that were so rich that the ore of inferior quality was sold at $12 and $15 per arroba (25 pounds), while the reihest sold for $200. These crests have been extensively worked. The gold is nearly pure, the lowest ore being 23 quilates, while it sometimes reached 3½ grains. A number of Indians at first worked the vein by being suspended by ropes from the side of the rocks from the crests above and picking out the earth with wooden sticks and knives. The mines were abandoned some years ago, but have since been denounced by an American company, who are working them so profitably, we understand, that they have lately refused $1,000,000 for them. The ores are reduced by an extensive stamp-mill, located on the Mulatos River, below the mine. This river has sometimes been called the Aribechi and Papigochi.

The district of San Xavier is distant from the port of Guaymas in a north-east direction, and about the same distance from Hermosillo, approachable from both points by an excellent wagon road. This is one of the oldest and richest mineral districts of the state. There are many mines situated within a radius of three miles—namely, Los Bronces, owned by Don Alsua of Guaymas; Las Cruzecitas, Las Aguas, Señor, Las Cumbres, La Division, La Naguilla, La Barranca, Las Animas, La Sierra, and many others. Among the most important, Los Bronces may be mentioned, which is worked by Don Matias Alsua of Guaymas, who has erected extensive reduction works, with stamps, barrels, furnaces, etc. His ores are worked by the German or Freyburg process, and the mine has yielded about $1,000 per day. Near this mine is located the La Barranca, in which a vein of coal was found nine feet in thickness. It is supposed to be anthracite, but this is denied by some experts, who claim it is more of the nature of bituminous coal. We examined a piece of this same coal, and it appeared to us to be similar to the bituminous coal of Pennsylvania.

About 200 yards above the Los Bronces mine is situated the Las Cruzecitas, which is owned by the Las Cruzecitas Mining Company. It has been extensively developed, and ten tons have been raised daily; and when further developed, will yield much greater quantities. The vein, which is particularly well defined, increases in width and richness as it descends; and at a depth of 145 feet, the vein was nine feet wide. The ore of the pillars is very rich; while that from the mine averaged over $150 per ton, all through. The "Petanque" has rich sulphurets of silver, which are extracted from the lower excavations, and assay over $3,000 per ton. The Company have erected reduction works at the mines. La Naguilla is situated on the highest hill in this region, in sight of the main road; its ores were formerly abundant, and their "ley" in silver, ten marcs to the carga. It however filled with water, and although an attempt was made to work it out, it was abandoned upon reaching a "caballo." Las Animas is also one of the old mines, and is now choked with earth; the "ley" of its ores was four or five marcs to four arrobas. Its vein was narrow, but contained an abundance of ferruginous ore, which, though rejected by the miners in former times, yield three to four marcs of silver to the carga. The amalgamating ores are also abundant, and of about the same "ley." In Los Afurnos, the vein is half a vara in breadth, and was profitably worked by Castillo. The mines of La Grande were equally rich with the others. The rest of the ores of San Xavier are smelting ores, or reducible by fire, with some exceptions. Enormous quantities of silver were remitted to the City of Mexico from this district, and prove it to have been very rich.

"The mine of Zubiate is situated eleven leagues (33 miles) south-east of Hermosillo. It was discovered in the year 1813. Its first owners were not able to pay their expenses, and sold out to two persons called Monge and Muñoz, who derived a handsome profit from a mine hitherto worthless. Muñoz, having acquired sufficient wealth, sold his interest to Francisco Monteverde, who continued the operation, in company with Monge, until the death of the latter, who left a large fortune. Monteverde then became sole owner of the mine," and worked it up to the time of his death, leaving it to his son, M. Monteverde, ex-Governor of Sonora, who is now in this city. "Its average ley did not exceed five to six marcs to three cargas of 300 lbs. each, or about from $36 to $45 per ton; but occasionally ores are found which yield two to three marcs ($3.20 to each marc) per arroba of 25 lbs. each, or from $480 to $720 per ton. Water flows into it, and for some time the sole profits of the owner were derived from furnishing supplies to his workmen." Governor Monteverde informs us, that since the publication of Francisco Velasco's work on Sonora, from which we quote the foregoing, that he has found the mine to become very profitable, and it now assays from $80 up to $1,000 per ton, having reached ores on a lower level that are very rich. This mine is for sale, and can be purchased of Governor Monteverde. He also informs us that $12,000,-000 have been extracted from the mine since its discovery, or in a little over 67 years.

San Antonio de la Huerta.

This district is located about 15 miles from San Xavier, and contains La Minas Prietas, Musidora, and other valuable mines, both of gold and silver. The Minas Prietas was purchased of Mr. R. D. Johnson, of Guaymas, by the Jannin Bros., of this city, and sold to a company in New York. The point of location on the maps of this mine is erroneous, and should be at the point marked Haygame, about 35 miles south-east of Hermosillo. A new 40-stamp mill is being erected for this mine. There was an old 10-stamp mill on it, which, with arastras, were used to reduce the ore.

Cieneguita District.

The following official report on the Mineral de la Cieneguita, of Robert L. D'Aumaille, official assayer of Sonora, is copied from the valuable work of Mr. Mowry, " on Sonora and Arizona"; our object being to give all the information available on the mines of Sonora, and also within the limits of the states of Chihuahua, Durango, and Sinaloa. On the mines of this district, his report reads as follows : " About 300 yards from the hacienda is the mine La Carjona, of trifling depth. The metal is plombiferous, vein one foot in width, and assays $16 to the 100 pounds. The water from the rivulet adjoining, has filled the shaft, which is not deep. Two miles distant in same direction, lies the hill that contains the veins of La Chipiona, La Colorada, La Plomosa, and another fallen in, whose very name has perished. The veins have been opened in many parts by the Spaniards, who content themselves almost invariably with sinking shafts for the extraction of the superior decomposed ores, abandoning the mine on reaching sulphurets, from ignorance of the process for the extraction of silver. In these sulphurets, and below the old galleries are situated the present workings. La Colorada, on the north side of the spur, is a portion of the Veta Madre (or main vein.) The workings are dry and firm; the galleries 50 feet in length and 45 in width. Another shaft, 22 feet, is opened 80 feet farther down the mountain, where the ores are uncovered to the same width. The vein in the lower places is about 18 feet in width, in parts 30; running north and north-west, with an inclination to the south-east of about 15 degrees, an excellent course and dip in Mexican mines. The assay was $172 silver, per ton, and traces of gold. La Chipiona is also upon the Veta Madre; vein same direction and dip as La Colorada; shafts, two, 30 feet apart; depth 30 feet, and partly full of water. The vein is 20 to 36 inches; same depth, and quality of metal uniform. The ores are more difficult of reduction, being bisulphurets of iron, with a compound sulphuret of silver, lead, iron, and copper; by the German process, assays 160 ounces per ton. The ores of La Colorada by same process, gave 212 to 320 ounces. There is not half the superficial excavations of the ancient mines, which have been cleaned out from this vein, and the falling in of the *labores*. The vein can be traced 250 yards, across the crest of the hill, up to the mouth of the La Colorada. Above the main vein is a cross-vein of 4 to 6 inches, cutting it nearly at right angles. The ore is said to yield 318 ounces of silver per ton. Nine hundred feet distant, in a straight line, in a spur of the same cerro, is the adit of La Plomosa; the upper workings being badly planned, have fallen in from the pressure of rubbish in the old drifts, and the miners have driven a level in the solid rock 150 feet farther down. The ores are argentiferous galenas, with a matrix of stratified ' calishe,' and are said to yield 18 per cent. of lead, and 96 ounces silver, per ton, up to 190 ounces. Both this vein and La Chipiona run across the valley and strike the opposite mountain. Old mining shafts are seen all the way across at different points. These mines can all be drained by a tunnel, as the Chipiona debouches upon an abrupt descent, by many hundred feet. The walls are firm and vein regular, presenting every indication of permanence. A quarter of a mile south-west of the Yerba Buena, are the mines of Los Tajos. The hill-side is covered with the buried workings of the ancients, and the superior position of the vein is in a very precarious condition. The vein is something like one-half a yard in width, with a heterogeneous medley of ores. It runs completely through the mountain, as very considerable works are visible on the opposite side; but whether ' en metales,' or not is unknown.

" The ores are said to yield 60 ounces per ton, but they are loaded with titaniferous and zinciferous metals. La Descomulgada is situated about a league west of south-west of the Yerba Buena. Its matrix is a very hard, silicious rock, which crumbles with great rapidity when exposed to air and moisture. The vein is said to be wide, and the superficial ores easily worked, costing $1.00 per 300 lbs., and to be easy of reduction.

" La Yerba Buena is a modern mine, said to have been very rich. The mouths have fallen in a few hundred yards from the Yerba Buena, on the road to the Descomulgada. Nothing more is known concerning it.

" Las Ostimuris, on the road to Yerba Buena, about half way from the Cieneguita, has two open mouths, and is full of water, the drifts running under the brook. Mr. Monge says it was abandoned on the outbreak of the Opatas, and as the shafts were shallow, the vein wide, and the ores yielding 450 oz. per ton, he entered into a contract with a skillful miner and put up whims and machinery for drainage. His partner died just as they were approaching completion; the Apaches drove off their animals; and, being ignorant of mining, he abandoned the mine.

" La Prieta is on the rancho of Matarchi, about six miles east of Cieneguita. The vein is from four to six feet wide. The opening is merely a trial pit. The ores of the outcrop are a melange of different sulphurets, heavily charged with copper.

" El Potrero, 24 miles distant, is said to be an immense 'clavo' of volcanic origin, and unknown extent, at the intersection of two veins. The ore is without alloy of silver, but contains much oxide of lead and spar. It forms an excellent flux for the ores of La Prieta, and Los Tajos. The cost of carriage is the only expense.

" La Viruela, east half a mile from the site of La Armargosa, is a lofty hill, from which large quantities of gold have been extracted, but the whole hill has fallen in.

" La Armagosa, and the rivulet which runs beneath El Realito, are constantly searched for gold. The water of the creek is not sufficiently abundant for machinery, and an examination was made of La Armagosa, one-quarter mile east, where a stream was found that is permanent and may be conducted by a tunnel. It furnishes a considerable volume of water, with a natural fall of 100 feet within a space of 100 yards in its own valley.

"Yerba Buena is three and a half miles south-east from the real, four and a half from La Chipiona, and four from Los Tajos. This district is located near Sahuaripa, about 50 miles south-east. The river is the Arroyo de los Ostimuris, which is permanent ten months, and sufficient to turn the wheels during the remainder of the year. Wood is abundant, and consists of oak, pine, juniper and ash. Pasturage, everywhere. Animals are said to fatten all the year round. Salt can be purchased at from $8 to $10 per carga of 300 lbs.; wheat, $6 per fanega. Freight from Guaymas, $80 to $90 per ton; from Sahuaripa, $3 per carga. Cattle are purchased from $10 to $15; hides, $1.00 each; mules and horses, dear; powder of the country, $7.00 per 25 lbs; flour, $7 per arroba." The ores are hard and require blasting, but, as seen before, are very rich.

"The Real of the Cieneguita embraces the mines known as La Chipiona, La Colorada, La Cajona, La Prieta, and the vein of copper in Matarchi, La Descomulgada and Los Tajos, La Viruela, and El Realito, San Rafael, Ostimuris, Yerba Buena, and El Potrero. All of these mines are within a radius of three miles.

"The principal vein appears to be that of La Chipiona. The origin of the real is unknown. The general belief is that it is the long-lost Real of Tayopa, famous in the early Spanish annals. The ores of the Chipiona, Colorada, and others, are refractory, being mostly hard ores and sulphurets. The titles to the mines, except those of El Potrero or La Prieta, and the copper vein in Matarchi, are on the ranchos of La Yglesia, a fine grazing estate of eighteen square miles in extent, belonging to and in the occupancy of Don José Yrenco Monge. The title is said to be perfect and undisputed, a Spanish grant of Carlos III. It is wooded and watered, and contains sufficient arable land. The rancho of Matarchi, which bounds it on the westward, is a beautiful pine forest, with some excellent cultivated land, containing nine square miles, well watered, and is likewise a Spanish grant of the last century. It contains the veins of La Prieta and the outcrop of copper.

"The mines Los Tajos, La Descomulgada, and El Realito, with four pertenencias, El Potrero, and La Viruella, are each the extent of La Chipiona's and La Colorada's possession, which was given by the Prefect of Sahuaripa on the 13th of September; is 1,800 feet in length; width, 600 feet on La Plomosa, and 1,350 feet in width, including all the present workings in the three mines. The sites called El Potrero, La Armagosa, La Cieneguita, and Yerba Buena, were denounced as "Haciendas de Benefico," or position for reduction works. The Real of Cieneguita is situated in a pretty little dell, embosomed among lofty mountains, almost at the foot of the Sierra de San Ignacio, and partly embraced by the unbroken ranges of the great Sierra Madre. These mines are now worked by a 30-stamp mill, and are producing immense profits.

"It is distant, perhaps, by the road, 42 miles south-east of Sahuaripa, nine miles south-east of Tarachi, and 72 miles west of Mulatos. The real contains about 20 acres of cultivated ground, and is supplied by a spring and perpetual brook, which traverses its center. The climate is mild. In winter, the snow falls occasionally two feet, and ice forms two inches thick. The road leads from Sahuaripa through mountain passes. From Aribechi to the real it is all mountain, except the plain of Las Cazadores, in the rancho Aoyua Blanca, and the valley of the Rio de Ostimuris, from which the road runs from Santa Fé to Tarachi. A considerable portion of the real is covered by the foundations of houses and ruins of smelting works, or immense piles of scoriæ and rubbish, proving incontestably to the practical eye the vast extent of the ancient mining operations." And another proof, we might add, of the former richness of these mines. We give this extended description, in order to show how an abandoned mine looks to the traveler as well as the mining engineers, although these same mines have since been reopened and worked by a 30-stamp mill, as before stated.

We are indebted to Mr. John A. Robinson, of this city, for the following:

"Some fifteen miles north-east from the famous gold mine of Mulatos, lies a cluster of mines known as 'Mineral de la Cieneguita.' There are some fifteen mines in all; the principal of them are the Chipiona, the Colorada, and the Plomosa; the two first being very rich in silver and gold, and the last in lead and silver. The country surrounding offers every facility for mining and reduction works. An abundance of water, heavy forests of pine, hemlock, various species of oak, juniper, etc. Building-stone and fire-clay in the immediate vicinity, with pasturage for the animals. The mines are at present worked on a small scale by some German gentlemen; but parties are now examining them with the view of establishing reduction works on an extensive scale by the lixiviation process. These mines are extremely rich in 'ley,' and abundant in ores. Some sixty miles to the east of the above are situated those extremely rich copper mines called 'Huacarbo,' in the Barranca de Tarrarique. Here also the facilities for working are great. The river Yaqui runs immediately at the foot of these immense lodes; and the country is thickly covered by heavy timber. The Yaqui River, in places, runs over the copper-vein, leaving the ores in sight for a long distance. Both of the foregoing mining districts were fully explored by Robert L. D'Aumaille, a most famous mining expert, chemist and amalgamist, sent there by Don Juan A. Robinson, formerly United States Consul for Guaymas, Sonora, and at present residing in this city. D'Aumaille reports that the copper vein is intersected in different places, by narrow gold veins of a very rich 'ley.'"

The district of Babicanora was discovered at the end of the last century, eight leagues south-east of Arispe and four from Sonoquipe, in the Sierra, running north and south. It was, at one time, very rich, and had a hacienda for the reduction of ores below Sonoquipe, one mile from the bank of the creek. It was abandoned by its owners some years ago, until Mr. Hunter, an American, lately obtained possession of two of the mines. One is called Mendoza, which has a vein three feet wide, and assays $80 per ton in silver. The other is Santa Ana, and has a vein one vara in width, (33 inches) with an assay similar to the other. Mr. Hunter has erected a ten-stamp mill, and is now working the mines profitably.

The hacienda of Gov. Pesquiera, called Las Delicias, is situated about 20 miles south-west from Arispe, and consists of about 30,000 acres of good land, about one-fifth of which is first-class agricultural land, and being in the neighborhood or west of the Sonora River, the soil is somewhat of the same nature, and produces wheat, corn and other cereals, as other lands on the Sonora River. The balance is good grazing land. The Santa Elena mine is located about four and a half miles from the hacienda, on a ridge of mountains, and is owned by Gov. Pesquiera, who erected a ten-stamp mill at the hacienda.

5

It is not in working order, and is fast going to pieces. The mine has been mostly worked by arastras, and produced, in one year, $200,000, but has never been properly worked. The best ore assays $5 per ounce bullion, gold and silver. The shaft is about 200 feet in depth, with a varying vein, sometimes reaching 15 feet in width. The mine is dry, with walls of porphyry and quartzite.

The Curcurpe district also contains many mines, among which may be mentioned the ancient mine of El Tajo, which is now full of water and in a ruinous condition, having been destroyed by the gambucinos.

The Santa Teresa de Jesus mining district is located 69 miles south of the boundary line of the United States, on the northern frontier of the State of Sonora, and 36 miles from Magdalena; the latter being only about 140 miles from Tucson.

We copy from a report of Mr. L. Jannin on the mines of this district, which has just been published, the following : " Leaving Cucurpe, and passing by the cultivated fields of its inhabitants, we find the road to the mines leading up the San Miguel River, sometimes emerging into an open plain. After following the course of this river some twelve miles, and passing El Pintor and the deserted Pueblo de Dolores, the road leads us over table-lands and meadows, the former adorned with oak and ash trees, the latter covered with waving grass, until we reach a broad belt of thickly wooded land, where the San Miguel first makes its appearance in the dry season. From this point the river always contains running water. In the rainy season it rushes violently along, sometimes overflowing its banks, but in the dry season it floats along tamely, scarcely covering its bed. All the land between Cucurpe and this point is of the richest description. It is unsurpassed in fertility by any portion of Sonora, and grain of all kinds can be raised without the slightest trouble.

In former times, the whole valley was populated, and the number of cultivated fields and the numerous herds of grazing cattle proclaimed the wealth of the inhabitants. But the continued incursions of the Apaches since 1832, by driving off the unresisting inhabitants and gathering the harvests they had planted, have depopulated and ruined the country. Deserted ranches are met along the road. No one lives here. No one dares to plant grain, and, as it is here, so it is also throughout the northern part of the State. Leaving the belt of wooded land that I have mentioned, the road still takes us over meadows and table lands, up the valley of the San Miguel and toward its source, the Cañon de Santa Teresa, a distance of 15 miles. Here, low ranges of hills, isolated peaks, and broken country, becoming more and more frequent, herald our approach to a mountain range, and soon we are in the cañon, with steep hills on each side.

The range of mountains in the foot-hills, in which are the mines of Santa Teresa, is known by the name of Sierra Azul, and its culminating peak is the Cerro Azul, which towers high above all the range, forming a most prominent object for a distance of over forty miles. The general course of the range is north and south, but spurs of the Cerro extend in all directions. The country is mountainous in the extreme. There are no table-lands, no valleys, and no open space of any extent, nor are the ranges of foot-hills continuous, but are broken up by side ravines and cañons, down which, in rainy seasons, the water finds its way to the various arroyos. These arroyos form the circuitous roads by which one point is reached from another. The position of the Mineral de Santa Teresa is correctly indicated by Colonel de Fleury's late map of Sonora. From it can be seen the relative position of the Mineral to the neighboring pueblos, owing to the mountains around it. The only broad road leading to the mines is the one I have described. All others are, and can only be, foot-trails. The mines are upon three distinct veins, known as the Trinidad, San Antonio, and the Santa Biviana. The openings on the Trinidad and San Antonio are in the Real de Santa Teresa, while those on the Santa Biviana vein are in a neighboring real of the same name.

The Real de Santa Teresa is approached by a cañon of that name, and is situated some three miles from its outlet. The bed of this cañon is a dry arroyo, and its sides are formed by a range of foot-hills rising up several hundred feet, and inclined towards the bed at an angle varying from 50 to 70 degrees. The arroyo varies in width from 50 to 300 yards, and forms the only road to the mines. In the rainy season, the water flowing down from the various ravines and from the Salto, (the source of the San Miguel) fills the arroyo and renders freighting in wagons difficult, but does not impede transit by mules and pack-trains. At the time of my visit it was perfectly dry, and generally remains so during nine months of the year.

The Cañon de Santa Teresa has a generally north-easterly

direction, although subject to many turns. In the neighborhood of the mines, its direction is as indicated, and the vein pursues a nearly parallel course. The mountain mass of this Mineral—in fact, the whole range—is a hard, dark-blue limestone, distinctly stratified, and dipping to the east at an angle of 50 degrees. Its strike is nearly north and south. The course of the veins is contrary to the stratification of the limestone, which forms its walls; and they have all the appearance of being true fissure veins. The walls are generally firm and enduring.

The Trinidad vein crops out at various places on the northerly slope of the cañon. Its general direction is northeast by south-west; but it changes its course with the slope of the hills, and at places it is heaved by faults and cross-veins. The outcroppings can be traced at various heights above the head of the cañon, until it reaches the opening called El Arroyo. Here the vein leaves the northerly slope of the cañon, crossing over the arroyo in a diagonal direction, and finally emerges on the opposite slope, still preserving the same general direction. The San Antonio vein, on the other hand, is entirely on the southerly slope of the cañon. Its general direction is north-east by north, but it also changes its course with the slopes of the hills. These two veins converge toward one another; but although they have been followed for many a weary mile, their point of junction has not been discovered. The general appearance of the outcropping is the same in the two veins, with some slight local differences. It is a hard, compact quartz, sometimes thickly impregnated with peroxyd of manganese, and at others, merely colored by its presence. It is seldom found with a honey-comb structure. At places the veins outcrop boldly to the height of several feet, and at others, disappear beneath the soil. The width of the vein does not remain constant; but the general average may be put down at two-and-a-half to three feet. The San Antonio vein shows somewhat larger at the various openings than does the Trinidad; but the ore in the latter is found more uniformly distributed. Wherever the veins outcrop, openings have been made. On the Trinidad vein there are six in number; and on the San Antonio, there are seven. The different mines opened, are the El Loreto, that assayed, at a depth of 30 feet, $70 to $80 per ton; vein small at surface, broadens out to 2½ feet in the shaft; angle of inclination, 40 deg. north-west. La Cruz lies north-east of the Loreto; depth of shaft, 30 feet; assay, $70 to $90, in first opening; second, depth 60 feet;

vein 2 to 2½ feet thick; dips about 45 deg.; assay, same as former. La Falda assayed $118 per ton. The Trinidad is the principal mine; shaft 150 feet deep, with some of the pillars extracted; some left standing, that would assay over $80 per ton, while the ore in the lower gallery assays $150. Water comes into the lower levels. The miners, in abandoning the property, have of course left no rich deposit in the mines; but the evidences are that an abundance of rich ore must have been extracted. The Arroyo mine was said to be very rich, and is 70 feet deep; filled with water, but could be cleared for about $600. The San Francisco is 30 feet deep; the ore sometimes occurs in large bunches and pockets (or " bonanzas "); sometimes in small nodules, and sometimes disseminated throughout the mass in minute particles. The vein is never free from metal. The San Antonio vein has seven openings, viz., San Pedro, La Burra, Consolacion, San Antonio, Corazon de Maria, Santa Gertrudis, and Las Animas. Of the first three I can say but little in their present state, as they all need clearing out. The Consolacion is in a better state of preservation than the other two, and a fair average ore can be taken from it. The San Antonio enjoys a great reputation; but at present it is in a dilapidated condition. The mine is filled with rubbish. In the Corazon de Maria the miners left nothing rich in sight. Santa Gertrudis contains good ores, and will assay $200 to $500 per ton. The average value of all I saw at the mouth is $270 per ton. The others will average $80 per ton." By comparing the locations on the map of Col. Fleury on Sonora, Sinaloa, Chihuahua, and Durango, it will be observed that these mines, of which we have reproduced a condensed description from Mr. Jannin's report, are located but a short distance, about forty miles, south-east of Santa Cruz, and in the neighborhood of the richest mineral and agricultural region of the state, outside of the rich lands of the Yaqui River.

La Alameda is situated in the Nacameri district, 21 miles west of the pueblo of Nacameri. This mine was discovered in 1835, and was once extensively worked. The mines of this district are all of silver, with a very good " ley," about $60 per ton.

Batuco also possesses some mines.

The Rio Chico district is in the south-western part of the state, 120 miles from Hermosillo, near the Yaqui River, is one of the most ancient mineral regions of Sonora, and in the last century produced great quantities of gold and silver.

Placers of gold were also discovered here. The gambucinos are still working some of the mines. El Aguaja is an
old mineral region of the last century. Its principal mines
are Guillamena, Ubarbol, and La Grande. These mines are
mostly abandoned, though worked by gambucinos. Suaque
contains many mines of gold and silver, which are but little
worked. La Trinidad is one of the oldest mineral regions
of the State, situated at the base of the Sierra Madre, on a
branch of the river Mayo. Its area is comprised almost entirely of mines, the principal ones of which are worked by
Mr. Alsua of Guaymas, by a modern stamp-mill, who is taking out in bullion, monthly, about $100,000. This district
is reached by a road from Sahuaripa through Babicanora,
south, on the Bapepito River, a branch of the Yaqui; thence
to Conichi, Ouava, Rio Chico, Nury; thence north-east to
Caraja, San Nicolas, Santa Rosa, and Trinidad.

The district of Bacuachi is in the northern part of the
State, as well as the copper mines of La Cananea. The gold
found in this district is coarse, and pieces were found weighing 25 mares. In fact, the whole of this region is covered
with veins of gold and silver, and are as yet undeveloped.
We have called especial attention to this district in another
place.

Among the old mines, we may mention the Cajon, six
leagues from the San Francisco placers and twelve
from Cieneguilla, and those of the hacienda of Santa Rosa,
near Cajon, which yielded great quantities of silver from
1798 to 1802. The average proportion of the ley of the
best or picked ores was six, eight and twelve mares to the
arroba; of the poorer or second class, two to four mares.
There was a scarcity of ore in the Santa Rosa mines, on account of the hardness and narrowness of the veins. In the
mines of San Francisco, water is scarce to the extreme, and
could not be obtained nearer than 21 miles, and sold in
the dry season at $1 per barrel. The timber, also, in the vi-
cinity, is unfit for building.

These mines are very rich, but the expense is too great to
work them profitably. The mines of Vado Seco, to the
north of San Ignacio Pueblo, on the road to Tucson, are reported to be rich, as well as the famous placer of Sobia,
on the main road to the city of Alamos, half way from Bar-
royaea.

The Cajon district contains a group of some three or four
mines, and are all owned by a New York company. The
nephew of General Magruder is the superintendent, and

owns one-half interest in the mines. The mine contains gold and silver-bearing quartz, which assays, on an average, about $65 to $70 per ton. The deepest shaft is only down about 125 feet. Rich spots are occasionally found in the vein, but after they get down a certain distance, the veins commence to pinch out. Some of the veins have entirely disappeared. The mine has, however, paid well, as they have taken out already enough ore to pay for the claim, mills and expenses, and have now on the dump, in sight, about $50,000 worth of ore. The mill has ten stamps, and is not quite completed, but will shortly commence to reduce the ore.

The Las Cedras, belonging to Don Santo Terminal, is situated in the district of Barroyaca, near the small town of Teropaco, 135 miles from Guaymas, in the direction of Alamos, south-east. This is a very rich mine, and has been extensively worked. It is surrounded by rich, arable lands, and a permanent stream of water flows in the vicinity of the mine. Negotiations are being made to purchase it.

During the years 1863 and 1864, many new mines were opened, among which were Las Cruzecitas, Corral Viejo and El Refugio, the latter on the border of Chihuahua, and the mines of La Cananea.

On the Cerro Prieto, between the ranchos de la Palma and La Casa Pintada, is an old mine, called Tarasca, almost forgotten. Tradition places it very rich, although it has not been worked for over a century. In this same neighborhood are many old mines, and vestiges of buildings may yet be seen on their antiquated sites.

In the district of San Jose de Gracias, a celebrated mine was worked in 1809-1810, by Juan José Carumina, who expended all his capital in bailing out the water from the old shaft, and in two or three hours, after clearing it of water, he took out a lump of ore weighing 75 pounds, which yielded 112 ounces of pure silver. The water began to gain on him again, so that in his effort to keep it down, he broke his bailing apparatus, and having contracted some debts, he could not return to his labor; the mine refilled in six or seven hours, and he abandoned the enterprise. A company afterwards undertook to clear the mine, but after expending a considerable sum, abandoned the mine on account of an accident to one of the workmen," says Velasco. This seems incredible; but for the fact that the mines are mostly worked by Yaqui Indians, who are very superstitious, and believe that devils inhabit the mines, says Ruxton, in his " Adventures in Mexico." The accident to one of their number would prevent others from working in a haunted mine, or one inhabited by evil spirits, in their imagination. Velasco further says: "Some of the old inhabitants of San José de Gracia, in speaking of this mine, testify that the vein in many places was of virgin silver; and that in others the ore yielded fifty per cent. of pure silver; also, that there was a stratum of red earth that yielded great quantities of gold, they having frequently witnessed the extraction of two or three hundred mares on one single occasion. The depth of this mine exceeds one hundred varas." Taking into account the unreliability of traditions, and the extravagance of some Mexicans, still there may be some truth in the tradition, as the famous mines of Batopilas, in Chihuahua, and others, have produced like results. If the mine is still in the condition that Carumina found it, a steam pump would soon reveal its hidden treasures.

The mines of La Cananea, 80 years ago or more, were worked on a large scale with great energy, by the house of Guea, of Chihuahua. We understand that these mines, or the principal ones, are owned and worked by Gov. Pesquiera, of Sonora, and are now bonded by him to Eastern parties. Nevertheless, we give a description of the district from the pen of the celebrated chemist, Robert L. D'Aumaille, mining engineer and official assayer for the State of Sonora.

General Pesquiera has worked five mines in this district, viz: El Ronquillo, La Chivatera, San Rafael, (or La Plomosa) La Terdilla, and La Cobre Grande. The report was written by M. D'Aumaille in 1860, and is as follows: "La Cananea is situated about 36 miles south-west of the Presidio of Santa Cruz, about 54 miles south-east of San Pedro, probably 35 miles southerly from Fort Buchanan, and not far from the American line. The mines worked are seven in number, of which the principal are El Ronquillo, La Chivatera, San Rafael, Santo Domingo, La Mina de Cobre Pobre, and La Mina de Plomo de Arvallo. In addition to these mines are La Mariquilla, (of white copper) El Tajo, (the ancient mine), and others—in fact, the whole region is strongly mineralized and of the most prepossessing exterior. The hacienda de Beneficio y Perez y Arvallo is on the El Ritto, a permanent stream at the foot of the mountains, about a mile and a half from the mines. The greater portion of the road is excellent, and the remainder can be readily made so. The hacienda is a mass of ruins, overgrown with rank vegetation. The machinery was destroyed by natives carrying away the iron available. The situation is pleasant, on the border of a vast plain covered with wild mustangs or horses, and which stretches away to San Pedro, and contains much arable, with any quantity of grazing land, and lies immediately around the site. Half a mile or so up the valley brings us to the mine of El Ronquillo, called also from its refractory ores, La Maletiosa, with its ancient hacienda. This mine was the property of Arvallo, but the miners were driven off by the Apaches. El Ronquillo has a thickness of from three and a half to four feet of very good ore, worked to a depth of 80 feet. It has several shafts full of water to the brim, which comes from copious springs in the lower workings, and a ravine which passes across the vein, and from its situation upon the gentle slope of a hill which gradually merges into the plain beneath, it cannot be drained by a tunnel, but recourse must be had to steam machinery. The ore of this mine assayed from $30 to $80 per ton. Passing through the ravine, copper croppings are seen. One-quarter of a mile further, is located the mine of La Chivatera, situated on a steep declivity, admirably adapted to tunnel drainage, and is half full of water. It bears every external evidence of being a powerful vein, but we are told that it is really an irregular deposit. Three hundred yards higher up lies a great open cellar, for I can compare it to nothing else, with a small pile of refuse lying at one side.

This is the mine of Tajo, of San Rafael. Judging from the small amount of earth visible, and the statement of the old administrador, it is nearly a solid mass of ore. You have ore on all sides in the level, so that it is impossible to tell where the vein is. This ore is ductile and most easily reducible. It flows like water in the furnace. The supply is apparently inexhaustible. Further up the glen is the Mina de Plomo de Arvallo, of the same character as San Rafael. The ores of these mines appear to consist principally of oxide and sulphate of lead; although vast masses of galena are found, and are so soft that a single barretero can throw down many tons a day, while the cost of extraction is nothing. The shafts appear of trivial dimensions, yet they have been worked from time immemorial, and the litharge or jugos, from San Rafael, have supplied all northern Sonora with that necessary article ; and they have even formed an article of export to Jesus Maria, and other great mining districts of Central Chihuahua. The ore of the Cobre Pobre Mine in the vicinity is boundless in extent, but of inferior quality. Near this point is also located the great vein of La Mariquilla. We have been assured that it was in the sierra of La Mariquilla, twelve miles to the north. This mine, from its alleged dimensions, and the richness of its ores, has great interest attached to it, as the cause of its abandonment was the fact of its producing white copper, something like the "paktong" of China, or the white copper of Heidelburghausen, the prototype of German silver. But the accounts of this mine are so obscure, conflicting and contradictory, that nothing can be made of it, but actual discovery of the mine. Some have denied the existence of this mine or vein, and others claim to have smelted it, who pronounced it an alloy of copper and silver.

El Tajo, the most ancient mine, is a huge rent in the earth like the Pamys mine in Iglesia, but the ores changed at the depth of 30 feet, suddenly, into pyrites. It is probable from analogy that these pyrites are argentiferous. Immense masses of black rock were abandoned by the ancient miners in the walls, under the supposition, probably, that they were black slate, which were subsequently assayed and proved to be a semi-stratified silicate of the dinoxide of copper.

Other mines of argentiferous galena, varying from 12 to 320 ounces per ton, are alleged to exist near the Ojo de Agua de Arvalla. Besides the oak, there are vast and most accessible forests of chamunque, a species of pitch pine of great strength and durability, excellently adapted for machinery and building materials.

The mines are accessible by a good wagon road via Santa Cruz from Fort Buchanan, Tubac, La Piedra Parade, and Guaymas, and are surrounded by the great depopulated haciendas of San Bernardino, El Ojo de Agua de Arvalla, another Ojo de Agua, Cuitahaca, El Agua Escondida, Las Animas, and Banamichi.

Another road, called a wagon road, but poorly deserving the name, passes by Bacuachi, Arispe, Ures, and Hermosillo, to Guaymas. Its position is romantic and delightful. Pastures exist green in Bacuachi all the year round, and of the most nutritious quality. Cultivable land of considerable extent is found in the same hacienda, which is the natural feeder of the real. The mines themselves are said, by Felipe Perez, to be on public land, a narrow strip or sobrante between two ranchos. All the necessaries of a great establishment—building material and fluxes—abound in excess. Building stone, granite, fine marble, tepustete, arcuillas, jugos and syndas are plentiful; and, during the search for the lost mines of Las Lamas, Espiritu Santo, on the road to Banamichi, a vast deposit of most refractory furnace sandstone was found, the first seen in Sonora. The water is good and the locality healthful, and in proximity to the American military stations of Fort Buchanan and Arritoypa," and the Southern Pacific R. R., which passes within about 150 miles of the district.

"Ange Robert L. D. Amuaille,
Ensayador Oficial de Estado de Sonora,
29 de Mayo de 1860."

La Basura is the first mining region discovered in the country of the Papajos, and is situated twenty-four miles north-west of Caborca. Its veins are numerous, especially those of gold ; but although they are of marvelous richness, this lasts but a short time, as the deposits extend but a short distance below the surface. San Perfecto was the second discovery made in the Papajo country. Quitovac was the third discovery, about seventy miles north-west from Caborca, and the same distance from the town of Guadalupo or Altar. The placers were first worked, they being very abundant in gold, which lay in grains on the surface, as at San Francisco and Cieneguilla. Afterwards many mines were opened to the depth of ten or fifteen varas, (about 33 inches to each vara) some of which yielded from four to eight ounces of gold to the bowl (or "batea"); others not more than a few cents. Occasionally pockets were found of large extent that yielded marvelously. Nuggets of large size were also found ; one weighed twenty-one marcs, (each marc weighing 4,608 grains). A large piece of gold-bearing quartz was extracted from a ledge, that was nearly all gold, and weighed over thirty marcs. San Antonio, another placer, about ten miles west of Quitovac, was discovered a few days after the latter, and was exceedingly rich at the surface. The discovery of these placers was owing to Father Faustino Gonzalez, who prevailed upon the Papajo Indians to reveal their locality, in 1835. Gonzalez made a large fortune, and he was soon surrounded by whites and Indians in great numbers. The placer continued rich for several years, and was worked until 1841, when the Papajos rose, and expelled the whites.

After quiet was restored, a few persons returned to Quitovac and worked some mines discovered after the placers, in the neighborhood of an abundant spring, capable of supplying a population of 30,000 or 40,000 inhabitants.

In the Sonoica Valley, which is situated about 36 miles north of Quitovac, on the road to Lower California, the gold discovered was very fine and light.

Alamo Muerto, about 48 miles west of Caborca, contains gold and silver mines and placers. It was discovered in the same year as Quitovac, and although its ores yield a fair proportion of silver, the scarcity of quicksilver prevented their being worked to any great extent. There were, however, ten mines in operation at the time of the rising of the Papajos, all of which were abandoned.

Las Palomas, six miles to the south of Alamo Muerto, were rich placers of gold, similar to those of Quitovaca. It was also abandoned for the same reason, and is now frequented by a few gambucinos, (poor miners) who are satisfied with enough to provide them with food.

El Zoñe was discovered in 1844, and contains numerous gold mines, some of them quite rich at the surface. From one of them was taken a mass of quartz of 25 pounds weight, yielding 50 per cent. of pure gold. A mine is located here called Ris Suena; eight or ten shafts are down about 300 feet. Ores are shipped to Aribaca, about 120 miles on the road to Tucson; pays about $200 per ton.

Cajitos is situated about 24 miles north-west from Caborca, and about 70 miles from port La Libertad, inland, north-east from the Gulf of California. The mines located here are in a low range of mountains or foot-hills. The mines were discovered shortly after the other mines in the vicinity, and have been worked in a superficial manner since 1842. In 1868, the hostile Indians drove the miners off, and the mines were abandoned until 1877, when small bodies of armed men returned and worked in the old drifts and inclines for a few weeks, then packed the ore on their mules, and slipped away quietly to Basura, about ten miles east, where reduction works were established. The richest spots were thus only mined until 1879, when the mines were again worked by the primitive arastra. The shafts are sunk on an incline following the course of the ore vein. Instead of using the windlass, the ore is packed on the backs of miners in raw-hide sacks, up ladders made by binding cleats of wood upon an upright pole, with raw-hide thongs. The ore is worked by an iron bar called "barreton," about six feet in length, which is used to throw it down, using it as a hand-drill and lever. One end is shaped like a drill, and the other is hammered flat and sharp like the larger end of a pick. The ore is broken into small pieces and thus transported to the surface, to the arastras. For shovels, the horns of cattle are steeped in water and flattened out, and attached to pieces of wood with raw-hide thongs.

In this manner, these mines have been worked for the last 35 years, and about four millions have been extracted from the four mines in the vicinity. The present depth of the shafts is as follows : The Tajilos, 275 feet; Puerte-citos, from 90 to 100 feet; Galilea, 80 to 90 feet; Oro Blan-co, 180 feet; Santa Rosalia, 200 feet; with two levels and stations.

" The gold has only been extracted, although a large per-centage of silver is found in the ore, which has been al-lowed to waste, owing to the lack of materials to save it. Mr. C. E. Hoffman, mining engineer of this city, although his residence is in San José, some months since was sent to Tucson to examine some mines in Arizona, and while there, met a Mexican, who showed him some of the ore from these mines, which, on being assayed, was found to be very rich. He accompanied the Mexican to the mines, was sat-isfied with their richness, and purchased the four mines, and thirteen others in the vicinity in the Juarez and Cajitos mining district, for himself and some gentlemen in this city, who subsequently organized the Caborca Mining Co. He re-turned again last April, and has been superintending their development, building reservoirs, and preparing a site for a 20-stamp mill. The water is abundant in the vicinity, which is caught in reservoirs, and the one now constructed has sufficient water to supply a 20-stamp mill for eighteen months.

" In this district the rancheros irrigate their lands by reser-voirs; though grain, if sown in season, and grass, thrive very well without. Mr. Hoffman has in his employ about sixty Yaquis. These Indians perform almost all the labor of Sonora, and are employed at from 50 cents to $1 per day. The ores of these mines assayed on an average $80 per ton. The ores of the Oro Blanco mine in this group, assayed as high as $224.94—about two-thirds being silver. The Santa Rosalia, about four miles from the Oro Blanco, west, went about $151; and the Alberca, $85.75, gold and silver, of about equal proportions. Thus we see the whole of this region surrounding Caborca is one of the richest in the state, and may be worked with enormous results. The price of transportation will not exceed $25 per ton to Port la Liber-tad, and may there be shipped to San Francisco for $8 per ton additional ; although Mr. Hoffman proposes to work the ore by a 20-stamp mill, until the mines are further developed; then add to their capacity 40 stamps more. Hay can be purchased at the mines at $16 per ton, and wood at $2.50 and $3.00 per cord. The hill-sides in the vicinity are thickly covered with a heavy growth of iron-wood, mesquite, and palo-verde. The location is such that the mines can be profitably worked, and yield rich returns to the owners. The Santa Felicita mine, twenty miles east of the Cajitos Mining Camp, is owned by Mr. Davis of Chicago, who has erected a 20-stamp mill, and is working in free gold ore. The Cajon mine, twenty miles south-west, is worked by a 10-stamp mill." (From report of Mr. C. E. Hoffman.)

We are indebted to Mr. Benjamin Rountree for the following:

"The principal mine of the mining district of La Barranca, in the jurisdiction of San Javier, is the Tarumari, a silver mine, which is owned by the Barranca Mill and Mining Company, of Guaymas. The owners are, N. Graff, F. R. Rountree, F. Ench, and Arturo Culicuro. This mine has reached a depth of 300 feet, and has produced bullion to the amount of $1,500,000. The width of the vein is from two and a half to four feet. The average assay has been, for all the working ores, about $100 per ton. The lowest workings are upon richer ore, reaching $160 per ton, with a vein at the lowest workings, 18 inches. The ore contains about five per cent. gold in bullion. A 20-stamp mill, concentrator, etc., are located at the mines. The ores are worked by the iixiviate process, or roasting, and then passed through a wet crusher. The ores are rebellious, and, consequently, have to be roasted before treating. This mine is located about 120 miles north-east from Guaymas, and about 100 east from Hermosillo, 10 from Los Bronces, 8 from San Javier." The same company owns the extensive coal beds hereafter mentioned, which are located 1,500 feet from this mine.

The region or mining district of Bolas de la Plata is supposed to be located in the northern part of Sonora, near the boundary line of Arizona. Its importance is chiefly derived from traditions of virgin silver having been found "at the place called Arizona, on a mountain ridge about half a league in extent. The discovery was made by a Yaqui Indian, who revealed it to a trader, and the latter made it public. At a depth of a few varas, masses of pure silver were found, of a globular form, and of one and two arrobas in weight. Several pieces were taken out weighing upwards of 20 arrobas, or 500 pounds; and one found by a person from Guadalajara weighed **140** arrobas, or 3,500 pounds," all of which has been quoted and given as a probable fact in many works, and is found referred to as a tradition in many Spanish and English works, and even quoted as a fact; since in the same year of the discovery, 1769, the Presidio of Altar seized upon large masses of silver in the possession of certain persons as the property of the crown, which was denied by the parties interested, and the matter taken into the audience chamber of Guadalajara, and from thence was referred to the court of Madrid. Seven years having elapsed, the crown decided that the silver pertained to the royal patrimony. The facts and all the data, in our opinion, can amount to no more, than that certain rumors were in existence, in relation to the products of one of the rich mines of Sonora, which had been seized by an officer of the crown: and had been found in a melted state in the mountains, at some mythical spot. The fact that the silver was in the shape of balls indicates that they were simply the ordinary products of one of the rich mines, and had been melted into the balls before mentioned, from the fact that formerly the silver in Mexico was thus melted, instead of into bars or bricks, as at present.

The following is copied from the Appendix of "Ward on Mexico," which contains a complete report of the district of Babiacora :

" In the neighborhood of Babiacora there are many silver mines, the most of which contain a greater or less proportion of gold. The principal are Dolores and San Antonio to the south-west of the town; Cerro Gordo, to the south-east, and Cobriza, on the Cerro de San Felipe, in the valley above Babiacora.

" The Cerro Gordo mine is situated four leagues southeast of Babiacora, on a very high hill, and appears to have been of considerable interest, from the great quantities of refuse ores thrown out on its sides. The quantity of water contained in it cannot be ascertained, as there is not any perpendicular shaft. From the steepness of the hill, a tunnel might be driven far below the bottom of the works, from a fine plain. The vein is about one-half yard in width. Some of the rejected ores produce from 12 to 30 marcs per 'monton,' (of ten cargas, or 3,000 lbs.)

"The mine of Cobriza de San Felipe, eight leagues north of Babiacora, and three from the town of Ituapaca, with the haciendas and ranchos of San Felipe, Agua Caliente, and Los Chinos, in its neighborhood, is said to have been abandoned when producing pure silver, which the miners cut out in small pieces by means of large shears and chisels. The Apaches drove the miners away, and, during their absence, the shafts became filled with water, and a large rock fell into the mouth, blocking it completely up." This was in 1827.

The mine of Tacapuchi is three leagues from Babiacora south-east. The ores produce 14 marcs per mouton, or about $44.80 per 3,000 lbs.

Dolores, one league from Babiacora, produces silver in the same proportion, with a mixture of gold. These mines are all advantageously situated, with wood and water in abundance adjacent, and are distant about 70 leagues from Guaymas.

About eight leagues from Oposura north-west, are the old and celebrated mines of San Juan Bautista. The Mineral of San Juan is a mountain of itself, encircled by others to the north-west and south of considerably greater elevation. It is 3,000 yards in length from east to west, and 1,500 wide at the broadest point, and is entirely surrounded by a ravine which opens into a large plain. The mountain or hill is 600 feet high, at the summit of which the principal vein, called Santa Ana, crosses from north to south. This is crossed by another vein on the northern slope of the mountain, and is called El Rosario. These mines have produced enormously, but now contain much water.

Twelve other distinct veins are found, with small threads of virgin silver permeating the centre. The azogues, (ores that contain quicksilver) which are very abundant, are untouched, though they produce from 24 to 96 ounces of pure silver to the carga of 300 lbs. or from $140 to $650 per ton. The ores, by smelting, have yielded 50 per cent. of pure silver.

Tradition says that when they were compelled to abandon Santa Ana from water coming in, they left off in a vein of pure silver one-third of a yard wide.

The twelve veins vary from one yard to six in breadth. The depth to which they were worked is as follows: Santa Ana, 140 varas; Rosario, 60; Cata de la Agua, 5; Guadalupe, 4; Gazapa, 20; Texedora, 20; Santa Catarina, 20; Arpa, 12; Prieta, 12; Bellotita, Coronilla, 12; Fontane, 10. Half a league further to the north of Santa Ana is the mine of Descubridora, with a vein of azogues, (heavily charged with quicksilver) 15 varas wide; depth of mine, 30 feet;

assay, 96 ounces to the carga of 300 lbs, or about $650 per ton, reduced by the amalgamating process.

One league to the westward is the mine called Bronzosa, or Los Bronces, with an immense vein, which may be traced one mile on the surface. It has been considerably worked, but has water in it. Two leagues further west is the mine called Cobriza, a new mine 20 varas deep. The two last have a good reputation.

The mining district of Nacosari is located 16 leagues from Oposura, and 14 eastward from Arispe. The entrance from the plain of Nacosari is up a narrow glen two leagues in length, through which flows a tolerable stream of water, which is lost in the sand.

About one mile from the entrance, during the rainy season, it reaches to Ojo de la Agua, the source of the Oposura River. Just before you arrive at Nacosari, the glen expands into a beautiful vale, planted over with a variety of ornamental shrubs, fig trees, pomegranates, peaches, and other fruits and plants, which were once arranged with order and taste, but now form a confused thicket. The remains of numerous canals are visible, through which water was conveyed to every part of the vale. This spot was once a residence of Jesuits. The remains of their dwellings and an old church at the upper end of the valley are yet to be seen. The surroundings are picturesque. The mountains on each side rise almost perpendicularly, and are intersected with strata of a great variety of colors. Some of them present a mixture of bright red, yellow, green, and other varied tints.

There are many excavations in the mountains, and the principal mine is called San Pedro de Nacosari. This mine is a phenomenon. The vein runs east and west, and is laid open from the surface for more than 1,000 varas, to the depth of 70 varas. The breadth of the aperture is about two yards; but on each side are immense quantities of rubbish thrown out. Much dirt and sand have washed in and covered the vein; but general report says that the mine has no water in the interior, and that the ores were so rich that the best yielded from 25 to 30 marcs of silver to the arroba (of 25 lbs.).

The mines of Churunibabi, Pinal, Huacal, Aguaje, and many others, are situated to the north and north-east of Nacosari, at no great distance from San Juan del Rio, built upon a stream which falls into the Yaqui. These minerals are equally rich with those already described. Pinal con-

6

tains a greater proportion of gold than silver. It is recorded in the archives of Arispe, that the former owner, a lady by name, loaned quite a sum to the government. Churuuibabi is a very old mine, worked in the same way as the San Pedro, as, indeed, are all the mines in this part of the country. The direction of the vein is east and west, width two varas. The last persons who undertook to work this mine, were named Escalante, Vasquez, and Coulla. They cleared away the rubbish at one end until they found a pillar left to support some of the old workings, from which they took ores that produced $70,000, and yielded 70 marcs of silver per carga of 300 lbs. The mine is laid open from the surface 400 yards in depth. Tradition says that the first discoverers found the vein of virgin silver one-half vara wide, (or about 16 inches) and that it was abandoned, on account of the Apaches, when the vein was two varas or 66 inches wide, (5½ feet) and the ores assaying 70 marcs per carga, or about $1,500 per ton. The richness of these ores appears almost incredible; but when we consider the great quantities of bars of silver the mines of Sonora, without the aid of quicksilver, have produced, the metals must have been very rich and abundant. Ten leagues to the west and south-west of Nacosari, and six to the north of San Juan, are the mines of Tonbarachi and San Pedro Virguillia, with ores of from six to eight marcs per carga. To the west of Arispe are the mines of Santa Teresa, of gold and silver completely virgin, and the Cerro or Mountain of San Pedro, which contains innumerable mines and veins untouched. In all the districts above described, the roads are only passable from the public roads for horses and mules. The country being very mountainous, but not of very great elevation, none of these mines are more than six or seven leagues from rapid streams of water, sufficiently considerable to work almost any machinery. The mines of Aigame, or Haygame, near Horcositas, are famous for the abundance and richness of their gold-bearing ores. Those of Lam Pozas and Palos Blancos, five leagues west of Tepachi, are likewise good mines, with considerable veins carrying rich ores."

On the Mining Districts of La Carita, La Iglesia, La Chipiona, La Amargosa and Los Mulatos.

All these districts comprise another seven hundred square miles of a very mountainous country, situated around the the head waters of the Rio de Guisamopa and those of the creek of Agua Verde, another tributary of the Sahuaripa river; as well as on the Rio de Mulatos, which is the most southern branch of the head waters of the Rio Yaqui, but already a powerful stream, where it rushes past the mining town of Mulatos. Some of these mountain ranges reach heights of 6000 and 7000 feet above the level of the sea. The whole seven hundred square miles are covered with most magnificent forest of pine, oak and a great variety of other trees. Water is in this extensive region by far more abundant than on the western slope of the Sierra Madre. Every now and then one meets a fine stream of crystal water, leaping from rock to rock, as if anxious to become of some use before leaving its birthplace. Grass is also more abundant and much sweeter than in the west, and provisions are full as near as to Trinidad and Guadalupe. But Guaymas is, by fifteen leagues, farther off from these latter districts. As in respects to the proposed Pacific Railroad, the seven hundred miles I here speak of are much easier reached than the seven hundred miles on the western slope of the Sierra, since said railroad would run close along the southern line thereof. The veins found in these districts are even more numerous than those in the more western ones; also more regular and extensive. But the ores, as taken on an average, are less rich and of a more complicated nature in respect to their metallurgical treatment. This is the principal reason why less mining has been carried on here than in the western districts. But the mines I am going to describe are, therefore, of less importance, since they seem to make up in quantity what they fall short in quality, at least as far as veins are concerned. The district of "La Carita," the most western of the group, is situated on the eastern side of the Sierra de San Ignacio, which is in that section of the Sierra Madre, the northern termini of its most western ridge. The principal part of this district is a bulky mountain, about five miles long and 5000 feet high. Its cap of porphyry is more than 1000 feet thick, but does not prevent the green stone porphyry, with its intermixture of iron pyrites as the precursor of the ores, from cropping out in a great number of gulches and ravines, from most of which the interior of the mountain could easily and cheaply be reached. With half a dozen of tunnels, hundreds of thousands of tons of valuable ores would become accessible, and make this mountain one of the most famous of the Sierra Madre. That it is an ore-bearing mountain is, in addition to what I have already said about it, proved by the astonishing number of veins cropping out in the cap of porphyry. Only a few of them have been worked, since their existence was but recently discovered. The ore on the surface of these veins is greatly decomposed, and is, therefore, very soft. It enters freely into the Mexican amalgamation process. But after a certain depth has been reached, from twenty to forty yards, the sulphuret of the ore makes its appearance. This, without being roasted, does not enter into the amalgamation. All the worked veins have on this account been abandoned, although the ores had become more abundant than they had been near the surface. The chemical character or compounds of the ore of the La Carita district I could not determine without putting it to an analytical test. In appearance it differs from all other ores in the Sierra Madre. In many of the mines of La Carita gold is found on the surface, and in quantities large enough to be worked for. Being the nearest mining district to the Rio de Sahuaripa, La Carita has all the mining facilities on hand, that is, as far as the country produces them. The small mining village of the same name is situated at the foot of the mountain, and close to the little streamlet which comes out of it. In the east the district of La Carita is joined by that of La Iglesia. About a century ago La Iglesia was a large mining village, but at the present it is but a small *rancho*, with but half a dozen families. As a mining district, La Iglesia calls the attention of the geologist as well as the miner. Its most important geological, or rather mineralogical, feature is, that wherever a vein has been worked, the ores on the surface were rich in silver, but soon changed into the metals, pyrites, with the extraction of which the Mexican miner never troubles himself. The succession of the ore strata is here, as far as it has been tried, the same as in Dios Padre, in Trinidad. Pure galena comes first, then galena and zinc blende, after this galena, zinc blende, and small pockets of gray silver ore. Now, judging by what follows this in Dios Padre, I have a right to infer that the same ore will follow here too, viz.: a rich gray silver ore, with perhaps a little zinc blende and galena. And if this really is the case, as I do believe it is, then immense quantities of pure and rich gray silver ore could be extracted from innumerable veins of the Iglesia district. In the whole district there is not a mountain over 1000 feet high, above the level of the Agua Verde Creek, which divides it into two equal parts. This creek is a powerful stream, with a good deal of fall, and therefore very well adapted to the driving of machinery and for other purposes. On its banks and on the hills near to it thousands of acres of land could be cultivated. They are now covered with an abundance of grass or a magnificent forest.

La Igelsia, as a whole, is one of the cosiest spots of the Sierra Madre, and a place on which at some future day a great mining town must spring up. The scenery all around the district is grand, sublime; one mountain rises higher than the other, and all trying to outshine one another with their dense and splendid forests of pine, oak, etc. The whole district of La Igelsia belongs to the same ore-bearing formation as Trinidad and Guadaloupe. One vein or mine of it I have to describe in particular; it is that of " El Tajo." It is situated on an elongated hill, above two hundred feet above the level of the Arroyo del Agua Verde, and but half a mile from its banks. The vein is an extensive one, was from two to three feet wide on the surface, but left in six feet at a depth of one hundred and twenty feet, in which the mine was abandoned some twenty-five years ago. Its history was, therefore, easily to be traced, and the condition in which it it was left ascertained. On and near the surface of the vein large quantities of galena were found, after which, little by little, zinc blende made its appearance, until at the depth of one hundred and twenty feet, nothing but zinc blende, with now and then a small pocket of gray silver ore was found. The vein, as stated, was six feet wide, and consisted of pure ore. Granted, now, that little by little the zinc blende will disappear, again to be replaced by rich gray silver ore. What, if such an event takes place, will be the value of this mine? Millions could be extracted from it every year, and incredble as this may sound, it is nevertheless probable that such should and would be the result if my theory stands good, which it will, since it is not a mere abstract theory, but one founded on a great number of established facts. The future development of the mine will show whether I am in the right or not. The rock of which the hill is composed is a rather soft one, and a shaft alongside the old works of two hundred feet would go a great way in telling what is to come after the zinc blende. The sinking of such a shaft would not cost over $1000.

The mine of Yerba Buena lies opposite that of El Tajo, and on the other side of the Arroyo del Agua Verde. From the surface of its veins rich silver ores were extracted. The saying is that it was abandoned on account of a large stream of water having been struck, but I rather incline to the belief that the appearance of zinc blende was the principal cause thereof.

A number of other veins have been superficially worked, but their history is more or less the same as that of El Tajo mine. All the mining facilities are here plentiful, and even the agricultural products could be raised alongside of the mines. I come now to one of the largest, most interesting, and most important mining districts in the Sierra Madre; I mean that of "La Chipiona." Unlike La Iglesia, it is formed by groups of mountains, from 4000 to 6000 feet above the level of the sea, but, through its peculiar topography, nevertheless accessible from all sides. Nay, the very height of the mountains and their size will contribute toward their development, in a mining sense of the word. In this district, as a rule, all the mountains are covered or capped by a thick stratum of porphyry. But in all the innumerable gulches and ravines, the green stone porphyry, with its never-failing iron pyrites, stands out in immense masses, and in one spot over twenty five acres of the very gray silver ore can be traced in a thousand small veins, running through the rock in every direction. The veins cropping out through the surface of the "caps" cannot be numbered, and are at the same time the most extensive ores in the Sierra Madre. The district of La Chipiona joins that of La Iglesia. It belongs, like this, to the ore-bearing formation, and even more so, as the description of some of its mines will show. If I say that more than a hundred mines have been worked here I do not say too much, since within six months, while I was residing in La Cienegita (the most inhabited part of the Chipiona mines), I could not visit half of them. Some of the veins I I traced for five or six miles, without coming to their terminal in any direction. They all run from north to south, or near to it, and their thickness lies between two and ten feet, but it increases as they go down, and, I believe, that in a depth of five hundred feet it will vary between ten and fifty feet. The ores of all these veins are, with the exception of a few, the same : a poor, gray silver ore, rich gray copper ore, intermixed with iron pyrities, and in some instances also with copper pyrites. To a depth of from twenty to fifty feet these ores were decomposed—changed into a kind of red or yellow ocre. They freely entered into the smelting as well as into the amalgamation process; but below that depth the sulphurets made their appearance. They are, without being well reverberated, untreatable, and consequently of no use. But I doubt very much whether this will be the process by which these ores can be treated to advantage, since lead is scarce and expensive, not only all through the Sierra Madre, but also over the whole of northern Mexico. The appearance of these sulphurets there was the cause why all these mines were abandoned again soon after they had been taken up.

I shall describe some of the most important ores as a mere sample of the nature and importance of the Chipiona district. As some of the most interesting ores, I have to point out a number of veins of the same nature as that of El Tajo mine, in the Iglesia district. The principal one is La Mina Grande, called so from a vein on which it was founded. On the surface it contained large masses of galena, which, little by little, changed into zinc blende. When it was abandoned, the vein was from six to eight feet wide. All I have said of the El Tajo mine, in respect of what it might become, may also be applied to this mine, and perhaps more so, since its veins are not only wider, but also more favorably situated as to working to advantage, running along the side of a high mountain, so as to be opened by the driving of a tunnel. Next to the Mina Grande comes that of Ostemuri, an extensive vein, in which a great deal of work has been carried on. Here, too, zinc blende was the cause of the abandonment. Provided that in either of these three mines, those of El Tajo, La Grande or Ostemuri, the sinking of a shaft or the driving of a tunnel would prove that I am correct in respect to the ores found below the zinc blende, what would these three mines be worth, and what dividends could a company in possession thereof pay ? Millions would stand arrayed against the small risk of $5,000. No further working capital would be required, as each mine, from the day of finding the rich ore, would become at once not only self supporting, but surplus producing. These three mines are so near one another, the greatest distance being but four leagues, that their works could be easily directed from the some point.

I come now to a description of a mountain peculiarly situated, of a peculiar shape. and peculiarly interesting. It is that of Cerra Colorado, or La Chipiona proper. I might call it a mountain peninsula, since on three sides it is separated from surrounding mountains by deep gulches. On the south side it is connected therewith by a low isthmus or small plateau. From that isthmus it increases in height until its summit is 1,500 feet above the level of the Arroyo de las Bronzas washing past its base. The cap of this isolated mountain is about three hundred feet thick, perhaps less. A very extensive vein (the principal one) crops out on its summit, and, following the ridge, loses itself in the isthmus, to reappear on the mountain coming down from the isthmus. Over this second mountain I have followed it for some three miles, without finding its termini. In this vein a considerable amount of work has been carried on, and in some places to no inconsiderable depth. All the ores extracted from it were decomposed ores (originally gray silver ores and iron pyrites). In all parts of the vein the working of it was given up as soon as the sulphurets were reached. Besides this, a hundred mines of the same nature were worked, and for the same cause abandoned.

Seven years ago, when I was for the last time in the Chipiona district, but one mine was miserably worked. I now come to the part of the mountain above described, to to which I would call the special attention of the geologist and miner. It is this: the immense base of it—the circumference, which comprises six to eight miles. Around all this base greenstone, porphyry with iron pyrites, stand out and on one side, the eastern, a thousand small veins of gray silver ore run in every direction through the rock, through the same kind of rock and in the same way as in the Dios Padre mine of La Trinidad. Besides this, the exterior of both mountains (not in shape) of La Chipiona and La Trinidad is the same. Why, then, should we not infer from all this that the exterior of the mountain bears the same relation to its interior as the exterior of the Dios Padre mine to its interior?

Geology would cease to be a science, and would be of no use if such inferences, based on so many facts, could not be drawn or would not be accepted. I have so far described four mountains, the heads or interior of which must be considered as bearing ore, and of a similar nature as that of the Dios Padre mine. They all four belong to the same formation, the same period of geological creation, and have the same rocks, ores and appearances in common. The most northern of these four mountains is that of La Chipiona; eight leagues from it lies that of La Huerta de Yulapa; four leagues from this that of Dios Padre, and seven leagues from that, the mountain of Guadaloupe Sierra de la Hierra, some eighteen leagues from one extreme to the other. Founded on these facts, since facts they may be considered, I ask the question, of what are the hearts or interiors of all the mountains lying between and around the four mountains mentioned and described composed? I boldly answer, of ore, some in a less and some in a higher degree; some with but very little of it, and some with a great deal; some with ore of a poor and others of a richer nature. The calculation of the sum total of the riches they may contain I leave to some mathematician who delights in such calculations, as some Americans do in calculating the population the United States will have in 6000 years from now.

All the mountains of which the district of La Chipiona is composed, comprising some two hundred and fifty square miles, are covered with the finest forests in the Sierra Madre.

Oak and pine abound everywhere, from the depth of the gulch to the highest peak of the mountains. Grass is no less abundant, since the whole two hundred and fifty miles form an almost continuous meadow.

Of water, the only stream of any consequence is the Arroyo de las Brouzas, a tributary of the Arroyo de l'Agua Verde. In the dry season it almost dries up, but there are a thousand places where artificial water reservoirs could be constructed, and filled to the brim in the rainy season, when water falls most abundantly. The projected Pacific Railroad touches this district as well as La Iglesia and La Carita.

Agricultural products for the maintenance of a large population could be raised in the low lands of Sonora, and within the mining districts, where good soil abounds.

The distance to Guayamas is seventy leagues. The Indian village of Taharachi lies inside the Chipiona district. In the east of the Chipiona district lies the district of La Cienegita Amargosa. It belongs to the same formation as all the rest of the Sierra Madre districts so far described. In it, too, a great number of veins crop out on the surface, some of them worked. There is one vein I discovered; it is one hundred feet wide, which has never been touched, and promises to lead into the interior of an ore-bearing mountain of great extent.

The surface of all the mountains of the Amargosa Cienegita district is, already stated, gold-bearing (in the description of the Sonora gold mines). The mountain described there as paying $12 per ton of decomposed porphyry and iron pyrites forms the most eastern part of this district. By all I know of the geology and mining of Sonora I am convinced that the interior of this immense mountain is very rich in silver ores, perhaps richer than any of the other ore-bearing mountains heretofore described.

The Arroyos of Amargosa and Cienegita have their rise in this district. They are tributaries to the Arroyo del Agua Verde, and small but permanent streamlets, of the best drinking water, are consequently of much importance in a region where most of the waters are impregnated with dissolved mineral substances. The brook of La Amargosa is the emanation of a mineral spring (steel water), and as such highly prized by the surrounding population.

The forests of Cienegita Amargosa district being very dense and the mountains above the elevation, where grass grows freely, this article is scarce in some parts of the district, but found in great abundance in the remaining parts. Leaving the Cienegita Amargosa district and taking the road for Mulatos one has to pass over the highest ridge in that part of the Sierra Madre. It is, like all other high ridges of the mountain ranges, composed of trachyte. Arrived on the other side, one looks down into a deep valley. It is the bed of the Rio de Mulatos, the southern branch of the Yaqui river, coming almost from the plateau of Chihuahua. It is a principal stream, and the day will come when it will be of immense value to mining. On the banks of this stream lies the mining town of Mulatos, with some some 1500 half starved inhabitants, although living on riches uncounted.

The gold mines of Mulatos were once, as I have already said, famous, not only through all Sonora, but also all through Mexico. As a silver mining district I cannot say less of it, since all its mountains showing gold near the surface will change into silver-bearing mountains after certain depths have been reached. There is a vein in the Mulatos district the ores of which produce the white copper heretofore only found in China. What its components are I am not aware of. Veins bearing silver ores on the very surface have so far not been found. Timber, wood and grass are rather scarce in the neighborhood of Mulatos, and all provisions must be brought from the Sahuaripa valley. The egress and ingress from and to the town are very difficult, and since a direct connection with the future Pacific Railroad is almost imposible, a mountain range 7000 feet in height lying between them, I must say that the district of Mulatos lies under great disadvantage. On the Eastern side of the river lies the mining district of Dolores, said to be rich in silver mines; but since I never saw it myself I pass it, and shall continue to pass all the mining districts of which nothing of importance is to be said. All that broad piece of country lying between the districts of La Trinidad and Guadaloupe and the boundary line of Chihuahua belongs to the same ore-bearing formation as all the districts of the Sierra Madre heretofore described.

But as nowhere veins of any nature (some gold-bearing

veins excepted) crop out on the surface, I shall not consider it a *bona fide* mining ground, although lying between the great eastern and western mining districts, the latter of which I have still to describe. Theoretically speaking, I must look on these hundreds of square miles as ore-bearing, and the future mining will prove that I was entitled to do so.

The most interesting and, perhaps, the richest gold mine of Sonora exists in the Sierra Madre, east of the Sahuaripa river, and behind the most western range of these mountains. It lies in the silver mining district of La Cienegita, and on both sides of the little streamlet of La Amagosa, the waters of which are charged with iron (steel water). This streamlet divides a long, wide and high gold bearing mountain into two parts. On the point where it comes out of it, or from between them, these mountains reach about 2000 feet above the level of the little flat in front of them. The rock which contains the gold is a kind of decomposed green stone porphyry and surcharged with oxide of iron (decomposed iron pyrites). Take away a ton of ore from these mountains wherever you may, and you will find that it pays you from $10 to $12 dollars a ton of 2000 lbs. By describing the geological character of this district when coming to the silver mines of Sonora, I shall refer once more to these two mountains, and tell my readers what their bowels contain. For the present I will add, that what is found on the surface of these two mountains is but an indication of what is sleeping in their interior. On different and exceedingly rich spots large quantities of gold were found, but the bulk of the ore has never been worked.—*The foregoing description of the districts of La Carita, La Chipiona, La Armigosa and Los Mulatos are from a report by Prof. Julius Miller, an engineer and geologist.*

In the Moctezuma district, the La Providencia, originally called La Palmita, mine is situated eighteen miles northeast of Oposura. This mine was discovered in 1803, and was worked by Spaniards up to 1811, by the records. At this date the records were destroyed, and it is unknown when the mine was last worked. The incline is irregular in the vein; depth, 100 feet; width, 4 feet; assay averages $125 per ton. Some of the surface croppings, we have been told, went as high as $806. The old shafts were abandoned and filled with rubbish; the pillars were extracted by gambucinos, leaving the mine in a ruinous condition. The intention is to sink a new shaft and put up a ten-stamp mill. A trail leads to the mine, but no wagon road. This mine was rediscovered by a Russian gentleman, who brought specimens of the ore to Harshaw, in Arizona and had them assayed, and there met a mining expert from this city, who examined the ore and found it rich, and placed the mine with some gentlemen in this city, who are now making preparations to extensively open it.

The San Antonio Mineral, in the Altar district, possesses some good mines. The Descubridora mine is situated in this Mineral, and is owned by the Sigs. Cipriano Ortega and Abelardo Ortiz, and is within the zone of twenty leagues of the frontier boundary upon the Territory of Arizona. The mine is developed by five tunnels. The vein runs north and south, and its width is from one to four feet. The depth reached is 313 metres, with an inclination of vein of twenty degrees. The metals contained in the ore are gold, silver and lead, and the ley is $16 in gold and $82 in silver, and 72 per cent. of lead. The ore is reduced by machinery established in the same Mineral, in which is located the American company, entitled the San Antonio Gold Mining Company. This mill puts in motion two batteries of five stamps each. The laborers engaged in the workings of this mine vary from twenty to thirty.

The mine of Cerro de Oro, or Hill of Gold, is in the Mineral of San Antonio. This mine is owned by Sigs. Cipriano Ortega and Abelardo Ortiz, and is situated within the zone of twenty leagues on the frontier bounding Arizona. The workings consist of two tunnels, the first 41 metres in depth and the second 45. The metals of this mine assay in gold $25 and $56 in silver, and carry 70 per cent of lead. The ore is reduced by the machinery of San Antonio. The vein of this mine runs east and west, with a width of $2\frac{1}{2}$ metres and an inclination of 35 degrees.

The mine of Vieja de Oro is owned by Sigs. Cipriano Ortega and Abelardo Ortiz, in the zone before-mentioned bounding Arizona. The mine is developed by one shaft 22 metres in depth. The assay of the mine reaches $40 per ton in gold. The ore is reduced in the mineral above mentioned. The vein of the mine runs east and west, and is 3 feet in width, with an inclination of 50 degrees.

The Rebozadero mine is owned by the same parties before-mentioned, and is located near the other mines. The mine has been developed by four shafts and one tunnel, and reaches in depth 56 metres. The vein runs southeast and northwest; width from 2 to 5 feet, with inclination of 20 degrees, and assays $15 per ton, gold. The Cobriza is also owned by the same parties, and is located near the others. The mine has one shaft, 12 metres in depth. The vein runs east and west; width, 1 metre; inclination 35 degrees. The assay is $25 per ton, in gold.

The Rosales mine is owned by Sigs. Francisco, Abel and Jose M. del Castillo, and is located adjoining the mines before mentioned, in the San Antonio Mineral. This mine has two shafts and four drifts, which reach the centre of the workings, about 180 feet. The vein runs from south to north, and its width is from 1 to 4 feet; inclination, 35 degrees. The ores by arrastras produce in gold $30 per ton, and is worked by four barreteros, or miners.

The mine of Ruisena is located in the Mineral of Plomosos and in the twenty-league belt, northeast of Altar. The mine is owned by Sr. Don Francisco Lizarraga. The vein courses east and west, and in width reaches 75 centimetres (one metre is 39.37-100 inches, and a centimetre is about .39-100 of an inch). The inclination is 40 degrees. The walls are firm, and the ores carry gold and silver. The workings are new, and consist of one tunnel, reaching the principal vein. The depth attained is 75 metres, and one shaft of 9 metres, and with other workings make in all some 327 metres. The present "labores" are in abundant metal; 25 laborers are employed in the mine. The metals are reduced in the works of the Mineral of Aribaca, in the territory of Arizona, distant from the mine about 30 leagues. The ley of the metal of the third class has assayed $801 per ton.

The mine Providencia is located in the Mineral of Sonoyta. This mine is owned by Sigs. C. Ortega and A. Ortiz, and is located within the 20-league boundary, northwest of Altar. This mine has one shaft and one drift, and the depth reached is 35 metres. The vein runs south and north; width, 1 metre; inclination, 35 degrees, and carries in the ores gold, silver, copper and lead. The ley is $8 gold, $40 silver, $20 in copper and $52 in lead per ton. The ore is reduced in the beneficio of San Antonio. This mine has ten laborers.

The Rosario mine is in the Sonoyta Mineral, and is owned by the same parties last mentioned. This mine has 4 shafts, and depth reached is 50 metres. The vein runs south and north; width, 2 feet—in some places 1½ varas; inclination, 70 degrees. The ore yields $180 per ton silver and is reduced by arastras. The mine is worked by five laborers.

The San Francisco mine is located in the Mineral of the same name. This mine is owned by Don Cipriano Ortega, and is also located within the twenty-league belt. The vein extends north and south; width 1 to three feet; inclination, 55 degrees. The ley is $40 per ton gold. The ore is reduced in Fremont, Arizona, about twelve leagues distant. The mine is worked by four shafts; depth reached 225 feet, and employs 30 men.

The San Francisco mine, in the Mineral of Corazon, is owned by Sr. Manuel Escalante and associates, and is situated about 25 leagues from the American line. The workings consist of shafts and drifts, which have reached 240 feet in depth. The vein runs south and north; width, 2½ metres; inclination, 75 degrees, and assays $20 gold and $56 in silver per ton. The ore is reduced by arastras, and occupies eight workmen.

The Mina Grande is located in the Mineral of Juarez. This mine is owned by Sigs. Modesto Borquez, Benigno V. Garcia and Justo Bon. It is located about 42 leagues from the American line. The vein runs southeast to northwest; width, 3 to 12 feet, inclination, 35 degrees. The ores contain gold and silver, and the ley is $50 in gold and $15 in silver per ton. The arastra is used, and 13 workmen are employed. The "labores" are new, and consist of shafts and drifts. The depth reached is 370 feet.

The Juarez mine is located in the Mineral of the same name. This mine is owned by the Sigs. Jesus Castro and Jose O. Velasco, and is about 42 leagues from the American line. The vein runs southeast to northwest; width, 3 to 6 feet; inclination 75 degrees. The ley is $30 per ton silver. The workings are new and consist of 2 shafts, depth 170 feet. The ores are reduced by arastras, and eight workmen are employed in the mine.

The San Felix mine is located in a Mineral of the same name, and is owned by Albert Sturges and brothers, and is within 56 leagues of the American line. The course of the vein is north and south; width, 6 feet; inclination, 15 degrees. The assay runs from $35 to $2000 per ton. The ores are worked at reduction works, called "Las Tanquas," about five leagues from the mine.—["Perito de Minas del Distrito de Altar."]—*From an official report on the mines of Sonora, in the Altar district.*

The Quintera mine is owned by a New York company, who purchased it last September from Mexicans. The principal owners are Messrs. McFarland and Morgan, of New York. The mine cost $210,000—$25,000 in cash, one half the balance in six months and remainder in one year. The property is said to be a good one. A 15 stamp mill is now reducing the ore, that has reached as high as $1000 per ton.

The Santa Juliana Mining Co. of New York, lately organized, have purchased the Santa Juliana and Mina del Padre silver mines. These mines are located in the municipality of Baroyeca, district of Alamos, about 65 miles from the city of Alamos, and 24 miles from the Yaqui river. The Santa Juliana is an old mine, formerly worked by the Spaniards and lately by the Mexicans. The old works are the Trojas, Dios Padre, San Francisco, San Juan, Santa Loreto, San Benito, Santa Rosa, Trousou Nuevo, Milagres, Congojas, San Ignacio, Salsipuedes and many others. The ores are docile and contain ruby-silver and sub-sulphides. The old pillars assay from $100 to $107 per ton. The Santa Juliana proper has a general E. 14 degrees N. course, with a dip of 45 degrees N. Its width varies from five to fifteen feet with walls firm and well encased. The gangue is principally quartz. It shows all the phenomena constituting a true vein, as far as explored from the surface to a depth of 700 feet, and in all the lateral works.

The Refugio mines are situated 25 miles east of Hermosillo, and about 25 miles from the Sonora railroad, 95 miles from Guaymas, on the Gulf of California. The mines are connected with Guaymas by the Sonora railroad. These mines were discovered by some prominent merchants of the district about a year ago and were purchased from them by the Refugio Mining Company of Santa Fe, N.M. The mines are situated on the Las Norias ranch, adjoining the celebrated San Juan de Dios mine, abundantly supplied with timber of good quality, and water sufficient for all milling and smelting purposes. The property is about 2700 feet long by 700 feet wide. The vein strikes apparently N. E. and S. W., and dips nearly vertically, although as no walls have, as yet, been encountered, actual data cannot be given. However, at the point where work has been done, the ore body has been proved to exceed 7 feet in width without meeting with the wall rock, indicating at any rate an enormous body of mineral. The surrounding country rock is composed of limestone and porphyry.

The mineral is carbonate of lead, carrying a considerable amount of silver. Numerous assays of the value have been made, varying from 35 to 75 per cent. of lead, and from 40 to 300 ounces of silver, also from $10 to $45 in gold. In the adjoining San Juan de Dios mine there exists an ore body of about 6 feet wide, reaching $1,850 per ton, also 10 feet of solid mineral at the end of the tunnel, none of which has a value of less than 150 ounces of silver.

It will thus be seen that the ore is essentially a smelting ore, and one that is perhaps more easily reduced than any the miner has to deal with. All necessary works for smelting the ore are now in course of construction within 1½ miles of the mine.

From the reports of W. A. Jones, on the Jesus Maria mines on January 1st, 1881:—"The mine is situated on one of the tributaries of the Mayo river, 40 miles northeast of Alamos, state of Sonora. The mine has a length of 2600 feet, by 600 feet in width, well defined ledge, and is enclosed between limestone and porphyry, the latter being the hanging wall. The ore-bearing material has a width of about 100 feet, samples of which assayed according to report from 15\frac{45}{100}$ to 19\frac{24}{100}$ per ton. Notwithstanding the low grade of the samples, from the nature and the great extent of the body of the ore, it is a property well worthy of development, with every promise of opening up into a large and valuable mine."

"The principal mine of the Plomo Mineral of the Altar district is the Ruisena gold mine and its continuation. This mine is located four miles from the village of El Plomo, and some 45 miles N. W. of Altar. The vein is a fissure with the hanging and foot wall of granite. Width of vein 3 to 3½ feet at a depth of 270 feet. The old workings cover an extent of over 3000 feet under ground, with surface workings extending over 5000 feet. The ores carry sulphurets of iron and copper and are refractory, with an average result of about $100 per ton. This mine has been worked for the last fifty years. The reduction works are located about four miles distant at El Plomo, and consist of a ten stamp mill, concentrators, and two water jacket furnaces. The refining works have a capacity of 20 tons per day.

This property is worked in connection with a large lead mine called "Abundancia," located near the works, the vein of which averages 4½ feet. The lead ores carry near 50 per cent. lead and 20 oz. silver, and about one oz. in gold.

The property is owned by a company incorporated in Chicago in June, 1882, the majority interests being held by Chicago capitalists. Mr. J. Sherman Hall is the Secretary of the company."—[Report by Mr. D. Tooker, M. E.]

About two miles from the Ruisena mine, a very rich pocket of gold was discovered some 20 years ago that yielded nearly a quarter of a million of dollars, all taken out in about three weeks. Some further prospecting has been done but this is the principal strike of this region.

The "Sonora Chief" mine is located in the Carbonera

mountains on the east side of San Miguel river, about 9 miles north of San Miguel, Carbonera Mineral, Ures district. The vein is a contact vein, formation, porphyry hanging wall and lime foot wall, width of vein 7 to 10 feet at a depth of 140 feet. The ores carry carbonate of lead and oxide of iron, and is a free smelting ore, carrying about 40 per cent. lead and from 80 to 100 oz. of silver per ton. The intention of the present operators is to ship the ore over Sonora railway direct to San Francisco, or Benson Reduction works.

The Jesus Maria mine is located at a point near Carbo station some seven miles distant, and is a large deposit of carbonate of lead and iron, lying nearly flat, which is developed by several open cuts and shafts, showing ore from 4 to 20 feet in thickness. The ores carry about 30 per cent. lead and 40 oz. of silver per ton. The ore will be shipped to Benson if reasonable rates can be secured.

The "Santa Felicita" mine is situated about 24 miles northwest from the city of Altar, and about 8 miles north of the town of Caborca, in the Altar mining district. The vein is a true fissure; width, from 5 to 18 feet, at a depth of 320 feet. The ore is a free-milling gold, carrying $30 to $80 per ton in gold, and from 70 to 80 ounces in silver. The ore body is decomposed quartz, with hanging wall granite, and foot wall porphyry. This property has been worked from 10 to 12 years. The "Santa Felicita Mining and Milling Co.," of Chicago, own and work the property, reducing the ore by a 20 stamp mill. This mine is said to be one of the most valuable in northwestern Sonora.

The Bonañea gold mine is located about three miles east of the Santa Felicita, and has a vein of ore from two to five feet wide, of the same character and about the same value as that of the Santa Felicita. This mine also belongs to the same company.

The above-named company are being amply remunerated for their investment. Dr. Davis, of Chicago, the Secretary, from whom we obtained the above data, says the net profits upon the working of the property reaches from $24,000 to $30,000 per month, and that the company is so well satisfied with their investment that they refuse to allow its stock to be quoted on the market, or the property to be sold.

In speaking of the old mines of Sonora, Francisco Velasco says that the old Spaniards generally confined themselves to the high grade ores, and when they were no longer in abundance they abandoned the mine, which then became choked or filled with water. "Windlasses or pulleys at that time were almost unknown; and where the mine could not be kept free of water by buckets, it was abandoned." All of which plainly indicates that old mines, as a rule, had better be very closely examined before any extensive outlay is entered upon; and since the mineral wealth of Sonora is almost unlimited, a good, new mine, with paying ore, or an old mine with present evidence of its richness, is better than abandoned or exhausted mines with a past reputation of almost fabulous wealth. *When a mine has produced its millions, generally there is not much paying ore left to warrant an extensive reopening.*

The Santa Clara Coal Fields of Sonora.

" These coal fields are situated in the district of Ures, Jurisdiction of San Javier, and Mineral or mining district of La Barranca, about 100 miles due east from Hermosillo, and about 120 miles north-east from the port of Guaymas, four miles east from the Barranca mine, about 12 miles east of the town of San Javier, and about three and a half miles west of the Yaqui River.

" These coal beds were first denounced by William Lubbert, Napoleon Graff, Thomas Mahan, Frank Ench, and Antonio Cubillos, on the 26th day of April, 1872. At the present date the property is owned exclusively by N. Graff, Florence R. Rountree, A. Cubillos, and F. Ench. The title of the above property vests in said parties, and is free from all incumbrances up to Jan. 1st, 1881, when, at that date, the property was bonded to Charles A. McQuesten, of this city. The property is held by the above-named parties as an association.

" The property consists of extensive deposits of anthracite coal," with some appearances of being partly bituminous, which indicates that there must be extensive coal beds of both anthracite and bituminous coal. " The coal beds denounced are contained in one square league of land. Up to the present date two well-defined veins of coal have been exposed.

" The first consists of a vein nine feet six inches thick, that has been developed by explorations and examinations on the side of a mountain.

" In some places, the vein is within about from one to four feet from the surface. This vein can be traced for about 1,000 feet horizontally, and about 500 feet above the base of the mountain, and extending toward the summit of the mountain. One extensive tunnel has been run on this vein, following its dip. No explorations have been m.de above the point above mentioned; but indications show that this vein has a much larger area. The incline of the vein is 20 degrees S. S. E., the dip east by north-east. At a distance of 22 feet below the point of location of the above-mentioned vein is another vein of about seven feet in thickness. This vein is reached by a shaft on the opposite side of the creek, on the side of the mountain opposite. On the side of the mountain, several excavations have determined the thickness of the vein. At the foot of this mountain is a cañon about 100 yards wide, on the opposite side of which rises a high and rugged mountain. This cañon is about six miles long, commencing at the Taramari mine and ending near the Yaqui River. The coal veins are about one-half the distance between these points, or about two and one-half miles from the Yaqui River bottoms.

"The bed of this cañon can be made into a good wagon road with little work, from the coal veins to the river. Water is found in the cañon at a depth of eight feet. In many places in this cañon, slate and many indications of coal are found. The geological formation of the vicinity and the character of the coal is as follows: The mountain ranges in the immediate vicinity of the coal are very rugged, with steep sides, covered with trees, cactus plants, and other tropical vegetation. The average elevation of the range of mountains is about 3,000 feet above the sea level.

"The range of mountains is continuous for over 100 miles running north, and about twenty south, of the location of the coal beds. They form the mountains bordering on both sides of the valley of the Yaqui River. Placers of gold that have yielded very richly, are located near the valley of the Yaqui, one man having in a single season extracted $30,000 from this same cañon where the coal beds are located. The Yaqui River is about three-and-a-half miles from the present workings of the mine; and the coal mine is very easy of access by a road to be constructed through the cañon, up a gentle incline. At present there is no road for wagons. Horses and mules are therefore used to reach the mines. With very little work a wagon-road could be constructed, or even a railroad, direct to the river's bank. For a distance of about ninety miles from the mouth, the Yaqui River is navigable for barges or flat boats; and at this point rocks and rapids impede a further passage, except for small boats, which are carried around the rapids by "carriers," at the mouth of the cañon opposite the coal fields. The river at this point is about 200 feet wide and four feet deep, during the dry season; but during the rainy season a considerable increase in the volume of water takes place. Engineers state that the river can be made navigable for barges from the point opposite the cañon before mentioned, to the mouth of the river, a distance, by following the course of the river, of about 120 miles. The Yaqui River lands, for a distance of 100 miles above its mouth, are noted for the richness of the soil, and the large crops, "as before mentioned." "A railroad can easily be built from the mine to the river, and following near the different windings of the river north, to enter the United States near Tombstone, where a market can be found for a large quantity of coal for milling purposes, and also for smelting furnaces, used to smelt the rich argentiferous and galena ores that abound in that region; and also through northern and middle Sonora, where hundreds of mines containing smelting-ore require a coal suitable for smelting purposes; or south, through the rich valley of the Yaqui River bottom, where millions of acres of the finest land in the world are awaiting the emigrant to cultivate its soil; and on to the port of Guaymas, where a market can be found for a large amount of coal for steamers that regularly ply from San Francisco and that port, and for vessels of war of England, United States, and other nations, that regularly touch at Guaymas.

"From Guaymas, barges can ply between that port and Mazatlan, or Cape St. Lucas, in Lower California, where a depot of coal could readily find a sale in supplying ocean steamers that ply between China, Japan, Australia, Panama and San Francisco, with a prospect in the near future of supplying coal to the fleets of steamers that will ply through the Isthmus of Panama Canal. Barges could also take the coal direct from the Yaqui, up the gulf, to the Colorado River, to Yuma; there supplying the steamers on that river, the several railroads that pass over this river, and the mills on and near this river, where steamers now go up a distance of about 200 miles from Yuma. Vessels could also transport this coal direct from the Yaqui to San Francisco, where a ready demand for anthracite coal will result in large sales, as at present all anthracite coal used in San Francisco comes from Pennsylvania." (Extract from the report of Charles A. McQuesten, of this city, on the Santa Clara coal fields of Sonora.) We might add that the Mexican Congress has lately approved of the concession to

Mr. Robert R. Symon for the construction of a railroad from the above coal fields to El Morrito, on the Bay of Guaymas. Thus it will be seen that this coal will soon be on the market.

Quicksilver, Graphite, Marble, Copper, Lead, Coal, Iron, Etc.

The ores of the mines of Santa Teresa and Santa Ana contain quicksilver, and tradition says that the mineral region of Rio Chico also produces this metal.

In San José de la Pimas there is a small hill entirely composed of graphite or black lead.

In San Javier is a vein of a dark color on the face of a hill, from which is extracted a compact substance which, when dissolved in water, produces a fine ink, which is similar to India ink, from China.

In Oposura, there is a hill composed of excellent marble, of which the altars and churches of Sonora are built.

At Ures, there is also another marble quarry.

The celebrated hill of "La Campana," in the city of Hermosillo, is composed entirely of marble as white as that of Italy, and it is used, in some instances, to pave the streets. Alabaster and jasper are found also at Oposura and Ures. Copper is found in the mountain range of La Cananea, north of Arispe.

Aduaña, (an old region of gold mines) Tonuco, 36 miles west of Hermosillo, and Bacuachi and La Cobriza, west of Horcasitas, all contain copper ores.

Lead abounds in Cieneguilla and Arispe, Batuco, San José de Gracia, Aduaña, and Promontorio.

Agua Caliente and Alamo Muerto contain lead, although it is found in the greatest quantities at Cieneguilla and Arispe.

Coal is found near Los Bronces and La Baranca, before mentioned, where a vein of from seven to nine feet is found.

Iron is found in abundance in the southern part of Arizona, in the range of mountains called Madera, and in the northern part of Sonora, and at Mogollon.

In the neighborhood of Cucurpe there is a vein of incombustible crystal.

SINALOA.

CHAPTER I.

General Description.

From the river Mayo to Alamos, in Sonora, the country is an extension of rolling hills, and from thence down to the coast and the valley of the river Fuerte, bordering Sinaloa. Here the "tierra caliente" plain is encountered that extends all the way down the coast, through the whole length of the State of Sinaloa. The town of Fuerte is located on the river Fuerte, about **80 miles** from the mouth. The river is navigable for flat-boats up to this point. An extensive valley below Alamos extends almost due south, between the mountains on the east and the low range of hills on the west, until it opens into the valley of the Fuerte and the plains located south. The Fuerte River is about 200 miles long, and rises north-east in the Sierra Madre, and flows south-west into the Gulf of California. The next river encountered is the Sinaloa, which rises in the neighborhood of the south-western part of Chihuahua, and flows in a south-westerly course, describing a section of a circle through placers of gold situated east of the town of Sinaloa, about 25 miles. Here the river winds in a curve to the east and again to the west, within a space of about eight miles, then continues its course, passing the town of Sinaloa, situated on its banks, and flows south-west into the gulf. A small peninsula completely hides its mouth from the open waters of the gulf. Another peninsula juts out in an opposite direction, forming a very good harbor for small vessels. The river is about **180 miles** in length. The Mocorito Arroyo or creek is next crossed, and another small stream, until the river of Culiacan is reached, which rises in the western part of Durango, near Tamasula, and flows southwest into the gulf, the mouth of which is also hidden behind an island, forming a very good roadstead, called the

Puerto de Altata. The city of Culiacan is located on the banks of this river, opposite the point where the Rio de Hamaya empties into the Culiacan River. This river is about 150 miles long, and on each side of it spurs of the Sierra Madre jut out into the plain within about 30 miles of the coast; the valley of Culiacan being at this point 15 miles wide. The Rio de San Lorenzo is next reached, that flows south-west direct into the gulf. The great mining district of Cosala lies south-east of this river, near its source; the town of Cosala being about 10 miles south from its banks. This river runs through a valley of narrow width, the whole distance, until it reaches the plains beyond.

A valley branches from the valley of San Lorenzo up to Cosala, with a gentle incline, when it again commences to slope on the other side down a valley or cañon to the Elota River. This river also rises in the western part of Durango, and flows south-west into the gulf. This river is about 110 miles long, and has numerous branches. In the neighborhood of its branches, in its cañons and ravines, and on the slopes of the mountains adjacent, are some of the most celebrated mines of gold and silver in the state. The Rio de Piastla also rises in Durango, in its western part, near the celebrated mines of San Dimas, and flows south-west, passing San Ignacio, and empties into the gulf. The valley of Piastla is also very narrow; but some exceedingly fertile lands are found in its bottoms, as in many other portions of the state.

Another small arroyo is reached, and we enter into the thickly-settled region adjacent to the city of Mazatlan. The port of Mazatlan is located on the coast, about half-way between the mouth of the arroyo last mentioned and the river of Mazatlan. This river also rises in the cañons of Durango, about 20 miles across the border line of the state of Sinaloa, and beyond the mines of Ventañas, and flows south-west about 50 miles, and then takes a course almost due south, and empties into the gulf, or rather Pacific Ocean; the mouth of the Gulf of California being now reached. The point where the river discharges itself into the sea is about 15 miles below Mazatlan City. The Rosario River also rises across the border line of the state, in Durango, and flows south-west, into the ocean, passing El Rosario, in the neighborhood of which are located some very rich mines. Above the mouth of this river, and lying in from the coast, is located the lagoon or lake of El Caimanero, which is about 12 miles long, and about 4 miles in width at its widest point.

The Rio de las Cañas, at the southern border of the State, separating Sinaloa from Jalisco, flows in the same direction as the Rosario River, and empties into the bay or lagoon of Boca de Tecopan, a narrow inlet of the sea which winds into the plain about five miles, and then spreads north in a narrow body of water about ten miles, and south about thirty-five miles, into an extensive body of water in the southern part. It is said it may be made one of the finest harbors in the world, and would contain all the fleets of the globe. With such a harbor as this at Mazatlan the most powerful city of the Pacific Coast would spring up upon its shores. This harbor is located about fifty miles below Mazatlan. The Tierra Caliente plain, before referred to, is about 300 miles long, and intersected by the rivers and streams before mentioned; and at its widest part is about forty miles in width, with extensive valleys branching up the banks of the rivers, some of which are 100 miles in length—the valley of the Fuerte being the largest. The foot-hills of the mountains are covered with timber, such as cedar, and the varieties of oak. The State of Sinaloa extends over an area of nearly 3,600 square miles, and has a population of about 200,000. The surface of the plains of the coast is low and somewhat sandy, though the soil is very fertile. Its productions are similar to Sonora, though to a less extent. Dye-woods abound on the coast and toward the Sierra Madre, and on the eastern frontier there abound extensive forests of pine and cedar covering the mountain sides adjacent to the streams. The rivers flowing into the gulf are used to irrigate adjacent land during the dry season. The state is divided into nine districts, viz., Mazatlan, Rosario, Concordia, Cosala, San Ignacio, Mocorito, Fuerte, Sinaloa, and Culiacan. The state is bounded on the north and northwest by Sonora; and north and north-east by Chihuahua; and east by Durango; and south-east by Jalisco; on the south-west by the mouth of the Gulf of California. The north and north-eastern portion is very mountainous, while it is more level on the coast, which is drained, as well as the mountains adjacent in the north-east, by the rivers before named. The interior contains mines of considerable extent, some of which are very rich, to which we will give some attention hereafter. The interior valleys are very fertile, especially the valley of Piastla, on the Piastla River, and the valley of Rosario, about twenty miles south-east of Mazatlan. There are about 100 towns in the state, and out of the latter, Mazatlan, Culiacan, Cosala, Rosario, Fuerte, and Sinaloa, are the most prominent. The first town reached of any import-ance is the town of El Fuerte.

The situation of the town is charming, being on the south bank of the Fuerte River. This river is about a quarter of a mile wide, and passes along the foot of a plateau that is elevated about 90 feet above its bed. There is a fair view both up and down the river, from this plateau. The town of Fuerte has about 1,000 inhabitants, and should be the principal inland town of the State.

There is no commerce at Fuerte, from the fact that its advantageous natural position is no protection from the competition of Alamos on the north and Mazatlan on the south. The valley in which the town is located is one that might be one of the most fertile in the State and can be easily irrigated from the river, and will raise corn, wheat, sugar-cane, cotton, and the various cereals, but the inhab-itants prefer to use this magnificent valley for grazing pur-poses, and raise chiefly stock. The mules raised here have the reputation of being the best in the State. The road from Fuerte is of the same character to Mazatlan, passing through Mocorita and Sinaloa.

The principal family at Fuerte are the descendants of A. Ybarra.

Ward, in his celebrated work on "Mexico," says of Fuerte:

"The situation is not particularly favorable, as, notwith-standing the vicinity of the river, the country about the town is unproductive, and the heat in summer intolerable.

"The Tierra Caliente of Sinaloa extends from El Fuerte, or rather from Alamos, to the confines of Guadalajara (Jalisco). It is one vast, sandy plain, destitute of vegeta-tion, except in the rainy season, or in spots where the vi-cinity of the mountains or the confluence of two large streams insure a constant supply of water.

"This is the case at Culiacan, the most ancient and popu-lous town in Sinaloa, situated upon a river of the same name, 80 leagues south of El Fuerte. It contains 11,000 inhab-itants, and the country about it is well watered and highly productive."

Of Cosala, he says: "Cosala, 35 leagues south of Culi-acan, is the next town of any note on the road to Jalisco. It derives its importance entirely from its mines, one of which, called Nuestra Señora de Guadalupe, is very celebrated. Gua-dalupe is free from water, and situated at a considerable ele-vation above the plain. It contains a vein of gold of considerable breadth, and its produce might be increased to ten times its present amount, etc."

From Cosala to the capital or City of Mexico, or the Central States of the Republic, there are two routes, the one by Rosario, the Cañas and Guadalajara, which is impassable during the rainy season, and the other due east from Cosala across the Sierra Madre to Durango. The distance from Alamos to Fuerte is 35 miles. This place was originally a military station, but the military are now removed to Mazatlan.

The town of Sinaloa is located on the river of the same name, and has about 1,500 to 2,000 inhabitants. The principal business of this place is in the production of Indian corn, pork, and lard, which is exported. The principal business men are Francisco T. Penna and N. Nuñez, who are in both the wholesale and retail trade, and H. Carubbio. The town of Sinaloa is located on a small river, and in the winter or dry season it dwindles to a very small stream. The seasons are reversed in the State. They have their dry season while we have our wet, and the reverse. The district around is fertile, and produces the usual agricultural productions, though the principal trade is as we have stated.

The town has but one street. The ladies of this town are celebrated for their beauty in the whole State, as those of Hermosillo are famous in Sonora.

Roads of the State.

A stage runs from Guaymas to Alamos over the old road, which runs east back of the bay, or north of the inlet formed by the mouth of the Yaqui River, crossing the small stream of San José, and the river Matape which flows into the gulf; thence to Torin on the banks of the Yaqui River, a distance of about 80 miles. The river is here crossed by a ferry in wet seasons, and forded in dry seasons, to Bocam, and thence north, following the course of the Yaqui, to Cocori, about 20 miles; thence to El Baihoca and south to Coraque, due east of Bocam, and distant in a straight line only about 15 miles. This short cut can be taken and save about 35 miles of useless travel. From Coraque the road runs south-east to Camoa on the opposite side of the Mayo River, which is here crossed at a distance of about 35 miles from Coraque; thence to Alamos, about 12 miles. From Alamos to El Fuerte the distance is about 35 miles, where the Fuerte River is crossed; thence almost due south to Sinaloa,

about 60 miles; thence across the Sinaloa River and on to
the Mocorito River and the small town of Mocorito; thence
south-east through Palmas to La Morita; and thence taking a
more southerly course to Culiacan across the Culiacan River,
distant from Sinaloa about 85 or 90 miles. Here two routes
are presented to Mazatlan, one by way of Cosala, which takes
a south-east course through the small towns and ranchos of
Las Arayanes, Las Flechas, El Vichi, Las Milpas, Santa Anita,
and Casa Blanca on the small stream of San Lorenzo; thence
crossing the stream east to Las Vegas, Carriscal, Higuiera,
and Cosala, a distance of about 60 miles; thence south, passing Calafanta, Conitaca, Salado, crossing a small branch of
the Elota River; thence to Laguna and Elota, about 40 miles
from Cosala. The other route from Culiacan runs south to
Aguarita and El Carriscal, El Salado, and San Lorenzo on the
river of that name. The river is here crossed and a south-
east course taken to Avaya, Vinapa, Higuerita, and thence
east to Elota on the Elota River. The former route is the
most traveled, though longer, as it passes through the rich
mining region of Cosala. The latter route is over a stretch
of about 80 miles, while the former is about 100 miles.
From Elota the road is direct to Mazatlan, distant about 55
miles south-east, crossing the Elota River, and Piastla River
at Piastla; thence to Coyotitan, Quebrachi, Quelite, Coma-
cho, Aval, Los Otates, and Mazatlan. From Mazatlan a road
runs south-east to the Presidio of Mazatlan, and east to El
Rosario on the Rosario River; thence south-east into the
state of Jalisco to Guadalajara and on to the capital of Mexico.

The road from Fuerte to Mazatlan and Rosario is a good
one, to which we have referred already, and is used for wagons and a stage line constantly during the dry season, but it
is impassable during the wet season on account of the lack
of the bridges over rivers that are swollen to a dangerous
depth and swiftness, and the roads being of clay and sand
become boggy. Another road, or rather mule trail, leads
from Mazatlan through San Sebastian east and then north,
passing many ranchos on the Mazatlan River, to Morito and
east, where the river Mazatlan is crossed twice on account of
a bend in the river, and on up the Mazatlan Valley into Durango; passing Favor in Sinaloa and Saulito in Durango,
and other towns up the cañon to the mines of San Antonio
de las Ventañas, and the celebrated mines of Guarisamay,
and from thence on to Durango, about 150 miles distant from
Mazatlan.

CHAPTER II.

Mazatlan.

The coast adjacent to Mazatlan, with its mountain peaks in the background, presents a grand and imposing scenery; and during the rainy season, when the valleys, hills and mountains are covered with verdure, it is one of the most beautiful spots on the coast. The small sugar-loaf mountains rise frequently, near and in the distance, presenting a variety of scenery to the eye that is very pleasing, and to lovers of scenery, it is delightful.

The port of Mazatlan is not capacious, nor surrounded by those safe landmarks characteristic of many of the ports on the Pacific Coast. For fear of the southerly or south-west winds, no vessels can be anchored long in the harbor, as the land is low adjacent, and on the south-west mostly open to the ocean. For this reason, vessels only stop long enough to unload, and proceed on their way. The inner harbor is far from admitting heavy merchant-vessels like the clipper ships arriving in the port of San Francisco. The approach is safe, however, for ocean steamers to approach and retreat when touching at this port. Larger ships anchor under the lee of the island of Creston, which is rather small, but much elevated. In this harbor there are two other islands, called Venado and Pajoros. The dangers to vessels during the stormy season detract much from the commercial position and advantages of Mazatlan; and, for that reason, Guaymas, in Sonora, will be the principal port for the vessels passing up the Gulf of California.

The city of Mazatlan is nearly surrounded by water, a mere tongue connecting it to the mainland. Near the water's edge, and back half a mile, the surface of the site is even, and also to the limits of the city, from the fort on the west, for more than a mile eastward; yet, farther back, it is uneven and ungraded. The fort commanding the inner harbor to the city is located on the side of an elevated plateau, near 1,500 feet above the sea. On its summit, one may enjoy the beautiful scenery spread out before him—a panorama of mountains, low undulating hills, and valleys. In this fort are planted some antiquated cannon, commanding the city and harbor. The streets are not laid out regularly. One main street runs from the water front out into the country beyond, on which are located both retail and wholesale business houses. Some are also situated on the streets of the water front. The whole number of shops and stores reach as many as 500. The buildings are mostly constructed of soft brick, one foot square, and, in some instances, there are stone buildings. Adobe houses are mostly occupied by the poorer classes in the suburbs. Most of the buildings are one-story; yet, in some few instances, the houses built by foreigners are two stories high. The houses are constructed roughly, and plastered inside and out, and afterwards penciled. The roofs and floors are made of brick. For the floor, the ground is raised, and surface leveled, and bricks laid in cement, which makes the floors both durable and cool in the summer. When the floors are carpeted, wool or common cotton is laid down first, then the carpet. Among the poorer classes, no carpet is used, but a native mat. Heavy joists and close together are laid across the walls of the building for the roof, and on these a tight floor of boards is laid, and on this the bricks are laid, one foot in thickness, cemented completely water-tight. The walls are commonly three feet thick, making each house a complete fortress, and, withal, very cool in the summer season.

The style of architecture is a mixture of the Moorish and Gothic. The doors are clumsy and large, generally fastened inside by wooden bars. The windows have mostly iron gratings of three quarters of an inch in diameter, and sometimes shutters, making the city look like a city of prisons. The inside walls are frequently papered, and the houses well and even elegantly furnished.

Most of the goods sold here are imported directly from Europe, and German houses seem rather to take the lead in commercial pursuits throughout the country. There are about 100 foreigners in the city, mostly engaged in commercial pursuits, and they are said to own most of the real estate in the city.

Gold, silver, and copper, and dye-woods are shipped from this point in large quantities. Many ship-loads are packed in from the interior on the backs of mules. "Burros," or she-asses, are used, to some extent, to pack mortar, bricks, lumber, etc.; but freight wagons and carts are also used, drawn by mules.

The streets are mostly paved with round cobble-stones, and in a concave form, so that the water drains off in the center. These stones are laid in cement, and become quite firm, so that they are not easily misplaced, except during the rainy season. The sidewalks are narrow, some made of hewn timbers, and laid so that two persons can walk side by side. Others are constructed of soft burnt bricks and flagstone. On any of them, but two persons can walk side by side.

The government buildings, such as the custom houses, forts, and arsenals, are well constructed, airy, and remarkably adapted to the torrid zone. These, as well as private buildings, have a species of rain spouts, which, in the rainy season, scarcely extend the dripping waters from the sidewalks. There is one church in Mazatlan. The composite architecture of beautiful constructions of arches and pillars give some of the buildings quite an imposing appearance. There are two principal hotels, kept by Frenchmen, who charge about $2.00 per day. Inside the court-yards, flowering shrubs, rare bushes, the hyacinth, and the trailing vine are frequently seen. The delicate and refined taste of the ladies of Mazatlan is well known in the republic, and their beauty rivals the maids of Hermosillo. A public plaza is tastefully laid out, with seats on the sides of the square, made of brick, having brick sides, and painted red, with brick walks through the center, coinciding with either point of the compass, and with a circular brick walk inside the seats around the whole circuit of the plaza; and to enhance the beauty of this, every 15 feet orange trees are set on the inside edge of this circular walk, which truly adds beauty to the whole scene. A beautiful fountain of crystal water plays day and night.

The marketing is done principally on Sunday morning on the market square, where purchases are made from the country people for the week. Indian corn, beans, Irish potatoes, sweet potatoes, eggs, red peppers, bananas, plantains, oranges, limes, several species of custard apples, squashes, pumpkins, watermelons, muskmelons, chickens, turkeys, and a variety of gallinaceous birds, such as the "hoco" or "curassow" and pheasants; also, crockery ware, chairs, and other articles are not unfrequently exhibited for sale. After the sales are ended, to the inhabitants of the city, the balance are bought by local hucksters at a reduced price. A theater is in the city, where the beauty and élite gather to listen to Spanish plays of love and tragedy.

Mazatlan is now a commanding commercial city of rapidly growing importance to Lower California, southern Sonora, Chihuahua, Durango, and northern Jalisco, and the state of Sinaloa.

Vast regions of agricultural, grazing and mineral lands are adjacent, untouched, that await development by foreign capital and industry. Most of the trade of all this region passes through Mazatlan.

This city has but few equals for its surrounding advantages, and invites to her municipal confines an intelligent class of immigrants, who will develop her latent energies and resources.

Sailing-vessels go leisurely up the gulf, carrying the productions of the south, though the greater part of the carrying is now done by steamers. The principal freight is sugar, coffee, rice and tobacco, with foreign and domestic merchandise. These are exchanged for flour, fruits, gold and silver, copper, pearls, salt, hides, and tallow. Some considerable sugar, cotton, rice, corn, beans, etc., and tropical fruits are produced in the rear of Mazatlan, in the Mazatlan Valley, which is 45 miles wide in its widest part, nearly one hundred miles in length, and well watered by the Mazatlan River.

Land can be cultivated three miles on each side of the river, on the river bottom lands. There are about 17,000 inhabitants in the town. The river, which empties into the sea, is 100 yards wide in rainy seasons, and is navigable for large barges, for five months, some distance up the river. The stage crosses in barges. The country east of Mazatlan is mostly level to the base of the mountains, diversified by rolling ground. There is one large cotton factory in the city, which manufactures the cotton raised in the vicinity, into goods that are purchased by the inhabitants of the region surrounding. This is a great cotton country, and timber is plentiful.

Coal has been found seventy-five miles from the city, with a vein cropping out three feet in width, something like anthracite. An interior valley, of 30 to 40 miles in width, at the widest point, lies beyond the Sierra Madre, east of the city, 40 miles from the river Mazatlan. Rich mines have been found near Cosala. Grazing is carried on extensively. The city commands the trade and supplies the wants of the country people and the inland towns within two-thirds of a circle from 200 to 1,000 miles in the interior.

Rich merchants come in from the country with packtrains, who have extensive haciendas, gold or silver mines, or who are exclusively engaged in commercial pursuits. The roads, or rather trails, through the mountain districts are not very good; and the rivers, in the rainy season, being mostly without bridges, present serious obstacles during that season for travel in the interior. The rainy season commonly includes the months of June, July, August, September, and a part of October; and during most of this time it rains a little nearly every day. Most of the flour used in Mazatlan, Tepic, and Colima, and the ports of San Blas and Manzanillo, is exported from Guaymas, in Sonora. The flour is nearly as white, possessing the same qualities, as California flour. From Mazatlan to the mouth of the Rio Grande, in Texas, near that point it is nearly six hundred miles; and a railroad from this city to the mouth of that river is practicable, and can be made by passing over a distance of 1,000 miles. To Loredo, in Tamaulipas, on the Rio Grande, it is not much more; the latter point being the point of connection with an eastern road running from the City of Mexico, almost due north. A better route, however, might pass Guadalajara, and connect with that road south of Loredo. The City of Mazatlan will be unquestionably a powerful rival of San Francisco. On the low land there is not much cultivation on a level with the sea.

The hacienda or rancho Tamaulipas of Piastla, on the road to Culiacan, contains about 80,000 acres, and is situated on the Piastla River, about seven miles from the coast, the whole of which can be cultivated, and is easily irrigated from the river. The stream, during the wet season, is navigable as far as the rancho. This rancho is owned by the Laveagas, but is not for sale. There are small ranchos, however, in the vicinity for sale. There are also very fertile lands near the Rio de Rosario, twenty miles south-east from Mazatlan. On this river, and throughout the country, land is cheap. Haciendas of one, two, and three leagues in extent, can be purchased for one, two, three and four thousand dollars.

Corn sells from 50 cents to $1 per bushel; beans, $9 per carga; oranges and limes $10 per thousand; sweet potatoes, 6 to 10 cents per lb.; beef, pork, and mutton, from 6 to 10 cents per lb. Poultry and eggs are high. Butter is sent here from Guaymas, but it is of a whitish color, and almost tasteless. The cheese is no better. Lower California furnishes large quantities of this cheese for the market of Mazatlan. An industrious American might settle in the vicinity of Mazatlan, and following most any pursuit, such as gardening, keeping a dairy, or even agriculture, he could accumulate a snug fortune, and in a short time retire from business, living in comparative ease and affluence.

The principal business houses are: Rogers & Marshall, Juan Cristobal Farber, Edward Coffey, Budwig & Rasch, Isaac V. Coppall, Charpentier, Reynard & Co., Peña & Co.,

Bartning Hermanos y Cia, Cannobio Hermanos, Diaz de
Leon Hermanos, J. Kelly y Cia, Echeguren y Hijos y Sobri-
nos, James Hermanos, Federico Koerdell y Cia, J. De la
Quintana, Jesus Escobar, Joaquin Redo, Haas y Aguiar,
Tepia y Ceballos, Gonzales Hermanos, Vicente Ferreira y
Cia, Charpentier, Reynaud y Cia, Duhagan y Cia, Melchers
Successores, Felton Hermanos, and Juan Somelleria y Cia.

The implements used in husbandry are of the most
primitive character in some portions of the state. The
plow consists of two poles, one six feet long, and the other
fifteen feet, fastened together by the means of a mortice and
tenon, at an angle of sixty-five degrees. Through, and
near the end of the short pole, there is a pin to steady the
plow; and on its end there is attached a pointed iron or steel
shoe to prevent it from readily wearing out. The yoke has
no bows, but is fastened on the heads of the cattle by means
of raw-hide thongs, and so is the tongue of the plow to the
yoke. With this rude instrument the ground is merely
scratched over about three inches in depth, and yet the soil
yields marvelously. The scythe, the cradle or the sickle,
even, are unknown in some places, with the hoe, or any
other common implement of husbandry. Reapers and
threshing machines are not even dreamed of in some isolated instances ; but they have been introduced in many of
the states of the republic. Here is a rare chance for our
agricultural implement manufacturers almost at their doors.

About one-twelfth of the population of Mazatlan is white,
and can trace their origin back to their Spanish ancestors.
Many blondes are seen who are direct descendants of the old
Castilians. In this city there are several wealthy merchants,
of different nations, who import goods largely from Europe,
many of which we have mentioned already. There are also
Mexican capitalists who have extensive ranchos and haciendas in the country, even one hundred miles back in the interior, and pass a part of their time in town. English and
German goods seem to be most used, and generally in demand; also French brandies and wines; but few articles manufactured in the United States are shipped into any of the
Mexican ports on the Pacific, although an extensive trade
with New York, Philadelphia, and Boston is springing up
by vessels and is landed at the ports on the eastern coast or
Gulf of Mexico. On the completion of the Texas and Pacific

8

and other railroads connecting with the east, a large trade will be established with the large eastern cities of the United States.

The principal business houses are engaged in both a wholesale and retail trade, dividing their stores into two departments. The principal buildings are the custom-house, a new church, municipalidad or city hall, containing court-rooms, etc.; Cuartel de Artilleria or barracks for the military, a cotton factory, gas works, and the hotels "Iturbide" and "Nacional."

Some trade has been carried on with San Francisco; in fact, much more than is suspected by many of our merchants. Two iron foundries are located here that have considerable trade.

Rosario.

The town has 6,000 inhabitants and takes its name from the Rosario mines in the vicinity. These mines are some of the oldest in the republic, and have produced an immense treasure for the owners. The shafts are now full of water. The Tajo mine by its richness is a great source of wealth to the town. This town is a place of considerable importance, and at one time was the depot of merchandise of Mazatlan. The merchants resorted to it to purchase their stock of goods and dispose of produce. It was the residence of the Commissary General of the state, and others high in official authority. The streets are narrow but well paved, and the houses built principally of stone. The town is located in a ravine, and much confined. The Rosario River, a small stream, runs below the town and empties into the Pacific a few miles further below. This stream is navigable for canoes from Rosario, by which people frequently go to Mazatlan, the distance by water being shorter. This town has considerable trade with Durango and some from Guadalajara. The distance to Mazatlan is 20 leagues or 60 miles, the Presidio of Mazatlan being a kind of half-way house or posta. The place is simply a large square surrounded by merchants' houses. The distance to Mazatlan Presidio is about 30 miles. In the northern part of the state the road from Alamos in Sonora runs over a level plain when it leaves the rolling hills, and requires no repairing, as the soil is made of sandy clay, almost without a pebble, and is perfectly even and smooth. The surface is level and excellent for coaches. The distance from Alamos to Fuerte is about 35 miles.

Culiacan.

The capital of the state of Sinaloa, Culiacan, is situated on a river of the same name, in the midst of a beautiful and rich agricultural country. The population of the city is about 10,000; its streets, with a great plaza, are laid out regularly, and it possesses much inland trade. The architecture and buildings are much the same as at Mazatlan.

The state government is located here, and during the session of the legislature, it presents a more lively appearance. The distance from Mazatlan is about 155 miles, and the intervening distance between, over the route by Cosala, is rough and mountainous, with but few ranchos on the line of travel. Cotton, sugar-cane, corn, beans, and rice, and vegetables of various kinds, and fruits common to this climate and a low latitude, are grown in great abundance in the vicinity. There are also some mines in the neighborhood. Coffee is also raised in the state, and brings from 30 to 40 cents per pound. The importation of coffee has at times been forbidden, in order to develop this industry in the state.

There is a cotton factory in Culiacan, owned by Redo, who resides in the same town, and is one of the principal capitalists. A stage road runs from Alamos, in Sonora, to Mazatlan—a five days' trip—also to Culiacan, as before stated.

There is also a mint in Culiacan. The principal business houses are, Redo, Valadez, O. Salmon, Robert R. Symon & Co., and Angel Urrea. Considerable business is transacted here. The road, after leaving Alamos, which is mountainous, or a rolling region, becomes almost level as it goes south to Fuerte, and passes down the interior about 60 miles from the coast, through the same level country, to Mazatlan. It also passes down a valley in the interior, beyond the mountains east of the former road, to Culiacan, over a very level road.

The Presidio of Mazatlan is located on the road to Rosario, and was formerly the principal place of residence for the merchants and custom house officers, who removed to Mazatlan, and left it almost deserted, with the exception of a large cotton factory which is there, owned by Echeguren & Co., of Mazatlan; and besides the operatives, the town has but few inhabitants.

The ladies of Culiacan are truly celebrated for their fair complexion, graceful forms, and modest demeanor. They

are very fond of music and dancing, and play very skillfully
on the harp, and are, withal, as intelligent and captivating
as any of the famous beauties of the republic. On the road
to Culiacan from Fuerte are situated Sinaloa, and Mocorito,
and La Muerito.

Cosala.

The town of Cosala is situated about 60 miles from Culiacan, to the south-east, and nearly 100 miles from Mazatlan.
The town extends over nearly as much ground as the latter;
but it is more interspersed with flower-gardens and small
orchards. The town is well built; but the streets are somewhat irregular. The number of inhabitants reaches 5,000.
Cosala is a mining district. Within about 20 miles of the
town, is located the Guadalupe mine, which is perfectly dry,
and at a good elevation from the plain.

The mines of Copala, Panucho, San Dimas, and San Ignacio are the principal ones located in the vicinity. The
Saragossa mine is situated north-east from Mazatlan and
north of Cosala. This mine is celebrated for its beautiful
specimens of virgin silver.

In this town, a peculiar disease that is attributed to the
water used exists, and is called " buche," and is known
with us as goitre, or swelled neck. One traveler describes
its unfortunate inhabitants as looking like pelicans.

From Cosala to foot of mountains, the distance is 15
miles due east. Santa Ana, a small rancho, and some
others, are located on the road. There are some six mines
near, bearing silver and magistral, and about one and a half
miles from the town, the celebrated Golconda gold mine.

The principal business of the state is mining, grazing, and
the raising of herds of cattle, horses, mules, sheep, etc., although the agricultural productions are considerable. The
mines of the state produce a large revenue. The Xocihuis-
tita mine, situated near Rosario, was bonded for three months
at $60,000, and the parties who had bonded it refused to
renew the bond. In a short time afterward the owners sold
a one-half interest for $500,000 to American capitalists of
San Francisco, who are now taking out from $50,000 to
$60,000 per month. Some ladies at Mazatlan were the
owners. Estacata is another old mine near Cosala that was
once extremely rich. Tradition says that its owners were
so rich and realized such fortunes from its possession that
they used to lay down silver bricks for their ladies to tread

upon on their way to church, and then take them up again by their servants—a piece of extravagant gallantry somewhat unheard of, even among the descendants of the Moctezumas. Some of the mines of Mexico are worked in what we would term an extravagant manner. The shafts in some instances are walled with timbers that are placed there for their imperishable qualities, and often the wood selected is of the most valuable character, and being the nearest at hand is used with a prodigal hand. One old mine, we are told by a gentleman who explored it, to which he gave the name of the old San José mine, was literally lined with ebony. He showed us a piece of this wood which he extracted from the mine, and had made into a rough cane. The timbers were as sound almost as when they were placed in the mine, and were laid one upon the other along the walls of the shaft, and some 15 to 20 feet in length. The origin of the mine was unknown, and the mouth of the shaft had fallen in, covering it up entirely until another drift from a mine near it in search of a vein of ore was run until they came to the ebony walls of the shaft of the old mine. It was cleaned out—rubbish, etc., removed—and found to be very rich. The ebony alone would be worth a small fortune in this country. The hacienda of La Labor, owned by the Laveagas, is situated about four miles from San Ignacio and contains 40,000 acres, about one-third of which can be cultivated. Sugar-cane, wheat, corn, and other productions have been raised upon its arable lands. It is located on the San Ignacio River, and the soil is very fertile.

Mining Districts and Mines of Sinaloa.

Rosario District.—The most important mine of this district is the celebrated Tajo mine, which is the second best producing mine in the state, and is located in a rolling country on the bank of the Rosario River. The depth reached two years ago was 1,200 feet, when Mr. Geo. S. Montgomery, of this city, visited it, and we herewith give his representation of the mines of this district, and some others.

This mine produces fair milling ore, with 60 per cent. gold; the balance, silver. The vein is six feet wide, until a bonanza is reached, that widens out the vein to about 100 feet. They were then taking out ore in a bonanza that assayed, on an average, $120 per ton, and ran sometimes in first-class ore up to $1,000. This mine is owned by Mr.

Bradbury, of Oakland, and Mr. Kelly and other merchants of Mazatlan. This is one of the best equipped mines in the state. One stamp-mill of 30 stamps was working the ore, and since, a 20-stamp mill has been added. The 30-stamp mill was then working 40 tons per day, which, with the 20-stamp mill now, is working about 60 to 70 tons per day. This mine is supporting about 6,000 population. There are other mines in this district of minor importance. The distance to Mazatlan is about 80 miles, in a north-westerly direction.

Plomosas District.—The principal mine is the Plomosa, located in this district near the border of Durango, and is owned by a Mazatlan Company, with the controlling interest in the hands of merchants of that city. The mine is valued at $1,200,000, and is divided into 24 shares, the usual number in Mexican mines. Mr. La Madrid was the former owner. The depth of the mine is over 800 feet; width of vein, 20 to 25 feet, well defined and apparently permanent. This mine has paid from the start, although the ore is somewhat rebellious, which could not be worked as easily as within the last year. The ores carried galena and zinc. The average assay was about $80 to $90 per ton, and is worked by a 20-stamp mill at the mine. This district is about 120 miles south-east from Mazatlan.

The Abundancia mine, in Plomosas, is situated in the gap which descends from the rancheria of Plomositas in a precipituous decline towards the northeast. The mountain on which the works are established, as well as the neighboring one of the Potrero Las Escaleras and El Arco, are of stratified rock, affected by metamorphism, and repose on the dyoritic formation in this locality. The aspect of all this zone, from the decline of the ground, from the elevated central table, is of a very favorable geological character for ores.

The Abundancia metaliferous lode detaches itself in part from the mountain that incloses it in a compact and elevated cliff, which has been prospected in great part by the ancients. The broad-vein prospect shows a horizontal breadth of at least ten metres. It is to be noted that where the matrix is found to be more quartzified are seen the best or more abundant ores, and as soon as the limestone aspect appears in small veins it seems that galena follows it, but without the concise relation taking place. I cannot consider the Abundancia lode as being a vein, properly so called, nor as an altogether irregular lode, for there appears a transition between both in its character.

The situation of the cliff above the adit is recognizable by the old shafts which communicate with the interior. It can be perceived from the pillars and some of the intervals that the ancients worked through means of a regular alloy, and the extent of these workings indicate the considerable quantities of ores that they extracted. Up to December 21st, 1881, the mine had yielded 27,354 cargas of different ores, containing, as per mining assay, 332,474 ounces of silver, averaging about 12.15-100 ounces per extracted carga. Of these, 554, averaging 65 ounces alloy, which has been exported, corresponding to two per cent. of the total in weight, and 10.08-100 in value.—*Extract from Report of Pedro L. Mouray on the Plomosas La Abundancia Mines.*

The Jocuistita Mine.

(From a Report by Wm. Ashburner, M. E., May 24, 1880.)

"The mining property known as the 'Negociacion Mineria de Jocuistita' is situated in the San Ignacio mining district, State of Sinaloa, Mexico, about 100 miles northerly from the port of Mazatlan. The property includes a group of nine silver-bearing lodes, lying within a short distance of one another, and on all of which work has been done sufficient to prove their mineral character. Of these, the principal one, so far as demonstrated, is known as "El Carmen." A narrow ravine extends northerly from the town of Jocuistita, down which runs a perennial spring of water, sufficient for about ten stamps in the dryest time, while during the rainy season the supply is indefinitely increased. The mill, or hacienda, is situated at the mouth of this ravine, while higher up, on the west side and less than half a mile distant, is the Carmen vein. This is the only vein now worked upon the property, and in it has recently been developed a body of ore which exceeds in richness and extent anything previously discovered. This vein has an east and west direction, running towards a steep outlying flank of the main mountain range, which rises abruptly to a height of several hundred feet, forming a sharp crest or divide. There apears little doubt that the lode will be also found extending to the east, upon the opposite side of the ravine, as from what was told me, a small shaft about 4½ feet deep was sunk 400 feet from the mouth of the Carmen mine, from which about one ton of ore was extracted, and worked with a milling result of 266 ounces of silver per ton. Subsequently, this shaft was filled, and a tunnel was commenced for the purpose of cross-cutting in depth several of the less known veins, so I was unable to verify the statement by sampling the shaft. The country rock is greenstone porphyry, lying in close proximity to a reddish trachyte. The vein dips toward the north at an angle of 83 degrees, and in places, particularly where the ore bodies are found, there is a well-defined clay wall; its width varies from a few feet to 17 and 18 feet. The ore is somewhat complex, containing frequently, besides sulphuret of silver and native silver, zinc, copper, iron and lead, in form of sulphurets, associated with a quartz gangue. Notwithstanding the presence of these base metals, the results obtained by amalgamation appear to be very satisfactory. As the ore comes from the mine it is first assorted by hand, richer portion being selected for shipment to Europe, while what is called the ordinary ore is sent to the mill. At the time of my visit, this shipping ore was estimated as being worth, by assay, about 750 ounces per ton, while the mill, running only fair samples, was producing nearly or quite $1800 per day. The proportion which the shipping ore bears to the milling ore bears to the milling ore is very variable, and depends upon the extent to which the former is segregated from the latter in the vein itself. The mine is worked by a vertical shaft, eight by ten feet, and which is now 133 feet deep. The ore is hoisted to the surface by means of a whim. From this shaft drifts 10 metres or 33 feet apart have been extended westerly on the course of the vein; leaving behind, however, in the form of pillars, most of the ore, which is of much lower grade than that recently developed in the west end of the mine, and under the mountain which rises above it."

A one-half interest in this mine was purchased for $500,000 by San Francisco capitalists. The ore of this mine has assayed about 50-per cent. silver. The vein, at a depth of about 250 feet, is 40 feet wide, and contains a small percentage of gold and galena. The mine has been worked for some years by Mexicans. The superintendent of the Guadalupe de Los Reyes negotiated the sale of this mine, being the principal owner. They have worked the mine by a 10-stamp mill, but are now erecting a 20-stamp mill, and are by the old stamp mill producing from $50,000 to $60,000 per month. The ore is rebellious, and is consequently more expensive to work than the ores of many other mines in the State, but the large percentage of silver makes it a very profitable mine. The distance from this mine to Mazatlan is about 80 miles.

"The mineral districts of San Ignacio and Cosala, in the State of Sinaloa, have in times past given millions of dollars yearly in silver and gold. The mines of Cosala, more particularly, have and still are, yielding large quantities of the precious metal. The ores are very rich and the veins very wide. These as a general rule will yield $500 per ton. The Guadalupe de los Reyes is surprisingly rich in gold and silver. For years this mine has been the source of many quarrels and numberless bloody fights between two families who claimed its ownership. The mine has been held in possession by the Vega family, whose wealth and political power enabled them to control not only this very rich mine, but the whole State of Sinaloa. The liberal party at length caused the political downfall of this family; they did not yield possession of this mine however, to its rightful owners. An English company once offered Vega for this mine one million dollars, which he refused, saying that he did not want any money at that time, and if he did he had only to work his mine, and that would yield him any number of millions —which was true."—*Chipman's Mineral Resources of Northern Mexico.*

"The district of Panuco is situated in the southern portion of Sinaloa. In this locality there are several mines; these, before the independence of Mexico, belonged to the Marquis of Panuco. The Marquis obtained from them many millions of dollars in silver. The ores of the richest class are argentiferous, and yield from $500 to $600 per ton. The ores that are treated by amalgamation (which forms the greater portion of the ores found) by the Mexican mode of treating them yield $200 per ton. After the death of the Marquis, the mines fell into the hands of a merchant of Mazatlan, by the name of Machado. He worked the mines very successfully for many years, until his death some 15 years ago, since which time his family have alternately worked them, squandered the products and ran them in debt, and finally abandoned them.

"A few miles northwest from Panuco, in the State of Sinaloa, and distant from the Pacific Coast some 30 miles, lies the famous mine of Tajo, situate in a town called Rosario. This mine owes its discovery to a herdsman of cattle. One day while chasing some wild cattle through the woods, a twig of a tree caught the rosary he had suspended to his neck and jerked it from him. Not wishing to lose it nor the animal he was in pursuit of, he threw off his hat to designate the spot. Upon his return night overtook him before he could find his animal; thereupon he concluded to spend the night. He built a fire and waited until morning to look for his rosary by daylight. In lighting his cigarette by the coals of his fire he noticed something which glistened in the ashes. Upon examination of this substance by his employer or master it proved to be pure silver. Excavations were made and a splendidly-formed vein was found, rich in silver and gold. The mine was worked and regularly opened, and for sixty years yielded immense treasures to the owners. Upon the expulsion of the Spaniards from the conntry, the mine was left unworked for many years. The church of Santo Domingo stands immediately over some of the prin-principal workings of the mine, and is now 110 years old. The ores of this mine yield an average of $120 per ton. The mine is now worked by an American company, whose headquarters are in San Francisco.

A few miles east from Rosario, in the State of Sinaloa, is located a mine called Plomosa. This mine was opened and worked many years ago to a depth of 250 feet by the Mexicans, producing while it was worked large amounts of silver. The ores gave $250 per ton. A large influx of water suddenly put a stop to operations, since which time nothing has been done to place the mine in working condition. It is a well-attested fact that the mine was yielding largely at the time of its abandonment. Nearly two years ago the mine was denounced, and possession given to some Americans, who now own it.

Northwest from Plomosa but a few miles, and in the same State, we find the Mineral of Copala. There are a great number of silver-bearing veins found in this locality, upon which many mines of good reputation are now being worked. Several American companies have erected reduction works here, and but for the advent of the French intervention would have been successfully prosecuting their operations. The ores are abundant, and give about $175 per ton.

Distant from the coast of the Pacific 150 miles we find the District of Ventanas. At this place some six or seven American companies are working, some with success, and all with good prospects, according to their respective means and skillful or unskillful management. The lodes are very numerous, and all the mines that have been worked gave good results. The average yield of the ores may be safely calculated to be $100 per ton.

The placer of the "Canoda de Banazagua" is situated about 16 leagues southeast of Alamos, in Sonora, on the north side of a tributary to the Fuerte River. The placer extends for about 12 miles in the canon, and has been worked to a considerable extent in the time of the Spaniards. The hillsides for all this distance have been perforated in many places, and shafts sunk and drifts run. Some of the works are recent, but the miners not being acquainted with the modes of getting out the water by pumps and flumes, have done all their work by washing in wooden bowls, and abandoning the shaft on encountering water. At the head of the canon drifting has been done to a considerable extent. The soil is composed of a red clay and decomposed quartz; the ore is worked by arastras. The mountain region of the Fuerte is so exceedingly rough and precipitous that no wagon road has ever been (or ever will be) made through it. All carriage is performed on mules, and a man is better off on foot than with an animal under him.

Mines of the Fuerte.

From Baneyagua east to Las Garobas is three leagues. This is a small place, but gold and silver mining is done here to some extent. Four leagues still further east is the Real del Rosario, another mining place, owned by Sr. Don Bruno Esquessa. The mine is situated on the side of a mountain, on the north side of the hacienda, and the diggings are surface diggings or excavations. The annual revenue of this mine, in net profits, is $70,000. There are some gold placers in the vicinity of Chinipas, about 30 leagues north, and the inhabitants are engaged in washing gold.

Palmarejo is a silver mine, distant about six leagues from Chinipas. It is worked by Don Miguel Urea of Alamos. This mine is worked on a more extensive scale than any in this section of the country. There are 20,000 ounces of silver taken out of it monthly. The ore is taken out by improvised forcing machinery. A four-stamp mill is run by water-power to reduce the ore. Abundance of water and timber is adjacent; the roughness of the country compels the owner to carry the ore on mules' backs for nine miles to the mill site.

Chois is situated in the valley of the stream of the same name, which empties into the Fuerte River. Its situation is very beautiful, being on a fine plain, with a very pretty view. This town is the natural outlet for all the mines of that country in the northern part of Sinaloa, and is one of the richest mineral districts of Mexico. Its situation at the base of the mountains, its easy access by good roads from the farms and ranchos of the lower valley, and its facility for communication with the Gulf, must make it an important place for trade as well as industry. The whole surrounding country is rich in gold placers, and even the spot on which Chois stands furnishes gold by washing the soil. All the streams in the neighborhood show the color on washing the loose soil of the banks. The town is about four miles from the junction of the stream with the Fuerte River.

Las Iglesias is located four leagues up the Chois, where the stream makes a bend, inclosing a mesa, or table land, of some 25 acres, which is perforated with shafts from 15 to 20 feet in depth, where gold has been sought after. There is plenty of it, and the dirt all pays alike, but the gold is so fine that the natives cannot save it. Above Las Iglesias, one league on the south side of the river, the Arroyo Sabina, or Cypress creek, is encountered, which runs a course due north; following it for four leagues, a branch of the same stream, called Los Pillos, is reached, where the valley bed forms a natural reservoir of waters. This stream heads, in an easterly direction, toward a high mountain, ranging north and south. A rich placer is also located here, which has been slightly worked by Indians. Placers have been found also on the Bayemene creek and at Yucorati. At this latter place are old Spanish diggings, the ruins of their works showing that here has once been a large population of gold-seekers. The country adjacent is perforated with shafts and drifts. The quicksands in the bed of the creek have hitherto prevented miners from reaching the ledge where the gold may be found.

The Mount Serat mine is located in the vicinity of Realito, one league distant. This is a famous silver mine, and is owned and worked by Sr. Don Juan Migloria. Its elevation on a high mountain makes it a very prominent object. Mount Serat has been extensively worked, and all around it, in the mountains, shafts have been sunk and drifts run. It is still worked on a small scale. Some of the most prominent mines are Todos Santos, All Saints Mine, San Jose and Santa Catarina.

The gold placers of Baconbirito are located at the junction of the tributaries of the Sinaloa River. The soil is apparently full of gold, and extends over a horseshoe bend of the river for some miles. The gold is coarse, and pays $18 per ounce. Many shafts have been sunk here; water and timber are in abundance. These placers have been considerably worked, and are undoubtedly not exhausted.

" The Candelaria mine is located nine miles northeast of the town of Rosario, Sinaloa, and is on the same belt as the celebrated Tajo mine—distant therefrom only some three leagues. The mining location embraces 2400 feet in length, by 600 in width. The mine was opened in 1860, and the only explorations consist of a shaft sunk to the depth of 100 feet, and the mine being filled water, I was unable to examine it. Samples of ore from the pillars yielded from $58 17 per ton to $583 20, Assay. In the process of sinking 100 feet and the stopes from the same, $35,000 was abstracted from the ore. The width of the vein is said to be from five to six feet, The conditions for cheap and econominal work are very favorable—both wood and water, the former of the very best quality—being close at hand."—*Thomas Price's Report on said Mine, April 14th, 1881.*

The San Francisco mine belongs to the family of Maria, and is located in the northwestern part of Sinaloa, upon the northern spur of the Chihuahua range of the Sierra Madre, about midway on the mountain, at an elevation of about 600 feet above the plain of that region. The mine is an old one, developed by shafts, with a depth of about 185 feet in the deepest shaft. The veins are numerous, cropping out of the mountain side, and can be readily traced.

The Veta Madre as about three feet wide, carrying free gold and some silver. From $40 to $500 is produced from the ore upon assays made by a competent expert. The average assay is said to be about $70 or $80. We are also informed by an engineer who examined the property, to whom we are indebted for the foregoing, that the mine is now worked by Mexicans, with some six or seven arastras. Besides the foregoing, a very rich gold mine has been discovered near San Ignacio, in this State.

The Panuco District.—This district possesses some very rich mines. The Panuco mines, especially, have lately been favorably reported upon by a mining engineer sent from San Francisco, and the mines have been bonded, with a view to to purchase and development. Dr. Holland has this report in his possession, and we are informed by him that the gentlemen interested are perfectly satisfied, and are assured that they have made not only a safe but profitable investment. Not having the data at hand we are not able to give the exact figures of the assay and the report is omitted, but we present in lieu thereof the following :

From a report by Mark Cornish of Nov. 3, 1881.—The Panuco Mining District, situated in the State of Sinaloa, Mexico, sixty-five miles from the port of Mazatlan, is surrounded by good agricultural lands, supplying all kinds of produce at the lowest prices. The climate is healthy, the temperature ranges from 60 to 75 degrees Fahrenheit, and the location 2,000 feet above the sea level. Work must have been commenced in the different mines of the above mining district as far back as the beginning of last century, because about fifty years later an Indian by the name of Vizcarra discovered the mine called " Faizan," and out of its profits built the churches at Rosario, Concordia, Copala, Panuco and Guadalupe, using in their construction hewn stone and cement, at an expenditure of over five hundred thousand dollars. The silver bullion of this district was at one time the main support of the Royal Treasury at Rosario, where there was an office for the collection of revenue to be paid to the Spanish Crown, on all bullion extracted from the mines. The following are the names of the mines of the district: "Animas Viejas," Faizan, S'ta Eduviges, Estufa, Covalenga, Cuevillas, Bomba, Chinanate, Nieves, Refugio, Amaloton Burrion, Animas Nueves, Faizanito, Santa Rosa, Fronteras, Las Remedias, Cuevillas de Charcas, Palo Blanco, Tiempo, Toro, Piojo, Dolores, and San Cayetano, and may be a few more of which we don't remember the names at present. Along the Panuco mine there are still six mills in a ruined state. "The San Nicolas" mill, which must have cost a good deal over $200,000, has, during six or eight months of the year, a water power of 150 horses.

The Panuco property also comprises 13 square leagues of the land surrounding the mining district, with plenty of water, abundant pasturage, and covered with pine, oak, and other kinds of timber.

We know but very little of the workings of these mines in olden times. By tradition we know of a Mr. Zambrano, who worked some of the Panuco mines at the end of the last century. This gentleman became famous for having erected, in Durango, a palatial mansion, covering a block 600 feet long by 400 feet wide, which is used as a capitol of the State Government at the present time. But what made him world-renowned was his extravagance in constructing the railing of all the balconies of solid silver. But the King ordered him to have them taken down, as, in the order, he said, that even his Royal Majesty would not permit himself to display such magnificence.

Regarding the workings of the present century, we know that a Mr. Remus, whose heirs reside in the city of Guadalajara, worked, from 1820 to 1830, the "Santa Eduviges" and "Santa Rosa" claims, with very satisfactory results. Mr. Remus conveyed some of these mines to Mr. Ornezagay, of Durango, and this last one to Messrs. Flores & Gadea, of Tepie. In the year 1844 they were conveyed to Mr. Juan P. Machado, who also bought several other claims, intending to develop more extensively the mining industry of the district. He worked these mines until he died, in 1848. The other mines have been worked by various parties, with excellent results. The average assays from the "Faizan" mine pay $70 per ton, which is the same as in the "Animas," "Santa Rosa," "Santa Eduviges," "Faizanito," "Fronteras" and "Mina Grande" mines. Rock has been taken out from the Faizan mine which assayed as high as $2,000 per ton, but there is not enough of it. The "Estufa" mine turns out a large amount of ore, but the assays don't average over $40 per ton. The ores from almost all the Panuco mines are free milling, with the exception of those of the "Covalenga." The Panuco mines generally have but little water, and the greatest depth attained in any of them is not more than 600 feet.

From a report by Mr. Frederic Weidner, Mining Engineer, on July 15th, 1881.—The gold mine "La Union" or Boles mine was worked during the first decade of this century; and whilst there is no official record of what it yielded, the unanimous testimony of surviving contemporaneous residents attest the fact that the mine was very rich, and only abandoned in consequence of the war of independence. A few years ago it was re-located and worked for a while by parties without means enough, who conveyed it to its present owners, viz.: Messrs. Maxemin Hermanos, Roman and Adelaide Osund, and successors of C. Fairbanks, who entered into legal possession in November last (1881), recording it under the name of "Union Mine." The mine is situated in the district of Mazatlan, 55 miles N.E. of this port (Mazatlan), on the western slope of a mountain range forming one of the first steppes of the Sierra Madre, near the source of the Nacaral and Guaymas creeks, which flow through the ravine called the San Juan, and empty into the Mazatlan river. Its summit rears 200 feet above the entrance to the mine, at an elevation of 1,550 feet above the sea, thus insuring a temperate, agreeable and healthful climate. The mine is situated in the heart of a forest of valuable timber, such as venadillo, mora, fig tree, apomo, and other species, affording an inexhaustible supply for building and fuel. Within a radius of a few miles, on both banks of the Mazatlan river, there are ranchos, farms, and grazing fields, which furnish supplies at reasonable prices. For instance: corn at $5.00 per carga (300 lbs.); beans, $3.00; cattle, $10.00 per head. Good labor for the mine and carriers for precious metals are readily secured at the neighboring town of La Noria.

The mountain containing the ledges of the Boles mine is granite, the same as the surrounding region. This kind of rock has the property here of decomposing or crumbling easily; on the surface forming a peculiar gravel, called by the native Indians "tucurubay," which is easily reduced by the point of the bar or "talacha;" but at a depth of 3 or 4 metres this same rock is so hard and solid that excavations of six or more metres in extent may be cut out, unsupported by timber and without fear of caving in. A considerable number of veins are traceable on the out-croppings. The only ones which have been worked heretofore are two, both quite irregular and varying in width and depth. The width ranges from 1 to 5 feet. The body of the ledge is composed almost exclusively of white, compact quartz, with a bluish tinge, containing more or less gold; it being a noticeable fact that the gold occurs here disseminated in invisibly small particles, foliated, or in round or angular masses, varying from fine powder to grains like rice. In some eyes and threads of the vein the quartz is accompanied by pyrites of iron (commonly called "bronce amarillo"), and talc of a dark cloudy green hue, resembling sometimes slate of chlorite, again serpentine, and in these cases these ores are always auriferous, and contain from twice to four times as much metal as the pure quartz. In addition to this auriferous ore, properly so called, there are found in the lower levels pockets of auri-argentiferous ore, containing antimonial sulphuret of lead, with a great deal of gold and some silver.

The owners of the mine are now building a new and improved mill, costing $5,000, in the same ravine which comes down from the mine at only 600 or 800 paces from the shaft. The machinery comprises a steam engine (8 x 16), 18-horse power, driving 5-stamp mill of 650 lbs., an apron, concentrator, Frue patent, and other auxiliary appliances. The yield by the arrastra from 1,204 cargas of the ore was $12,217.60, or over $10.00 per carga.

La Joya Mining District.—The group of mines comprised within the boundaries of the "La Joya" property are known as the "Refugio" or "S'ta Eduviges," the "San Juan," the

"Gloria," the "Rosario," the "Hilos," the "Relis," the "Virginia," and the "San Eugenio" mines. They are situated in the mining district of La Joya, prefecture of Sinaloa, State of Sinaloa, and distant about 120 miles from Culiacan, capital of the State, or 60 miles from the city of Sinaloa, and 90 miles from Plaza Colorado, a safe port in the Gulf of California, through which all high grade ores from the mines are exported, and where mining machinery and materials destined for La Joya are regularly landed. The climate is exceedingly healthy, the temperature ranging from 60° to 75° Fahrenheit. Grain and produce abound in the neighborhood, at very moderate prices, the property being located within 4 leagues (10 miles) of the best agricultural lands in the country.

The width of the veins (of the above property) vary somewhat in the different mines. Thus the "S'ta Eduviges" or "Refugio" averages from 7 to 13 feet; the "San Juan," 13 feet; the "Gloria," from 6 to 14 feet, and the "Rosario" more than the "Refugio." The veins are encased between good solid walls of dioritic porphyry intercepted by crystallized poryhyry, in small quantities, combined with decomposed granite in large masses. Along the entire length of the location numberless small veins crop out and traverse the ground in different directions, but no evidence is shown that the main lodes are broken anywhere upon the surface. Mr. Muñoz lays great stress upon the fact that the geological formation of this district favors the production of extensive bodies of rich ores. He decribes the same as appertaining to the trappeanic period, which is of a porphyritic nature, showing a greater ejection of precious metals than other metalliferous zones.

The two most interesting mines are the "S'ta Eduviges" and "Rosario." They have been somewhat extensively opened and much valuable ore taken out of them, and still it is easily shown that their mineral wealth is merely skimmed, as the average depth of the works does not exceed 420 feet. At this depth the veins are more defined, and the ore chutes become more regular and permanent, and the ore averages a greater richness than nearer the surface.

Mexicans never touch a vein which does not pay from its very surface, and then they only follow the ore body encountered, until the excavations become dangerous or expensive from want of ventilation or drainage. No dead work of any consequence is ever done. Perpendicular or hoisting shafts are seldom met with in any mining district; no explorations underground are undertaken to any extent, with a view to discover ore chutes other than the one originally followed in the same vein. No matter what treasures a mine may contain in its lower levels, no cross-cuts are made, and it is simply by accident that more than one ore body is developed in a single vein. And then how often do we see a mine with many mouths or openings, started one after the other, abandoned as the ore body in the previous excavation would pinch or break off, or as water would be encountered.

The ores contain mainly silver with a small percentage of gold. The expense of milling does not exceed $1.31 per carga of 300 lbs., including freightage from the mine. The yield varies according to the quality of the ores, but only such ores are worked as assay a minimum of 40 ounces of silver to the ton, of which there are always great quantities.

There is never any scarcity of workmen. The *Barreteros* or drill-men get $1.00 per diem, and the same wages are paid to timberers. The ore carriers get 75 cents per day, and all other common laborers at the mill only 50 cents for 10 hours' work. The workmen are paid weekly, and receive 75 per cent. of their wages in merchandise and 25 per cent. in coin. The present owners keep a store for the purpose, and reap a benefit of 75 per cent. upon their investment. The ores exported, for account of Messr. Martinez de Castro, show a total of 8,818 sacks, weighing, net, 1,263,447 lbs. The same foot up a gross yield of £55,771 (sterling), 8s., 3d., and equal to about $269,931.64.

San Francisco, May 15th, 1882.

From a report of Mr. J. C. Turner, made on Feb. 12th, 1881, to the Mexican Exploring and Mining Syndicate, we quote the following :—The Cuatro Señores mine is situated in Copala mining district, judicial district of Concordia, 65 miles from the port of Mazatlan. Work was first commenced on this mine August, 1868, and has since been carried forward, and it has never failed to yield ore in paying quantities. The ledge crops out about 600 feet below the apex of a very high mountain, elevation being 6,000 feet above sea level. The croppings can be easily traced for a distance of 4,000 feet. A tunnel was run in from a point 200 feet below the croppings, cutting the ore vein at a distance of 300 feet. At this point the ledge was found to be dipping at an angle of 60° to the north, the course of the vein being east and west. At the point where the ore was first encountered in the tunnel, it was extracted by opening a large chamber, which is still being continued, and at the present time extends in length on a line with the vein 300 feet, following the foot wall on the south side across the vein for a distance of 170 feet, with ore still in

the face and no appearance of any hanging wall as yet. The
highest place of the chamber or stope is 70 feet above the
tunnel, through the entire face of the slope. The vein looks
well and yields large quantities of high grade ore. The ore
has run from $50 to $364 per ton. An eight-stamp mill is
reducing the ore on the Panuco river at the rate of ten tons
per day. The mill is about one and a half miles from the
mine, and the ore is transported by pack mules from the mine.
This mine is one of the valuable properties of Sinaloa, and is
mostly owned by Mexicans residing in Mazatlan.

The Nuestra Señores mine is located north-east of Cosala,
on the Elota River, near the source, and almost on the
boundary line, and is owned by Mauricio La Madrid, and is
about 20 miles from Cosala. This mine contains two classes
of ore; one being lead and silver, while the other is free
milling silver ore. The depth attained is about 200 feet.
The lead-bearing ore assays about $80 per ton, and the free-
milling ore nearly $120, on an average. This mine is
reported to have reached a "bonanza" that assays as high
as $1,000 per ton. An attempt was lately made to purchase
this mine for $500,000, an expert having been sent to exam-
ine the property, who reported very favorably upon it. A
small, four-stamp prospecting mill, for the purpose of prospecting the mine, has been reducing the ore, and the result
is said to have been very satisfactory. This is an old mine,
and very celebrated; and Mr. Ward tells us that its former
owner, Don Francisco Iriarte, at one time (in 1825) refused
an offer of $1,000,000 for the privilege of working this mine
for three years, by a foreign association. The mine is free
from water, and situated at a considerable elevation above
the plain. It contains a vein of gold of considerable
breadth, and its former reputation was fabulous.

Barreteras Mine.—This mine is celebrated. The town
of Cosala was built up by it, and a church founded upon its
productions. The mine has produced many bonanzas,
yielding rich results. The character of the ore is native
silver. The mine is developed by a shaft of 500 feet in
depth, and by a tunnel over 1100 feet in length, from the
side of the mountain into the heart of the vein. The mine
is located at the summit of the mountain, in the Sierra
Madre, distant from Cosala about six miles west. The view
is grand from this point, extending over a hundred miles, as
far as the eye can reach, over mountain-tops. The vein is
about two feet in ore deposits. It reaches only six or eight
inches with seams of native silver, that are extracted by the

barraton, or a chisel. The pockets reach, sometimes, 20 or 30 feet along the vein at irregular distances. The mine is owned and worked by Mexicans. The character of the rock surrounding the vein is a granite formation, easily worked. The ore is smelted by furnaces. The ore is almost virgin silver, as at Batopilas. The lower levels are filled with water.

At one extremity of the district of Cosala is found a great number of gold and silver bearing quartz mines that are said to be very rich. The ore carrying gold is mostly free milling, and the mines have yielded very largely in the past. They have been worked extensively by natives and Spaniards; but on reaching water, could not go any farther, in the absence of machinery, and the mines were consequently abandoned, after a large expenditure of capital upon them. Another cause of abandonment was continual revolutions, or organized robbery, that forced the owners to pay a tribute on their wealth, and at last drove them away; and either fearing to return, or finding lucrative employment and mines elsewhere, the mines, consequently, became entirely abandoned and filled with water.

There are many of these old mines closely grouped together that are not adjacent to any settlements, but in the midst of one of the wildest regions of the mountains, that is hardly ever entered, save in the search for lost cattle. A good wagon-road may be constructed from these mines to the river, and reach a railroad that is to be built, passing within 15 miles of the mines. Wood is abundant, and water sufficient to run an ordinary mill the year round.

There are quite a number of extensive veins of rich gold and silver bearing ores in this region that have yielded largely wherever they have been worked, within a radius of 12 miles, and all contain ores easy of reduction.

To the east of this locality is located another rich mineral region, called Vetillas, from the large number of rich veins that have been found in the neighborhood. The ores are more uneven and rebellious; but the location is good, with a perpetual stream passing through the district and adjacent to the location of the mines. The mountains are of high elevation, with hard-wood trees covering their sides that would be valuable for timbering the mines, etc. Here are located furnaces for smelting the ores, which were abandoned with the mines by the former owners.

The celebrated Guadalupe de Los Reyes mine is located within about 24 miles of these antiquated haciendas, north-east, and other mines that are being worked with good results. This is an old mining region, that was worked by Spaniards under the Spanish regime; but the owners were obliged to flee in the war for independence. The ruins of ancient arastras and furnaces are numerous, and prove the locality to have been extensively worked. These mines have not been worked for about 70 years. The old mill-site could be restored, and the mines reopened, providing an expert should deem the enterprise profitable. The arastras were run by water power, and the veins opened as close as possible to the stream, which naturally filled the shafts with water. One of these old mines was called Mina de Plata. The residents nearest to these mines report that they were very rich, and contained bonanzas.

The adjacent river bottoms are planted with orange, lime, and plantain trees in different places, with other tropical fruits.

A wagon-road can be constructed from this point to Mazatlan, at a small cost, passing through or near large ranchos that are cultivated extensively, producing corn, beans, sugar-cane, and other productions. This region is located north from Mazatlan, distant about 70 miles.

The Palmarajo is another old district; also, the ancient mining district situated in the northern part of the State near the boundary line of Sonora, called the De Chois and Ycora districts, that were, at one time, extensively worked, and contains some good mines; also, the celebrated ancient mining district of San José de Gracias, which is located in the midst of an almost inaccessible mountainous region, in the northern part of the State. Since their abandonment years ago, they have scarcely been worked but by gambucinos. This region formerly had a fabulous reputation.

CHIHUAHUA.

CHAPTER I.

General Description.

The State of Chihuahua is bounded on the west and south by Sonora, west by Sinaloa, on the north by New Mexico and Texas, and on the north-east by Texas along the Rio Grande, and on the south by Sinaloa and Durango, and on the east by Coahuila. The area of the State extends over 100,000 square miles, with a sparse population of about 190,000.

The state is divided into 18 cantons or departments, as follows: Iturbide, Aldama, Abasolo, Victorio, Rosales, Meoqui, Morelos, Bravos, Hidalgo, Allende, Camargo, Balleza, Jimenez, Guerrero, Galeana, Rayon, Matamoras, and Arteaga.

The great plateau west of the Rio Grande region consists of undulating prairies, with here and there a conical shaped hill, and extends to the Sierra Madre mountains on the west and south-west. There are some depressions in the plains which, if opened, would supply water. Then we have the large body of water south-west of El Paso, known as Lake Guzman, and the River Mimbres. This river rises in the Rocky Mountains, in New Mexico, and, after coursing through the plateau, discharges itself when full into Lake Guzman. It seldom reaches the lake, however, its waters being absorbed or lost in the sandy plains. Its sources have never been traced out, as far as known. It must flow about 130 miles, when full.

Lake Guzman, during the wet season, is about 30 miles long and from five to six miles wide, and seldom dries out entirely, although it is almost surrounded by sterile tracts of land covered with sand plains and alkali, interspersed with sand-hills. It is located about 60 miles south-west of El Paso, more in a westerly direction. These sand plains extend the most of this distance, after leaving the Rio Grande region, until the neighboring lands of the lake are reached.

134

The whole water system of the state embraces, besides Lake Guzman, four other small lakes or pools, called Maria, Candelaria, St. Martin, and Patos, and are all located north of the central part of the state, in depressions of the table lands, with the exception of lakes St. Martin and Candelaria, nearer the center and south and south-west of the sand plains. In the mountain ranges and spurs of the Sierra which are cut with deep gorges and cañons, and which are located in the western, south-western and southern part of the state, there are many mines of the precious and useful metals, containing gold, silver, copper, lead, iron, tin, saltpeter, bituminous coal, and cinnabar. This region is also noted for forest trees of great value which cover the mountain sides, especially near the water-courses and between the ranges. The Sierra Madre range extends along the western boundary of the state, and is almost impassable except at the northern and western, south-western, and southern, part of the state, through the cañons of these localities. The Mulatos River, sometimes called the Papigochi, which is a branch of the Yaqui River in Sonora, rises in the Sierra Madre, south-west of Cahuahua City, and flows north-west through a pass in the mountains east of, and near Aribechi in Sonora. The tributaries from the neighboring valleys flow into this stream (Mulatos) near the pass. The river Buenaventura also rises in the Sierra Madre and flows north of the Presidio of Buenaventura into the small lake or pool of St. Maria, while another small stream loses its waters in the table lands near the Presidio de Janos, which is connected with a road to Bapispe in Sonora on the west, about 40 miles distant. The river Carmen rises west of lake St. Martin and empties into lake Patos in a northerly direction. South-east of lake Patos is located another extensive sand and alkali plain on the table lands that reache to the hills bordering on the valley of the Rio Grande and the river Conchos, over a territory of about 120 miles long and 40 wide. The latter river has many tributaries taking their rise in the mountains south of the central part of the state, and flows by Santa Rosalia, San Pablo, and other towns in a northerly course, with many windings, into the Rio Grande at the Presidio del Norte, and is about 300 miles long. East and south-east of the river Conchos and south of the Rio Grande extends the vast desert called "Bolson de Mapimi," which embraces all the extreme eastern part of the state south of the Rio Grande and also a portion of the state of Coahuila on the east. In this plain are dried-up lakes, and the whole is completely covered up with a vast tract of sand and alkali plains which are sterile and completely deserted, and entirely destitute of water. Near the rugged sierras are mesquite - covered plains, but beyond them lies the vast desert of Bolson de Mapimi, extending over 250 miles from north to south and 100 miles in width, through which no traveler ever passes, as the road to Durango and Mexico lies to the south-west. Thus it will be seen that a large portion of Chihuahua is absorbed on the east by the desert lands, and north-east and the south-west by mountains and broken regions, the latter taking up about one-third of the state, and the former, or about one-fourth, is desert wilds. The balance of the region on the Mexican side of the Rio Grande to the Gulf of Mexico is mountainous through Coahuila, New Leon, and Tamaulipas, bordering on table lands that are intersected with rivers flowing through small valleys into the Rio Grande, and is very sparsely settled until the slope toward the gulf is reached.

Oak, pine, ash, and other forest trees are found in great abundance in the southern and southwestern portion of the state : wheat, corn, and other cereals are raised on the Encinillas Rancho, and at El Sauz, Alamos de Peña, Ojo Caliente, and other localities.

Mr. Ruxton says that "the State of Chihuahua produces gold, silver, copper, iron, saltpetre, and other minerals; but it is productive of mineral wealth alone, for the soil is thin and poor, and there is everywhere a scarcity of water; but it is a paradise for sportsmen. In the sierras and mountains are found the black and grizzly bear of the Rocky Mountains, the latter of which is very abundant in the neighborhood of Chihuahua. The big horn, or Rocky Mountain sheep, and black-tailed deer, the ' cola prieta,' (a large species of fallow deer) a species of pheasant and quail in abundance, and birds of brilliant plumage are found. Among the reptiles are the rattlesnake and copper-head, and scorpion, the latter of which is found all over the republic. The characteristic shrub of the elevated plains of Chihuahua is the mesquite, a species of acacia, which grows to the height of 10 to 12 feet. The seeds contained in a small pod are used by the Apaches to make a kind of bread or cake, which is sweet or succulent to the taste. The wood is extremely hard and heavy.

" In Durango and Chihuahua, the ranchos are supplied with such simple goods as they require by small traders, resident in the capitals of those states, who trade from one village to another, with two or three wagons, which, when their goods are sold, they freight with supplies for the cities or mines."

There are about 200 villages and towns in the state, the principal ones being Chihuahua and El Paso del Norte. The former is the capital, and is located south of the central portion of the state, about 230 miles from El Paso del Norte and El Paso Texas on the Rio Grande.

Soil, Productions, and Grazing.

The soil is fertile, especially on the water courses between the mountain ranges and along the Rio Grande. Outside of mining, grazing forms the principal pursuit; though the vine, wheat, corn, peas, beans, barley, cotton, and sugar-cane, are cultivated to some extent. This is a great grazing state, abounding in stock, which are disposed of in Texas and Kentucky. Good grazing is found on the table lands in many places, where immense herds of stock of all kinds are raised: although along the water-courses the best grazing is found. Along the Las Casas Grandes, and Conchas, and other streams, which almost entirely disappear in the sands during the dry season, immense herds of stock are raised. In the neighborhood of Chihuahua, about 170 to 180 miles south-east of Lake Guzman, are located extensive ranchos. One of these is called Rancho Encinillas. This rancho has about 300,000 head of cattle, sheep, horses and mules, on its grazing lands. Some agricultural productions are also raised in the state on the banks of the streams which are used to irrigate the lands.

The mines of the State constitute almost its sole feature of importance, outside of the grazing or raising of stock on the fertile table lands and banks of the water-courses. The climate of Chihuahua is varied; cold in the winter, and in the mountainous districts it reaches the freezing point; and snow falls about two feet deep. In the valleys the temperature varies from the cool and pleasant in winter to heat in the extreme. The climate of the state on the whole can be said to be much cooler than either that of Sonora or Sinaloa.

CHAPTER II.

Chihuahua.

The city of Chihuahua is the capitol of the state, and is located west of the Conchos River, near the centre of the state, and is distant from Mexico city in a direct line about 1,250 miles; from El Paso, in a southwest direction, 225 miles, by rail; and from Guaymas, by way of Baleza in Chihuahua, and Alamos, in Sonora, 500 miles. It is reached by the Mexican Central Railroad from El Paso on the north and will soon be connected with Durango on the south by the same line, opening in that direction communication by rail with Mexico City on the completion of the Mexican Central line.

The road through to Alamos has not yet been put into complete condition for wagons; hence, the most of the travel in that direction is on the back of mules. The city of Chihuahua was built toward the close of the seventeenth century, although the State was originally inhabited and occupied at Las Casas Grandes by the Aztecs many centuries ago. No one knows the date, farther than by the records of the ancients, which say that the state was occupied by the Aztecs at that place in 1160, or over seven centuries ago.

The city of Chihuahua is well laid out, with the streets crossing each other at right angles. They are broad, well paved, and kept quite clean. The square called the Plaza Mayor is quite extensive, and ornamented on one side by the famous cathedral, which has been pronounced by American traders to be one of the finest structures in the country. This building cost $800,000, and is constructed of brown stone masonry. It is surmounted with a dome and two towers, and is in imitation of the modern Gothic, mingled with the Moorish style of architecture. It is a large building, having a handsome façade embellished with statues of the Twelve Apostles.

On the other side of the Plaza, there are public and private buildings, including the ancient State House.

The unfinished Convent of San Francisco also looms up from the other buildings, a " conspicuous mass of masonry and bad taste," says Mr. Ruxton. In the center of the plaza, which is adorned with flowers and orange and other tropical trees and shrubs, a beautiful fountain plays day and night, which is supplied with water continually by a well-constructed aqueduct a little over three miles long, which carries water from a tributary of the Conchos River or stream. This aqueduct supplies the town with water, and is supported on several stupendous arcades, which adds much to the massive architecture in the town.

The large cathedral was built out of the proceeds from one mine in the vicinity, which struck a bonanza that continued for nine years, and was apparently inexhaustible. One real was laid aside for each marc of silver produced, and a fund was formed, out of which this magnificent cathedral of Chihuahua was built, and a reserve fund formed of $100,000. A mint is also located here. Much trade is carried on between this city and San Antonio, Texas, and St. Louis, and Santa Fé. It is also the resort of many strangers from New Mexico, California, Texas, Sonora, and Sinaloa. The city contains about 18,000 inhabitants. The Jesuit Convent of San Francisco before mentioned is celebrated as having been the place of confinement of the patriot Hidalgo, the Mexican Hampden, who was executed in a yard behind the building, in 1811. A monument has been erected to his memory in the Plaza de Armas, and is a pyramid of stone, with an inscription eulogistic of his character and patriotic record.

The shops are filled with goods from the various points before mentioned, and it is not unusual to find the finest of imported silks, and other costly articles from Europe and India. Traders arriving in Chihuahua either sell their goods in bulk to resident merchants, or open out a store on their own account. The goods are brought across the border from the United States in wagons; and some years ago, a law was passed by the state, charging a duty of $500 for each wagon-load, without taking into account the value or nature of the articles. The result was, that one wagon was made to carry three loads, to evade the duty on two loads. This has been abolished since, we understand, and the laws relating to duties are general throughout the republic. The city of Chihuahua supplies all the surrounding country.

Las Casas Grandes and its Legend.

The famous Las Casas Grandes, or Great Houses, are located towards the north-western part of the state, on the west bank of the Las Casas Grandes River, which flows into

Rio los Conchos. Here lie, decomposing and moldering under the luxuriance of vegetable growth, the ruins of Aztec greatness.

A legend is related by Spanish historians of the migration of the Aztecs to Chihuahua and Arizona, where a portion also located and built the Casas Grandes, ruins of which are now seen in that territory. The legend is found in the work of Antonio Garcia Cubas, and in the works of many other Spanish writers, and is as follows:

"Huitziton, a person of great authority among the Aztecs, heard in the branches of a tree the trilling of a small bird, which in its song repeated the sound 'tihuc,' the literal meaning of which is, 'let us go.' Huitziton being struck at this, and communicating his impressions to another personage, called Tecpaltzin, they both induced the Aztecs to leave their country, interpreting the song as a mandate from divinity. Even to the present day, there is a bird known among the Mexicans by the name of 'Tihuitochan' (Let us go home).

"In 1160 they commenced their peregrination, and passing by a large river in which historians concur in being the Colorado and which discharges itself into the Gulf of California, they advanced toward the river Gila, after remaining for some time at a place known to-day by the name of Casa Grande, not far from the shores of that river. From thence they continued their road and again took up quarters at a place to the north-west of Chihuahua, now called like the previous stopping place, Las Casas Grandes, and whose ruins show the vast proportions of the ancient building and fortress. Leaving behind them the wide " Sierra de la Tarahumara," they afterward went to Hueycolhuacan, now Culiacan, capital of the state of Sinaloa, and there remained for three years, during which time they made the statue of their god Huitzilopochtli, which was to accompany them in their expedition.

"During their peregrination the tribe was divided into two factions, one faction settling on a sandy promontory called Tlaltelolco. The name of Mexico was given to the new city, in honor of their god who was born of a virgin belonging to the family of Citli, and he was cradled in the heart of a maguey plant (or metl); hence the name 'Mecitli,' afterward changed into 'Mexico.' The popular drink of the Mexican people is made from this same plant, and is called 'mescal,' a strong intoxicating liquor."

From the appearance of the Las Casas Grandes or the

AN AZTEC IDOL.

great houses, it would seem that their outer proportions were the lowest, and not above one story high; while the central ones were from three to six stories high. The ruins are constructed of adobe, though these are much larger than those in use among the Mexicans at the present day. From a report touching a close examination of Las Casas Grandes, it is to be inferred that they occupied a space of at least 800 feet from north to south, and from east to west near 250. On the south side a regular and continuous wall or fortification may be traced, while the eastern and western fronts are extremely irregular, leaving projecting walls. Within the inclosure there appear to have been several court-yards of greater or less dimensions. Las Casas Grandes here resemble those near the Pimo villages on the Gila in Arizona. The town near, of the same name, has about 1,500 inhabitants.

CHAPTER III.

RIO GRANDE REGION.

Near El Paso del Norte there is a good agricultural country. This town is located in the extreme north-western portion of the state on the Rio Grande. The products of this region are grapes, fruit, wheat, Indian corn, and other cereals. The bottom lands along the Rio Grande are extremely rich, and extend back from the river about one mile; beyond this rolling hills into the table-lands, which continue until broken by the valleys of the four lakes and their streams before mentioned. About 70 or 80 miles from El Paso del Norte, in the interior, in a southern direction, the land is sterile, as before mentioned. Then as the country nears Baranca, a small town situated east of Las Casas Grandes, the country grows better, and the soil extremely rich, in places. South of these sand plains there is a good grazing country. There is no water to be found near these sand plains, and water has to be carried in crossing them. The Rio Grande region extends along the Rio Grande the whole extent of the north-western boundary, and small towns are occasionally met with on the road, among which may be mentioned El Presidio del Norte, and San Vicente. Much stock is raised all along this region, and some agricultural productions.

From El Paso to the City of Chihuahua.

Mr. Julius Froebel recounts as follows a trip from El Paso
to Chihuahua City in 1859. He was in company with some
merchants, and we give his description for the benefit of our
readers:

" For the first five or six days journey from El Paso to
Chihuahua, a choice of two roads is presented. The one
is considerably shorter, but dangerous and difficult, as it
takes a southern direction over the notorious medanos, or
quicksand hills, the other avoids these by following the
course of the river two days journey' as far as the village
Guadalupe, and again joins the high road somewhat to the
north of Carrizal. We chose the last, and our caravan proceeded down the valley to Guadalupe.

The road, at first, passed close along the base of the alluvial terrace, through thickets of mezquite and a scrubby
plant of the order of compositae, then it wound up the terrace, which consists of sand-gravel and fragments of rocks
overgrown with mezquite, larrea, fouquiera, artemesia, shrub-
by labiate, cacti yuccas, etc. In some places the river had
formed its channel close to the terrace, forming a perpendicular sand cliff, rendering the road at its very edge in no
slight degree dangerous."

The town of Guadalupe is reached in three days travel
from El Paso. About six miles lower down the river, a new
village named San Ygnacio has been founded by the settlement of New Mexico immigrants.

From hence (Guadalupe,) the Sierra de Cantarrecio on the
left and the Sierra Guadalupe on the right, the road rises
gradually to the higher ground south of the Rio Grande.
The space between the above named mountains is a plain
rising somewhat to the south, and covered with the common
chapparral of these localities. At noon we stopped at Cantarrecio, a watering-place, where we found only a tittle muddy water. In the evening, when dark, we passed—turning
to the west, by a slow ascending plain of firm clayey soil,
which contracted to a small mountain pass—the chain of hills,
by which the terrace of Centarrecio is separated from that of
the medanos, and encamped for the night on the opposite
side, on a grass covered plain. The mountain peaks, near
the pass, are bare, rocky and in some places of grotesque
form. On the right an opening passes through the rock
from one side of the mountain to the other, and one of our
Mexican drivers told me that this part of the mountain is

named from this circumstance Sierra de la Ventana, "Window Mountain.', This name, however, did not appear to be generally used, for a gentleman, who had accompanied us from El Paso, called it Sierra de los Medanos, or Sandhill Mountain. Behind this road, as we approached it from the East, the needles and peaks of the Sierra de la Rancheria, which bears a striking resemblance to the Sierra de las Organos. Farther on eastward appears another similar mountain group called Sierra del Candelario. In the plain at the back of the former are the Charcos del Grado, pools surrounded by mimbre bushes. (Mimbre is a beautiful shrub which in Northern Mexico, from Rio Grande to California, flourishes on the banks of intermitting streams. It is a biquoniaceous plant, with pink and white blossoms, and long pendant lanceolate leaves—a chilopsis.)

In the afternoon we distinguished as we thought, the smoke of five fires in a southerly direction, but the next day we discovered that they had been clouds of dust caused by whirlwinds. In the evening we advanced over a level plain towards a mountain chain of perpendicular rocks, among which one remarkably angular and defined in its form, the Cerro de Lucerr o attracts attention. We encamped next morning at Ojo de Lucerro, a spring near the Laguna de las Patos. This is a lake on the left of the road. The plain is mostly covered with grass, but near the Cerro de Lucerro tracts of clay or sand are covered with an effervescence apparently of carbonate of soda.

One road, at least, took us over places of this nature, and from appearances, it seemed probable that, to the right of the road, they existed to a considerable extent. It was over this portion of the plain, that we had seen, and now saw more closely, those columns of dust. Their recurrence in the same locality may be accounted for by the nature of the soil.

At no great distance from the Ojo de Lucerro we met with another spring, Ojo del Coyote, remarkable as rising in the summit of a sandhill about twenty or thirty feet high. This curious circumstance is however easily explained, the sandhill being built up by the spring. It is surrounded by the same kind of efflorescence. The Mexicans call this salt, which they collect for soap-boiling, "Tequesquite," evidently an Aztec word. A few miles farther, at no great distance from the Laguno de los Patos, a warm spring rises in several eddies from the white sand. It forms a clear, tepid brook, which flows into a piece of water, surrounded by tall reeds, on the side of the road. This place was frequented by numbers of waterfowl—ducks, coots and a large black, web-footed bird, with very long legs, long neck and long bill, called by the Mexicans "Gallareda." They flew, when disturbed, in wedge-shaped flocks, with outstretched necks, like geese. The spring and piece of water are called Ojo de la Laguna. The water is slightly alkali, and a white efflorescence collected at its edge. In eight days travel Carrizal is reached.

The situation of Carrizal is one of the most beautiful on the North Mexican table land. An extensive plain, watered by several streams, is surrounded in the distance by a girdle of bare, steep mountains. A clear mountain stream, dispensing fertility to field and meadow in its course, flows through lands between varied banks for miles through the plain, its course marked by rows of poplars. Twenty years ago herds of many hundreds of thousands of cattle grazed upon the plain; now they have dwindled to the mere shadow of their former numbers, and, comparing this locality with the wealth it was known formerly to possess, the conclusion is irresistable that, of all destructive animals, man is the worst. The place, indeed, is full of ruins, and lies on a raised platform, consisting of hard red clay, with pebbles and fragments of sandstone, evidently changed by the influence of heat; black sloamaceous lava, yellow and green sienna, much resembling pumice, and numerous pebbles of chalcedon. The country is bare of trees, with the exception of the poplars along the irrigating canals, so that they are literally the only trees visible throughout the whole journey from the Rio Grande to Chihuahua. We reached towards evening, two days later, a warm spring of rather high temperature, named Ojo Caliente, which rises at the base of a group of phonolitic hills. The water, which is clear and pure in taste, forms a considerable stream, but I am not sure whether it reaches the Laguna de los Patos, or is retained in the plain for purposes of irrigation. Numerous fish sported in its waters.

We traveled next day from morning till evening between bare mountains, over rocky, treeless, but grass-covered hills, and passed a portion of the night on the broad, level pass of Chinate, a notorious place, where numerous bones of men and animals warned us not to leave hold of our arms. Many parties of travelers have been attacked here by the Indians, with much loss of life.. The rocks consist of a green and grey hard phonolitic porphyry. We started at two o'clock in the morning, in order to reach the Laguna de Encinillas without a halt. Toward eight o'clock we came to a descent in the rocks which, from the name of a hacienda on the other side of the mountain, is called the descent of Agua Nueva, and leads to the lower level of the lake. The hacienda of Agua Nueva is one of the few large grazing estates in North Mexico, where the herds still exist on the old Mexican scale of cattle keeping.

As we descended the hill, the largest herd of antelopes passed, that I have ever seen. It must have numbered more than 1,000, and extended from one mountain to another straight across the valley, vanishing as quick almost as thought from our sight. The plain in which the Lake of Encinillas lies, is surrounded by steep mountains, and is one of the richest and most valuable localities in the world for cattle grazing, in times past supporting innumerable herds; now it is almost a dessert. The trip consumed fourteen days.

Los Medanos.

The medanos or sand-hillls are a peculiar feature of the northern part of Chihuahua, and are encountered on the road from El Paso to Chihuahua City. These hills stretch in a line from northwest to southeast for some twenty miles, and are about six miles across from northeast to southwest. Nearly destitute of vegetation, their light yellow-whitish appearance presents a strong contrast to the deep brown of the adjacent mountains during the dry season. This sand is very light and fine and forms deep ridges resembling the waves of the ocean, which are continually shifted about by the winds. entirely obliterating the tracks of passing caravans or stage. The whitened bones of mules and cattle project here and there from the sand, with an occasional carcase which was dried up before the wolves discovered it. Although this route is the shortest by some sixty miles it is invariably avoided by trains or loaded wagons. These, take the river route which passes entirely beyond their farthest southern extremity. Persons on horseback, pack-mules and light pleasure wagons, or the stage, alone attempt to cross the hills. This place is also attended with great danger from the attacks of the Apaches, who well know the helpless condition of animals passing and take the opportunity to attack parties.

From Correlitos there is no other road to El Paso for wagons, except by making a complete circuit around these hills.

10

This point is one of the favorite places of attack of the Apaches, and is peculiarly dangerous on account of the late hostile demonstrations by these murderous bands of savages. Travelers are warned to avoid this point of all others while traveling through Chihuahua.

From Chihuahua to Durango.

The distance between the cities of Chihuahua and Durango is from 390 to 400 miles. The most of this distance is only traveled by mule pack trains, although a wagon road could be easily opened. The direct route leads through small towns and villages. The trail takes a southeast direction over the plain, about 40 miles when a small pond or lake called La Cieneguilla and a small stream that empties into the Rio Florido a branch of the Rio Conchos, about 30 miles traveled, reaches the rancho Alamito, which is situated about 8 to 10 miles from the banks of another stream emptying into the Florido. A stretch of about 55 miles takes the traveler to Hidalgo, at one time quite an important town. The trail then continues almost due south to San Jose del Parral, distant, about 35 miles. Here the line of travel takes a southwest course, crossing the headwaters of the Rio Florido, about 25 miles further. The Fuerte Cerro Gordo is reached about 8 miles beyond. The distance to Las Pinoles is near fifty miles, over a dry barren region. The trail following the same course, it here takes a southerly course to Fuerte de Gallo, nearly 30 miles distant, 35 miles further reaches the Rio Mapimi, near which is located on the road the rancho San Lorenzo. Crossing the valley of the Mapimi, taking a southerly course, brings us to Cuencame, a stretch of 40 miles.

Cuencame is a busy little place, whose industry makes it flourishing. Large smelting furnaces are here in operation for the smelting of the ores of silver which abound in the mountains. The furnaces are well built, of brick, on the English plan. The inhabitants are engaged at their different occupations in the most assiduous manner, quite different from most Mexican villagers. It is fifty leagues to Durango in a southwest direction. The first portion of the road is over a range of volcanic hills, and the latter is along an elevated table land. It is easy for the traveler to come from Eagle Pass, on the Rio Grande, to Cuencame by wagon, but to Durango from this place a good riding mule or sure-footed horse is much better, and for the conveyance of baggage pack animals will be necessary. Animals can be purchased cheaply at Cuencame, and those that are used to strong, rocky ground, as the country there is very gravelly. The first twenty miles after leaving Cuencame are pretty rough traveling and bring us to a stock-raising rancho, where plenty of mules are bred of a fine quality. Here water is elevated to the surface by a drum propelled by mule power. Twenty miles north of this place is a valley where cotton is raised, and where there are some factories at work manufacturing the "manta," an unbleached cotton cloth much used by the Mexicans. It is a flourishing little place. From here the road leads over a valley covered with a growth of the vinasgas, whose fruit is much relished by the people of the country. The valley also affords fine grazing, but water and timber are very scarce. Twenty-five miles takes us to a fine prairie, at the lowest part of which is a deserted rancho called El Saucito, or "The Willow." A large willow tree shading a spring of cool, refreshing water gives the place its name. From El Saucito to El Sauz is twelve miles, over a high country slightly timbered. El Sauz is in sight for ten miles before reaching it. This is a stock and grain rancho, as is also Laguna, twelve miles on the road, where a lake or lagoon is found. The next forty miles of road are over an undulating country. There are four miles of road in one place so stony that you are forced to dismount and lead your mule. It appears that a hail storm of stones had fallen on those four miles. Beyond this bad road are some water wells, but the water is brackish. A little further on is the haicenda of Los Chonos, or the Water Spout, where water flows abundantly out of the ground. This is really a fine place, built of solid masonry and whitewashed. There are large droves of sheep and mules on this rancho. The residence of the "Amo," or owner, is a pretty piece of architecture, the colonades being in the Corinthian style and all else about it showing unusual refinement. The country around Los Chonos is thickly wooded with mesquit and the soil rich. One or two farms may be discovered in the clearings. From this place to Durango is thirty miles. Three leagues from Durango is the crossing of the Rio de Hautruipi, near which is situated a fine hacienda, but it is not visible from the road. Between this one and Durango is a large haicenda, said to be one of the richest in the State. From here a fine road leads into Durango, which is seen at a distance from the plain.

El Paso del Norte.

This town was named from the ford on the river and the pass between the mountains, and literally means the "passage of the nor'h." This is the oldest settlement in the northern part of Mexico. A mission was established here by El Padre Fray Augustin Ruiz, one of the Franciscan monks, about 1585. The colony was composed of twelve families from Old Castile, under the leadership of Don Juan Oñate. Several years after the first settlement the Spanish colonists of New Mexico were driven to this settlement, where they erected a fortification and maintained themselves until the arrival of reinforcements from Mexico. The population of the place has not increased much since the year 1848, as there were then 5,000 to 6,000 inhabitants — about the same number as now. The colony divided the lands bordering the banks of the river, into small plats of twenty acres each, and gave one to each family, on which they raised corn, potatoes, beans, and vegetables, and planted small vineyards and fruit trees; and the river was dammed up in dry seasons, about a mile above the ford, and water conveyed by an aqueduct or main canal to irrigate the bottom lands. The whole settlement was intersected in every direction with dikes. They manufactured the grapes into wine and brandy, or "aguadiente," the latter of which is much esteemed in Chihuahua and Durango. Under proper management, wine-making here might become a very profitable branch of industry, for the soil is especially adapted for the vine, and the interior is supplied with French wines at an enormous price. Wine may be made of the El Paso grape, equal to the best growth of France or Spain. The river bottom is timbered with cottonwoods, where it is not cultivated for a few hundred yards on each side of the stream.

The town of El Paso del Norte is located opposite the town of El Paso, Texas, on the American side, and runs down the river about three miles, and back one mile. The region is thickly settled for several miles farther down, and back five miles from the river. There are a number of vineyards in a high state of cultivation. The town has two or three principal streets, on which most of the business is transacted. The streets are narrow, irregular and dusty. The houses are built of adobe, and the windows are barred with iron gratings. The doors are fastened with wooden bars inside, and are clumsy affairs. Carts with large wheels, hewn from logs, are still used here—the same clumsy and heavy vehicles so often seen in Mexico.

This town, although presenting a somewhat unsightly appearance to the visitor, is destined to be one of great importance, and will soon serve as the distributing point for the whole of north-western Mexico, including Sonora, Chihuahua, Sinaloa, and Durango, on the completion of the railroads centering here.

The Rio Grande River is a shallow, muddy, sluggish stream, and not over two or three feet deep at this point, during the dry season, but assumes large proportions in the wet season. The banks are low and sandy, and the course of the stream often changes, and, for this reason, the towns on its banks are mostly situated high up on its banks and on the neighboring plateaus or bluffs. The water in the river is very good for drinking and cooking purposes, and not so impregnated with alkali as the well water in use by the inhabitants.

The river, at this point, is small, but in the time of the rainy season it swells to six times its width in the dry season. It is fordable in almost any part, but from the shifting bars and quicksands, the passage is always difficult for loaded wagons, and often very dangerous. The stream abounds in large fish of an excellent flavor, and large eels. During the rainy season the ford is crossed by a ferry-boat. The settlements extend down the river some distance, in little groups or towns, for some 15 miles, and are mostly inhabited by Mexicans, with here and there some few exceptions. Some enterprising Americans having planted vineyards, are carrying on a very good trade in wine and brandy with the interior.

Mining Districts and Mines of Chihuahua.

The principal mining districts of Chihuahua are, the Guadalupe y Calvo, Zapuri, Batopilas, Urique, Guazaparez, Jesus Maria, and Potrero, Morellos, Chinapa, Pinos Altos, Concepcion, Cusihurriachic, Magurichic, Hidalgo y Tenorivo, San Francisco del Oro, and Hidalgo del Parral.

The Guadalupe y Calvo mines, which are located in the southern part of the state, are mostly owned by a New York company, who purchased them from an English company, who obtained vast profits from working them. The mines of this district obtained their great reputation from the immense wealth brought to their English owners. The Zapuri District is also very rich, and is owned by Becerra Hermaños. The mines of this district, which are now being worked, are said to be the richest in the state of Chihuahua. The Batopilas District is mostly owned by several American companies and individuals, and is located in the south-western part of the state, about 90 miles from Fuerte, in a north-east direction.

The celebrated San Miguel mine is owned by the Batopilas Consolidated Mining Company, of New York, with other mines in this district. Mr. Shepard, of Washington City, owns the controlling interest of this company, which is amassing immense profits from their mines.

The San Miguel, which is now yielding from $7,000 to $8,000 per day, is located near this point; and while working the mine, they reached one of three veins that produced bonanzas of from 50 to 90 per cent. pure silver; the rich places being found sometimes in one ledge, then in another.

The Santo Domingo, which is located on one side of the San Miguel, and is owned by Mr. Kirk, of Philadelphia, struck a bonanza upon the same ledge that was passed through by the San Miguel, without finding rich ore, though the latter mine struck a bonanza on the next vein beyond.

The Nevada Tunnel Company's mine, owned by Becerra Hermanos & Co., was opened near the converging point of the different veins, expecting to strike it rich on the other side, to the right of the San Miguel mine; they reasoning that if the veins all converge at this point, which the angles of the ledges or veins indicate, they will find one solid bonanza of all the veins in one. If this is true, the result will be millions to the owners. These mines are all located in the Batopilas district, the veins of which produce virgin silver, with little or no alloy with copper or base metals. We were shown specimens of ore taken from these mines, and found them to be from 50 to 90 per cent of virgin silver. These specimens are to be seen at Mr. J. F. Schleiden's office, of this city, who very kindly gave us valuable information in relation to the mines of Sinaloa, Chihuahua, and Durango.

The Urique District contains many rich mines, and is owned by the Becerra Hermanos.

The Chinipas District is on the road to the Guazaparez district, and possesses some very good mines. The latter district contains some rich mines, and is entirely owned by Mexicans.

The Jesus Maria District may be mentioned next, to which we have given special attention in the reports of assayers and mining experts; the greater part of which information is found in the valuable book of Mr. Mowry, on Arizona and Sonora. The mines of this district are all owned by Mexicans, and are now worked to great advantage.

The Pinos Altos District is mostly owned by English and American companies.

The district of Morelos is also, with the Pinos Altos, very rich in ores that yield marvelously.

We might add that the Batopilas district is completely surrounded with mountains containing milling ores. The silver is almost entirely native in this whole region. The celebrated Tajos mine is located in the Batopilas district, and is famous for its beautiful specimens of ores. This mine is also owned by the Bacerra Hermaños. There is another silver mine in Parral, that has a shaft 300 feet deep, that pays $175 per ton, according to the assay of Salazar, assayist, of Tucson, Arizona. This mine is located in the southern part of Chihuahua, in the Sierra Madre range, in the vicinity of other silver mines. The vein, Mr. C. Orcilla, the owner, who is now in this city, says, is from 12 to 24 feet wide, and is located in the town of Parral, that has 6,000 inhabitants. The river, or Parral Creek, runs through the town. There is good grazing in the vicinity, and it is surrounded by cattle ranchos. It is in a region well settled. The mine is an old one, and the extent of possession is 600 by 200 varas. The ore is milled near the same place by the primitive arastra. The ore is carried to the arastras on the backs of mules. The mine is for sale, and can be purchased of Mr. Orcilla. The *El Minero Mexicano*, of December 9th, says that the mines of Hidalgo del Parral might be explored by the expenditure of $500,000.

Mines of Jesus Maria and San Jose Districts.

"The Nuestra Señora del Rayo mine, in the district of Jesus Maria, was discovered shortly after the discovery of the mine of Jesus Maria, from which the mining town derived its name, in the year 1823, and is situated in the western range of mountains of the creek of Jesus Maria, at one-and-a-half miles from the town.

"The Rayo was discovered at the same time as the celebrated Santa Juliana Mine, from which it is about 500 varas distant. Its first owners were Messrs. Tomas Suza and Tomas Rivera, who worked it successfully, with good re sults, in gold and silver. It was abandoned on the discovery of a bonanza in the Santa Juliana mine, of which they were part owners. This happened in 1826. It was afterwards worked by the Siquerio Bros. until it became filled with bad air, caused by careless management. The mine was afterwards almost ruined by gambucinos. Sr. J. C. Henriquez, in 1858, denounced it to restore it, which he subsequently did, and it is now being worked.

The extent of possession of this mine is 700 varas vertically, the vein having an inclination of from 15 to 20 degrees, and running east and west. A drift shaft 25 varas long and 5 wide has been opened, with firm walls, from whence two shafts have been sunk, leaving a pillar of 14 to 15 varas between. A drift was run from them of large extent.

There is also a vein of auriferous, argentiferous quartz in the vein proper. It runs from 2 to 10 inches in thickness in four different veins, running parallel with each other. The ley of the ores was 24 ounces of auriferous silver per carga, or 160 ounces per ton. The intrinsic value of the silver of this mine, according to the statement of the government assayer of the district was 11 d. 2 gr. silver, 100 gr. gold, realizing 11 d. per marc at Jesus Maria prices.

The ore discovered in widening the walls, when these auriferous veins were first discovered, contained more silver than gold, yielding at the rate of $1,500 silver to $100 gold per carga of 300 lbs. It afterwards changed into more gold, and yielded over $100,000 per ton. Later, this vein changed into its former state. More or less rich pockets are found at uncertain intervals. The ores are easily reduced under the common Spanish amalgamation process. This Rayo mine is situated near the top of a mountain range, from 300 to 500 varas above the creek. The entrance to the mine is on an almost perpendicular side of the mountain. Timber is abundant, and at three miles distant. It is hardly half a mile to the hacienda of Quintana.

Santa Margarita is situated at the Rosario, about three miles distant from Jesus Maria, and was formerly owned by Messrs. Gutierrez, Guerreña & Co. The vein is steep, slanting from one-half to one vara wide, its gangue being limespattle with virgin gold of 960 m. ley per ton. The vein runs east to west 2 degrees, incline north; extent of possession, 800 varas. The mine has filled with water, and has three shafts. The common ore always paid $72 per ton. The better class reached $25,961 per ton, and the best ore,

$71,680 per ton, with gold selling at Jesus Maria at $12 to $14 per ounce. The improvements on the mine are one stone building—a "malacate," or large horse-windlass. An outlay of $4,000 to $5,000 would put the mine in working condition, providing the malacate windlass was used.

"**San Jose.**—The Rosario gold mine is adjoining the Santa Margarita mine, and is supposed to be the same vein. The vein is almost perpendicular, and from one-half to one vara in width. Several shafts and drifts have been run. The best and second-class ore has paid a similar ley as that of the Santa Margarita, while the common and inferior ley pays from $3 to $4 per carga, or from $20 to $25 per ton, while the heavy residue of the ground and worked ore pays six ounces to the arroba, of 25 lbs. "Zaroche" is the name for gold of low color, containing silver. On one occasion, a carga of 300 lbs realized $10,000, having reached a rich pocket. Extent of possession, 800 varas. This mine is now full of water.

"The Candelaria mine is situated about half a mile from the town of Jesus Maria. The vein runs almost perpendicular from one to two feet wide, The ore is hard, but docile under the amalgamation process. The lowest yield has never been less than $48 per arroba of 300 lbs—$320 to $3243 per ton as the highest.

"The gold of this mine sells at Jesus Maria at $10 per ounce. The mine is on the top of a mountain range 400 varas above the creek, and was full of rain water; extent of possession, 800 varas.

"The San Rafael mine is distant three-quarters of a mile from Jesus Maria town. The vein is nearly perpendicular, direction south to north, inclination from 15° to 20° east, and is about one and a half feet wide, on an average. The gambucinos filled up the most of the shafts with rubbish and destroyed them. The balance of the shafts from the first drift are filled with water. The lowest ley has never been less than one marc to the cargo, the residue or "polvillos" paying from two to three marcs silver per arroba, or about $110 per ton. This silver is auriferous, and sells at Jesus Maria at $16 per marc; extent of possession, 800 varas.

"The Hacienda Quintana is the point established for the reduction of the ores, and is situated in the center of the mining town Jesus Maria. It consists of three stamps and eight arastras, all the machinery of which is moved by an overshot wheel run by water. The hacienda reduces three and a half tons per 24 hours, and is fed by the creek Jesus Maria."

The principal mines of El Parral, situated at the city of Parral, are six in number, known as the Prieta, Mercaderas, Tajo, San Antonio. Leona and Ronquilla. These mines are famous in history and have a national reputation, having yielded over \$60,000,000 in silver, and are with those of Batopilas and Jesus Maria the most important in the state of Chihuahua. The mines are located on a small mountain of the foot-hills of the Sierra Madre range called "Cerro la Cruz," which overlooks and is within walking distance of the city. The Prieta and Tajo mines have been extensively worked by the Spaniards and Mexicans. The workings in the former, following the body of the ore, have left an immense hall or chamber, showing the amount of ore that has been extracted. The height of the chamber reaches 260 feet and width following the vein, extends from seven feet two inches to over twenty feet, and length from 150 to 200 feet. At the bottom the vein is from seven feet two inches to fifteen feet wide. At the extreme north end the ore as shown by assays made last year carried 67 ounces of silver to the ton, a few feet further south 82 ounces, in other parts 146 ounces, 77 ounces, 66 ounces, 139 and 180 ounces. The Mercaderas mine is next to the Prieta, not being however connected with it. At the point where is situated the Mercaderas mine the same vein is narrower, but from this mine a very large quantity of silver was taken, very rich ore having been found. At the Tajo, however, the vein is wider than it is at the Prieta, having in the Tajo, and from there to the Ronquilla a width of from twenty-five to sixty feet, the ore being quite as rich as that found in the Prieta.

The above described property was bought by Hon. Joseph Knotts while U. S. Consul at the city of Chihuahua, from different parties and consolidated by the company known as the Knotts Mexican Silver Mining Company of Chicago. A ten stamp mill has been erected with suitable storehouse buildings and all the necessary appurtenances in the shape of furnaces, pumps, etc.

The city of Parral, which is called Hidalgo del Parral, is a place of about 10,000 inhabitants and is over 200 years old. It is as orderly and quiet as any city of its size in the United States and has a considerable trade in supplying mines in the vicinity. The foregoing report upon the mines of Parral is taken from a report of A. J. Howell on the consolidated mines of Parral.

From a report on "Pastrana," in the Batopilas district, by Jno. C. F. Randolph, M. E., we quote the following data:

"The diorite is the rock in which the productive silver veins in this locality are found. Extending from the northeast corner to the southwest corner of the belt, a distance of perhaps four and a half miles, there seems to be a bonanza line of white panina, on which all the great bonanza veins of Batopilas lie. No great bonanza veins have as yet been found outside of this line.

The peculiarity of this district lies in its containing veins of calc spar in the diorite carrying native silver. This occurrence is only known in one other locality in the world, while near the surface chlorides of silver, black silver and ruby silver are found. The eventual ore has always been found to be native silver highly crystallized and often massive. This ore is richer and more cheaply and easily treated than any other ore of silver. In this district the cases are many in which veins have gone into bonanza over and over again, and this indeed is the usual experience with bonanza veins. These veins do not bear one blossom and then stop bearing. This is notably the case with the Veta Grande vein on the property whose history has been given (San Miguel of the Consolidated Batopilas S. M. Co.). This vein gave a bonanza netting in four years almost $3,000,000. Within eighty feet of this bonanza, a new bonanza was struck into last year which has already produced $200,000 to very slight efforts, and in the portion already developed contains upward of $400,000 more in place, waiting for the arrival of a mill to treat it. The rule with all the mines of this district has been that, although they may carry chloride of silver on the surface, the eventual ore at a depth is native silver in all its grades of massive, Brossa, Cispeado, Clavo, and Azogue."—[J. C. F. R. in "Silver Mines of Batopilas."]

From same: "At the greatest depth as yet attained by any mine in the district, viz.: 200 feet below the level of the river and 900 feet below the actual surface, this native silver still remains the final ore, and that no other class of ore will be found is undoubted. The classes of ore of this district are different from anything else in the world: 1st, Massive silver in pieces of 100 pounds and upwards; 2d, Brossa silver, three-quarters silver and one-quarter calc spar, $20,000 per ton, and daily produced in the district; 3d, Cispeado silver, one-third silver and two-thirds calc spar, $10,000 per ton, and daily produced in paying quantities in the district; 4th, Clavo silver, calc spar carrying isolated nails of silver, $500 to $5,000 per ton; 5th, Azogue, or amalgamating ore, with finely disseminated native silver, from $50 to $500 per ton, in large quantities. The veins which have up to date (October, 1881) produced the principal bonanzas are the Pastrana, Carmen, San Antonio, Veta Grande, Arbetrios, Roncesvalles, Camuchin, Descubridora, San Antonio de las Tachos, Santa Teresa, Guadalupe and Trinidad. All these bonanza mines are found on a diagonal line running from the northeast corner to the southwest corner of the belt, and are embraced within an area of a few hundred feet in width and some four miles in length.

The most convenient connection for supplies is from San Francisco to Mazatlan by steamer, thence by schooner to Agiabampo, on the Gulf of California, and from thence to Batopilas by pack train. Lines of stages make regular trips from El Paso and San Antonio to Chihuahua, and on the Pacific side from Mazatlan to El Fuerte. The cost of shipping silver from Batopilas to New York, including insurance against every risk, is but 3½ per cent."

"The Todos Santos Mining Company own two mines, the Todos Santos and Arbetrios. The first was denounced in 1875 and a shaft was sunk to the depth of 150 feet with six levels, and which worked by Mexican processes yielded nearly $120,000. It is said a lump of silver ore which assayed over 90 per cent. weighing 285 pounds, was taken from this mine. Another now in the company's office in New York weighs over 65 pounds, extracted in the early part of 1881, is estimated to be at least one-half silver in weight. The company now are driving a tunnel into the side of the mountain 150 feet below the old works, to tap the vein. The other mine, Arbetrios, is an old mine, that, according to the mining records of Batopilas district, in one year produced over $500,000."
—[From prospectus of the Todos Santos Silver Mining Co.]

Twelve miles east of Chihuahua, Mexico, is the marvelous Santa Eulalia silver mountain, from which $447,000,000 have been taken in times past. It is now in the hands of New York and Philadelphia capitalists. The El Paso *Times* has a description of the mine at present, from which we quote as follows: "A road has been built through a very deep arroyo leading to some of the old mines, while another one has been completed thence to the hacienda, along which a ditch has been run, bringing up the water of the Chihuahua river to the works for reduction purposes. Another gigantic operation is the cutting of two tunnels, one of five miles in length and the other ten miles, which are to pierce the old mines. Even before reaching any pockets, or leads proper, the ore taken out already is of sufficient value to pay the expenses of this colossal work as it progresses. Two hundred men are now employed, and when the hoisting works, stamp mills, etc., are completed, the former yield, fabulous as it may appear, will be easily surpassed. The records of the Tribunal of Mines and the Mint at Chihuahua, show that this mine, first opened in 1703, has yielded the enormous sum of $447,000,-000 in silver. But the church records of the Cathedral of Chihuahua would lead one to believe that even more was extracted. That cathedral was built by a tax on this mine exclusively. A sum equal to 7 cents on every marca ($8) of silver taken from the Santa Eulalia constituted the only building fund for this cathedral; and when it is borne in mind that this edifice cost not less than $900,000, as estimated by the ecclesiastical and civil officials, $447,000,000 is a modest figure.

In speaking of this region, Ward, in his work entitled "Mexico in 1827," says: "Near the surface of the earth all the lodes contain a considerable quantity of gold. This diminishes as the workings increase in depth, while the proportion of silver augments." And of the Santa Eulalia: "To the north of El Parral, and about five leagues to the southeast of the city of Chihuahua, is the ancient mining district of Santa Eulalia. It has been long abandoned, and the mines are in a ruinous condition. The ores were generally found in loose earth, filling immense caverns, of which some are stated to be sufficiently large to contain the cathedral of the City of Mexico; but there can be little doubt of their magnitude, since the last bonanza extracted from one of them continued for nine years." "The ores of Santa Eulalia are generally mixed with a considerable quantity of galena, which renders them fit for smelting."

Intending investors in mines in this country should only buy mines that, at least, have been partially explored and show metal. It is impossible for anyone to see into the ground, and no one is competent to state specifically the value of an undeveloped property. Good miners judge of the value of a mine by the amount of ore in sight, and from the indications of vein, rock, etc., draw inferences as to the amount that is hidden. A vein is more likely to extend than to "peter out" suddenly from a good prospect.

While there are many rich mines in Mexico one cannot be too careful in investing. As a case in point: A mining company in San Francisco purchased an inaccessible mine which they could not reach with expensive machinery which they had purchased, and a 10 stamp mill now lies scattered along the sides of a mountain in Chihuahua, in a ruinous condition, and the property was totally abandoned after some $90,-

000 were expended in the experiment. These mines are undoubtedly good mines, but are inaccessible, and therefore will not pay the expenses of working them.

Guadalupe y Calvo, in the Guadalupe y Calvo District, is the largest mine in the State of Chihuahua. It was leased in former years to an English company for a period of 20 years, and supported a population of 10,000 people. This is a celebrated mine, on account of its producing immense fortunes for the English company. When the lease expired, the original owners, who are Mexicans, took possession, with all the improvements, and continued to work it. While it was in possession of the English company, they secured the erection of a mint by the Mexican government, to save the expense of transportation. A 20-stamp mill was used to reduce the ore, and about 80 arastras. The latter were run by Mexicans on shares. The depth reached in the mine is about 900 feet. The width of the vein averages from 20 to 25 feet, and is well defined. The average assay was about $200—the lowest, $40, and the highest, $2,000. The ore was free milling. The mine is located on the side of a mountain, 500 feet above the creek; but it is now abandoned, and the shafts and drifts are filled with water on the lower levels.

The Carmen mine is located just beyond the border line of Sinaloa, in the State of Chihuahua, on the side of a mountain near the summit, in the main range of the Sierra Madre. The depth of the mine is about 300 feet or more; width of the vein about 5 feet. The average assay about $120 per ton, and the ore runs pretty even from $80 to $300 per ton. It is owned by a Mexican. The ore is rebellious, and contains but a small percentage of gold. The mine is not a mile distant from the border, and about 25 miles from the town of Cosala in Sinaloa.

The Pinos and Altos is worked by an English company, Mr. Hepburn is the principal owner. A 15-stamp mill is now reducing the ore and arrangements are being made for another 15 stamp mill. The depth attained is 800 feet. The average assay is about $100 per ton. This mine is situated on the top of a mountain about 15 miles from Jesus Maria Northwest. Several shafts, crosscuts and tunnels have been run. The present owners have worked the mine for about three years. The mine was purchased from Mexicans. The ore produces a larger percentage of gold than silver.

The La Soledad has reached a dept of about 90 feet, and and width of the vein about 15 feet; average assay, about $100 per ton. This is developed by a shaft but a short distance above the Arroyo, and about 20 feet from the bank of the stream. The mine consequently became filled with water and was abandoned.

Santo Domitius mine is situated southwest of Jesus Maria, about five miles. The mine is developed by a shaft at the surface, and a tunnel at the foot of the mountain, tapping the vein. The principal owner is Jesus Solis. A ten-stamp mill is being erected to reduce the ore at the mine. A small five-stamp prospecting mill has hitherto been used. The tunnel reaches the heart of the vein and is over 1200 feet in length. The ore is abundant and assays on an average about $75 per ton.

Good accounts continue to come from the Batopilas mines in Chihuahua. Ex-Govenor Shepherd writes that he has ready over $600,000 worth of ore, and that the mines are working now in "bonanza." A piece of ore, weighing 148 pounds, and valued at $1,680 has been forwarded as a sample of the mine's production. It is stated that the Batopilas mine, during its first year, without machinery, paid $160,000 besides the sum of $57,000 set apart for mills, and a balance of $180,000 retained in its treasury, Mr. Robinson, formerly of Durango, whom I met recently, fully confirms the reports of the richness of the Batopilas mines.

The San Jose de Bravo mine is located 23 miles form Jesus Maria, in a southwest direction. This mine was first discovered and worked about thirty-two years ago, by Sigs Devaley Y Lopez Y Cia. Reliable information as to the history of the mine is difficult to obtain. It is reported that $700,000 were extracted from this mine in two years, while in bonanza. The population of Bravo at that time was about 1000. The owners of the mine squandered the proceeds, and died in comparative poverty- The manner of working, was the usual Mexican style of extracting the rich ores only, and on the abandonment of the property, the gambucinos completed its ruin by extracting the pillars and thereby causing the destruction of the workings. The mine is now owned by Mr. Hepburn.

The Pertenencia extends 2400 feet. Eighteen hundred N. N. E. of the mouth of the lower tunnels, and Six hundred feet in a S. S. W. direction. There are three parallel veins, named respectively; San Franguilino, San Bonifacio and San Antonio. The first has an average width of 8 to 14 feet

of ore varying in **richness.** The second is completely **cover-**
ed with the veins of the old workings, so that no exact re-
port can be had of it. The third vein is also in like manner
covered. A tunnel 250 feet long, and two or three shafts
have been sunk. One **of these** shafts is called the San Fran-
guiimo, and the other the San Bonifacio. One of the workings **was called the Dolores,** and the other Dulces Nombres.
The first is about 200 feet above the Arroyo Bravo, and **the**
second about 500 feet. The assay reaches from $20 **to** over
$2,500 per ton. Abundance of wood and water **are** adja-
cent.

The La Soledad **is** about three milles due north of Je-
sus Maria. The vein of this mine runs southwest and north-
east, and dips southerly at an angle of 40°. The walls are
more or less well defined, and are of porphyhy and green
serpentine. An old mine, called the Jesus Maria mine adjoins the Pertenencia, that carries a low grade ore in great
abundance, assaying from $30 to $35 per ton. Tunnels and
shafts have been sunk on the vein of La Soledad, but they
are filled with water, and mostly caved in. Mr. Theo. A.
P. Brown who reported on this mine from which we obtain
the data states in his opinion "that there exists still large
quantities of ore, and of considerable value, there is not the
slightest doubt . The tunnel of Soledad commences about
15 feet above the Arroyo. It is run on the vein which is a-
bout 6 feet wide, but pay ore is only found on the foot wall.
and is about 12 inches wide throughout the upper works.
At bottom of mine, now under water, the owner says the pay
ore is a vara wide. I have made an average assay of 400
cargas, equivalent to 60 tons, the result of which was silver,
$67 86; gold, $19 94; total, $87 80. Later assays by same
report, showed as high as $196 from mouth of tunnel."

DURANGO.

CHAPTER I.

Physical Features.

A large proportion of the state of Durango is situated upon the table-lands, and the capital, though surrounded in most maps by mountains, lies in the midst of a vast plain, which, to the north-east, extends, with few interruptions, as far as Chihuahua and Santa Fé, in New Mexico. To the west, both north and south, the Sierra Madre extends, forming a barrier upon the Pacific side, and the hot low lands of Sinaloa occupy the space between the foot of the mountains and the Pacific Ocean. The state is bounded on the north and north-west by Chihuahua, and on the east by Coahuila, and on the south-east by Zacatecas, and on the south by Jalisco, and south-west by Sinaloa. It is completely surrounded by Mexican territory, and is not considered as one of the border states, though we have included it in our work on account of its location and important interests connected with those states on the frontier.

The state of Durango is divided into 13 districts, as follows: Durango, Nombre de Dios, Mesquital, Cuencame, Uzas, Mapime, San Juan de Guadalupe, San Juan del Rio; Indee, Papasquiero, El Oro, Tamasula, and San Dimas. The state has but few manufactures. Its riches consist almost entirely in mines and agricultural produce, which last is so considerable that the lands already brought into cultivation are supposed to be sufficient for the support of a population five times as large as the State now contains. Consequently, it has considerable trade with the surrounding region.

The raising of stock is carried on extensively also; most of the estates, besides being devoted to agricultural products, are also devoted to the raising of large herds of horned cattle, horses, mules, and sheep, of which last 150,000 are sent every year to the Mexican market. The Hacienda de la Sarca alone possesses a stock of 200,000 sheep and 40,000

11   161

mules and horses. That of Ramas, which consists of 400 "sitios" or sheep ranches, has 80,000 sheep, and the Guatimape 40,000 oxen and cows. The valley of Poanos, about 45 miles from the capital east, contains nothing but corn lands. It is watered by a river which runs through the center of the valley, and on this river are nine "haciendas de triego" (corn estates) in immediate succession, which supply the capital with flour of the very best quality, at from $6 to $8 per fanega. Sugar might be extensively raised in the valley of the Sierra Madre, where water abounds and climate might also be selected at pleasure. Sugar is at present brought from the valley of Cuencame at a distance of 250 leagues. It sells at an enormous price — $5 per arroba, and often at $10. Indigo and coffee might likewise be reckoned among the natural productions, as they are found wild in the barrancas or ravines of the Sierra. Sugar, we believe, is raised to a small extent in some of the valleys.

Mr. Ruxton describes the ranchos and haciendas as follows: "The ranchos and haciendas in Durango and Chihuahua are all inclosed by a high wall, flanked at the corners by circular bastions loop-holed for musketry. The entrance is by a large gate which is closed at night, and on the azates or flat roof of the building a sentry is constantly posted day and night during Indian troubles. Round the corral are the dwellings of the peones, the casa grande or proprietor's house being generally at one end and occupying one or more sides of the square." He goes on to speak of large herds of cattle and horses to be found on the plains, but of one district he says: "From El Gallo to Mapimi a mule track leads the traveler through a most wild and broken country, perfectly deserted, rugged sierras rising from the mesquite-covered plains, which are sterile and entirely destitute of water. This part of the country is far out of the beaten track from Durango to Chihuahua." Thus it is seen that sterile tracts are also to be found in this state. The whole of the state is mountainous and contains no rivers, except a few small streams.

CITY OF DURANGO, MEXICO.

CHAPTER II.

City of Durango.

Of the City of Durango he says: "The City of Durango was founded by Velasco el Primero, and it may be considered the 'ultima thule' of the civilized portion of Mexico. Beyond it to the north and north-west stretch away the vast uncultivated and unpeopled plains of Chihuahua, the Bolson de Mapimi, and the arid deserts of the Gila." The distance to Mexico City is 650 miles from Durango, the capital of the state, which is situated 65 leagues north-west of Zacatecas. The population is 22,000. The state had, in 1876, 185,000. Both the city of Victoria and most of the other towns of Durango—Tamasula, Sianori, Mapimi, San Dimas, Canelas, Cuencame—take their origin from the mines.

The town of Victoria, or Durango, is situated in the plain heretofore mentioned, and is the principal town of the state. The streets are pretty regular, and the town contains a large plaza called the Plaza Mayor, one theater and other public buildings, which were built by Zambraño, a rich mine-owner, who is supposed to have extracted from his mines at San Dimas and Guarisamey, upwards of thirty millions of dollars.

The capitol is located here, a mint, and the Casa del Apartado, (a place for the separation of gold from silver) a glass manufactory, a tannery, and a fabrica de tobacos. The police of the town is well organized, and robberies almost unknown. Legal proceedings are summary, the legislature having passed a law which concludes legal proceedings in three days, in cases of robbery.

Tobacco is produced, also, in the State, to some extent.

There is much trade at this point, principally in bullion from the mines, and among the principal business firms may be mentioned, Julio Hildebrand Succesores, Doorman & Co., Giron, Stahlknecht & Co., Francisco Gurza & Co., Juambels Hermaños, and Francisco Alvarez & Co.

The towns of Villa del Nombre de Dios, San Juan del Rio, and Cinco Señores de Nazas, are almost the only cities in the State connected with mines. The two first are supported by an extensive trade in "vino mescal," (a sort of brandy distilled from the maguey or American aloe, sometimes called the century plant, which requires from seven to ten years to develop.

The last-named town is supported by the cotton plantations situated upon the banks of the river Nazas. The alacran (or small scorpion) excepted, Durango is very pleasant, and the climate is delightful and healthy, and the people fairer and finer-looking than in any part of Mexico I have yet seen.

Bath Houses of Durango.

We are indebted to Dr. Benjamin of San Jose, for the following. "The hot springs located at the upper part of the city, furnish water for nearly the whole city. A stone aqueduct conducts the water through the centre of the principal streets. The stream is about three feet wide, by one and one-half feet deep. Near the source of this stream, are built a great many bath houses, all built of stone. The bath tubs are of masonry and a number of them are 12 by 12 feet in diameter and 5 or 6 feet deep. The temperature of the water is about 80°. You can take a bath in the large rooms for twenty-five cents, There are a great many small rooms—prices, six to twelve cents. The population are very fond of bathing, and I do not wonder, when I remember how fine and clean are the bath tubs, and how pleasant is the temperature of the water."

From Durango to Mazatlan.

Further than Durango no wheeled vehicle can go, so we disposed of our ambulances, and took it mule back, paying at the rate of $12 per mule for passenger and baggage. Four miles from Durango the wagon road gave out, and we took a path which wound up rugged cliffs until near camp. When we came to a mountain mesa. Our course lay to the westward, and for the first few miles, our road was good and we had a comprehensive view. In consequence of the dangers which beset the road, it is customary for travelers to rendezvous at Durango, and travel in large parties. We made a terrific descent to-day, at the bottom of which dashed a beautiful mountain stream, and up we climbed again to the top of another mountain. Our camp is among beautiful pines, and flocks of noisy parrots are flying over us, on their passage from the nut forests. Here is said to begin our dangerous road; near by are the skulls and bones of some murdered travelers, placed on a pile of stones. The road next morning is quite rough; in fact, a mere path, winding through dark woods, and over precepitous heights. These wild solitudes are charming, the pine forming arches over head, the earth carpeted with green grass, and at short intervals cool springs of water. The days are warm, the night cool. On the next day we camped in a beautiful pine grove, on an eminence, overlooking a pretty little vale. In the midst of the grove stands a high rude cross, said to mark the spot where the banished bishop of Durango performed mass. A grand temple, whose pillars are the forest-monarchs, and whose dome blue Heaven. The next day our path passed through a beautiful mountain country of pine woods and gushing streams, our every step still beset with the melancholy sight of human skulls. Our next encampment, was in the bend of a beautiful bold mountain stream,—a desirable location for a settlement, soil good, building material abundant, and a natural site for a mill. Shortly after leaving camp the next morning, the foot passengers and some of the horse-men separated from us, taking a nearer but rougher route to Mazatlan.

The roads parted near the piloncillos, a collection of curious, cone-shaped rocks. Among the footmen were some mountain cargadores now carrying loads of apples. They carry their loads on their backs, keeping them in place by means of a strap across the foreheads. These men are employed to carry heavy machinery where it is impossible to use animals; they also carry the mails between Durango and Mazatlan, making the round trip in eight days, for which they are paid $15. They keep up a brisk trot all day, munching their tortillas as they run, pursuing their way over places impassable for even the sure-footed mule. They do not wear shoes, but sandals or guaraches, as do also the muleteers, merely pieces of rawhide cut to fit the sole of the foot, and kept in place by thongs; these they prefer to shoes, their feet becoming very hardy, suffering neither from cold nor the gravel which is continually sifting between the sandals and their feet. We had traveled but four hours the next day before the order to halt was given. We have reached the jumping-off place and must give the mules a good rest for the morning's arduous task. For the last five days we have been shut up in dark primeval forests, pursuing our rough path over heights and along ravines, but now we have reached the pinnacle to which we have been ascending ever since we left Durango, and in the morning will commence to descend.

A Grand View.

By ascending a little eminence near camp, and walking a short distance through the woods, I came upon one of the grandest and most sublime displays of mountain scenery, I ever beheld. Standing on a rocky peak, I hung, as it were, over an abyss extending below me for thousands of feet—I may say for miles—I could see a stream, which resembled a silver thread, and farms along its bank; it seemed I could throw a stone so that it would fall within their peaceful premises; far below hung white clouds, and the blue ether seemed to envelop me, and on every hand, rose mountain peak on mountain peak, in awful sublimity. But, from my lofty perch, I could command them all, and far to the westward the mountains sank away and the sun's slanting rays reflected from the Pacific Ocean. From this place, although our destination is almost within the scope of our vision, it will take us seven days to reach it, and truly when I cast my eye over this rough vista, it seems the mountain barriers could never be passed.

We began the next morning to descend from our lofty eminence, and reached Duraznito about 2 o'clock P. M. Our road was a winding, terrific stairway of twelve miles; the glimpses of the grand and beautiful filled me with awe and ecstasy. We have changed climates in the course of a few hours. This morning we were shivering from cold, and now we seek the shade of the fig tree and bless the soft wind. Peach trees are in bloom about us. This little place is situated, as it were, on a shelf of the mountain, by which it is shadowed, and still beneath it lies a deep gorge or valley. We are now in one of the finest gold and silver-bearing regions in Mexico.

A short distance from Duraznito, and at the foot of the mountain, we found ripe blackberries. Upon reaching the summit of the mountain we had a fine view. Far beneath us was Duraznito, the smoke of its humble, tile-roofed domicils ascending in spiral columns, and the deep valley still further down, and the grand mountains, that seemed like the giants of creation, basking in the rosy dawn. Here is certainly mountain scenery unrivaled by any in the world. The lakes of Switzerland would be but drops in the infinity of the natural grandeur about us. A narrow trail winds for the most part along the sides of immense mountains, which is just wide enough to admit our mules single file, with tremendous heights rising perpendicularly above us—an awful gulf of space below us. One false step would cost a life. The sun was intensely hot whenever we were exposed to it, but for the most part we were protected by the shadow of the mountains, around and over which we were winding, looking, in comparison, like a procession of ants upon the dome of St. Peter's, Rome. This tiresome and perilous road was cheered by the sound of laughing rivulets and there is something exquisitely pleasant about these mountain solitudes. We had traveled hardly an hour along a more fearful trail than ever, a portion of the road called Buenos Ayres, when one of the mules lost his footing and fell, bounding down the mountain side as an india rubber ball would down a flight of stairs, and dashing to pieces below. The train moved on as if nothing had happened, it not being an unusual occurence, and camped for the night upon a level eminence a short distance further on.

We broke camp early next morning, and commenced our day's travel by ascending, as usual, and passing along more frightful cliffs—warily, from yesterday's accident. Passed Piedra Gorda, quite a rancho, beyond which we came in view of a mountain called El Pyramido, or The Pyramid, a magnificent freak of nature; the base is covered with dark woods, from which shoots up a shaft of solid bare stone, tapering gradually to the top. It is certainly grander than all the pyramids of Egypt combined.

As we descended the climate became warmer, and instead of pines, we passed through groves of flowering trees and lemon trees bending with yellow fruit. By midday we had reached the bottom of the gorge, or base, as it were, of the main range of the Sierra Madre, and on the banks of a stream running westward. Our road lay along this stream, crossing and recrossing it several times; we camped at Agua Caliente. Before reaching camp we passed some mud huts and by El Favor, where an arastra, or atana, was in operation, working silver ore. It is sunset, and thousands of parrots and flocks of birds of beautiful plumage are floating down from the adjacent mountains to roost in the woods along the stream. We started early next morning, to take advantage of the cool of the day, to cross the El Espinaso del Diablo, or "The Devil's Backbone"—(hereafter described)—a fearful mountain ridge, and said to be the last of our very bad road, camping on the river at El Palmar. The next day our trail lay, for the most part, through dense tropical woods. Our attention was attracted by the strange varieties of trees, and especially the banyan, whose roots

spring from the upper branches, and trend down to the earth
and then take root. Great numbers of parrots flocked
through the woods, almost deafening us with their screams.
Our party shot several, and we made a feast of parrot, which
we found very palatable—in fact delicious.

After a warm day's travel we arrived next day at Puerto
San Marcos, our road pursuing the river all day. We camped
at a miserable little rancho, one day's travel from Mazatlan.
The weather was quite warm, but the trail was more tolerable, passing several ranchos and plantain groves, and fields
enclosed with hedges of orgona cactus, planted like posts in
the ground. On the next day we reached a broad wagon
road, within a few miles of Mazatlan, and on an eminence
near the city the sea broke upon our view. Just before entering the city we underwent the scrutiny of the Custom-
House officers.—*From a traveler's report.*

The Devil's Backbone.

On the road from Durango to Mazatlan one of the grandest scenes presented by nature is the ridge that juts out
from one mountain to another, called "El Espinaso del Diablo." It seems that the surroundings suggested the not
very euphonious connection with the anatomy of his Sa-
tanic Majesty. The traveler cautiously picks his way
over a road over this ridge with precipices falling
almost perpendicularly for thousands of feet on either
side. The trail is very narrow and over hard, smooth
rocks that the storms of thousands of years have failed to
wear away. It gives the traveler a sensation that he will
never forget, as he looks upon either side into an abyss
yawning at his very feet, and the sight is so fearful that he
hastens over, shuddering at depths that make the stoutest
fear to peer into. One traveler describes his feelings by
saying that he involuntarily closed his eyes to shut off the
fearful sight before him. Another says the precipices on
either side are immense chasms or clefts in the mountains,
which are so deep that you can hardly see the bottom if the
attempt is made to peer into their depths. In every direction high and lofty peaks extend as far as the eye can reach,
lifting their rugged mountain tops with bare rocky summits
heavenwards for hundreds of miles. This high ridge is really the summit of one of the mountains and presents the
only route practicable for pack trains over the mountains.
It is the highway that has been used for many years, in fact

ever since communication was opened in this direction between Durango and Mazatlan. A former soldier in the Mexican army says that he was in a company that went over this route, and while crossing the ridge the soldiers were ordered to cross on a run. Singularly no accident occurred, though he said he shudders yet as he recalls his feelings while keeping his place in file with his comrades rushing behind him.

The Short Route to Mazatlan.

One of the early pioneers, who came to California at an early day by way of Durango and Mazatlan, describes a trip he made in taking the short route from Durango to Mazatlan. This same gentleman is one of the prominent citizens of Sacramento, and from his own lips we learned the following Says he: We had heard that there was a shorter route, and, being impatient, concluded to risk the trip. We had heard that it was a fearful ride and too dangerous for horses or even mules, and that none but cargadores, or footmen, dared to undertake the trip, but we concluded that we could go anywhere a Mexican could, and so started upon the route, the narrator acting as leader. We found that the road was rough enough at the start, and that it led along a trail on the side of very precipitous mountains, so narrow that it was impossible to pass should any one be met on horseback. At last the trail seemed to dwindle to almost nothing upon the side of one of the steepest mountains; in fact a fearful precipice yawned at our very feet on one side, on the other and above us rose an almost perpendicular wall. Just ahead a smooth, slanting rock jutted out with its slippery, polished surface inclining into the abyss beneath us. I did not see it until I had passed around a jutting portion of the mountain, and my horse stood upon such a narrow ledge that I dare not dismount; I knew that if I did that my horse might topple over and we both be hurled to destruction, so I concluded I must take my chances and make my horse climb over that smooth surface that appeared almost certain death, although my hair stood on end, as my horse, a faithful and sure-footed animal picked his way carefully across. I arrived safely, but it was the most foolhardy act of my life. Fortunately my companions had not yet arrived at the narrowest point and I was enabled to warn them to dismount and lead their animals across. He concluded by saying that he found afterward that a Mexican and his mule had tumbled off that same rock only a few days before. The balance of the road was the roughest we had ever traveled, in some places covered with large boulders that it seemed almost impossible for a horse or even a mule to cross over them. We publish this as a warning to the many travelers who might by mistake undertake to travel over this same route,

Rancho de Morteros.

The greatest part of Durango is mountainous in the extreme. In but few instances throughout the whole of the State are ranches found that make any pretenses at agriculture, the principal object being to supply the immediate wants of the owner of the property, and perhaps a limited local trade. Cattle-raising and mining form the principal pursuit. The buildings are mostly of adobe. Among the exceptions to this rule may be mentioned the buildings upon the Rancho de Morteros. All of the improvements are of solid masonry and were built by one of the Spanish nobility long before the independence of Mexico drove its wealthy occupants from their possessions. This rancho is situated in the southern part of Durango, some twenty miles north of Nombre de Dios. The main buildings contain two stories and are built of solid freestone masonry, and form an immense square with eighty rooms, the largest of which are twenty feet square. The floor is inlaid with tiles of burnt clay, both on the upper and lower floors. The whole building has the appearance of a fortress or square castle with bastions on each corner loopholed for musketry. The only entrance is through a door of solid timbers four inches thick protected completely with nail heads, entirely covering the outside. An inner square, or court, with no roof is in the center of the structure, with a porch bounding it on all sides, the roof of the porch being supported by solid stone pillars about one foot in diameter. This court admits the only light into the building through inner windows. The upper story is reached by a stone staircase from the lower floor. The ceiling is made of massive timbers, upon which are laid the tiles of the upper floor. The roof is covered with tiles of the same material, and is flat with barely enough incline to drain the water from the roof. Adjoining this building is the church, also of solid masonry, with tower containing four bells. Stone acqueducts extending for two miles conduct water from a spring to the hacienda and also to a large mill built of the same durable material. The corral for the stock, and even the fences extending for miles, are all built of stone. Six large granaries 20x100 feet each are constructed for the grain that is grown on this ranch. The grain patio or threshing floor is also of solid masonry. The huts of the peons surround this feudal castle who labor for their master in the fields surrounding. These large cornfields extend for miles and are cultivated in the primitive Mexican fashion with immense returns to the owners. Dr. Benjamin Cory, of San Jose, while visiting Durango, stopped for some time at this rancho, and we are indebted to him for the above description. The Doctor was much pleased with his visit to this princely estate and rode over the land with a view to its purchase for parties in San Jose. He describes it as the most desirable of any property he found in the State of Durango.

Mines of Durango.

The gold mine of La Republicana is located on the side of a high mountain near Guadalupe. It is said to be a very valuable mine, as far as richness is concerned, but the vein is narrow and the rock of the greatest possible hardness. It is owned by the Yriarte family, who, unable to work it for lack of capital, merely keep the mine worked just enough to hold possession. The mine might pay well, as one traveler reports its assays at about 70 per cent. Five leagues southeast by south of Guadalupe is the old mine of Espiritos Santo, another mine of the Spanish times now under water. There are several other old mines in the vicinity of Guadalupe, but they are so filled up with rubbish that it is difficult to speak of their richness with any certainty, although fabulous stories are told of some of them, which seem probable enough from the fact that Guadalupe stands in their midst, a proof of mineral wealth and successful mining.

The Vaca San Marcus and Bismarck mines are described by Dr. Benjamin Cory of San Jose, as follows: "These mines are located in the district of Parrillis, about sixty miles south of the city of Durango and about twelve miles from the town of Nombre de Dios. In 1848 these mines yielded in silver ore $700,000, according to a certificate which I have from the Superintendent of the Mint in Durango. The owners at that time were only 450 feet deep in the mine, but were forced to abandon the works on account of the quantity of water. Our company organized in Sacramento some three years ago have denounced the mine and have been in active prosecution of the work ever since the denouncement. We have steam hoisting-works and pump in operation, the first ever seen in the State of Durango. By the latest news our pump has lowered the water about 400 feet below the surface, and we expect to get into the old bonanza in a short time. We have but a few weeks since shipped from Sacramento a pump of large capacity. We have at the mine an engineer, four California miners, a carpenter, a blacksmith and a number of Mexicans employed in and about the mine. Wood and timber, we find, is very cheaply and easily obtained. I had two assays made of the ore from our mines, one by the Professor of Chemistry in Santa Clara College, who reports his assay at $250.08 per ton and lead 43 per cent. Thomas Price, of San Francisco, assayed a piece for me, and he gives as a net result: silver, $325.02 per ton."

Dr. B. Cory, from whom we obtained the foregoing, is one of the directors of the company, as he states, organized three years ago under the name of the "Vaca, San Marcus and Bismarck Mining Company," with Mr. Fred. Werner as President; P. A. Grace, Secretary; and E. R. Lyle, Lewis Goodwin, Geo. W. Chesley, Dr. B. Cory and Fred. Werner as Directors.

The Guarisamey mines are located north of the mineral Guarisamey. "There are eight mines in this mineral district which are known as Serano, Copalaja, Encinillas, Cobres, La Gallera, Baragon, and several others, belonging to Mr. Frank McManus, an American resident of Chihuahua. These mines yield ore, the average of which gives $140 per ton. The last person who worked them regularly, Mr. Sanchez, extracted yearly a profit of $78,000 in silver. His mode of working was in the old Mexican patio amalgamating manner—grinding his ores with the arastra. Still, with all the disadvantages attending the want of proper machinery he was, as can be seen from the figures above, enabled to realize a handsome yearly profit. Upon the advent of Maximilian he sided with the Imperialists and took flight to save his life, having sold his mines for a mere pittance. Some tin placers are also found in this State.

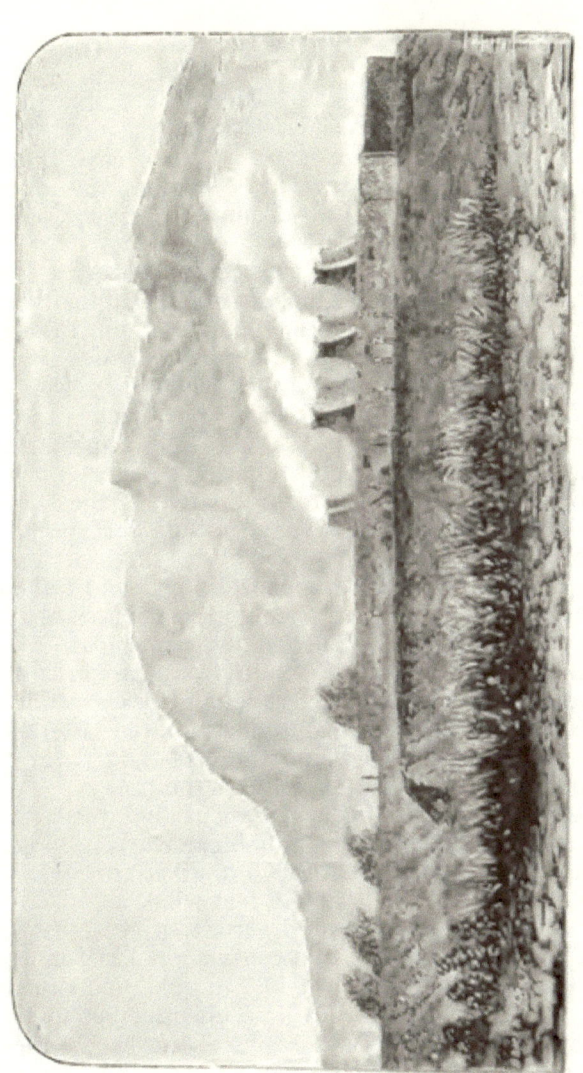

SMELTING WORKS OF THE DURANGO MAPIMI MINING COMPANY.

(Looking South.)

SITUATED IN MAPIMI, STATE OF DURANGO, MEXICO.

The principal mining districts of Durango are : San Dimas, Gavilanes, Guarisamey, Tamasula, Canelas, Sianori, Topia, Picachos, Biramoa, Bajada, Papasquiera, Guanacevi, Indee El Oro, Cuencamé and Mapimi. The other mining districts given by Garcia Cubas are: Topia, Tominil, Corpus, Comitala, Durango, Noria, Avino and Coneto.

The Mapimi mines have been worked for centuries, enriching their owners for several generations. Originally these mines were worked largely by the Spaniards, until their expulsion in 1829. Since that time they have been worked by the Mexicans until a few years ago, when they were purchased by Mr. A. B. Sawyer, and have since been worked by him with very gratifying results. The following statement of Mr. Sawyer we herewith present as his report upon the Mapimi mines, that have been consolidated by the Durango Mapimi Mining Company of Council Bluffs, incorporated at Council Bluffs, Iowa:

There are eight separate mines consolidated and owned by this company, viz.: Ojuela, San Vicente, Socobon, Santa Rita, El Carmen, Santa Maria, La Soledad and San Judas.

Ojuela mine is situated five (5) miles from the works, and is 870 feet in depth, with a shaft 768 feet deep. It is a great deposit of lead carbonates from eight (8) to one hundred (100) feet in width, and carries gold from $5.00 to $6.00, and silver from 24 to 33 ounces, and lead 15 per cent. to the ton.

San Vicente is similar ore, lying about 360 yards to the south. This mine is 675 feet deep, and carries from 15 ounces to 42 ounces in silver, and from $2.50 to $9.00 in gold. The ore body is from five (5) to fifty (50) feet wide.

Socobon is situated two hundred yards south-east of Ojuela, and yields from fifteen (15) to twenty-eight (28) ounces in silver, and carries from $3.00 to $4.50 in gold, and runs from 15 per cent. to 50 per cent. in lead. This mine has a tunnel 150 feet long, and has a depth of about 825 feet. At the bottom of the shaft, on the Ojuela mine, at a small expense, this mine can be made to communicate by a "cross cut," and also with the San Vicente, working advantageously these three mines through this one shaft, saving two additional shafts.

Santa Rita, one of the principal mines, is a continuation of the Socobon, and connected with it; yields from twenty (20) to seventy (70) ounces of silver, and carries from $2.50 to $20.00 in gold to the ton. The ore body is from three (3) to forty (40) feet wide, with a depth of from 300 to 450 feet.

El Carmen is quartz and carbonate of lead; new mine; yields from 50 ounces to 140 ounces in silver, with an ore body from two (2) to ten (10) feet wide. This mine has been worked to the depth of 75 feet, and is located six miles from the works.

Santa Maria or Tecolotes is a new mine of quartz ore, worked to the depth of twenty-five (25) feet. It is situated in the main body of the Bufa Mountains, with an ore body from one (1) to four (4) feet wide. This mine has yielded very rich ore, as high as 1,000 ounces to the ton. However, as will be seen, but little work has been done so far on this property.

La Soledad and Las Arcos, one mine with two entrances, not communicating one with the other, is quartz ore, and yields from 24 to 120 ounces of silver per ton, and is from three (3) to eight (8) feet wide, and in some places twenty (20) feet wide, and is about 300 feet deep, lying to the south-east of the Santa Rita.

San Judas is lead carbonates, ranging from 15 to 24 ounces per ton in silver. It is a great body of ore communicating with the Santa Rita. It carries gold from $2.00 to $4.50 per ton, and has been worked to the depth of 900 feet.

The company in possession of the above property are making extensive preparations for the thorough working of their mines. They have purchased a large engine, two large boilers, two No. 5 Baker blowers, and three large smelting furnaces, with all the outfit, to be sent to their mines, which have cost the company about $50,000. This, with the smelters and works they already have at the mines, should make a handsome return from the investment. We have herein given illustrations of the works at these mines, that are among the most celebrated of Durango.

"Guarisamey, the head of the surrounding district, owes its discovery to the lode of Tecolota, which crosses the high road to Cosala, in Sinaloa. The abundance and richness of its ores soon brought prospectors, who discovered the veins of Araña, Cinco Señores, Bolanos, Pisamide, Candelaria, Dolores, and Topia, with many others, every one of which was worked profitably. These lodes, or the most of them, were denounced by Zambraño, and all produced bonanzas, some of which were very rich.

"The mine of Araña was remarkable for containing between two small strips of rich ore, a cavity filled (like the bovedas of the mine in Zavala at Catorce) with a rich metalliferous dust, composed almost entirely of gold and silver. It was also distinguished by many of those rich spots commonly called 'clavos,' which, although of small extent in a hori-

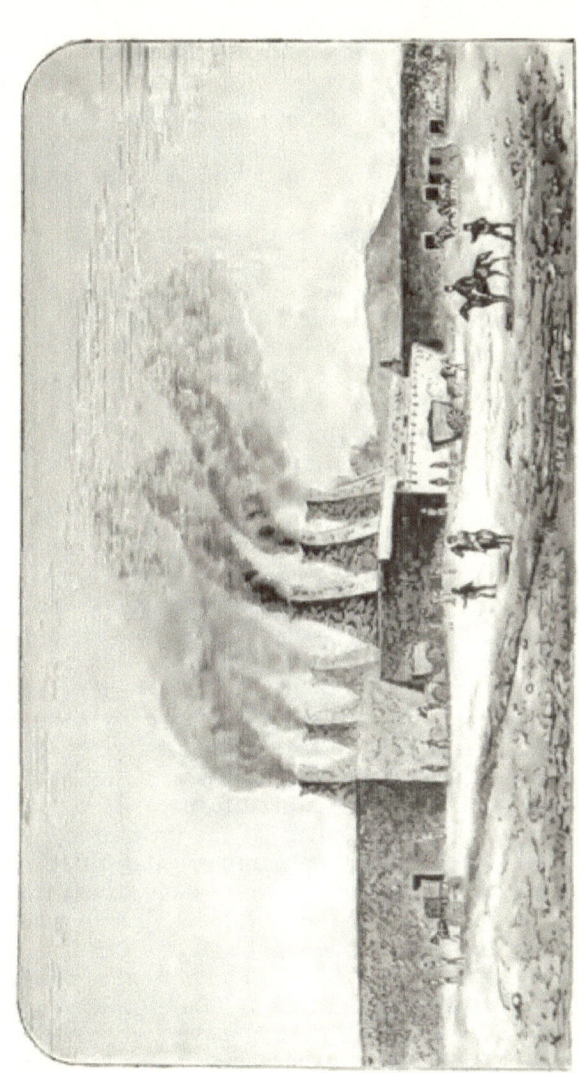

SMELTING WORKS OF THE DURANGO MAPIMI MINING COMPANY.

(Looking Northeast)

SITUATED IN MAPIMI, STATE OF DURANGO, MEXICO.

zontal position, were constant in perpendicular depth. The 'clavos' were worked to the depth of 180 varas, though the mine had no shaft; and during the whole of this space, the most ordinary ores yielded from 10 to 15 marcs to the monton of fifteen quintals, while the richest are said to have produced from 70 to 105."—[Ward on Mexico in 1827.]

The tin mines of Durango have lately been opened by the Durango Tin Mining Co., a large amount of capital having been invested. It is stated that the Durango Tin Mining Co. is working some 75 men, and in March last began smelting. No shipments of tin have yet been made. Mexican wagon freighters have offered to put the tin down at Laredo, Texas, for two and a half cents per pound, and a German firm has offered to deliver it to New York from the mines at four and a half cents per pound. The Mexican Central Railroad will reach the mines during the present year, and another, the Mexican National, at a later period. When these roads are completed the company can ship its tin by way of El Paso, Eagle Pass, or Laredo. Some specimens of the ore assay as high as 75 per cent. pure tin.

Iron Mines of Durango.—The *Journal of Charcoal Iron Workers* furnishes the following interesting account of the Piedra Azul (Blue Stone) Iron Works, situated on the banks of the Rio Tunal, some five miles south of Durango, Mexico. These works consist of a blast furnace, 35 x 8 inches; a heating furnace, a puddling furnace, one train of rolls, two sinking fires, one wooden helve hammer, and three smith fires. Power is obtained from a masonry dam across the Rio Tunal, giving a head and fall of 17 feet. There are four wheels—two over-shot, one under-shot and one turbine.

The blast furnace is built of stone. The bottom of the crucible is 24 inches square; the top, which is 5 feet 6 inches higher, is 32 inches square. The bosh then slopes, at an angle of 55° from the vertical, to 96 inches diameter. The crucible and bosh are built of sandstone, brought by wagons 200 miles. The shaft of the furnace is constructed of a silica fire-brick, made from clay and crushed quartz. It runs nearly straight for the first ten feet above the bosh, and is then drawn in by curved lines to the open top, 32 inches in diameter.

Blast is delivered cold from two $2\frac{1}{2}$-inch open tuyeres, the air being supplied by two iron blast cylinders, 60 inches diameter and 5 feet stroke, placed horizontally, and operated by an over-shot wheel. The charge is raised by hand winch, on an inclined plane, to the tunnel head, and consists of one buggy of oak charcoal, seven to ten "batteas" of ore, two batteas of a rotten limestone, and one-half battea of clay. These batteas are wooden dishes, and each contains two arrovas (50lbs.) of ore.

The charge may, therefore, be considered at from 350 to 500 lbs. of ore, 50 lbs. of limestone, 15 lbs. of clay to 20 bushels of charcoal.

The average daily product of the furnace is 60 quintals (6,000 lbs.) pig iron, the ore yielding 60 per cent. in the furnace, and requiring one and three-quarter quintals of charcoal to one of iron — to 175 bushels of 20 lbs. to one ton (2,000 lbs.) of pig iron.

Connected with the furnace plant there is a puddling furnace and a heating furnace, in both of which pine wood is used for fuel. There are also two sinking fires, in which pig iron and scrap can be converted into blooms. A short wooden helve trip hammer, raised by four cams on a wheel revolving at right angles to the hammer helve, is used for shingling the loupes and puddle balls. The cams strike the helve back of the hammer head, and a spring piece assists in intensifying the force of the blow.

The smith fires use pine charcoal for fuel. The charcoal is made in the Sierra Madre Mountains in small heaps, by Indians, and most of it is brought in upon the backs of burros. As these animals carry only 8 to 10 arrovas (200 to 250 lbs.), and in some instances can make but a trip to and from the iron works in three days, it is not surprising that oak charcoal sells at 12½ cents, and pine charcoal at 15 cents per arrova. Reduced to a bushel of 20 lbs., this would equal 10 cents per bushel for oak, and 12 cents for pine charcoal.

The charcoal is of good quality, but much reduced in size by handling and transportation. The price of the charcoal could be considerably reduced if the iron works produced its own fuel from wood more convenient to it.

Besides the iron works before described, the Iron Mountain Company, of Durango, Mexico, was incorporated in New York, and now proposes to erect extensive works, consisting of a blast furnace, with capacity of 200 tons of iron per week, and a large foundry. This last-named company hold the title to the whole of this immense iron deposit, called the Iron Mountain, near Durango, with the exception of one seventy-third, which is held by the former company.

Ward, in his work on Mexico, in 1821, says, in speaking of the iron mines of Durango: "Durango might in two years be rendered the depot of iron for Sombrerete, Zacatecas, Catorce, Batopilas, and all the mining districts south of Chihuahua [We might add, for the whole Republic], nor would the suc cess of the iron mines already taken up at Encarnacion interfere with this prospect, as their market would be confined to the central mining states, beyond which, from the difficulties of communication, their operations would hardly be extended." (Ward on "Mexico," in 1827.)

This subject has attained more importance since the construction of railroads has been commenced throughout the Republic, and the cost of iron imported for rails is as follows, taken from the "El Minero Mexicano" of December 9th, 1880:

	Per Ton.
Steel rails in England	$28.00
" United States	31.00

COST OF RAILS IN MEXICO.

Price in England	$28.00
Freight to Vera Cruz	9.00
Landing	2.00
Freight to Mexico according to tariff	54.32
Total	$93.32

COST OF RAILS IN SAN LUIS POTOSI.

In England	$28.00
Freight to Tampico	9.00
Landing	4.00
Freight to San Luis Potosi	60.00
Total	$101.00

Cost of rails in New York	$31.00
Freight to Tampico	15.00
Landing	4.00
Freight to San Luis Potosi	60.00
Total	$110.00

The *El Minero Mexicano* very naturally deduces from this that the rails had better be purchased in England, and imported to the ports of the republic, on account of the difference in the price of the rails as well as the freight. But if the extensive iron mines of Durango were developed the rails could be manufactured in the republic at a less price than they can be imported from either of the points mentioned, since the rails could be transported over the table lands of Durango, south-east to Mexico, over a railroad now

12

being built on a highway that is comparatively level, that puts the state in direct communication with the City of Mexico and the numerous railroads that are being built from that point throughout the republic. Then the rails could also be transported north to the Southern Pacific or Texas railways and shipped to El Paso, and from thence to Guaymas and Mazatlan, or to Chihuahua, to the railroad that is being built from that point to El Paso, and through a practicable pass in the mountains to Mazatlan, by way of Fuerte and Culiacan, or to Alamos and Guaymas. A large proportion of the territory of Durango, as we have seen, is situated upon the table lands, and the capital is in the midst of a vast plain, or rather in the south-western portion of the plain, that opens up a communication both to the north-east, and south-east to the points designated. On the west, however, and the south-west, the Sierra Madre extends, reaching the valleys and plains of Sinaloa by immense steppes or elevated plateaus, one above the other, which forms a barrier that is almost inaccessible, although a pass is reached on the north-west leading into Chihuahua, where the descent is more gradual, making communication practicable with Chihuahua and Alamos, in Sonora, thence to Fuerte, and from thence to Culiacan and Mazatlan, and Cosala, a new wagon road having lately been built from Mazatlan to Cosala. The iron industry is a most important one to Mexico; and foreign capital, invested properly, would be of great value to the republic, as well as very remunerative to the owners. A foundry could be built at the mines, and rails manufactured, and all kinds of mining machinery, and thus a vast trade could be opened. Says Mr. Ward:

" Iron abounds within a quarter of a league of the gates of Durango. The Cerro de Mercado is entirely composed of iron ores, of two distinct qualities. (crystallized and magnetic) but almost equally rich, as they both contain from 60 to 75 per cent. of pure iron. The operation of smelting these ores is attended with considerable difficulty An iron foundry, lately set up upon the banks of the river, one league from Durango, has failed, from the want of knowledge of the proper mode of treating the ores. A hacienda has been built in a situation where there is both water for machinery and an abundant supply of timber and charcoal; but as the proprietors do not possess the means of constructing a road for carts, (although from the nature of the ground, it might be accomplished with a very inconsiderable outlay) the conveyance of the ores on mules to the reduction works materially diminishes the profits of the speculation. With regard to the difficulty of working them, it might undoubtedly be overcome, as from the affinity of the iron of El Mercado to that of Dannemora, Swedish forgemen would understand the nature of the process at once."

Since the writing of Mr. Ward's book, the ore has been successfully treated, and manufactured into excellent mining tools, etc.

Mr. Geo. F. Ruxton, in his valuable work, entitled, "Adventures in Mexico and the Rocky Mountains," published in 1848, says that "this enormous mass of malleable iron, as he terms it, is isolated on the plain, and is supposed to be an aerolite, and is, consequently, not connected with any ledge or bed of ore. He also says its composition and physical character is identified with certain aerolites which fell in 1751, in Hungary. It contains 75 per cent. of pure iron, according to the analysis of a Mexican chemist, and some specimens which Humboldt procured were analyzed by the celebrated Klaproth, with about the same result."

We obtain the following data from a valuable pamphlet published in Mexico in 1878, entitled, "El Cerro de Mercado de Durango por Federico Weidner," in which the writer compares very justly the difference of the price of iron used in the foundry at Mazatlan with the price in England and also at Durango, as follows:

"At the port of Mazatlan, for example, in all iron of second fusion (pig iron) which is used in the establishment of Señor D. Joaquin Redo, as well as first material (or iron ore) the price per ton of 2,240 lbs. which is manufactured or melted in England, is as follows:

First price of the invoice, per ton..........$15 to $25
Freight by water, per ton .... 5 to 7
Unloading and carriage by mules, per ton... 5
Custom house duties, at 30 cts. per hundred, 5
                                            ———
        Total...............................$36

a little more or less per ton, or $1.60 per quintal.

"In the place of English iron, if they want to use Durango iron, the cost at the foundry of Flores would be $3 to $4 per quintal, or $60 to $80 per ton.

"Adding to this the freight between Mazatlan and Durango at $3.50 per quintal, or $80 per ton, with the purchase price at Mazatlan, at $60 to $80 per ton, makes a total of $156 per ton, more or less, or $7 per quintal."

The iron of Mazatlan, at $6 to $10 per quintal, when cast by the piece, costs $12 to $16 for complicated work; but when half-finished or plain, it costs $8 per quintal, or $180 per ton; so that in Durango, the minimum price is $15 per quintal, or $336 per ton. Adding to this the freight to Mazatlan, makes the minimum price for finished iron $20 per quintal, or $448 per ton."

This is sufficient argument, we take it, for the establishment of a foundry at Durango alongside of the Cerro de Mercado, or mountain of iron, in the immediate vicinity. The author goes on to show that since the first cost in England is $20 per ton while it can be procured in their neighborhood for $4 to $6 in ore, and carriage to a foundry erected would not make it more than $5 to $7. He also mentions the existence of furnaces, retorts, and other apparatus which were abandoned by various parties up to 1856, on account of their being unable to successfully reduce the ore, and points out the fact that the ore of the Cerro de Mercado can be successfully treated and manufactured at a very great profit. He also publishes a scientific examination of the ore and the surrounding locality, its extent and analysis, which we condense below. He goes on to explode an error that exists on the part of travelers and scientific men that this immense mass of iron is an aerolite, and publishes in the pamphlet the geological structure or formation around and underneath it, and pronounces the aerolite theory a *cabal* on the Cerro de Mercado, and further that it is of volcanic origin; and points out the fact that the iron mines of England have produced 15,000,000 of quintals annually for the last 330 years, amounting to $9,900,000,000, or more than seven times the amount of gold and silver coined from all the mines of Mexico from 1690 to 1803. He says the Cerro de Mercado is 1,750 varas in length from east to west, and 400 varas in width, and the height from the surface of the plain of San Antonio 234 varas, which cuts it, as it were, in the middle horizontally, and the resulting estimate in cubic measurement is 60,000,000 cubic varas, and by analysis of the contents or percentage of pure iron it contains, estimates the amount of ore in the whole mass at more than 5,000,000,000 of quintals, from which he calculates that, taking the percentage of pure iron to be 50 per cent., although it assays 75 per cent., the whole mass will then produce 2,500,000,000 quintals of metallic or pure

CERRO DE MERCADO DURANGO MEXICO.

iron, and, estimating its value at $5 per quintal, it would represent not less than the enormous sum of $12,500,000,000, or more than three times all the products of the mines of Mexico from 1772 to 1880, which we have estimated to be about $4,000,000,000.

Further, in order to fully comprehend the immense amount of iron in this solid mass, by calculating the amount produced in England at fifteen millions of quintals annually for the last 330 years, the whole amount is 4,950 millions of quintals, or only a little over one third of the amount of pure iron contained in the Cerro de Mercado (calculating the amount at 12,500,000,000 of quintals, valued at no less than from 60 to 70 billions of dollars), which has been aptly termed a mountain of iron, and lies almost untouched, while the same metal now so much in demand within the boundaries of the Republic is imported from England (outside of late importations of machinery, locomotives, etc.), as we have already shown ; the difference in freight as well as first cost, giving the trade to England.

The amount of iron which Mr. Weidner calculates to be in sight, or cropping out of the ground, is, as we have seen, 2,500,000,000 quintals (or cwt.) of pure iron ; but there is a much larger amount which will be seen as follows : —

While, by actual measurement of this enormous mass, we have on the surface of the ground the above results ; yet we must remember that the great bulk of the ore lies beneath the surface, according to all precedents in iron deposits. Mr. Weidner himself says :

" Thus it is, speaking only of the metal which is in sight on the surface of the ground. But it may be supposed that the quantity which is found below the surface is much greater, because it is thus with all metallic beds of this class ; and it is also proven by a little hill of the same nature, distant easterly from the Cerro de Mercado about a quarter of a league (or three quarters of a mile); it rises about ten varas above the plain that extends towards the ranch of San Ignacio. This little hill, which looks like a forest on the right-hand side of the accompanying plat, must form, with the principal "Cerro," a subterranean connection, and the conduits of both must penetrate like the roots of a tree to the very depths of the earth, there uniting with one great deposit of metals, of which both " Cerros" do not form more than a small part, which, giving way at some remote time to the pressure of subterranean vapors, burst in a liquid state, breaking and tearing to the surface of the earth and spreading itself over it."

"This idea that the Cerro de Mercado has emanated from the bowels of the earth through some crevices, and that its subterranean mass extends to great distances and depths, is even corroborated by the fact that, in the extension of its central line towards the west, we find in the lands of the farms of Tapias and Murga a number of ferruginous veins, and extending the same line towards the east, it passes by a little hill, also of iron, which, it is said, is on the road to Panuco, and finally it enters the centre of Breña, whose volcanoes, by their black color, the great specific weight and quantity of alloy of its basaltic rocks, we may consider as contemporaneous, or the immediate precursors of the eruption of the Cerro de Mercado." Suffice it to say, that we may safely calculate that but one fifth of the amount of iron contained in this mountain crops out on the surface of the plain, and that beneath it lies an immense body of ore that is practically inexhaustible, extending for long distances, and that the mass must have been enormous to produce by its own irresistible bulk, aided by vapors, this most wonderful of all the mineral deposits of the world. Enough iron lies in this deposit to supply all the foundries of both hemispheres for centuries to come, and the railroad communication now under headway will enable Mexico to place her iron in every market. While there are many mining enterprises in the republic worthy of investment, with promises of fabulous returns, we do not hesitate to say that the iron industries of Mexico will in the near future assume an importance that will equal, if not surpass, her silver productions, which are well known to have exceeded all other nations, and that the Cerro de Mercado will give this great iron future to the Mexican Republic.

Curious Caves of Durango.

From Cosala, in Sinaloa, to the foot of the mountains, a distance of five leagues due east, Santa Ana, a small rancho, is situated, and near it are some mines of silver and magistral. The road here enters a cañon, and the traveler soon gets enveloped in the mountains, which rise almost perpendicularly. Strata of porphyry, granite, limestone and alabaster are found on each side.

A small stream runs along the bottom of the cañon, and leads up to the table-land, which soon commences. On the boundaries of Durango, immense herds of cattle are seen grazing on the plains, mingling with elk and the fallow deer, and black-tailed deer; the latter, however, frequents mostly the inaccessible mountains.

The celebrated caves of the state are located 30 leagues from San Antonio, and 16 leagues from Cosala, or about 48 miles. The caves are situated in a small circular valley or basin 100 yards in diameter. The road lies down the cañon, 14 leagues below, to this basin.

The caves are called Las Cuevas de San Miguel. The largest is called San Miguel, and is 240 feet in length and 80 feet high, and 150 feet wide, forming a large room. The roof is a regular arch in formation or curvature. In the back wall opposite the entrance, are found openings of different sizes. One of them was penetrated by a traveler, who describes them in a book entitled, "The Northwestern part of Mexico." He says he penetrated 130 feet, and found intricate windings and subdivisions or openings on each side.

The origin of the caves is unknown, but it is supposed that they were inhabited by the aborigines or ancient Aztecs. They have never been completely explored, as near as we can ascertain, and the attention of antiquarians is called to them, as relics of the former inhabitants might be found. From the caves, the distance to Plomosas is 40 leagues, and to the city of Durango, 40.

Coahuila de Zaragoza.

CHAPTER I.

Boundaries and General Description.

The State of Coahuila de Zaragoza takes its latter name from General Ignacio Zaragoza, one of her distinguished citizens and patriots of the 5th of May, 1862. The state was formerly united with Texas and was erected into a department in 1837, and admitted as a state in 1847. It was united to Nuevo Leon in 1857, and assigned its present boundaries as one of the states of the republic in 1868. The state is bounded on the north by the Rio Grande, on the east by Tamaulipas and Nuevo Leon, and on the south by Zacatecas, and on the west by Chihuahua and Durango. The state contains 9,500 square leagues, or 42,066,000 acres, and claims 125,400 inhabitants (in 1883). It comprises the districts of the Centre, of Parras, Nazas, Monclova, and Rio Grande. The greater part of the state is covered with the vast plains called the Bolson de Mapimi on the west, while the remaining portions are mountainous. The principal mountains of the northern part of the state are El Pico, Etereo, La Sierra del Carmen, and Lomerios de Peyotes; in the central and southeastern, Santa Rosalia, San Marcos, La Fragua, La Paila, Sierra Azul, Coahuila, Chiflon, Angostura, and Sierra Madre. In these mountains many small streams are formed, which take an easterly direction and empty into the Rio Bravo (or Rio Grande). The Sabinas River forms the Salado River in the State of Nuevo Leon, which uniting with the Saltillo and Patos rivers, form the Sabinas, which empties into the San Juan, and thence carries the waters into the Rio Grande at Camargo, in the State of Tamaulipas.

The state has been less developed than any state of the republic; but its resources are none the less wonderful. Its agricultural productions in 1878 were $1,286,274. The amount of corn was 39,100,000 kils., value, $650,000; coffee, 900,000 kils., value, $225,000, and cotton, 1,500,000 kils., value, $156,250. The wines produced in this state are of a superior quality. A gold medal was awarded at the

Philadelphia Centennial for their excellence. Large forests of timber exist in the state containing all the valuable woods and timbers for building purposes.

The Bolson de Mapimi, which extends throughout the western part of the state, is a deserted region and uninhabitable. The agricultural districts of the state, however, are in possession of a rich soil with a wonderful fertility. The lands along the banks of the Sabinas River and its tributaries, as well as the Nadadores, its largest branch, are exceedingly productive, producing corn, coffee, sugar-cane and cotton, and all the vegetables in great profusion. The grazing regions are also confined to the streams and their immediate vicinity. The principal agricultural regions are regions around Nava, on the road from Piedras Negras in the northeastern part of the state, to the old presidio of Lampazos, in the state of Nuevo Leon, and the regions around the city of Saltillo, in the southern part of the state, where some wheat is also raised; and Sabinas, situated north of the centre of the state, and Progresso, and the region near Monclova, on the Nadadores River. The surface of the country around Saltillo is mountainous, diversified by valleys and cañons, through which small streams pass. The grazing districts are near Saltillo, Arizpe, Agua Nueva, Patos, Sauceda, and San Antonio in the southern part of the state, and Cienegas, Nadadores, Abosolo, Panuco, and Progresso, near the centre, and on the large number of tributary streams of the Sabinas River, near Sabinas and Santa Rosa, north of and northeast of the central part of the state, extending along the banks of the Sabinas in a southeasterly direction, and on the small stream called the Rio Escondido and its tributaries, extending northeast, and reaching to the Rio Grande at Piedras Negras.

CHAPTER II.

Cities, Towns, and Factories.

The city of Saltillo is the capital of the state, and possesses about 17,000 inhabitants (in 1883); perhaps 20,000, since the connection with the Mexican national railway, which has brought it into communication with the American system of railways. The city is well built, with paved streets, and is situated on the slope of a ridge which crosses the whole valley on the road from Monterey. There are several hotels and stores in the city, and quite an extensive trade is carried on from the United States, both by rail and the usual pack-train transportation; and some traffic in agricultural productions, among which may be mentioned corn and wheat, as the principal trade. Sheep and goat skins are also extensively trafficked in the immediate vicinity.

The city is sixty or more miles nearer the city of Mexico than Monterey, and is on the direct line of the Mexican National Railway, which commences at New Laredo on the Mexican side, and is now being built to Mexico city. Saltillo is situated on the summit of the Sierras, some 8,000 feet above the level of the sea. It is destined to be a favorite resort for pleasure seekers, and is even now claiming to be the Saratoga of Mexico. The railroad officials look upon it as one of the important places upon the Mexican National Line. The climate is delightful, and it is the intention of certain capitalists to build a large hotel here for the accommodation of American winter travel. The railroad from Monterey to this point has some magnificent scenery, and the tourist will not fail to find in the trip many attractions, more particularly mentioned hereafter. There are in the district of the centre, formerly called the Saltillo District, several cotton factories, viz.: "La Hibernia," "La Esmeralda," "La Aurora," "La Libertad," "El Labrador," and "Palomas."

The city also contains a fine church, fronting the main square; the church of the convent of San Esteban, a convent for the Sisters of Charity, in which young ladies are educated; an abandoned church, used as a soldiers' barracks, which was formerly built by the Jesuits, and a fine amphitheatre, situated on the square of San Esteban. The Alameda is celebrated as one of the beautiful parks of Mexico. On the hill, to the southward, is a small fort, built during the empire. The tourist and traveler will find much here to interest him. The site of the battle of Buena Vista lies only five miles from Saltillo. The old hacienda still remains as one of the historic places of the republic, and will well repay a visit.

The town of San Fernando de Rosa, lately called Zaragoza, has about 6,000 inhabitants, and is located thirty miles southeast of Piedras Negras. The lands around the town are irrigable, and produce wheat, corn, sugar-cane, beans, and the various vegetables.

In the district of Parras, the thriving city of Parras de la Fuente is found, containing some 8,000 inhabitants. The town is well built; many of the houses are of two stories,

being quite spacious, with courts in the centre, and built
with much taste. It is an old settled place, and has always
been noted for the excellence of its wine and brandy. The
city takes its name from a species of vine called Parra.
The city extends a couple of miles along the side of a hill.
The smaller vineyards run along the declivity, the larger ones
beyond the town on the plain. The hill consists of porous
limestone, abounds in water, which is collected in tanks, and
conducted by acequias through the vineyards and the principal streets of the town. Many of the houses have wells in
their courts. The surplus water is conducted by aqueducts
or ditches to the plains, where it is utilized in irrigating, first
the gardens and vineyards, and beyond these, the fields of
wheat and maize. The town is surrounded by a fine agricultural district, covered with orchards and gardens, plantations of maguey, and grain fields.

The city is situated about eighty-five miles southwest of
Saltillo. Considerable business is here transacted in the
staple Mexican products. A cotton factory, called the "La
Estrella," is located in this place. The cotton industry of
the state has been, and is destined to be one of great importance, with increasing demands for the home market, as well
as a more extended trade. The district of Nazas produces
most of the cotton of the state, and has great capacities for
cotton culture; indeed, we have been informed by a competent engineer, who made a careful examination in the interest of one of the railroad companies, that the district of
Nazas was the great cotton region of the whole republic.

Monclova has 4,236 inhabitants (in 1883), and does considerable business. One cotton factory, called "La Abundancia," is located here, which runs 500 looms. The other
principal towns are San Buenaventura, with 3,500 inhabitants; Candela, with 3,037 inhabitants, and Cuatro Cienegas,
with 3,200 inhabitants. The principal vineyards are owned
by Senores Aneceto del Castello, Jesus Carranza, and Albino
Morales.

Mineral Resources.

The mineral wealth of this state in the near future may
become one of its greatest sources of revenue and profit. It
has all the advantages of the other mining states in its geological formation, and mining was at one time very profitable
to the old Spanish miners, as appears from the following
record: —

In the archives of the Presidio of Santa Rosa, now a town called Villa de Musquiz, an official report is recorded as having been made by Don Felipe Torralva, president of the mining board of the department in which Santa Rosa is situated; it is dated Nov. 24, 1844. It shows that, at that time, 51 mines were worked in said mineral district, with a result as follows, viz.: eighteen mines produced ores yielding from 4 to 6 ounces of silver per carga, or $28 to $42 per ton; 17 mines yielding 1 marc to the carga, or $56 per ton; 5 mines yielding 3 marcs to the carga, or $168 per ton; 1 mine yielding 6 marcs to the carga, or $336 to the ton; 1 mine yielding 8 marcs to the carga, or $448 to the ton; 1 mine yielding 30 marcs to the carga, or $1,680 to the ton; and 1 mine yielding 100 ounces to the carga, or $5,600 to the ton. In the latter mine, which is known as the San Juan mine according to tradition, large pieces of pure silver were found. In the mines of Santa Gertrudés and El Pabellon, which produced ores yielding as much as 30 marcs of silver per carga, or $1,680 per ton, pieces of virgin silver weighing one ounce and more were found. Leaves of silver as thin as paper were also found between layers of slate.

Gold, silver, copper, lead, salt, nitre, onyx, alabaster, and a large deposit of iron, have been already discovered, although but little attempt has been made to develop this important feature of the state's resources.

There are no less than eight cotton factories in the state, and fifty flour and corn mills, besides several saw-mills. This state is the least known of any part of the republic, the northern portion especially being marked in the maps until lately as an unknown region. Although it has a large territory, and rich soil, a large proportion of which may be irrigated, it has a small population, and hitherto has had no means of transportation other than that by horses, mules, and burros. This is now being entirely changed by the railway development. The amount of the assessed value of real estate, city and country, has been reported at $5,346,476.

The Mexican National and Exploring Company of Philadelphia have, among other claims, purchased the Bolsa de Judas silver and copper mine. The mine is located about ten miles from Cándela, upon the mountain of the same name, and has four pertenencias. The assays show some "six dollars of silver, and some 15 per cent. copper to the ton, of outcropping ores." The ore is a carbonate, and promises well. The mine was formerly worked by the Aztecs. Two shafts were found to be sunk sixty feet, following the carbonates.

The Panuco claims of the same company are situated "about thirty miles from Cândela, and some distance from Monclova, near the former mine. The large body of ore developed, showing "40 per cent." of copper, makes the mine one of great promise.

After the declaration of independence, four mines were worked in the district of Viezca, viz.: Sierra de Ramirez, Sierra de Timulco, Cañon de Ribera, and Sierra de Hornos. The mines of Matchuapile, situated in the mountain, and near the hacienda of the same name, of the estate of Salado, are reported to have been in bonanza between 1720 and 1735. Near this rancho a town formerly existed of several thousand inhabitants, who were engaged in mining; but the people were driven out by the Indians in 1735.

Iron has been found near Monclova and Viezca; copper and lead in Reis and Guadalupe; nitre is found at San Blas, and sulphur and copperas in the Peyote hills.

Coal has been found at Santa Rosa of a good quality, lying in an immense bed, from the indications, with a vein from four to six feet in thickness. The coal seems to be bituminous, and is easily coked. At Piedras Negras, and also on the American side, large fields of coal have been discovered. At Eagle Pass the supply is so abundant that it may practically be said to be inexhaustible. It may thus be seen that Coahuila, so much unknown heretofore, is assuming great prominence on account of its great mineral wealth.

NUEVO LEON.

CHAPTER I.

General Description and Agricultural Resources.

Nuevo Leon is bounded on the north and west by Coahuila ; on the north and east by Tamaulipas; on the southwest by San Luis Potosi, and on the south and east by Tamaulipas. The area of the state is 6,695 square miles, or 4,000 square leagues ; the population in 1882 was 194,861. The state is mountainous, and for the first sixty miles after crossing the northern border, the route over the Mexican National from Laredo to Monterey, leads through poor sandy country, where nothing seems to grow but mesquite, cactus, and withal presents an unfavorable impression. After this distance is reached, the country begins to improve ; in fact, as soon as the mountains are reached, beyond the plains just passed. For a hundred miles or more we ride through a beautiful valley that is showing some evidences of agriculture. and stock-raising, and pass into the more cultivated districts, which are very fertile. Along the streams, and in the cultivated districts in their immediate vicinity, orchards containing peaches, pomegranates, apples, pears, lemons, oranges, mulberries, aguacates, figs, bananas, grapes, etc., are found. The chirimoya, so celebrated, is found throughout many portions of the state.

In 1878, the amount of corn produced was 751,200 bushels, value, $250,000 ; maguey, 1,098,000 plants, value produced, $144,250 ; tobacco, 45,750 cwt., value, $4,490 ; piloncillo, 1,368,250 cwt., value, $437,840 ; ixtle, 3,811,875 cwt., value, $86,475 ; sugar, 300,000 cwt., value, $96,000 ; total amount of products, $1,329,138 ; value of stock of all kinds, $868,021. The principal streams of the state are the Salado, El Candela, El Sabina, and the San Juan. The latter is about 130 miles long, and empties into the Rio Grande. Ebony, Brazil wood, beech, oak, ash, coyotilla, huisache, cedar, palmetto, frijalillio, huiachillo, elm, cypress, pine, and other species of timber, are found in the mountains. The elevation of the state reaches from 1,010 feet above the sea level, to 2,350 feet. The climate is therefore temperate or semi-tropical.

CHAPTER II.

Cities and Towns.

Monterey, the capital of the state, is on the line of the Mexican National Railway, and is reached in about ten hours and a half from New Laredo. The city is situated on the Santa Catarina River, 602⅔ miles from Mexico City, and is 1,626 feet above the level of the sea, and is built in a basin formed by the great mountains surrounding it. Splendid springs flow through it in several directions, pouring out streams of pure and healthy water, large enough to run a mill, or irrigate all the country around it. The streets are well paved, and are kept quite clean. The city is built mostly of stone, and has several fine churches, an hospital, a college, a convent of the Sisters of Charity, a city hall, several beautiful squares, hotels, and 37,000 inhabitants. The Bishop's Palace is situated on a hill, west of the city, on the right hand side of the Saltillo road.

Monterey has a fine trade that is continually increasing. The future of this city seems to be a promising one, and its importance as the largest city of northeastern Mexico, has added much to its future, by drawing the attention of the railroad. "Nature, as if to complete and perfect Monterey as a sanitarium, in addition to her magnificent climate the year round, has placed, within a distance of three miles, and at the foot of one of the mountains adjacent, a series of thermal springs, whose curative qualities are well known. The diseases most benefited are rheumatism, gout, scrofula, diseases of the liver and kidneys, dropsy," etc.

The other principal towns are Cadereyta Jimenez, of 16,000 inhabitants; Montemorelos, of 10,000; Linares 12,000; Galeana, 6,500 inhabitants; Doctor Arroyo 1,800, and Lampazos de Naranjo of 7,000 inhabitants. The factories of the state are "La Fama," "La Leona," "El Porvenir," "La Constancia," "El Lucero," and several sugar factories. The state produces also cotton, and is well adapted to most of the productions that any other state of the republic may raise.

Mineral Resources.

The town Villadama was founded as a mining settlement in 1646, under the name of Mineral de San Pedro Boca de Leones. The mine Chihuahua is located in this district "with an inferior tunnel of 500 feet, and a well-defined vein of galena ore, running from three to nine feet in width, and carrying from forty to sixty ounces of silver to the ton." The mine Coayache contains "a valuable vein of earth ore, running from one to three feet wide, which produces from 200 to 350 ounces of silver to the ton." The mine Moreno contains "a rich vein of galena ore, carrying silver running from one to three feet in width, and producing from $200 to $300 per ton." The Farandula was reported by the Spaniards as a good mine, but that it contained rebellious ore. The above-named mines are owned by the Anglo Texas Mexican Mining and Smelting Company, of Houston, Texas.

The Rosario mine, which contains low grade ores, is situated within six or eight miles of Salinas Victoria, and is owned by the Rosario Mining Company, of Dallas, Texas. The San Juan Chico mine is located in the district of San Antonio. The Spaniards in 1756 worked the old claim, and it is said found a silver bonanza. The new claim is on the old vein, and at ten feet depth, the width was from twelve to fourteen inches, and composed of argentiferous galena, with gang of heavy spar. The dip is twenty degrees, with blue limestone on hanging wall, and siliceous bastard limestone on foot wall. Assays show from $50 to $300 per ton, and of lead sixty-five to seventy per cent. The Boludo copper mine is situated about twelve miles from Candela, on the Boludo Mountain, in the San Geronimo gap. A large body of ore has been found that assays $7\frac{11}{100}$ per cent., or $143\frac{4}{10}$ lbs. per ton of copper, with traces of silver and gold. The mine has not yet been developed.

The Buena Vista mine is located in the Minas Viejas belt, on the Minas Viejas Mountains, about fifteen miles from Villaldama. "The formation is much broken up, and in cracks, crevices, and joints of rocks, of a yellowish ochre clay, very abundant, and assaying $20 per ton. The ore is rich argentiferous galena, assaying $150 to $350 per ton."

The Yguana silver mines are located about twenty-five miles from Lampazos, near the line of the Mexican National Railroad. The district was worked from 1756 to 1812, by the Spaniards, when they were driven out by the Mexicans.

The Minas Viejas mine is located fifteen miles from Villaldama, State of Nuevo Leon, adjoining the Guadalupe mine. The mine has two shafts, called "San Jose," and "El Carmen," and is reputed to be a valuable property, with large bodies of ore in sight; assay from $18 to $270 silver per ton. The mine was formerly worked by the Spaniards.

The Rosario mine is situated six miles from Salinas, near the line of the Mexican National, and is reported to have developed good ore. The above mines are owned by the Mexican National Exploring and Mining Company of Philadelphia.

The state contains also iron, lead, sulphur, nitrate of potash, alabaster, white and colored marble, and muriate of soda, and a large bed of coal. A large deposit of magnetic iron ore has been found upon the Carisal Mountain, about twelve miles from Candela, and nineteen miles from Lampazos, at a point named Piedro Yman Gap. The mine proper lies about eighty feet below the crest of the mountain, where the deposit on the surface is about 50 to 120 feet in width. The ore is found in a vein. This deposit of ore is almost wholly magnetic oxide; a slight proportion of other varieties, and runs, it is said, sixty per cent. pure iron.

TAMAULIPAS.

CHAPTER I.

Description; Cities and Towns, Free Zone and Mineral Resources.

The State of Tamaulipas is bounded on the north by the United States or Rio Grande River, and by Nuevo Leon on the northwest and on the west, and southwest by San Luis Potosi; on the south by Vera Cruz, and on the east by the Gulf of Mexico; area, 4,228 sq. leagues, or 11,102 sq. miles. The state is traversed by part of the Sierra Madre range, which crosses the state from the northwest to the southeast, from the town of Villagran, near the divisory line of Neuvo Leon on the line between this state and San Luis Potosi, to the Hacienda del Chaburo Mountain; spurs extend in different directions, forming many beautiful valleys,—the Santa Barbara and Chamal being the principal ones. The low, flat lands along the coast and Rio Grande River are unhealthy, that on the coast being subject to yellow fever. That portion west of the mountains, however, is cool and dry and healthy. Most of the streams of the state carry their waters easterly into the gulf; one or two small streams only reaching the Rio Grande on the north. The state is fertile on the banks of streams and produces corn, cotton, rice, sugar-cane, beans, peas, sweet potatoes, and other vegetables. The maguey is extensively raised, as in almost all parts of Mexico.

The principal fruits are peaches, bananas, mangos, the goayaba, citrons, the aguacate, and the chirimoya. Abundance of timber fit for building purposes, and fine cabinet work, including ebony and other valuable woods, are found on the mountain sides.

The eastern part of the state and the northeastern on the Rio Grande is admirably adapted for stock-raising. Horses, cattle, sheep, and goats are raised in large numbers, as well as large numbers of mules. The total amount of agricultural productions in 1878 was $2,174,280, of which $1,677,120 was

194

of corn, and wheat, $82,000. The amount in kilograms in corn was 79,383,680, and wheat, 1,455,500.

The state is divided into four districts; Del Norte, Del Centre, Del Sur, and Cuarto Distrito.

Matamoras is one of the principal ports of entry of the republic, and contains about 18,000 inhabitants. The city is located on the west bank of the Rio Grande, opposite the town of Brownsville, Texas, and about thirty miles from the river's mouth. The trade of the whole state is considerable, and Matamoras controls the most of it, and is recognized as the centre of the large trade of the free zone. On March 17, 1858, the free zone was established for the benefit of Matamoras, Reynosa, Camargo, Mier, Guerrero, and Nuevo Laredo, in which these towns were to be free from all duties except municipal duties and state taxes. The decree was first issued by the legislature of the state, and on July 30, 1861, was approved by the general government. The facilities of the "zona" added to its location, made the American side from 1861 to 1865 a great depot for supplies of all kinds going in, and for cotton, etc., out. Matamoras at that time had 40,000 inhabitants. The present annual exports of the zone to the United States are about $2,000,000; about one half of which is silver; the remainder being hides, skins, ixtle fibre, wool, live animals, etc. For the year ending Sept. 30, 1880, the imports at Matamoras were $2,176,772, of which $1,052,255 were bonded goods, and $1,124,517 were American goods. Probably 25 to 40 per cent. of these imports are consumed within the limits of the "Zona Libre," and the remainder are sent to the interior, mostly to Monterey and Saltillo, San Luis Potosi, Durango, Zacatecas, Victoria, etc. The present limits of the "zona" are from the mouth of the Rio Grande up the river to the state lines, a few miles above Monterey, Nuevo Laredo, and back from the river a narrow, but rather indefinite distance, not exceeding in any place about 25 miles. The ports of first entry are Matamoras, Camargo, Mier, and Monterey (Nuevo Laredo). The towns of Reynoza, Guerrero and other villas and ranches within this limit are entitled to receive from the ports of first entry. The population of the zona is about 50,000. The following we copy from Consul Sutton's report of February 28, 1881 : —

"All goods imported into any one of the ports of first entry must be regularly entered at the custom-house under the exacting conditions of the tariff. All goods which are not by the Mexican tariff free of duty must pay one half cent per pound on the gross weight and one and thirty-seven hundredths per cent. of the regular Mexican tariff. Any error in the declaration as to weight, value, description, etc., is punishable by the same heavy fine as on goods entered at other ports where full duties are exacted. When these goods have passed the custom-house they may be held in store by the merchant an unlimited time or may be consumed free of any further charge.

"When any goods thus imported are to be sent to any point inside the 'Zona Libre' they must be again regularly manifested and a bond given to produce and file within a certain prescribed time the "guia," properly indorsed by the various custom officers along the route and at the destination. No charge is made except for the paper, stamps, etc. The goods once arrived at the point of destination may be there consumed free of further tariff duties.

"Goods destined to the interior are regularly entered and are then subject to the full Mexican tariff, less the amount already paid. These are sent with similar restrictions as to return of "guia," etc., as in the 'Zona.'

"In the paying of duties on goods to the interior one thing has to be considered, although it does not strictly concern the 'Zona Libre.' This is the possibility of buying what is called custom-house paper and using the same in paying a portion of the duties. This paper is of a variable character as to quantity, availability, and price. At present a small supply is said to be obtainable at about 80 cents on the dollar. I understand that this year it may be used to pay 84 cents on the dollar of the amount of duties which have not been paid on entering and which are due when goods are manifested for the interior.

"If the 'Zona Libre' did not exist, the local frontier trade would be almost entirely transferred to the American bank, and only those goods intended for the interior would be entered at the custom-house. This was plainly shown by the condition of affairs at Piedras Negras, which is above the limits of the 'Zona Libre.'

"Although calico was freely used by the residents of that city, I found but a single piece in stock, and that had not come over in the regular way. The merchant who had it, said he would sell five or six yards per annum in cases of emergency; that is, in cases where there was not sufficient time to send to Eagle Pass, Texas, just across the river, there to buy and smuggle across. Nearly every article needed for local consumption, which was not free of any import duty, was thus bought in Eagle Pass and smuggled across to Piedras Negras. The legitimate business is thus confined to free imports, to imports intended for the interior *via* that custom-house, and to the exports and consumption of Mexican products. The same conditions obtain all along this frontier and would doubtless have the same results. As matters now stand, the 'Zona' merchant pays the local charges previously noted and the very high occupation taxes or licenses and can sell at equal advantage American or foreign goods. The American merchant on the other bank can only sell to good advantage American goods,— foreign goods which are free of duty and those which pay but a small import duty. Those foreign goods which pay high import duty in the United States can be purchased cheaper in the 'Zona.' Of late years the increased demand for American goods, the lower taxes, greater security, lower import duties on many foreign goods, have aided to make trade in many articles more profitable on the American than on the Mexican bank. This condition prevails to-day along the 'Zona,' and is likely to continue, although it may be modified by the opening of railways."

The American Bonded System.

" The privileges of the 'Zona' are materially aided by the facility and cheapness of bringing European goods to this city *via* the United States. The port of Brownsville (Brazos de Santiago) is nearly as much a Mexican as an American port of entry. The European goods which passed through that district last year all came to this city, and lacked less than $100,000 of equaling the imports of American goods. (See Table A.)

" In former years most of those European goods came to Brazos in American vessels, having been first entered at New York or New Orleans. Of late years, owing to the high freight rates between those ports and Brazos, it has been found more profitable to bring more of them direct from Europe in European vessels.

" For the year ended Sept, 30, 1876, the direct imports at Brazos were 47 per cent., while in the year ending Sept. 30, 1879, they had increased to 68 per cent. of the total imports of such goods. As the customs charges for this class of goods are very small, they are laid down in Matamoras almost as cheaply as American goods.

" As many correspondents have inquired of me if the 'Zona Libre' had been abolished, I would state in this connection that at the present I know of no effort being made to secure its abolition. On the contrary, as previously stated, two ports of first entry have been reopened to commerce with the United States with all the privileges of the 'Zona.'"

Victoria is the capital of the state, with about 6,000 inhabitants, and is beautifully situated at the foot of a high mountain. It is well watered by a large, clear stream and lies in the midst of gardens and fields of sugar-cane.

Tampico is one of the important ports of the republic, second only to Vera Cruz, and is situated at the mouth of the Panuco River, which is navigable to Altamira, over a distance of about eighteen miles. The population of the town is about 5,000. A large trade is carried on here with Europe and the United States. There are six mining districts in the state, *viz.:* San Nicholas, San Jose, Bustamente, El Zique, La Miquihuana, and Villagran. San Nicholas has twenty-five abandoned mines and four worked. The Miquihuana district has four abandoned mines. The district of Bustamente has twelve abandoned mines. The duties paid to the Spanish crown on record indicate that the mines were good mines. Silver, copper and lead were produced for the Spanish owners. The district of Villagran, known when first discovered as Real de Borbon, contains some old abandoned gold and silver mines. Iron ore has been found in Victoria, and in the vicinity of Aldama, silver, copper, and iron, and slate quarries, and in the vicinity of Ornelas, alabaster of a fine quality, and near Santa Ana of Tamaulipas, jasper and marble have been found.

Near San Carlos, Morelos, Guerrero, and Camargo, a mineral belt has been discovered containing copper, and at Guerrero and Carmago, coal has been discovered, and near Guerrero, red ochre and red lead.

VERA CRUZ.

CHAPTER I.

General Description, Cities and Towns, and Agricultural and Mineral Resources.

The State of Vera Cruz has an area of 5,501. square leagues, and except very near to the coast is mountainous. The district of Orizava is occupied with the Sierra Madre, which penetrates the state from Oaxaca and extends into the district of Zacatlan, of the State of Puebla. The principal mountain peaks of this Cordillera are the volcano Citlaltepetl; elevation, 5,295 metres above the sea, and may be seen from the vessels entering the port; in fact, is used as a landmark by navigators. The second peak is the Cofre de Perote, formerly called by the ancient Mexicans Nanchampatepetl, which signifies the square mountain; elevation, 4,088 metres. A grand scenery may be enjoyed from its summit. The port of Vera Cruz and the Castillo de San Juan de Ulloa, and a wide expanse of coasts and Mexican scenery, diversified by tropical vegetation on the margins of the principal rivers, at once presents a view to be enjoyed by sightseers. In the districts of Cordova, Orizava, and Jalapa, productions of the hot, temperate, and colder climates are raised.

The State of Vera Cruz is bounded on the north by the State of Tamaulipas, on the east and southeast by the Gulf of Mexico, on the east by Tabasco, southeast by Chiapas, on the southwest by Oaxaca, west by Puebla and Hidalgo, and northwest by San Luis Potosi. Area, 3,501 square leagues. The city of Vera Cruz derives its name from the first city built on this continent by Cortez in 1519-20. From the sea the coast on each side of the town presents a dismal view of sand-hills, which appear almost to swallow up the walls. The town, however, sparkling in the sun with its white houses and numerous church spires, has rather a picturesque appearance; but every object, whether on sea or land, glows unnaturally in the lurid atmosphere. We take the following description of the town from the report of a traveler writing to the *Boston Herald:* —

"Daybreak of the next morning found many an anxious gazer on deck speculating on our chances of landing. To the delight of all, the screw revolves, and on a comparatively smooth sea we ride into the open harbor, flanked on the left by the city of Vera Cruz, and on the right by the old fort San Juan de Ulloa, which lifts its ancient battlements high above the surrounding reefs. This fort was begun in 1569, and was finished in 1633, remaining in the hands of the Spaniards until several years after the independence of Mexico had been proclaimed. It marks the spot where Hernando Cortez landed on April 21, 1519, and is now used as a state prison. The old scenes of Havana and other ports are repeated as soon as we have dropped anchor. Numberless lighters and sailing craft of all kinds are soon at hand. As the steamship company allows passengers to land themselves and their luggage as best they can, we secure a sail-boat and are speedily conveyed to the single pier that graces the city's front and over whose granite length the white-coated waves dash in fury, making the landing anything but pleasant in all save the calmest weather. But, as though old Neptune had determined that our trials had been sufficient and that our parting should be a pleasant one, he granted a brief respite, during which we were safely landed within the inclosure of the custom-house. It was well that we quickly availed ourselves of the opportunity, for a less fortunate French steamer, following in our wake only three hours later, found the "norther" again in full blast, and was compelled to seek the shelter of Sacrificios. So suddenly do the winds and waves rise as though in protest against the stranger's setting foot in this city of the True Cross."

The city is well planned and was until lately surrounded by an adobe wall. It has wide streets, crossing each other at right angles. There are also several large and handsome buildings fast mouldering to decay. The few foreign merchants who reside here remove their families to Jalapa in the season of the vomito. The city has been subject to an annual quarantine, which begins about May 1 and continues during the sickly season. In spite of this great drawback, the city maintains its own and receives the greater proportion of foreign goods imported into the country. The population of the city reaches 9,647, and includes a large number of live business men who recognize the importance of the city and its great opportunities for trade.

Jalapa is a beautiful place, situated on the side of the Macuiltepec Mountain and enjoys a fine and temperate climate. The old convent of San Francisco, the church of St. Joseph, an hospital and substantial public buildings are the principal architectural features of the city.

Cordova is a town of 9,500 inhabitants, and is situated in a small valley, surrounded by mountains and near to Rio Seco, the waters of which have an average temperature of 80 degrees Fahrenheit. As it is only at a moderate altitude, and not far from the sea, it enjoys at the same time the daily tropical heat and the evening sea-breeze. The "Vomito Negro" is seldom engendered there, so that all the advantages attract each year a great number of Vera Cruzians. The town is surrounded by rich coffee plantations.

Orizava is situated eighty-two miles from Vera Cruz, on the Mexican railway, which runs from Vera Cruz to the City of Mexico. The distance to Jalapa is also eighty miles. This city is the capital of the state, and has about 12,500 inhabitants. The valley of Orizava presents to the eye the appearance of an immense luxurious garden, in the middle of which the town detaches itself, with its flat-roofed and white houses and haciendas, varied now and then with domes and steeples. The peak of Orizava stands in view, 17,375 feet above sea level, with its snowy head glittering above the clouds, forming with the surroundings one of the delightful views of Mexican scenery. Three rivers or streams run near the city,—Ojo del Ingenio, Rio Blanco, and the Rio de Orizava. There is a large spinning and tissue mill, a paper factory, and several flour mills in the city. The climate is rather humid, but healthy, the easterly wind predominating. The plateau on which it stands is 4,027 feet above the sea, and the average temperature is seventy-two degrees Fahrenheit. In the environs there are several waterfalls. Orizava contains twelve churches and four hotels. Diligencias — prices, $2 per day; San Pedro, De las Cuatro Naciones, and Del Ferrocarrill; the latter three hotels charge but $1 per day.

The State of Vera Cruz is chiefly an agricultural state, although some mines have been discovered and are worked. The amount of corn produced in 1878 was 286,817,280 kils., value, $8,079,360; wheat, 781,000 kils., value, $44,000; coffee, 5,880,000 kils., value, $1,470,000; sugar, 12,420,000 kils., value, $1,552,500; tobacco, 3,391,180 kils., value, $884,376; vanilla, 28,900 kils., value, $346,400; sarsaparilla, 87,445 kils., value, $11,400, and other productions, $1,026,522; total, $19,295,425.

Besides the above, petroleum has been found in this state in large quantities, flowing from the ground and mingling with the streams in many ravines, and filling gulches at the base of the mountains. This will add another element to the resources of this wonderful country, and become an important part of the traffic upon the railroads.

The coast lands of Vera Cruz furnish just such climatic conditions as are favorable for cotton crops. The soil is of a sandy-clay character, thoroughly disintegrated, and with a good sub-soil, is the most desirable, and is found in all the coast districts. The heavy north winds of the coast would, of course, be dangerous to the maturing crop, but at some distance from the coast this danger disappears as well as that from the coast fever, while all the advantages of soil and climate continue. The soil of the state is well adapted also to coffee and tobacco. . Large crops of the best of coffee are annually raised. The tobacco of Vera Cruz is already celebrated among tobacconists, and we predict for Vera Cruz cigars a run that will be .flattering to the Mexican tobacconists. Gold, silver, copper, iron, lead, and coal have been found in various parts of the state. Coal has been found in the Chicontepec district and denounced by Messrs. Craviato. The Jalapa district is attracting some attention by its gold mines. One of these, the Miqueta, has been opened by the local owners and has disclosed a vein of rich gold-bearing ore. There are good smelting works at Zomelahuacan and Tenepanoya. Amozal is also in possession of large coal beds whose deposits are open to view in the walls of the cañon La Mira.

Capt. H. W. Burdett, the manager of the Boston and Mexican Oil Company, now working at Chapopote, near Tuxpan, states that the first well is down 600 feet, with indications of a heavy body of oil. It is reported that five oil springs have been discovered and denounced at Tansime, in the State of Vera Cruz. ;

SAN LUIS POTOSI.

CHAPTER I.

Physical Features, Cities and Towns, and Agricultural and Mineral Resources.

The State of San Luis Potosi is bounded on the northeast by the States of Nuevo Leon and Tamaulipas; on the south by Guanajuata, Queretaro and Mexico; on the west and northwest by Zacatecas; area, 4,262 square leagues. Several chains of mountains cross this state, forming many fine valleys. The valley of San Luis is the largest, but the valleys Del Maiz and Rio Verde are said to be the richest. This state is one of the most important of the republic, for it is not only rich in agricultural resources, but its mineral resources have made it one of the famous states of the Republic.

The city of San Luis Potosi is the capital of the state and is situated on the east side of the great plateau of Anahuac, in a valley extending from north to south, some forty-five miles in length. The streets are narrow, and run at right angles. The city contains some very fine buildings, viz.: "El Carmen," the Cathedral, San Francisco, San Augustin, La Merced, the College of Loretto, and San Nicolas, the Hospital of San Juan de Dios, the Chapel of El Rosario and Los Remedios, and the Sanctuary of Guadalupe. The city is easy of access, and is connected with Mexico City by the Mexican Central Railroad, and by stage or Mexican diligence. also, with Zacatecas, and Tampico. The city has 45,000 inhabitants and a large trade. The climate is healthy, on account of its elevation; is never very cold or very warm. Matehuala is situated within a few miles of the Cerro de las Frailes and the Catorce Mountains, and has a population of 25,000 Cedral is situated six miles north of Matehuala, and is the centre of a flourishing mining district; population, 15,000. Catorce, one of the great mining districts of the state and of the republic, is situated four leagues from Cedral, in the mountains of Catorce; population, 20,000.

El Venado is a city of 10,000 inhabitants. A cotton factory with two hundred looms is located here. Charcas is a mining town, with a population of 4,000 inhabitants. The other principal towns are Ciudad del Maiz, Rio Verde, Valle de San Francisco, and Moctezuma.

One of the largest haciendas in the republic belongs to the jurisdiction of this state. It is known as the hacienda de Salado, and is situated on the main highway, between the city of San Luis Potosi and Saltillo. Its lands belong to the four States of Zacatecas, Coahuila, Nuevo Leon, and San Luis Potosi, and contains an area of over 200 leagues in one block, or 885,600 acres. It is one of the best properties situated on the table-lands of Mexico, being well adapted to all kinds of stock-raising, and to the cultivation of all small grains, and corn, the grape and all the fruits of the temperate climates. The hacienda is well watered by spring wells and tanks, and water is found at a depth of from 5 to 50 feet. Its mountains, which are really the foot-hills of the Sierra de Catorce, contain over 2,000 metallic veins; some of its mines produced immense bonanzas during the last century. They are principally silver, lead, copper, cinnabar, and some gold, and a rich iron deposit. The building materials, such as marble, rock suitable for hydraulic lime, fire brick and earth for the best kind of brick and crockery, are found in abundance for all purposes. Maguey, the lechuguillas, the zotole, the zolmandoque, the palmetto, the cactus, abound over the hills and valleys of the estate, all of which produce valuable fibre, and whose roots or fruits can be distilled profitably into alcohol. The above description of this great estate will give an idea of the immense resources of San Luis Potosi. The estate formerly belonged to General Don Juan Bustamente, Ex-Governor of San Luis Potosi, but has lately been sold to English capitalists for $2,500,000.

The principal agricultural productions of this state amounted to $7,921,984 in 1878, of which $6,081,600 is the value given to corn raised, or 287,862,400 kilograms. The amount of wheat was 12,780,000 kilograms, valued at $720,000.

The mining resources of the State of San Luis Potosi ranks it as fourth in the list of mining states. It had eight mining districts with sixty-five mines which were worked in 1878, with a result of $3,404,745. There are fourteen mines of gold and silver, forty-six of silver alone, six of copper, five of lead, and nine of quicksilver. The amount of gold and silver coined in the mint of this state up to 1865 was $48,745,584. In 1880, ninety-nine mines were worked, which shows a steady increase in her mining interests. Mr. Ward, in his work on "Mexico in 1827," has given an extended description of the mines of San Luis Potosi, and we shall content ourselves by referring our readers to his description, with the following summary : —

In the mining districts, viz. : Real de Catorce, Guadalcazar, Charcas, Ramos, Ojo Caliente, San Pedro, and Santa Maria del Peñon Blanco, many rich mines were discovered. The Real de Catorce produced immense wealth, and a mint was established to coin the silver of its mines. The whole amount of silver coined by the mint of San Luis Potosi, up to 1867, was $52,699,902.25. Of this amount the various districts of the state supplied the metal. The mining district of Guadalcazar possesses some very rich mines. The Ascencion de Alvarado, Veta Viscaina, San Pedro, Santo Tomas, Tercias Partes Corcovada, San Clemente, Remedios, Estaquillo and San Amaranto, mines, were overflowed by a water spout in 1622. They are all situated on the eastern slope of the San Cristobal Mountain. The San Francisco del Ramillo, San José, El Cascajol, La Cocinera, Santa Catarina, La Angelica, La Compania, and the Sacramento mines, are situated on the west side of the same mountain. The above mines were reputed to be rich mines, but contain rebellious ores. The San Juan Stanislao mine, situated at the foot of the mountain, produced a bonanza in 1850. Its ores produced $80 per carga of 300 pounds, or about $500 per ton.

The following mines are located near the aforementioned property, viz: Jesus, Promontorio San Juan de Encino, Marquerate, El Muerto, La Cruz, and La Manavilla. The San Rafael, formerly called the Santo Domingo, San Vicente, La Encaracion, San José, La Concepcion, El Carmen, Guadalupe, and San Miguel el Gato, are all situated on the south slope of the mountain. The mines mentioned above have produced on the average about from $80 to $100 per ton. These mines have been often flooded, hence their abandonment. In 1574, the mines of San Cristobal were found in the Charcas mining district situated about a league north of the old town of Charcas. The ores produced large quantities of metal by smelting. The San Carlos and Sabino mines were discovered, with some others of lesser importance, in 1600, and produced large quantities of metal. The principal mines of the Ramos mining district are La Cocinera, San Juan, San Jose, San Vicente, Animas, Aura Valenciana, San Geronimo, Cinco Senores, and San Nicolas. They produce native silver, ruby silver, pyrites and galena. These mines are also flooded. In the district of San Luis eight mines are worked and sixty-six are idle. In the district of Charcas and Sabino, eight mines are worked and sixteen are idle. In the districts of Peñon Blanco and Ramos, twenty-three mines are idle. In Catorce, sixty-five mines are worked, and twenty-six are idle. In Guadacalzar, eighteen are worked and ninety-nine are idle. Thus out of 321 mines in the state, ninety mines are worked, and 231 are lying idle. Quicksilver mines have been found and worked in the districts of Ojo Caliente and Gudalcazar. Salt has been produced from the district of Santa Mario del Peñon Blanco.

QUERÉTARO.

CHAPTER I.

Description, Cities and Towns and Resources.

The state of Querétaro is in general very mountainous, and more especially in the northern part. The hills are almost lacking in vegetation, but the mountains and cordilleras, are covered with forests of timber. The districts of Querétaro, San Juan del Rio, Caderyeta and Amealco, with but few exceptions, are covered with rich and fertile agricultural lands. The state is bounded on the north by Guanjuato and San Luis Potosi, east by Hidalgo and Mexico, southwest by Michoacan, and west by Guanajuato, and south by Mexico. The state has six districts, viz. : Querétaro, San Juan del Rio, Amealco, Jalpan, Toliman, and Cadereyta ; area, 500 square leagues. The climate is temperate and healthy. The city of Querétaro is the capital of the state, and has 48,000 inhabitants. It is reached by the Mexican Central railroad from Mexico city. The city is surrounded by gardens and orchards, and has a temperate climate. The principal buildings are the convents of San Francisco, Santa Cruz, San Antonio, Santo Domingo, San Augustine, and El Carmen. An aqueduct carries water from the neighboring hills, some of the arches of which are 90 feet high. The aqueduct was built by Don Juan Antonio de Urutio y Arana, and cost $124,000. The city has a fine Alameda, and presents a beautiful appearance to the eye of the visitor.

Querétaro enjoys the distinction of having the most extensive and best equipped establishments in Mexico. They are owned by the celebrated and wealthy Rubio family, and are immensely profitable. The first mill that is reached, about a mile from the city, is La Purisima Conception, or the Immaculate Conception. This is run by water, and employs some 300 operatives. The largest mill is the Hercules, superior, certainly, to any other in Mexico, and probably equal to the best to be found anywhere in the United States. It is a vast establishment, giving employment, a few years ago, to 1,800 people, and running 18,000 spindles. Since then I

understand that additions have been made to the establishment, so that now it runs 5,000 more spindles, and employs
fully 2,000 people within its walls, and a large number of
common laborers outside, who directly find their support
from it. The annual product of these two mills is said to be
about 1,200 tons of cotton cloth, besides large quantities of
yarn and wick. In the production of these goods nearly
2,000 tons of raw cotton are annually used. This is largely
brought from Vera Cruz, Morelia, and Colima, and the distant provinces of Durango and Chihuahua are also drawn
upon, while even the borders are crossed and Texas made to
supply a share of the necessary staple. The Hercules mill
is a model establishment in every respect. Its spacious buildings stretch out over a vast extent of land, and are fitted up
with all the most improved machinery to be had from the
United States or England. The works are run by two double
oscillating engines of 100 horse power each. For protection
against robbers and against revolutionary parties, the owner
keeps a standing army of seventy foot soldiers and twenty
cavalry. These men are neatly uniformed in white, and are
on duty all the time. They are paid about sixty cents a day
and provided with uniforms, and the cavalry with horses
also. In addition, in cases of emergency, an army of 500
from workmen can be mustered, all drilled, equipped, and
fully trained. The arsenal of the establishment is well
stocked, and two light guns are conveniently stored in the
engine room. Sentry boxes are mounted on the roof, and in
times of disturbance or apprehended danger a constant watch
is kept. The buildings of the factory are of stone, and are
surrounded by fine gardens, with artificial ponds. Among
the statues that adorn the grounds is one of "Hercules,"
which cost in Italy $15,000. There are several hotels in the
city and a theatre.

This state produced in corn alone, in 1878, 103,547,000
kils., valued at $1,456,000, and some other agricultural pro-
ductions, reaching to $1,726,055, upon 100,000 hectares of
land under cultivation, or only 248,000 acres under the rude
processes of cultivation. This, however, does not include
some other productions, among which may be mentioned
sugar to the amount of 2,250,000 kils., valued at $281,250.

The mining in this state has as yet been undeveloped to
any considerable extent. The mining districts of the state
are Atarjea, San Pedro, Escanela, Maconi, El Doctor, or
Las Aguas. Silver, galena, grey copperas, copper, malachite,
antimony, iron, cinnabar, native mercury, lignite, anthracite,

opal, calcedonia, rock crystal, copperas and many other minerals are found in the state. The Santa Inez silver mines and Sombrerete, of the mining district of Las Aguas, which produces silver, are being worked. The mines of La Sojonia and Nuestra Señora de las Nieves, of the mining district of Vizarron, and the five quicksilver mines, viz., San Joaquin, Senor de la Esperanza, San Jose, and San Lorenzo, of the mining district of Tierra Colorada, are also worked. There are sixty-nine mines abandoned and idle in the state.

GUANAJUATO.

CHAPTER I.

Topography, Cities and Towns, and Agricultural and Mineral Resources.

The State of Guanajuato is bounded on the north by San Luis Potosi, on the east by Querétaro, south by Michoacan, and west by Jalisco. The area of the state is 1,755 square leagues. Two ranges of mountains extend through the state; in the northeastern part the Sierra Gordo, and the Sierra de Guanajuato in the central. Beautiful and fertile plains are found in the state, among which may be mentioned Bajio, situated between the Sierra de Guanajuato and the Penjamo mountains, and the valley of Santiago Yuriria.

The city of Guanajuato, which is the capital of the state, is situated ninety-four leagues northwest from the city of Mexico, in a canon, surrounded by a rich mineral region. The city has 63,000 inhabitants, an imposing governmental palace, a theatre, a college, and other public buildings. Leon, situated west of the city of Guanajuato, is a manufacturing city. The best saddles and leather in the republic are manufactured here. The city has a large trade; population, 100,-000. San Miguel de Allende is a beautiful city situated on the declivity of a high hill, with a population of 25,000. The streets are well paved. There are several churches, hotels, and beautiful squares, and a college in the city. Dolores Hidalgo is one of the principal towns of the state, and has well paved streets, several fine churches, and plazas. Padre Miguel Hidalgo y Costilla, at this place first proclaimed for independence, on Sept. 16, 1810. In the city of Salamanca there are several cotton factories, which manufacture unbleached cotton. In Salvatierra there are factories of cotton thread, and in Celaya there are several woollen factories.

The great State of Guanajuato is the second great mining state, with no less than 45 mining districts, and 238 mines, which were worked in 1878; and 317 mines in all, 150 of which were of gold and silver, 91 of silver alone, 16 copper, 17 lead, and 43 of quicksilver. The amount produced in these mines during that year reached $5,487,791. There were no less than 18,415 of its population engaged in mining, while Zacatecas had 19,850. The amount of gold and silver coined in its mint up to 1865, was $179,685,745.

The amount of its principal agricultural productions for the same year of 1878, was 581,410,300 kils., valued at $13,-652,031, of which 478,396,000 kils. was of corn, valued at $10,107,000, and wheat, 35,199,000 kils., value, $1,983,040.

The past wealth of this state in its mineral productions will be found very fully set forth in Ward's work on Mexico; but in order to give an idea of the present status, we quote the following report by a competent engineer on March 28, 1881:—

"The district of La Luz, which some thirty years ago was selling over $200,000 weekly, besides remitting ores to the haciendas for reduction, is now almost abandoned; for although various of the once famous mines are still being worked on a small scale, there is but little hope of their ever producing anything of importance, being in reality worked out. In this category may be included San Juan, Santa Lucia, Santa Clara, Refugio, San Vicente, Los Locos, and Jesus María. Those which offer more hopes at some future day, are Purisima, Rosario, and San Pedro, as they have grounds still to be explored; but they are all inundated, and the cost of drainage, with the present means of effecting it, is too costly for the capitalists which at present exist here. Megiamora is a mine with an ample territory, the greater part of which is unexplored. It is being worked on a limited scale, and is not covering its expenses.

"The adit of San Cayetano, which was opened from the river of Santa Ana, and has been driven some 1,500 metres through the ground of the mines of Buenos Ayres, San Antonio, and San Calletano de Ovejera, toward El Diamante and Megiamora, is still being carried forward, though slowly. It is worked by the United States Mexican Mining Company, which has continued its operations for a long series of years with the greatest constancy; and although up to date it has not been rewarded by the discovery of any important deposit of ore, may be compensated, it is to be hoped, at some future day, for its perseverance and heavy outlay.

"La Joya, which at various periods has given handsome returns, is at present very poor. The ore in this mine has been generally met with in rich deposits or 'clavos,' with intervening spaces of 'borrasca,' so that at any time it may present a favorable change.

"The drainage at Valenciana is still maintained, but the produce from the mine is far from covering the outlay. Cata is at present giving some very good ore, and Mellado is leaving profits, though not large ones. Rayas is very poor, and with no immediate prospect of improvement. El Nopal maintains its extraction, and it has been reported that some rich ore has been lately cut there.

"A large number of small mines are being worked in all directions, the names of which it would occupy too much space to enumerate. On the result of these, the future of the district depends, as little can be expected from the old and worked-out mines; while on the contrary, should one or more of these new undertakings be attended with favorable results, we might regain our past prosperity.

"The district abounds in mineral deposits, wanting only capital and enterprise to develop them, and it is to be hoped that the opening up of the country by the railways now in construction, may make the interior better known to foreigners, and induce them to invest some of their capital in mining speculations."

On Jan. 8, 1880, a mining company was formed, called the "Society for the Exploration of Mines in Guanajuato." On account of the decay of mining in this state, in the exhaustion of the old mines, this company was formed, with a "fund of $1,000,0 0," subscribed by Mexican capitalists, "to be dedicated exclusively, and with the object of prospecting *for new metallic* veins." The old veins have so long been worked that no attention has been given apparently to prospecting for new veins hitherto.

ZACATECAS.

CHAPTER I.

Description, Cities and Towns, Agricultural and Mineral Resources.

The State of Zacatecas is bounded on the north by Coahuila, southeast by San Luis Potosi, and east by San Luis Potosi, Aguas Calientes, and Jalisco; on the south by Jalisco and Aguas Calientes; on the west by Durango and Jalisco. Area, 6,270 square leagues. The surface of the state has the same aspect as Durango,—unequal and mountainous on the west, and plains, interrupted by mountain chains, on the east. The descent is gradual from the Sierra Madre to the plains, and diversified by elevated table lands, wide valleys, and deep cañons. The region in the southeastern part of the state, along the course of the Tlaltenango and Juchipila rivers, present a great contrast by their fertility, to the northern region, which is arid and dismal, excepting that portion devoted to cattle raising. The climate is cold in the mountains, and semitropical in the valleys. The city of Zacatecas is the capital of the state, and contains 62,000 inhabitants. It is built in a ravine situated in the middle of a mountain, consequently its streets are irregular. The government palace, city hall, markets, hospital, mint, a theatre, and a cathedral, are its principal buildings. It has besides fourteen churches, an amphitheatre for bull-fighting, and thirteen squares. The city of Fresnillo has about 15,000 inhabitants, and is the centre of an old mining district discovered in 1569. It has a handsome theatre, a parochial church, market, and several squares. The city of Sombrerete is the centre of one of the first mining districts of the republic. It is situated in a cañada near the boundary of the state, on the road to Durango, thirty-six leagues northwest of the city of Zacatecas, at an elevation of 2,369 metres above the sea level. It has a city hall, various churches, chapels, and a population of 5,173. The city was founded in 1570, fifteen years after its discovery as a mining district. The city of Garcia was founded in 1531; population, 7,255. The city of Villanueva was founded in 1691; population, 6,065. The city of Nieves is an old mining centre established in 1579; population, 1,500.

This celebrated state is not only a great mining state, being the first in the products of its mines, but its agricultural resources are of no inconsiderable value. The amount of corn alone in 1878, reached 234,941,840 kils., valued at $5,063,560, and wheat to the amount of 21,300,000 kils., value, $1,200,000; the balance of the principal agricultural products swelling the amount to the grand total of 276,043,764 kils.; value, $7,030,717.

Although many fine and extensive haciendas and ranchos are under cultivation, on which are raised wheat, barley, corn, beans, peaches, pears, pomegranates, guavas, melons, tomatoes, etc., it has vast tracts of table and agricultural lands, and some extensive pastures, on which are raised immense herds of cattle, sheep, and horses.

CHAPTER II.

Mineral Resources.

During the last few years the mining interests in Zacatecas have been on the increase. For the year 1879, the amount of gold, silver, and copper coined in the mint of the state, which was produced in its own mines, was $5,791,812. There are three rich silver and gold bearing lodes running through the state, which have produced for the mint up to 1865, $204,784,949. There are 16 mining districts, in which 240 mines were worked in 1878. Of the mines in the state, 21 were of gold, 67 of gold and silver, 146 of silver alone, 15 of copper, 37 of lead, and 16 of quicksilver. The principal mining districts are Zacatecas, Espiritu Santo, Chapala, Los Arcos, Norias, Ipala, Santa Lucia, Nuevo St. Martins, and Naranjal. All of these districts have been worked extensively, and continue to produce yearly an immense amount of bullion, both gold and silver, the principal part of which goes to England. The great mineral wealth of this state has made it the most celebrated of the republic. Here are located some of the oldest and largest mines of the republic. Many of these mines have been worked steadily for 300 years, some of which have been exhausted, while many others are yet rich in metal. The district of Zacatecas is a network of large fissure veins, with "cross-cuts," "off shoots," and "hilas." Ward, in his work before mentioned, gives an elaborate description of the mines of this state, and we add the following : —

"Pinos is a town of from 3,500 to 4,000 inhabitants, situated at an average altitude of 7,775 feet above the sea. It lies on a sloping plane at the base of a ridge rising some 2,000 feet higher. This range of mountains is the 'divide' between the 'gulf slope' and that of the Pacific Ocean ; Pinos being on the eastern or gulf slope. The town at present is barely kept alive by the Candelaria mining and reduction works, which furnish employment to a large force of men. The valley south and west of the town is a vast overflow of volcanic rocks, chiefly trap and trachyte. Ascending towards Pinos, we come across a series of low, broad, white hills of cretaceous or tertiary age. This bed of sedimentary deposits is very narrow here,— not more than five miles,— but widens to the northwest. I have traced it up through Piñon Blanco, and beyond Real de Angeles. · There are two distinct systems of veins observable here,— one differing but little from a north and south direction, and the other being essentially east and west. The veins of the former do not penetrate the porphyry, disappearing immediately the latter is encountered, showing that they were formed anterior to, or were coincident with this outflow. The east and west veins, on the contrary, are frequently traced through the limestone into the porphyry, and, in fact, seem to be more numerous and larger in the latter than in the former." These veins have lately been explored by Mr. Nelson W. Perry, a mining engineer of Cincinnati, Ohio (from whose report we take the foregoing), and various assays were made of the ores, which ran from $13.56 per ton to $143.37. He found that the Esquipulas mines of the Almiranti group "had been not extensively worked, nor are the ore surfaces now exposed of much value. The manner in which it has been worked, too, would seem to indicate that no rich ore bodies had been encountered. The Almiranti mine lies directly north of and adjoining the Esquipulas. The upper portions of the mine have been pretty thoroughly picked over by the late owners, and it is only in the lower portions that much good ore of good quality is now to be seen. The vein extended from a few inches to 6½ to 7 feet thick, according to location and development, and gave the result by assay as before stated. At the bottom of the Almiranti the gangue rock is chiefly a hard white quartz, associated with more or less calcite or gypsum. The ores produce gold and silver. The gold is free and of a high grade, and in the highest assay ran $124.02 per ton, and $19.35 silver. The Ave Maria mine adjoins, and lies directly north of the Almiranti. This is an old Spanish mine, but the old workings "nobody of late years has been able to find." "Of late years considerable work has been done on a small vein dipping strongly to the west. At a depth of about 100 feet vertically, this stringer unites with a more prominent vein standing more nearly vertically, and corresponding in many respects to the principal or old vein of the Almiranti mine. Here considerable work has been done, but of late years it has been so filled with foul gas that nobody has attempted to enter." Mr. Perry attempted to explore the mine, but failed on account of the gas to reach a satisfactory conclusion, further than "demonstrating the presence of a strong vein, which had been extensively worked by the Spaniards, at a considerable depth. "This mine is located near the old Carmen mine, now the property of the Candelaria Mining Company. The samples from near the surface of the Ave Maria assayed $40.67 and $77.49. The above properties are owned by the New York Mexican Mining Company of New York. The district of Mazapil, which lies in the northeastern part of the state, was discovered in the first years of the conquest and worked at intervals until the beginning of the present century, when it was abandoned by the Spaniards who were expelled from the country. "The San Eligio is located on the Albarradon lode, northeast of the town of Mazapil, some five or six miles. The mine is an old one, and has reached a depth of 450 feet; drifts have been run from 800 to 900 feet in extent. In the interior, the great chamber, called 'Salon del Bronce,' which is greater than that of the 'Panilla Grande,' shows that of the two metaliferous chimneys in it, the one to the east is very important, extending into virgin ground. This salon is 300 feet high. Forty-five feet deeper, 120 feet east of this salon, is found the little chamber 'San Augustine,' which is 75 feet high and 20 feet wide. The light-colored oxidized ores, with green copper, are found to a depth of 400 feet. The chamber 'San Fernando' is the one farther east. The chamber 'Caracol' is 200 feet deeper than the San Fernando, but is 600 feet farther west, with no opening between them. The mine has the advantage of being entirely dry." [Extract from an official report of Trinidad Acuña, M. E.] Samples of the ore taken from the old works assayed $49.84 and $78.09 per ton. "The Albarradon mine is located in the same district," about five miles west of the town of Concepcion del Oro, and just over the crest of the range of mountains of which Temeroso is the chief. The mine was extensively worked by the Spaniards in the early history of the country, and since that time has been worked constantly, but with varying activity, by the natives. This mine has been opened to a depth of 800 feet, and samples directly from the vein assayed 25.75 ounces of silver per ton." " Entering the mine by another opening I found a body of lead ore 12 feet wide, 50 feet from the surface, which assayed $29\frac{5}{16}$ ounces silver per ton. Descending 250 feet from this point I found a body of ore exposed on three different levels, which averaged 8 feet in width and assayed 50 ounces in silver to the ton. The 'Santiago,' about one mile east of the Abarradon, is practically a new mine on the old workings, with an incline about 30 feet deep; below the incline, about 250 feet, a tunnel has been started on the vein. At present it is only about 20 feet in, but shows a strong vein of 4 feet in width, with a streak of good ore about 18 inches wide. The 'Promontorio,' situated about one mile from Concepcion, has been worked in a similar manner to the mines already described, the openings showing that a great deal of ore has been extracted, while large bodies of rich copper ore are still to be seen, the mine having been chiefly worked for the sulphurets of copper, they finding a readier market here; while the oxidized ores, carrying from 20 to 30 per cent. of copper and 11 to 15 ounces of silver to the ton, have, when possible, been left standing. The 'Cabrestante' is about one-eighth of a mile from Concepcion, but presents in the old workings the same features as the other mines. At the old shaft two veins intersect each other, one of which was formerly worked for gold, and gave to the town its name " Concepcion del Oro " The other was worked for copper, and as depth is obtained the copper in both veins increases. In the old openings large bodies of ore, rich in copper and with 50 ounces of silver per ton, are still standing." [Extract from a report of H. F. Wild, M. E. for the Mexican Syndicate of New York.]

AGUAS CALIENTES.

CHAPTER I.

Physical Features, Cities and Towns, Agricultural, and Mineral Resources.

The State of Aguas Calientes is bounded on the north and west by Zacatecas, south by Zacatecas and Jalisco, on the southeast by Jalisco, and northeast by Zacatecas; area, 327 square leagues.

The eastern part of the state is covered with plains, the western part by mountains. The capital of the state is the city of Aguas Calientes, which has 35,000 inhabitants. The city has thirteen churches, one hospital, one penitentiary for women, a city hall, a market, and fine public walks.

The state is small and its agricultural productions are proportionally less than the states surrounding. Its productions in the staple articles amount to 39,918,000 kilograms, value $1,048,916. The products comprise corn, beans, wheat, pepper, lentils, tobacco, potatoes, all the fruits and vegetables of warm and cold climates, pulque, also a liquor made out of the cactus fibre, called colonche, wines, alcohol, cheese, etc. The soil is rich and well adapted to agriculture; value of its real estate, $2,827,179. The state possesses twenty-seven schools, an institute, a catholic seminary, and two libraries. The mineral wealth of the state is as yet undeveloped. In the mining districts of Asientos and Tepezala, fifteen leagues northeast of the capital, are the old abandoned mines of San Francisco, Romana, and the Descubridora, Cristo, San Antonio de los Pobres, which tradition says were formerly rich mines. In the Descubridora a vein 11.7 metres wide was worked. In the district of Calpulalpan the mines of San Pedro del Bosque and La Purisima are found.

218

JALISCO.

CHAPTER I.

Topography, Cities and Towns, and Agricultural and Mineral Resources.

The State of Jalisco is one of the first states of the republic. It is bounded on the north by Sinaloa and Durango, Zacatecas and Aguas Calientes; on the east by Zacatecas, San Luis Potosi, Guanajuato and Michoacan; on the south by Colima and Michoacan, and on the west by the Pacific Ocean. The Sierra Madre range runs almost through the centre of the state, from north to south. Large and rich valleys, well watered, are found on both sides of the mountains. The state is well timbered with all the trees indigenous to the soil, and it has a climate which varies according to the altitude,— cool at Lagos, La Barca, and Cololtan, temperate at Guadalajara and Etzatlan, warm at Aultan and Tepic and San Blas, and variable in Sayula; area, 8,324 square leagues. The city of Guadalajara is the capital of the state, and has 93,875 inhabitants. The city is well laid out, with paved streets crossing each other at right angles, generally with an average width of about 30 feet, but with narrow sidewalks. The city extends over two miles square, and has sixteen public squares, most of which are ornamented with rows of beautiful trees. The cathedral of Guadalajara has a spire 200 feet high, and presents in its architecture a combination of the Arabian and Moorish, or modern Gothic style, with its pointed arches, clustered pillars, lofty towers, and flying buttresses. This building is located on the north side of the Plaza de Armas, the principal public square, and is situated in the centre of the city. The government palace is a commanding edifice, of the Doric style of architecture, presenting a massive and grand appearance, nevertheless rich and graceful. Los Portales de Comercio, consisting of arcades around three large square blocks of houses, are also numbered among the principal architectural features of the city. The streets opposite the plaza are wide and well paved. There are, aside from the cathedral, nearly twenty other churches, the bishop's palace, the government mint, custom house, and the public theatre.

Guadalajara is the principal seat of the cotton and wool manufacturing industries of the country. There are a large number of mills here and in the immediate vicinity. They are all outside the city limits. Four are particularly prominent,— the El Escoba, with 3,300 spindles, the Atanupac, with 5,000 spindles, the Salto, with 500 spindles, and the Experience, with 1,000 spindles. These are most all on the banks of the beautiful stream that supplies them with water, in the midst of charming scenery and gardens of tropical fruits and flowers of every conceivable variety. There are other mills of lesser importance, most of which have been erected within a few years past. As a general thing, these mills are what are known as the 120-loom mills, and employ in the vicinity of 300 hands. There are, however, quite a number of 60-loom mills, and some smaller and a few larger ones.

The city is located 150 leagues from the city of Mexico, and does a large trade. It possesses a university, a college, an academy of painting, drawing, architecture, sculpture, and a seminary. The city of Tepic is located about twenty-five miles from the port of San Blas, and has about 15,000 inhabitants. The custom house was for many years at Tepic, located there on account of the unhealthy climate of San Blas, the principal port of the state. The city has some importance as a manufacturing place, and is celebrated for its good quality of cigars. The city seems to be situated on a level plain, and laid out somewhat with a view to right angles; notwithstanding, near the town rolling eminences protrude in various shapes. The streets and sidewalks are narrow. The private dwellings among the rich or wealthier classes have court-yards in the centre of their residences, with columns, arches, balconies, balustrades, suitable to the construction and number of stories. The valley in which the city is located extends over an area of 10 miles square, and possesses a very fertile soil, and is devoted to the production of sugar-cane, coffee, cotton, rice, sweet potatoes, and corn. The port of San Blas is situated about 25 miles west of Tepic, and 116 leagues from Guadalajara. Through this port most of the foreign trade of the state is carried on. The city of Lago has about 10,000 inhabitants, and is an important manufacturing place.

This state is one of the rich mining and agricultural states of the republic. The production of corn in this state reaches

748,410,000 kils., valued at $15,811,479, and wheat, 88,910,-
000 kils., value, $4,877,957, with some other agricultural prod-
ucts, making a grand total of $20,862,066. Vast herds of
live stock are raised in the state, no less than 470,460 head
being reported in 1878.

The mineral wealth of this state is well known. Some of
its mining districts have produced immense wealth. The
mining districts have been described by Ward, in his work
on Mexico, and we refer our readers to his account. The
principal minerals are those of Bolaños (an old district formerly very productive, but now almost exhausted), Copala,
Hostotipaquillo and Anonas, Reyes, Estancia, Cuale, San Sebastian, Socorro, Favor, Limon, and Comanja. The district of
Tepic contains 8 minerals, and 56 mines. The mining district
of San Sebastian, 60 miles south of the city of Tepic, is almost abandoned. Some 36 mines are worked in the district
of Talpa, and 54 in the district of Tequila. There are no
less than 47 mining districts, in which 303 mines are being
worked, out of 415 mines in the state.

"Las Animas group of silver mines are 6 in number, and
are known as the 'San Julian,' 'San Antonio,' 'Colorado
de Los Tapos,' 'De San Francisco,' and 'Las Animas,' and
are situated in the mineral district of Acaponeta, State of
Jalisco, some 120 miles southeast of Mazatlan, and 36 miles
from the port of Las Flores. This group of mines has
been worked by the early Spaniards. The veins average from
3 to 9 feet in width; at the present time, all of them are filled
with water excepting the Las Animas; here a shaft has been
sunk to the depth of 95 feet. The vein at the bottom was
4 feet wide; samples obtained from these points gave from
$106.15 to $1,406.25. The ore is free milling, and very similar in character to that produced on the Comstock, Nevada.
The extent of mining ground embraced in all of these locations is 1,800 feet in length, by 600 feet in width. The
topography of the country is such, that the veins could be
tapped the depth of 300 feet by means of a tunnel some
250 feet in length. In addition to the mining ground, there
belongs to the property one square league of good timber
land, with abundance of water for all the purposes of mining
and milling by steam." [From a report of Thomas Price,
San Francisco, April 14, 1881.]

COLIMA.

CHAPTER I.

Description, Cities and Towns, Factories and Agricultural **Resources,** Coffee Plantations, etc.

The State of Colima, so celebrated for its coffee, is bounded on the north and northwest by Jalisco, southeast by Michoacan, and southwest by the Pacific Ocean ; area, 9,700 kils. square, or 552 leagues square. This state is an agricultural and manufacturing state, and is covered with a good soil extending over a plain which is diversified by many isolated hills and spurs of the Sierras. The state is well watered by streams, and is highly cultivated. The valley of Colima possesses a large scope of productive land, adapted to growths of hot climates. Apparently it is situated in a basin surrounded with mountain ridges, except on the southeast and northwest, and extending to the base of the volcano of Colima. It is computed to embrace the superficial area of 100 square leagues of arable land, or near 5,000 acres.

The city of Colima has 31,774 inhabitants, and was founded by Cortez after his return from Spain, between the years 1522 and 1524. The city is situated on the plain of Colima, 80 miles from the port of Manzanillo, the principal port of the state. It is the capital of the state, and is laid out regularly, with narrow streets crossing at right angles. The style of architecture observed, with reference to the church, the residences and the stores, is an imitation of the modern Gothic and Moorish order. Many of the courts are ornamented with fountains, and tropical trees and plants.

Colima is also quite a centre for the cotton manufactures. The one-story buildings of an establishment near this city surround a square which blooms with all the glory of tropic vegetation, poetizing even the prosaic occupation of cotton weaving. A wheel, 42 feet in diameter, is required to run the looms here. Two thousand spindles are worked, and give employment to 250 men and women. Another mill near by, the Armonia, has 800 spindles, and gives employment to 80 hands. Still another, the Atrevida, has 25 looms, 800 spindles, and 80 operatives.

Manzanillo is a town of some 1,000 inhabitants, very prettily situated, and about 90 miles from Colima, a city of 16,000 population; is rapidly rising, and has good trade with San Francisco.

The annual imports amount to between $800,000 and $900,000, consisting principally of English cotton goods, assorted hardware, and groceries from Germany. The English goods are brought here per steamers *via* Panama; while the heavier articles, such as hardware, groceries, etc., are brought in sailing vessels around Cape Horn. The entire trade is in the hands of the Germans, who have their principal establishment or home office in Hamburg, which furnishes the capital; with branch houses in Manchester for the purchase of goods, and others in Colima and Guadalajara for the sale of them.

The general run of all the import business is as follows: The Hamburg house sends every month through their agents in Manchester a certain amount of English dry goods, common prints, etc., per steamer *via* Panama, and annually one or two cargoes of assorted merchandise *via* Cape Horn; these goods are sent either in consignment, or joint account with the Colima house, who pay their invoices in remittances in eagle dollars to the bank of England. A consignment of goods by steamer, if sold promptly, requires from 16 to 18 months time to be finally settled, while a consignment per sailing vessel requires fully two and a half years for final settlement. The interest for this long time is added to the prices of the goods at the rate of one per cent per month. This monotonous system of business — abstaining strictly from any other enterprise — has been carried out by the German merchants ever since their trading with Mexico, for over 30 years. Their head house in Hamburg prohibits the investment of funds in any other enterprise, and not a cent of their capital is employed in mines, agriculture, or mechanical industry.

The State of Colima and the surrounding country has plenty of fertile soil well adapted to the culture of tropical productions, such as cotton, coffee, rice, sugar, etc. The present annual production is about 5,000 bales of cotton, at an average of 18 cents per pound; 1,000 tons of sugar, at an average of 8 cents; 800 tons of rice, at an average of 4 cents; 40 tons of coffee, at an average of 22 cents, and 20 tons indigo at an average of 75 cents; with the exception of small lots exported to Mazatlan, Guaymas, etc., this whole production finds consumption in the States of Colima and Jalisco. The State of Colima alone has sufficient rich and fertile lands to produce 50 times the above mentioned quantities of tropical productions. Agriculture is here in its first infancy, and besides American axes and shovels, no modern implements are in use. The difficulties of moving the products to a market are great drawbacks, for even wagon roads are almost unknown; everything has to be carried by pack-animals for distances of from 50 to 500 miles. Coffee plantations are considered one of the best investments for capital; abundant lands well adapted to coffee culture, and situated near the City of Colima, can be had at $10 per acre. The average cost of a coffee tree four years old, including cost of land, labor, planting, etc., is calculated at 35 cents; a tree will furnish 1 pound of coffee the 4th year and 2 pounds every subsequent year. According to these calculations capital invested in a coffee plantation would give the handsome interest of 25 per cent. the 4th year, and 50 the year following.

The exports consist principally of Mexican eagle dollars, 5 or 6 cargoes of cedar, and small quantities of hides, and the annual export amounts to about $400,000 in round figures.

The amount of corn raised in 1878 was 39,100 kils., value $650,701; coffee, 900,000 kils., value $225,000; cotton, 1,500,000 kils., value $156,250; total productions, 43,808,250 kils.; value $1,206,274; value of real estate, $2,789,515.

MICHOACAN.

CHAPTER I.

Topography, Cities and Towns, Factories and Agricultural Resources.

The State of Michoacan possesses great mineral and agricultural resources. Its surface is covered with vast inclined plains of gentle grade sloping towards the Pacific coast, which are intersected by branches of the Cordillera. The Sierra Madre enters the state in the district of Coalcoman. The state is bounded on the north by Jalisco, Guanajuato and Querétaro; on the east by Mexico and part of Guerrero; on the south by Guerrero and the Pacific Ocean; on the west by Colima and Jalisco; area, 3,487 square leagues. The principal cities are Morelia, the capital, with 25,000 inhabitants, Zamora, Uruapan, Puruandiro, Tacambaro, Zitacuaro, Maravatio, Ario, La Piedad, Patzcuaro, and Jiquilpan. Maruata is the principal port of the state, situated on the Pacific Ocean. In the city of Morelia considerable trade is carried on. Two cotton and woolen factories, called "La Paz" and "La Union," a large candle manufactory, tobacco manufactories and breweries are located here. Patzcuaro is the third town of the state, and is situated on the margin of a beautiful lake of the same name, which Baron Humboldt declared to be one of the most beautiful on the globe. The lake contains five small islands, covered with a rich tropical vegetation and flowers. Uruapan is one of the most flourishing towns of the state. The soil is very rich around the town, and among other productions an excellent quality of coffee is raised. A cotton factory called the "El Paraiso" is also located here.

The state is great in its unbounded resources, and while its mineral wealth is well known, the mines producing in 1878 $1,554,820, the agricultural productions for the same year were $11,979,917. This includes corn, $8,630,790; wheat, $569,000; sugar, $1,068,750. Thus we may see, that besides her mines, Michoacan has many other elements of wealth; in fact, this particular section seems to be one with

which nature has been singularly prodigal in her most choice
gifts. Within the limits of this state we have every climate,
from the torrid to the moderately cold, the vegetation being
as varied as the climate. Near the coast, sugar-cane, cotton,
rice, indigo, cochineal, vanilla and every variety of tropical
fruits grow with a luxuriousness unsurpassed anywhere. On
the table land, wheat, barley, Indian corn, tobacco, and all
the fruits and vegetables of the temperate zone grow in the
greatest abundance.

Taking everything into consideration, notwithstanding the
many and various attractions of other favored sections,
Michoacan is perhaps the most attractive state in the Mexican republic. Here there are many large haciendas and
villages and towns, yet the country is sparsely inhabited and
presents a most attractive field for colonization. Here emi-
grants have a choice of climate and products, and thousands
of industrious settlers could, within a very few years, make
for themselves comfortable, happy homes, and all such emi-
grants would be welcomed with open arms by the people.

CHAPTER II.

The Mineral Resources of Michoacan.

In the interest of the Michoacan Syndicate, which is composed of a number of New York and Mexican gentlemen of
high standing, Mr. Le Row proceeded to Morelia, in company
with Messrs. Foote and Simpson, mining engineers sent out
by the syndicate from New York. The mines of the following districts were minutely and scientifically examined by
these three gentlemen: Chapatuato, Ozumatlan, and Zinda.

Chapatuato contains what Mr. Le Row pronounces one of
the finest mines he ever saw, the San Nicolas. This is a
mine which was abandoned by the Spaniards on their expulsion from the country, but had not been extensively
worked. The principal vein in this mine is nineteen metres
in width, and assays from $100 to $1,000 per ton, with a
slight percentage of gold which of itself is sufficient to pay
all the expenses of the extraction and reduction, thus leaving
the silver clear profit. The ore is both hard and soft, but all
easily worked. The syndicate owns 3,200 metres on this
lode. In this district the following other mines have been
secured by the syndicate: Santa Rita, La Purísima, La Providencia, and Guadalupe, all of which are very promising.

The Chapatuato River furnishes an abundant supply of water, and timber is plentiful. The ruins of an old Spanish reduction work are still standing, and there is a splendid site for a modern mill. This district is situated fifteen leagues nearly south of Morelia, in a spur of the Sierra Madre.

Ozumatlan, which was formerly a large town, is situated fourteen leagues southeast of Morelia, and was at one time the centre of one of the most prosperous mining regions in Mexico, all the remaining indications attesting the enormous scale on which mining was at one time conducted. There are still in existence reliable records showing that the sum of $4,800,000 was paid by the mines of this district in church tithes to the cathedral in Morelia, which building, although despoiled of its wealth by General Miramon, still retains many evidences of its former magnificence. The district of Ozumatlan contains many old and very extensive mines, the veins in which are large and of a very good quality of quartz ore easily treated. The syndicate owns the San Vicente mine, the vein of which is twenty-one feet wide, the ore being very good, containing both silver and gold. The following mines have also been purchased by the syndicate: La Purísima, El Carmen, San Cayetano, San Pedro, La Concepcion, San Juan, La Melchora, San Antonio, and others. Wood and water are found here in abundance, as in the district of Chapatuato. The Mexican National Railway will pass within seven miles of the town of Ozumatlan.

The district of Zinda lies high up in the pine country, and is essentially a gold producing region. Here there is a regular network of gold-bearing veins or fissures on the surface, and the indications are that they all meet at a depth of about 2,000 feet. The ore is hard, but very easily worked. All the mines in this district are comparatively new. Wood and water are abundant. The syndicate has purchased the following named mines in the district of Zinda: Santa Gertrudis, El Caiman, San Miguel, La Purísima, and many others. Roads at present can hardly be said to lead to either of the above named districts, and transportation is usually conducted by means of pack-mules. However, good wagon roads can be made to all at a comparatively small expense.

Mr. Le Row visited the districts of San Diego and Curucupaseo, 35 leagues distant from Morelia, in company with Sr. Maximiniano Rocha, the prefect of Morelia. In the San Diego district are situated, on opposite sides of the San Diego River, the Eureka and Nevada silver mines; the latter is located on an immense lode of galena ore; the former has three veins, all exceedingly rich. There are also some gold mines in the vicinity. At Curucupaseo, the Cal y Canto, La Soledad, and El Caiman mines are very good, having an abundance of very rich ore, but the mines have been worked a great deal and are very deep. Here are ruins of an enormous reduction work, several churches and numbers of large houses; everything showing that the work must have been carried on on a large scale and very profitably. The mines which have been mentioned in the above named districts belong to Governor Octaviano Fernandez, and Messrs. Solorzano, Rocha, and Gravenhorst, all of Morelia.

Mr. Le Row visited 12 miles southwest of Morelia a tract of land where may be seen an immense deposit of what by a casual observer would be thought red clay. This deposit was discovered in April last by Mr. William Denton, and has proved to be an immense body of decomposed gold-bearing quartz, which assays from $100 to $200 a ton. Mr. Le Row had pits from 6 to 8 feet deep, and from 30 to 50 yards apart, sunk over a large area of country, from which 29 assays were made with the result already stated. A tract of 4,000 metres was "denounced" by Mr. Le Row, Mr. Denton, and three other persons.

Mr. James Sullivan, of the Mexican National Railroad Company, says of the mines in the state of Michoacan, one of which, although worked by the old and primitive methods, yielded in February last $4,000,000 of bullion, that the famous mines of Chihuahua were nothing in comparison to the mines of this state. They would, he had no doubt, in time attract capitalists from the states; and when worked with modern machinery, and by Americans, would treble their present yield.

"The Tlalpujahua mining district is one of the principal districts of the state. The first mineral that was found in this district was by a "Vaquero," a herder of cattle named Corona, in the latter part of the sixteenth century. He found, on what is now known as the Corona's vein, some native silver outcropping on the surface, for a distance of 9 feet; of this, he informed his employer, who began work. The Corona's vein is about 3 miles in length, by about 26 feet in width, outcropping almost the entire length. On said vein there are several mines. Among them are the Concepcion group, composed of four contiguous claims, which are worked by a company composed of the following gentlemen: Mr. Sotero Peña, Daniel W. Kline,

Rafael Sanchez, and three other gentlemen of Chicago. The mine is now in *bonanza*, taking some 10 tons of ore daily, that run on an average 600 ounces silver, and from one-half to two ounces in gold per ton ; and very often they take ore that runs over $4,000. The latter sometimes has been shipped to Germany. This company have a Hacienda de Beneficio, or reduction works, composed of two arrastras, and a five-stamp mill, by which they only work about 5 tons of ore in 24 hours. Their reduction works will be increased by ten more stamps in a very short time. On the same vein, and adjoining the Concepcion, on the southwest end, are the Aztec group, composed of four and one-half claims, amongst which is found the great "Descubridora," where Corona found the native silver. These mines are only 500 feet in depth, of which 300 are in water. The principal owners, Messrs. D. W. Kline, M. J. Peña, and Sotero Peña, are now making arrangements to drain them and put up a ten-stamp mill. The ore found on the old workings above water level, is very much the same nature as the Concepcion ore, but in some places it is found much richer in gold than any other group on the same vein. The southwest end of the Aztec group is joined by the Coloradillas, which is composed of four claims. These mines are under water, and have but recently been re-located by some rich miners from the mining districts of Pachuca Real del Monte. It is understood that they will develop them in a very short time, and place on said property a forty-stamp mill. On the northeast end line of the Concepcion are located the Santa Rosa claims, or group, which have been re-located for over a year, by a Frenchman, who is trying to organize a company. This group is composed of four claims.

The great Borda vein is over two miles long, and it is a very well-defined fissure, about 15 feet wide. It outcrops almost the entire length, showing its high grade ores from the surface. The ores found in this vein are black sulphurets and ruby-silver, carrying a good percentage of gold. The latter is more abundant from the surface down 500 feet. On this vein there are the "Borda Mines," a group composed of seven claims, well developed by several shafts and tunnels. This group is owned by a company composed of Americans and Mexicans, the owners being Mr. H. Z. Culver of Chicago, Sotero Peña of Tlalpujahua, M. J. Peña of Colorado, L. F. Burrell, and A. M. Culver of Chicago. These gentlemen are working their mines up to water level until their pumps reach the district. The pumps to be used on these mines are of large dimensions, as they are about 250 feet under water in some places. These gentlemen have on the way machinery with a capacity of 75 tons, to reduce the ores already on the dump, from some of the old workings. This group of mines is one of the richest in Mexico, according to the records kept by the " Deputacion de Mineria," and also the records kept by the general government, which show that the said mines paid taxes on $35,000,000 worth of bullion besides $2,000,000 expended by the owner of them at the time, in building a church and charitable buildings, which still are in existence at said town of Tlalpujahua.

The richest ores extracted from these mines were taken from the surface 550 feet down. The richest ores that are found on the vein began at a depth of 500 feet, where native silver was found in great quantities. It is ascertained that at the actual depth there is a body of ore, 3 feet wide, that will yield very profitably. On the same vein are other mines, owned by some of the natives, who do work only to hold them. At the same time they take out ore enough to make their living, mining and working it themselves, by the primitive processes. Some of them are in hopes to get capital to work them for an interest, or by leasing the properties.

In the same district there are several other veins of smaller width, but are probably not as rich as the two main veins of the district. On said veins there are a great number of mines located and owned by natives, some of whom have arrastras, and others not even those, to beneficiate their minerals extracted.— [Report of Sotero Peña, November, 1882.]

GUERRERO.

CHAPTER I.

Description and Resources, Cities and Towns.

The State of Guerrero is bounded on the north by Puebla, Mexico and Michoacan ; on the east by Oaxaca ; on the south and south west by the Pacific Ocean ; and on the west and northwest by Michoacan.

The northern part of the state, north of the river Balsas, is a rough and uneven, inclined plain, jutting out from the Sierra Madre range. The surface of the state from the coast rises in successive table lands, which continue until they reach the mountain range, which run through the centre of the state from the northwest to the southeast. The whole state is mountainous, but has many fertile lands on the elevated lands and in the valleys. The climate is on the whole quite warm, and very unhealthy on the flat lands of the coast. The area of the state is 3,564 square leagues. All the tropical fruits are produced and the various cereals. Timber is found in a great variety on the mountain sides. The mineral wealth of the state is very great ; no less than 460 mines were known to exist in the state in 1880. Among the principal mining districts may be mentioned, Cuitlanapa, Tasco, Hidalgo, Aldama, Brazos, Morelos, and Chilapa. In Huilzuco are found rich quicksilver, silver and coal mines. Gold placers have been discovered recently which promise to be richer than those found in California in the United States in 1849 and 1850.

Chilpancigo is the capital of the state, and has 3,000 inhabitants. Atoyac has a cotton factory. Tasco is a mining town, celebrated for its rich mines of gold and silver, and excellent climate. Acapulco has an harbor nearly land-locked, and one of the best in the world. Vessels can anchor almost alongside the granite rocks, so deep is the water. This used to be the great emporium between the Spanish East Indies and the Spanish dominions in Mexico. It now bids fair to recover its former importance. It has a population of 3,500 inhabitants, and similar to other Mexican cities in appearance

231

with its narrow streets, and long, low buildings, and roofs of
tile. The exports of Acapulco with various countries for the
year ending Sept. 30, 1878, amounted to $139,336.28, and the
imports for the same time amounted to $578,924. While
the exports of Acapulco with the United States alone for
same date were $38,441.28, and the imports, $44,800. This
country is rich in mines of untold wealth, consisting of gold,
silver, marble, etc.

This is the starting point to the great metropolis, the city
of Mexico, which is only about three hundred miles away.
The conveyance is by horseback, or rather, that of mule or
donkey, to Cuernavaca, and thence by stage to the city. The
length of time from Acapulco is eight to ten days for travellers, but the mail is taken in about half that time. The scenery all along this route surpasses in grandeur that of any
other portion of the republic.

The agricultural products of the state in 1878 was of corn
170,229,000 kils., value, $3,063,800 ; cotton, 1,980,000 kils.,
value, $495,000. Total amount of productions, 183,018,060
kils., value $4,087,750.

MEXICO.

CHAPTER I.

Topography, Cities and Towns, Agricultural and Mineral Resources.

The State of Mexico is bounded on the north by Hidalgo; northwest by Querétaro; west by Michoacan; south by Guerrero and Morelos; east by Puebla and Tlaxcala. The federal district, in which is located the federal capital, the city of Mexico, was originally a part of this state, and is surrounded by the districts of Tenango, Lerma, Tlalnepantla, Tetzcoco and Chalco, of the State of Mexico. The area of the state is 20,300 square kilometres. The state presents a succession of beautiful valleys or plains, surrounded by mountains. These valleys nestle in the highest table lands of the whole republic, and possess a climate from a pleasant temperature to the cold. The valley of Toluca is the highest inhabited land of Mexico, being 8,638 feet, or 3,110 varas above the level of the sea. The climate is consequently cold. The district of Tlalnepantla is composed of rich plains, and has a fine climate. The city of the same name is the summer resort for the inhabitants of the city of Mexico. The district of Tetzcoco comprises the lowest portion of the valley of Mexico, where all its waters unite and form the two great lakes of Tetzcoco and Chalco. The waters of the lakes are unfit to drink, and, according to analysis, contain carbonate of soda, sulphate of soda, marine salt, and vegetable matter. The other portion of the district of Tetzcoco is a rolling country with a fine climate. The city of Toluca is the capital, with 11,376 inhabitants. The state has 16 mineral districts, with 127 mines that are being worked, 21 haciendas de beneficio, 3 iron foundries, 4 cotton and woollen factories, 24 distilleries, 2 breweries, 3 gas works, 1 salt factory, 1 tobacco and 2 varnish factories, 34 molinas de caña, 57 flour mills, and 5 acid manufactories.

The mineral resources of this state have proved of immense wealth; and on account of their proximity to the great mint of Mexico city, which originally by law coined all the silver of the republic that was coined, the mines have been worked at considerable depth, and in many instances with no evidences of exhaustion. There are many old and abandoned as well as exhausted mines, but the production is great from the mines at present worked. Mr. Ward has given, in his work before referred to, an elaborate description of the old mines, to which we refer our readers, as well as his description of the mines of other states, and confine ourselves to the following summary from a report made at New York, May 15, 1880, by Mr. Louis Janin, one of the best mining engineers in the country: "The Mineral del Oro is situated in the Canada del Oro, which is one of a number in the neighborhood of the mountain called Somera, and is upon the western or Pacific side of the mountain chain that separates the waters which flow into the Atlantic from the waters which flow into the Pacific Ocean. The district is in the northwestern portion of the state, near the boundary line of the State of Michoacan. It is held by some that these mines are on the course of the great mineral belt which passes from the famous mines of Guanajuato to the equally renowned mines of Real del Monte. The distance from the city of Mexico, in an air line, is about 60 miles, or by the stage road to Morelia about 120 miles. The neighborhood of the Mineral del Oro is lovely. The mountains are well wooded with oak and pine and cedar, and the valleys are under excellent cultivation. The population of the town of El Oro and the adjacent villages is usually about 3,000, and the productions of corn, barley and wheat is ample for a much larger number. The altitude of El Oro above the sea is, I believe, about 9,000 feet; the climate is cool and agreeable at all times, though there are occasionally heavy frosts in winter. The veins of this district were known, and some of them successfully worked, long before the independence of Mexico. Probably they were among the first which the Spanish exploited after the conquest of the country, nearly 360 years ago. Several bonanzas were encountered which yielded good profit; but those mines, like many others in the country, were abandoned during the war of independence. The same mines were, in 1825, worked by an English and Mexican company. The expense entailed by an extravagant management in some years later led to the abandonment of the property. The mines then became the property of Don Manuel J. Madrid, who sold them to the El Oro Mining Company of New York. The San Rafael is the easternmost of a group of veins which are more or less parallel to one another, and which have a general northwesterly course and a dip to the west of 70 to 80 degrees. The Chihuahua, San Acacio, Descubridora, Mahomeros and San Rafael are the leading ones, and all have been worked to some extent. The Descubridora vein was from 5 to 15 feet wide, which yielded about $50 in silver and $35 in gold, per ton. A shaft 950 feet in depth was sunk at a point some distance to the west of the Descubridora, upon the hanging wall side between that vein and the San Rafael, which struck the vein. A drift was then run 1,100 feet in length, which cut the San Rafael vein 600 feet below its present working. Other tunnels and shafts have been carried on, showing an extensive working, that of the San Rafael vein being worked over a length of some 1,500 feet in the aggregate. The country rock is a clay slate, with occasional bands of slate of a more micaceous and chlorite character. This slate is in horizontal layers, and is overlapped by a heavy deposit of conglomerate, and this again is covered in places with an overflow of trachytic porphyry. The vein breaks through the slate, but is covered by the conglomerate and other superimposed masses of rock. The gangue of the vein is a compact cellular and crystalline quartz, intermixed with a good deal of carbonate of lime, which in some places is highly silicious. The metals found in the vein are native gold, generally in a very finely divided slate, and native silver in small quantities. Both the silver and gold occur as free milling ores. The body of ore (which in the San Rafael was 50 or 60 feet wide) found in the San Antonio mine or shaft was 20 to 24 feet wide. The ore in the San Antonio yields on an average from $12 to $14 per ton. The amount of ore left standing in the San Antonio is very large. Along the bottom of the lowest level of the working there is a shoot of ore of unproved dimensions, but which carries high grade ore for at least 45 or 50 feet. This ore assays $45 in gold and $40 in silver. Along the bottom level of the foot wall seam of the San Rafael is a large and even richer body of ore, 4 to 6 feet wide, that assayed $86.32 in gold, and $28.85 silver."

In 1881, there were 39 mines worked in the Temascaltepec district. The La Magdalena was the principal mine, which yielded 50 marcs of silver to the carga of 300 pounds. The other principal mining districts are Sultepec, Cristo, and Zacualpan. The agricultural productions of the state in 1878 were corn, 437,142,030 kils., value, $9,235,395; wheat, 11,650,-980, value, $820,490. Total, 495,758,955, value, $11,282,127.

HIDALGO.

CHAPTER I.

Topography, Cities and Towns, and Agricultural Productions.

THE state of Hidalgo is one of the richest states of the republic, both in mineral and agricultural productions. The state is bounded on the north by San Luis Potosi; on the east by Vera Cruz and Puebla; on the south by Tlaxcala and Mexico; on the southwest by Mexico, and northwest by Querétaro; area fifteen hundred and twenty-one square leagues. The surface of the state is crossed by numerous Cordilleras, especially in the northern part, and is mountainous, and well timbered by numerous forests. It has many fertile valleys. The most mountainous part is that occupied by the Sierras de Huejutla, de Huchuetla, and Alta de Zacualtipan, at the base of which, and extending to the south, is an extensive and beautiful, as well as fertile valley. Gigantic monoliths crown the summits of the Actopan mountains, overlooking the valley, which are termed "*Los Organos*," or "the organs," a name given on account of the resemblance to large pipes of an organ. The name of "*los Frailes*" is also given to the same mountains. The whole valley is surrounded by a scenery that is pronounced to be one of the grandest of the whole country. The principal plains are those of Atotonilco el Grande, which is found between the grand barranca and the Sierra de Pachuca, the plains of San Javier and Tizayuca, situated southwest of the same Sierra and the plain of Mezquital, which is diversified by extensive mountain ridges, isolated and mountainous hills, and occupies the districts of Ixmiquilpan, Actopan, and Huichapan.

The city of Pachuca is the capital of the state, and has a population of fifteen thousand. The great mining company of Real del Monte, the largest of the republic, has its works located here. The city lies about fifty-seven miles northeast of the city of Mexico, in a gap of the mountains. The plains lying south of the city are under high cultivation. The city is reached from the city of Mexico and Vera Cruz by railway, recently completed. The state ranks as the third in its mineral productions. It has twenty mining districts, and in 1878 had one hundred and four mines in activity, which pro-

CITY OF PACHUCA. MEXICO.

duced $4,739,656. The agricultural products reached $4,382,050, of which the amount of corn produced was $3,456,000. The assessed value of real estate was, in 1878, city and country, $15,311,600.

CHAPTER II.

Mineral Resources.

THE mining district of Real del Monte is one of the celebrated mining districts of Mexico, and contains some very rich mines.

The Rosario mine contains a vein seventy-five centimetres in thickness, which assayed one hundred *marcs per monton;* and although it has well paid its owners, its workings are now suspended mainly on account of foul air in the mine. In the Encarnacion one of the shafts has cut a vein that assays eighteen marcs, with the ore carrying copper besides silver.

The Real del Monte Mining Company, originally an English corporation, is now controlled principally by Mexican capitalists. This company owns many mines in this district and the Pachuca mining district. The Dulce Nombre mine in this district was first located in 1820, and was recorded then. A shaft was sunk on a north and south lode, which at a depth of five hundred and fifty feet dipped to the east. The vein averaged ten feet, with firm hanging and foot-walls of porphyry. A very rich-paying streak in the vein averaged two feet six inches, but the ores were very refractory, and under the old system much of their value was lost. This mine has been relocated recently.

The Bizcaina and Tapona veins run east and west. The former is the largest vein in the district. The Santa Inez and Santa Brigida veins run north and south, and the Moran system of veins crosses the others diagonally. All these veins crop boldly, and on them are located the many mines which have made this district historical. The water-level is twelve hundred feet from the surface, and the Real del Monte Company have dug a tunnel which discharges four thousand gallons of water per minute, and has its mouth in the village of Omiltan, four and one fourth miles from the Real del Monte, yet the lower levels are unwatered. The elevation at the Velasco Works is eight thousand two hundred feet, at Pachuca eight thousand two hundred and fifty feet, and at Real del Monte ten thousand feet above the sea. The other principal mining districts are Pachuca, Jacala, Zimapan, Cardonal y Bonanza, Pechuga, Tepenene, and Atotonilco el Chico.

The San Miguel del Tajo mine is situated in the Pueblo of Azoyatla, municipality of Pachuca, in the Pachuca mining district. Its workings consist of a vertical shaft which measures 73 varas in depth. The vein was reached in 40 varas from the mouth of the shaft, and the ore assays from 40 to 50 marcs. The mine is said to contain very rich ore with a vein from 4 to 5 varas in thickness. Pachuca is the centre of one of the great mining districts of Mexico which has given to the state its great mining reputation.

In the mining district of Pachuca the mines in 1881 which were being worked numbered 45, and 138 were idle. For the reduction of the metals the city of Pachuca has five *haciendas de beneficio*. The Santa Gertrudis mine was reported to have reached a bonanza in 1878. A vein 2 metres in thickness which assayed as high as 50 marcs per monton of 30 quintals or 3,000 lbs., was being worked. The San José de Gracia mine has a vein 9 varas in thickness, which assayed 15 marcs per monton. The mine "La Luz" is located in the mining district of Zimapan, in the barranca of Toliman, two leagues from the town of Zimapan. Two veins have been discovered called "La Luz" and "La Pastora." At a depth of 105 metres ore was found that assayed from 12 ounces of silver to two marcs per carga. The Santissimo mine is located in the barranca of Verdosas, four leagues from Zimapan. Three veins were found in this mine which produced 3 ounces of silver per carga, and 10 to 12 per cent. lead. Some samples produced 10 ounces of silver and 33 per cent. lead per carga. In the Mineral of Jacala a mountain called "Cerro de las Maravillas" was discovered that contained veins of gold, silver, carbonate of lead, magnetic iron, oxide of manganese, and carbonates of copper. Many mines were worked upon these veins during the Spanish control. The principal mine was called El Carmen, in which a large body of ore was found containing oxide of manganese, and carbonate of lead and silver. The assay ran from 2 to 20 ounces of silver per carga, averaging mostly about 5 ounces. Placers of silver and platinum were found in this district, about 24 leagues from Zimapan and 12 leagues in a direct line from Encarnacion. The mineral of El Chico is also a rich district. The mining district of San Nicolas del Oro is the rich gold-bearing district of the state.

MORELOS.

CHAPTER I.

Description, Cities and Towns, Agricultural and Mineral Resources.

THE state of Morelos is bounded on the north by the Federal District, and part of the State of Mexico; east and southeast, by Puebla; south, by Guerrero, and west by Mexico; area, two hundred and sixty-two square leagues. The whole state is mountainous, with some few plains, valleys, and barrancas. The plains of Cuernavaca and the plain of Amilpas en Cuantla are the principal plains. The climate is tropical in the valleys, which are very fertile. Cuernavaca is the capital of the state, and has twelve thousand inhabitants. This city was founded in 1432, and contains the ancient palace of Hernando Cortez, the parochial church built in 1713, the Church of Guadalupe and of Las Tepetates, San Pedro, and San Pablo, the immense gardens of Borda in ruins, an hospital, a garden in its principal square, two Protestant churches, a literary institute, the Stage and San Pedro Hotel. This city was the favorite resort of Maximilian. The city of Cuantla de Morelos is the principal city in the district of Morelos and has three thousand inhabitants. It possesses a fine city hall, a public garden, a parochial church built in 1605, and the churches of San Diego and Señor del Pueblo. Yantepec of Zaragoza is the principal city of the district of Yantepec, and has a population of forty-five hundred. The city of Tetecala de la Reforma, in the same district, has twenty-five hundred inhabitants. The city of Jojutla de Juarez has forty-one hundred and seventy-five inhabitants. Sugar is manufactured to some extent in this state. Its principal productions are coffee, sugar, fruits, corn, rice, alcohol, wheat, etc. One mine is being worked in the mining district of Oaxtepec, and five mines in the Huantla mining district. There are seven silver mines, one of quicksilver, one of alabaster, two of jasper, and four of marble, which are not worked at present. The amount of agricultural productions in 1878 were, corn, 89,232,800 kils., value $1,885,200; sugar, 26,400,000 kils., value, $2,750,000; total, 119,240,-000 kils., value, $4,838,825.

TLAXCALA.

CHAPTER I.

Physical Features, Cities and Towns, and Resources.

THE state of Tlaxcala is bounded on the north and north-west by Hidalgo; and north and northeast, east and southeast, and south and southwest by Puebla; and west by Mexico. The state is mountainous, but has many fine valleys, the principal one of which is the Huamantla valley. Part of the state is well irrigated by the Zahuapan and Atallac rivers; area two hundred and fifty-three square leagues. The city of Tlaxcala is the capital of the state, and has thirty-six thousand four hundred and sixty-three inhabitants. The business of the city is confined to its woollen factories, traffic in grain and hides, and the importation of groceries and linens. The other important cities are Huamantla, Apizaco, Santa Ana Chautempan, and San Pablo. The productions of the state are corn, wheat, barley, oats, peas, lentils, and Chili pepper. Fruits of all the climates are produced in the varying altitudes of the state. The climate is on the whole pleasant and healthy. The mineral resources of the state embrace, as far as discovered, silver, lead, copper, and coal. The celebrated mountain called Malintzi, or Matlacuezatl, which is seen by tourists over the Mexican Railway from Vera Cruz to Mexico city, will attract the eye by its shape and the beautiful scenery around it. The summit has a resemblance to the corpse of a woman lying wrapped in its shroud at full length. The immense plain right and left, behind and in front of this, as far as the eye can reach, is planted with maguey. The mountain rises out of the plain some 4107 metres in height, and at once attracts the attention of every visitor. The mountain occupies an important place in Mexican or Aztec mythology, and bears the name of one of the favorite gods of the Aztecs. The state in 1878 raised 75,828,100 kils. of corn, value $1,602,100; wheat, 22,265,600 kils., value $940,800; total amount of productions, 166,334,200 kils., value, $3,918,150.

PUEBLA.

CHAPTER I.

Topography, Cities and Towns, Factories, and Resources.

THE state of Puebla is bounded on the east by Vera Cruz, southeast and south by Oaxaca, south and southwest by Guerrero, west by Morelos, Mexico, and Tlaxcala, and Hidalgo, and north by Tlaxcala and Vera Cruz. A wide chain of high mountains, cut at intervals by fertile valleys or plateaus, extend through the state. On the eastern boundary of the state are situated the Cofre de Perote and the peak of Orizaba; on the west, the volcanoes of Popocatepetl and Ixtaccihuatl. The first is 5400 metres, and the second 4786 metres above the sea. The climate is hot in the southern, temperate in the centre, and cold in the northern part of the state.

The city of Puebla is the capital of the state, and is situated in a beautiful valley seven thousand feet or more above the sea. It is a city fair to see, and fair to see from. It has a population of 76,817 inhabitants, a famous college, and a curious museum, many factories of cotton, porcelain, and glass, foundries and flouring mills, and is the second city in point of wealth and importance in the republic. The city is well built, its streets are wide, its churches numerous, many of them grand and imposing. It has its plaza and alameda, and there is an air of brightness and order everywhere. The principal churches are the cathedral, which is smaller than that of Mexico, but the interior is one of great magnificence; the Campana or Jesuit's Church, and that of San Francisco. The cathedral occupies one side of the plaza, and, like that of Mexico, stands on an immense stone platform, raised four or five feet from the plaza. It is built of dark porphyritic stone, with massive buttresses and lofty towers. Within the effect is very imposing. Vast columns, ninety feet high, support a well-lighted and graceful roof. The altar is of polished pillars of marble, with each groove edged with gold-plate. Inside these columns is a mass of polished, green, and almost translucent marble, and above and around it hang all manner of images. The chapel in the rear of the high altar is a mass of gilded and graven images, as are all the chapels in the chief churches in all the cities. Every crevice of the large chapel is covered with carved wood, tossed up into airy forms like the filigree work of a gold setting. Its chapter-room is hung with tapestries worked by the ladies of the court of one of the Spanish kings, who presented them to the cathedral. In the sacristy are some fine old paintings; the lavatory for the priests, with its beautiful marble, is finer than that in the cathedral of Mexico.

The city lies four square. Its streets are paved in broad blocks, which look as if washed daily, so lustrously do they shine in the rays of the sun. Most of the streets are raised at the crossings on each side of a narrow channel that runs through their centre under a single broad, flat stone, which channel lets the torrents in the rainy season flow to the river without disturbance of travel. The straight streets terminate in green groves or brown hills, which gives a very pleasant effect to the vista that opens to you whichever way you gaze. The branch of the Mexican Railway reaches this city, connecting at Apizaco on the Vera Cruz and Mexican Railway. Much trade has been opened with the United States by some of the most wealthy merchants. A railroad connects this city with that of Mexico and the port of Vera Cruz. It has five hospitals, two public libraries, containing over 50,000 volumes, several cotton and woollen factories — no less than nineteen in the state — three paper factories, and five iron foundries. The state has one college, a medical and pharmaceutical school, a normal school, an academy, and a school of art. The state is rich in the remains of Mexican antiquities. The fortifications of Tlaxcallan, and the celebrated pyramids of Cholula are worthy of a visit. The pyramid of Cholula is similar to the Egyptian pyramids.

The state of Puebla produced in 1878 the sum of $12,522,-485 in agricultural products, of which the amount of wheat raised was 23,075,000 kils., valued at $1,300,000; sugar, 5,250,000 kils., value $656,250; corn, which is one of the staple products, 400,093,520 kils., value, $8,452,680. The mining interests of this state are as yet but little developed. A superior quality of stone coal has been discovered in the department of San Juan de Los Llanos, besides many veins of silver and copper-bearing ore. Petroleum has been found in large quantities in no less than ten different localities. Immense quarries of marble have been discovered that are already one of the wonders of Mexico. Value of real estate, — city, $14,380,690; country, $15,458,774; total, $29,-839,464.

OAXACA.

CHAPTER I.

Physical Features, Cities and Towns, and Resources.

THE state of Oaxaca is bounded on the north by Puebla and Vera Cruz, and northeast by Vera Cruz, and east by Chiapas, south by the Pacific Ocean, and west by Guerrero. The whole state is mountainous, and traversed by cañons, barrancas, and narrow valleys; the climate varies with the altitude, but is on the whole mild, and varies from the semi-tropical to the temperate; all kinds of stock are raised; game and fish are abundant, and pearls are found in the fisheries of the coast. The city of Oaxaca is the capital of the state, has twenty-six thousand seven hundred and eight inhabitants, and is located in a beautiful valley. Its streets are laid off at right angles. On the main square are located the government palace and the cathedral. The latter is much praised on account of its style of architecture. The other principal towns are Teotitlan, Huahuâpan, Ejutla, Jamiltepec, Tepozcala, and Villa Alta. The principal ports are Puerto Angel and La Ventosa, Chacahua, and Huatulco.

This is one of the principal states of the republic, and has four thousand nine hundred and fifty-three square leagues. It has 233 sugar factories, 29 brandy distilleries, 368 brown sugar factories, 400 flour mills, 17 tobacco factories, 266 soap factories, 476 mezcal factories, 5 iron foundries, 200 earthenware factories, and 3 cotton and woollen factories. The public institute of the state has 34 professors, and departments of jurisprudence, medicine, pharmacy, commercial school, etc. The Seminario Tridentino has 8 professors. The state has 167 schools and colleges, including the State Institute, Seminario Tridentino, and Catholic College. It has also a public library containing 13,479 volumes, and two hospitals.

The state of Oaxaca has large forests of valuable timber, including dyewoods and all the fine cabinet woods, besides pines, oaks, and other timber for construction. In the list

243

of agricultural productions are found, beside the products of the India-rubber tree and vegetable dyes, Chili, or red and green peppers, bananas, oranges, lemons, and all the small tropical fruits, corn, wheat, barley, and the fruits of the temperate zones. The soil is rich and produces marvellou-ly. The amount of corn raised in 1878 was 416,662,080 kils., value $8,802,720; wheat, 7,693,908 kils., value $541,820; total amount of agricultural productions, 446,940,878 kils., value $10,469,530. Sugar cane is raised so largely that the common brown sugar sells for one cent per pound. Cochineal at one period was the chief product of this state, reaching the aggregate value of $2,500,000 per annum. This state has deposits of gold, silver, copper, iron, lead, and quicksilver, as yet not developed to any considerable extent owing to the lack of capital and the improved mechanical appliances; yet in 1880 no less than one hundred and thirty-eight mines were worked and thirty-two reduction works were running. Petroleum is also another element of wealth of this state, having been discovered in two localities. This state has an abundant rainfall, and has a greater number of constantly flowing water-courses suitable for irrigation and for motive power than is found in other states, which, with railroad facilities, added to the many advantages it already possesses, will place this state among the most important of the republic. Value of real estate — city and country, $8,630,589.

CHIAPAS.

CHAPTER I.

Physical Features, Cities and Towns, and Resources.

THE state of Chiapas is bounded on the north by Tabasco; east by Tabasco and the Republic of Guatemala; northwest by Tabasco, Vera Cruz, and Oaxaca; south by the Gulf of Tehuantepec; area 2,474 square leagues. The Sierra Madre mountains, in three chains almost parallel, traverse the state from east to west. Between the mountain ranges, extensive plains are found, and lowlands on the coast. The climate is hot on the coast and generally temperate in the rest of the state. There is no part of the state in which they do not cultivate all kinds of cereals. The state is well timbered, but its magnificent forests of valuable wood are being destroyed; cattle-raising and the cultivation of all cereals are the great industries of the state. The city of San Cristobal las Casas is the capital of the state, and has 10,205 inhabitants. Comitan with 6,286, Tuxtla with 6,963, Chiapa with 4,324, Tonala with 6,707, Ococingo with 4,019, Palenque with 2,554, Simojovel with 2,548, Pichucalco with 5,264, and San Bartolome with 4,591 inhabitants, are the other principal cities. San Benito in the department of Soconusco, and Tonala in the department of the same name, are the principal ports. The department of the centre produces flour enough to supply the whole state, and largely exports to the neighboring state of Tabasco. One of the richest industries in this department is the manufacture and export of linseed oil. The department of Simojovel is the chief source of the tobacco supply of the country. It is in very large demand throughout this state, and also in Oaxaca, to whose factories large quantities are shipped. The department of Chilon raises large quantities of sugar-cane and furnishes most of the supply of the state. The department of Libertâd possesses several large saline streams from which salt is evaporated. Cotton is grown extensively in the same department. In the department of Palenque sugar-cane is raised, and mahogany and cedar logs are delivered at tide-water. The departments of Tuxtla, Gutiellez, Chiapa de Corzo, and Tonala are specially devoted to the cultivation of the Jiquilite plant, from which an excellent aniline dye is manufactured and largely exported. The department of Pichucalco is largely devoted to growing cocoa, which is exported in large quantities to the various interior states, and also to foreign markets. Soconusco is specially noted for its excellent coffee. Lead, iron, sulphur, and talc have been found in this state. The amount of agricultural productions in 1878 were, — corn, 42,950,000 kils., value $796,000; sugar 335,600 kils., value $42,000; total 45,882,570 kils., value $1,045,500.

TABASCO.

CHAPTER I.

Physical Features, Agricultural Resources, Cities and Towns.

The State of Tabasco is bounded on the north and northwest by the Gulf of Mexico, west and southwest by Vera Cruz and Chiapas, northeast and north by Campeche, and east by the republic of Guatemala and Campeche, and south by Guatemala and Chiapas. The surface of the state is occupied by a vast plain lying along the coast with a few elevations; area, 1876 square leagues. The principal streams are the Usumacinta, Mescalapa or Grijalva, Istacomitan, Tacotalpa, Puscatan, Teapa, and a few smaller streams. This state is better supplied with water than any other of the republic, and is covered with a luxuriant tropical vegetation. The climate is hot and unhealthy. The state is divided into 12 partidos, and has 16 municipalities, 2 cities, 11 towns, 59 pueblos or Indian settlements, 67 haciendos, and 118 ranchos. The productions of the state are cocoa, sugar-cane, coffee, tobacco, cotton, corn, vanilla, yucca, sarsaparilla, pimienta, amber, hule, tolu, achicote, añil, fine woods, etc., and a large number of balsams and medicinal herbs, as well as a great variety of fruits of the tropical climate. The agricultural

productions in 1878 were, corn, 53,062,560 kils., value
$1,121,040; cocoa, 1,056,000 kils., value $880,000; coffee,
176,400 kils., value $58,800. The city of San Juan Bautista
is the capital of the state, and is situated on the banks of the
Grijalva river. It has 8,000 inhabitants. The principal port
is Frontera. The other principal towns are Cardenas, Comal-
calco, Teapa, etc.

CAMPECHE.

CHAPTER I.

General Description, Cities and Towns, and Resources.

The state of Campeche is bounded on the north and north-
east and east by Yucatan and Belize, south by Guatemala
and Tabasco, on the southeast by Tabasco, and northwest by
the Gulf of Mexico; area 3801 square leagues. The northern
part of the state is occupied by hills, which gradually rise
from the coast. The city of Campeche is the capital of the
state, and has 26,000 population. It is an old fortified Spanish town, situated in a fertile valley adjoining the gulf. It
has a fine theatre and several institutions. For many years
it was the only port of Yucatan, and was sacked frequently
by filibusters. The land is gradually invading the bay, so
much so that only boats of light drafts can navigate into the
port. The principal productions are sugar, brandy, henequen, tobacco, carey, shells, sponges, dye-woods, fine cabinet woods and timber, corn, etc. Amount of agricultural
productions in 1878, 4,303,360 kils., value $173,880. Value
of real estate is $2,746,591. El Carmen, the capital of the
partido of the same name, is situated on an island of the
same name in the Lagua de Terminos. It is a port of some
importance for the exportation of fine wood and dye-woods.
The climate is hot and unhealthy.

YUCATAN.

CHAPTER I.

Topography, Cities and Towns, and Resources.

THE state of Yucatan is the extreme eastern limit of the republic, and forms part of an immense peninsula, its own territory of which, is bathed by the Gulf of Mexico on the northern and northwestern, and the Carribean Sea on the eastern part of the state. On the south it is bounded by Guatemala, on the west by Campeche. The state is traversed by the Sierra Alta in a northeast and southwest direction. The surface gradually rises from the coast into foothills, and merges into the afore-mentioned Cordillera. The climate is extremely hot on the coast and throughout the whole peninsula. The city of Merida is the capital, and has 56,000 inhabitants. It was founded by Francisco de Montejo in January, 1542. Its principal buildings consist of a government palace, hall of justice, city hall, hospital, a theatre, a literary institute, conservatory of music and oratory, college of jurisprudence, school of medicine and pharmacy, and a normal school. It has also a public library, museum of antiquities, a cathedral, four parochial churches, and nine other churches. Progresso has 1900; Matul de Zepeda Paraza, 2900, and Valladolid has 3000 inhabitants. The latter city was founded by Francisco de Montejo in 1543, and removed to its present site in 1544. The city of Zical has 6000 inhabitants. The city of Ixamal has 4797 inhabitants. The state has 7 cities, 13 towns, 152 villages, 1133 haciendas, 363 ranchos, and 831 farms. This state (as well as Chiapas at Palenque) has some very interesting ruins that will well repay a visit. The state produces corn, rice, fruits, añil, tobacco, coffee, cotton, vanilla, gums, and dye-woods, sugar, henequen, logwood, etc. The productions in 1878 were, — corn, 164,952,850 kils., value, $4,446,560; henequen, 29,040,000 kils., value, $2,420,000; total, 202,381,760 kils., value, $7,489,075.

AN ANCIENT AZTEC TEMPLE.

THE FEDERAL DISTRICT.

CHAPTER I.

Topography, Cities and Towns, and Resources.

THE Federal District of the Mexican Republic occupies an extensive plain called the Valley of Mexico, which measures 45 miles in length and 31 miles in width. The district is bounded on the north, east, and west by the state of Mexico, and south by Morelos; area 50 square leagues. It is divided into the prefectures of Xochimilco, Tlalpam, Tacubaya, and Guadalupe Hidalgo. The principal cities are the city of Mexico, the capital of the republic and of the Federal District. The other principal towns are Guadalupe Hidalgo, Tacubaya, Xochimilco Tlalpam, San Angel, Mixcoac, Coyoacan, Atzcapotzalco, Tacuba, Santa Fé, Milpa Alta, Actopan, and Tlahuac, etc. The climate of the district in general is moderately cool and agreeable. The district in general is fertile, especially in the southern part, where the rich haciendas of San Antonio and Coapan are situated. The Valley of Mexico is diversified by many isolated hills — the Sierra de Guadalupe, and the Ixtapalapa or Estrella hill, the Sierra de Ajusco, and the cerro or hill of Chapultepec. The streams coursing through the district are those of Tlalpam, San Angel, Guadalupe, Consulado, and Tacubaya. The lakes of Tetzcoco, Chalco, Xochimilco, and Zumpango, receive the waters of the afore-mentioned streams, and of the whole valley. In 1878 the following were produced in the district: Corn, 12,254,600 kils., value, $215,750; wheat, 2,392,700 kils., value, $101,100; straw, 1,215,520 kils., value, $19,300; fodder, 3,055,200 kils., value, $38,190; alfalfa, 8,400,000 kils., value, $28,000; total amount of productions, 30,380,750 kils., value, $591,906, and 89,440 maguey plants produced $44,720.

CHAPTER II.

The City of Mexico.

THE city of Mexico, the capital of the republic, is situated in the middle of the valley of Mexico, 19° 36′ 26″ north latitude, and 99° 6′ 39″ longitude west of Greenwich, and contains about 280,000 inhabitants. Its altitude above the sea is 2282.5 metres. Its climate is temperate, never being over 70° nor under 50° Fahrenheit. The barometer stands at 22½ inches, and water at boiling-point marks 190°. The longest day is 13 hours and 10 minutes, and the shortest 10 hours and 50 minutes. The city is beautifully located. Beyond its white buildings, quaint and massive architecture, extends the rich and fertile plain, with its fields of grain, and maguey plantations, arbors and orchards, until the eye rests upon the distant volcanoes — Popocatepetl and Iztaccihuatl. The lakes, sleeping near the city, glitter in the sun like burnished silver, or, shaded by the vapors which often rise from them, lie cool and tranquil on the plain. Here is a scene long to be remembered by the traveller and tourist who has been permitted to rest his eyes upon the capital city of the Montezumas; a city the origin of which is hidden beneath old and almost immemorial Aztec legends; a city that was once the metropolis of a continent and the centre of a forgotten American civilization, which to-day from its former isolation of prehistoric splendor greets and welcomes all that modern civilization can add to its own accumulations through an unknown period of time.

The streets are at right angles, running north and south and east and west. Their names change at every block. At the extremity of each line of streets the mountains which surround the valley are plainly seen. The city stands on part of the old bed of the lake of Tetzcoco, out of which it sprung, but the borders of which are embanked at a certain distance from the capital. The six lakes cover fifty square miles of the valley. During the rainy season, in June, July, August, and September, in which the rain falls mostly in the afternoon or night, the streets are flooded for several hours on account of the current through the sewerage being insufficient. The valley should be drained, the sewerage of the city being almost on a level with the body of water from the lakes which lie beneath the city. Fruits and flowers grow in profusion, but the European fruits have not the savor of their original country; neither have the flowers the vivid colors or odor which they possess in lower regions. Although the altitude gives the city a climate that is between a temperate and semi-tropical, it is rarely cold or excessively warm, and will make the city a popular winter resort, the only reminder of the colder climates being the perpetual snows upon the mountain peaks. The commerce and industries of the republic are mostly carried on by foreigners, Mexican capital being invested in real estate, mines, and agriculture. From 10 A.M. to 10 P.M. the fares for carriage-hire are 25 cents per half-hour or less, and 50 cents per hour or over a half-hour, and from 10 P.M. to 6 A.M. the fares are doubled. The republic contains three archbishoprics and fourteen Roman Catholic apostolic bishoprics. The cathedral, so celebrated, is situated on the Plaza Mayor, and was erected on the very spot where Cortez found and destroyed the Aztec teocalli or temple, which was dedicated to the Mexican god Huitzilapoctli. The first cathedral was built in 1530, but was replaced by the present cathedral, which was commenced in 1573 and finished in 1667. It cost $1,762,000. This building is the most prominent of the city, and is the most elaborate of all the cathedrals of the republic. There are nineteen other Roman Catholic churches and one Protestant Episcopal, and four Methodist Episcopal churches. The other principal buildings are the national palace, the palace of congress, palace of justice, the municipal palace, and post-office. Chapultepec, the ancient palace of Montezuma, since the residence of the presidents, and afterwards a military college, is now the National Astronomical Observatory, and is situated but a short drive from the city, and at the extremity of the Calzada de la Reforma. There are four principal theatres and several smaller places of amusement. There are also the Academy of St. Charles, or fine art school, a mining school, colleges of jurisprudence, of medicine, a military college (at Tacubaya), college for young ladies or seminary, a school of agriculture, conservatory of music and oratory, school of commerce, school for deaf and dumb, and seminary school, the Mexican society of geography and statistics, architects' society and industrial arts, national museum, several clubs, an archiepiscopal palace, the mint, custom-house, houses of correction and a general prison, hospitals of infants, a general hospital of St. Andrew, hospital for insane women, and another for men, and others, and an asylum for the blind. There are several hotels and restaurants, and public drives and walks. The Alameda contains 70 fountains, 30 avenues, and 34 gardens. The Mexican Central Railway's handsome buildings are located in the northwestern part of the city.

Railroads.

THE principal railways of the republic are the Mexican Railway or Vera Cruz Road, the Mexican Central, Mexican National, Sonora Railway, Sinaloa, and Durango, and the Tehuantepec Road. The Mexican Railway opened its continuous line from Vera Cruz to the city of Mexico in 1873. It has a branch also to Puebla, and operates in all 365 miles. The directors' report for 1881 shows an annual average earning for the eight years of $1,310,882, or $4,473 per mile, net. This is six per cent. on $74,000 per mile, a moderate estimate of what it should have cost. The actual cost of the line has been officially announced as $36,319,526.52, or over $123,000 per mile.

The Mexican Central is destined to be the great trunk line of the republic, and will, when finished, bring the city of the Moctezumas nearer by rail than San Francisco is to New York. The company's main line extends from the city of Mexico, northerly, to El Paso, Texas, where it connects with the Atchison, Topeka, and Santa Fé, the Southern Pacific, and the Texas and Pacific railroads. There are two principal branches, one running westerly through Guadalajara and Tepic to San Blas and the Pacific Ocean, and one running easterly through the city of San Luis Potosi to Tampico, on the Gulf of Mexico. The distance from the city of Mexico to El Paso, by the best route, is 1,231 miles; from the main line to the Gulf, 318 miles; and from the main line to the Pacific, 430 miles.

The company began construction in the summer of 1880, and the track is now completed 350 miles north from the city of Mexico, and in operation to Lagos, a distance of 295 miles, passing within 12 miles of the city of Guanajuato, and connecting with it by a spur track, which is also completed and in full operation. The company is also constructing from the northern end of the main line, and the track is completed 382 miles south from El Paso, and is in full operation to the city of Chihuahua, a distance of 225 miles. Rapid progress is also being made from Tampico, westerly, towards the main line, 62 miles of track, beginning at Tampico, having already been completed, and recently work has also been commenced at San Blas. The line from the city of Mexico was opened for business to Tula, 58 miles, Sept. 15, 1881; to San Juan del Rio, 118 miles, Dec. 15; to Querétaro, 153 miles, Feb. 15, 1882; to Celaya, 182½ miles, April 15; to Irapuato, 219 miles, May 1; to Leon, 258 miles, Aug. 1; to Lagos, 295 miles, Dec. 15, 1882; and from El Paso to the city of Chihuahua, 225 miles, Sept. 15, 1882.

The road will connect the capital of Mexico with the eight largest state capitals, viz: Aguas Calientes, Chihuahua, Durango, Guanajuato, Guadalajara, Quérataro, San Luis Potosi, and Zacatecas, the aggregate population of which has been estimated at 608,767. The lines follow pretty closely the great highways upon which have grown up cities and towns, and pass through many of great size and importance, in addition to the capitals already named, such as Tula, San Juan del Rio, Celaya, Salamanca, Irapuato, Silao, Leon, Lagos, Fresnillo, Las Nuevas, Jimenez or Huajuquila, Santa Rosalia, La Barca, Ocotlan, Tequila, Ahualulco, Etzatlan, Tepic, Tampico, San Blas, and El Paso. The total population of the states through which the lines pass is estimated at 5,673,531, and the agricultural products, exclusive of cattle, for the year 1879, according to official figures recently published, were in weight 3,842,982 tons, and in value $89,100,976.

This great enterprise was originated and has been carried on mainly by Boston brains and capital, but Chicago has been an important factor, and strong support has also been given by Cincinnati, New York, and Philadelphia. Mr. Thomas Nickerson, of Boston, under whose management the Atchison, Topeka, and Santa Fé roads were built and made successful, is president of the company; vice-president, Robert R. Symon, New York; second vice-president, Levi C. Wade, Boston; official attorneys, R. G. Guzman and Sebastian Camacho, Mexico; treasurer and clerk, S. W. Reynolds, Boston; assistant clerk, M. de Zamacona é Yuclan, Mexico; auditor, J. N. Goodspeed, Boston; general manager, Rudolph Fink, Mexico; general superintendent, D. B. Robinson, El Paso; supt. Tampico division, E. H. Whorf; supt. Pacific division, Charles E. Payne.

The Mexican National Railway is built in pursuance of a decree of the Mexican Congress, known as the "Palmer-Sullivan concession," which contracted for the construction of a railway and telegraph lines from Mexico City to the Pacific Ocean at the port of Manzanillo, or between that port and Natividad, passing through Toluca, Maravatio, Acambaro, Morelia, Zamora, La Piedad, and thence to the Pacific, following the line most favorable; also a line and telegraph from

Mexico to the northern frontier, this line taking its departure from that to the Pacific at a point between Maravatio and Morelia, and passing through the cities of San Luis Potosi, Saltillo, and Monterey, arriving at the northern frontier at Laredo, or between that point and Eagle Pass. The other lines, since added by additional concessions, are to extend from Matamoras to Monterey, via Mier, and from Zacatecas to San Luis Potosi, and from Zacatecas to Lagos, making in all a system of over 2000 miles. The work of actual construction began in the fall of 1880, and the road is now in operation from Laredo (where it connects with the Texas Mexican Railway) to Monterey, making the run in 10 hours and a half. The Sonora Railway runs from Guaymas on the Gulf of California, via Hermosillo, Magdalena, and San Ignacio, to Nogales on the Mexican frontier of the state of Sonora, where it connects with the New Mexico and Arizona Railroad. The latter connects with the Southern Pacific at Benson, Arizona. The distance from Benson to Guaymas is 352 miles; from Nogales to Guaymas, 264 miles. The road runs through a part of the richest and most fertile portion of Sonora. Along its route are found numerous wealthy estates and old Spanish settlements, and many rich mines. The Sinaloa and Durango Railroad concession was granted Mr. Robt. R. Symon and associates for the construction of a railway from the port of Altata on the coast of Sinaloa to the city of Durango, via Culiacan and Cosala, and also a branch to run down the coast from Culiacan to Mazatlan. The road is now completed from the port of Altata to Culiacan. The Tehuantepec Railway concession was granted to Mr. Edward Learned and associates for the construction of a railway across the Isthmus of Tehuantepec. Part of the road only was completed, and the concession was then declared forfeited and turned over to the Mexican government. Many other concessions have been granted, some of which are being carried out, but the above roads are the principal ones of the republic.

Mexican Tariff and Trade Regulations.

The Mexican tariff by its excessive rates, and the governmental regulations controlling foreign intercourse and trade, have long been a source of annoyance to foreign merchants, and the primary cause of official delinquencies. The high rates have not alone been the cause of smuggling, but the peculiar intricacy of the custom house regulations, which have caused the confiscation of goods of well-meaning merchants, has also added to the temptation to evade the revenue officers and thus defraud the Mexican government. Independent of the annoyances attending a new trade, it will repay our merchants to examine carefully the following facts in connection with the list of goods mostly exported from the United States to Mexico. The duties thereon are calculated by the French standard of weights and measures. A metre is 39 inches, a kilogram is 2⅕ pounds. The figures enclosed in parentheses is an additional charge per 100 kilograms, gross weight, imposed by the law of June 25, 1881.

Wine, white, of all kinds, in bottles or demijohns, without allowing breakage, kil. net wt. (50 cts.)_____$ .29
Wine, white, of all kinds, in wooden vessels, without allowing leakage, kil. net wt. (50 cts.)_____ .19¾
Wine, claret, all kinds, in bottles or demijohns, without allowing breakage, kil. net wt. (50 cts.)_____ .18½
Wine, claret, all kinds, in wooden vessels, without allowing leakage, kil. net wt. (50 cts.)_____ .11¾
Wines, medicinal, all substances, and authors, kil. net wt. (50 cts.)_____ _____ 1.50
Liquors in bottles or jars, without allowing breakage, kil. gross wt., .23 and .08 additional net, (50 cts.)
Acids, of all kinds, either gaseous or liquid, kil. net wt. including inside packing, (50 cts.)_____ .25
Acids, powdered or in glass vessels, kil. net wt., including inside packing, (50 cts.)_____ 1.00
Billiard tables of any material, not including cloth, upon appraisement, 55 per cent.
Billiard balls, kil. gross wt. (50 cts.)_____ 3.72
Billiard sticks and caps, kil. gross wt. (50 cts.)_____ .43
Books, bound in velvet, shell, tortoise, ivory or metal, kil. gross wt. (50 cts.)_____ 1.15
Blankets, cotton, plain or stamped, square metre, (50 cts.) .48
Blankets, wool, not stamped or figured, square metre, (50 cts.)_____ .96
Blankets, cotton and wool mixed in average proportion, plain or stamped, square metre, (75 cts.)_____ .72
Brushes, scrubbing, shoe blacking and horse cleaning, gross wt. (50 cts.)_____ .19
Brushes for table, clothing, hair, teeth, nails and hats, set on wood, bone, horn, or gutta percha, gross wt. (50 cts.)_____ .29
Same, set on ivory, shell, tortoise, or gilded or silver plated metal, gross wt. ($1.00)_____ .86

Bags and sacks, ready-made, common, of any material, upon appraisement, 55 per cent. (50 cts.).........

Clocks, fine, not gold or silver, gross wt. ($1.00)...... .86

Clocks, common, with or without wooden box, gross wt. (75 cts.)... .29

Coffee, net wt. (75 cts.) .... .10

Cloves and spices, net wt. (50 cts.)................... .60

Cotton, ginned, gross wt. (50 cts.)................... .07

Cotton, seed, gross wt. (75 cts.) .... .02

Curry-combs and iron combs, gross wt. (50 cts.) ...... .19

Codfish, dried or smoked, and any other fish prepared in the same manner, net wt. (75 cts.)............. .10

Combs, Chinese cane, all kinds, gross wt. ($1.00)..... .23

Combs, ladies' varnished iron, horn, gutta-percha, bone, or wood, with or without common metal, gross wt. (50 cts.) .... .29

Cloth, all kinds and colors, with woolen base and woof, plain, figured or striped, sq. metre (75 cts.)...... 1.56

Cotton goods, common white and colored, sq. metre ($1.00) .... .09

Cotton goods, white and colored, not embroidered or perforated, sq. metre (50 cts.).................... .16

Cotton goods, plain, brown, unbleached, sq. metre (50 cts.)... .09$\frac{40}{100}$

Cotton goods, bleached or unbleached, serged or twilled, sq. metre (50 cts.)................................. .16

Cotton goods or textures, white or colored, embroidered or perforated, sq. metre ($1.00) .... .19

Thread, per doz. ($1.00) .... .20

Cassimeres and similar woolen goods, sq. metre ($1.00) .80

Carriages, open, and coupés, each (50 cts.)........... 176.00

Coaches, phaetons, landaus, each (50 cts.)........... 396.00

Buggies, each (50 cts.) 132.00

Sulkies, each (50 cts.)................................ 33.00

Wagons, each (50 cts.) 66.00

Harness for carriages, fine, kil., gross wt. (75 cts.) 2.00

Harness for wagons, ordinary, kil., gross wt. (75 cts.).. .86

Furniture, 55 per cent. *ad valorem* (50 cts.)...........

Pianos, kil., gross wt. (75 cts.) .... .43

Drugs, medicines, natural and chemical products, and vessels and commodities used therefor not specified in tariff, 88 per cent. *ad valorem* ($1.00)......

Earthenware and porcelain, except those specified, and toys, gross wt., without allowing breakage (50 cts.) .14

Same, ornamented with white or yellow metal (75 cts.) .29

Flour, kil. net. wt., (50c)	10
Wheat, kil., net wt., (50c)	04
Barley, kil., net wt., (50c)	03
Rice, kil., net wt., (50c)	07
Hops, kil., net wt., (50c)	18
Hams, smoked, net wt., (50c)	25
Meats, salt and smoked, net wt., (50c)	24
Lard, kil., net wt., (50c)	18
Butter, kil., net wt., (50c)	24
Cheese, kil., net wt., (50c)	14
Candles, tallow, gross wt., (50c)	08
Candles, stearine, gross wt., (50c)	19
Candles, parafine, gross wt., (50c)	38
Crackers, gross wt., (50c)	12
Canned fruit, cans included, net wt., (50c)	50
Canned meats and fish, cans included, net wt., (50c)	72
Pickles, jars included, kil., net wt., (50c)	48
Soap, toilet, kil., gross wt., (75c)	1 15
Soap, common, kil., gross wt., (50c)	15
Glass, common, kil., gross wt., (50c)	24
Gun powder, kil., goss wt., (75c)	2 00
Nails of all kinds, iron, kil., gross wt., (50c)	12
Tools, iron. steel and wood, kil., gross wt., (50c)	19
Clothing, ready-made, all kinds, per suit, ($1) 132 per cent.	
India rubber clothing, kil., gross wt. (75c)	1 43
India rubber shoes, etc., kil., gross wt., (50c)	43
India rubber cloth, for tables, kil., gross wt., (50c)	29
Oil cloth, for floors kil., gross wt., (50c)	29
Leather, boots, yellow, dozen, ($1)	16 50
Leather boots, calf or morocco, dozen, ($1)	27 00
Leather shoes, common, men's, dozen, ($1)	7 00
Leather shoes, fine, men's, dozen, ($1)	16 50
Leather shoes, women's dozen, ($1)	10 00
Leather shoes, women's common, dozen, (75c)	5 50
Carpets, two and three-ply, sq. metre, ($1)	80
Carpets, Brussels. sq. metre, ($1)	97
Carpets, velvet, sq. metre, ($1)	1 40
Cocoa matting, kil., gross wt., (50c)	16
Vinegar, barrels, kil., net wt., (50)	05
Vinegar, bottles, kil., net wt., (50c)	10
Whisky, barrels, kil., net wt., (50c)	37½
Whisky, bottles, net wt., (50c)	46
Beer, barrels, kil.. net wt., (50c)	10½
Beer, bottles, kil., net wt., (50c)	21

17

Petroleum, cans included, kil., net wt., (50c)........ 09
Resin, kil., gross wt., (50c)............................. 25
Tar, kil., gross wt., (50c)............................... 03
Salt, kil., gross wt., (50c(............................. 05
Potatoes, kil., gross wt., (50c).............. 02
Onions, kil., gross wt., (50c)............................ 02

Free List.

Articles exempt from import duties at the Maritime and Frontier Custom houses of Mexico, as revised in accordance with the law of 1st of June 1880, and also with the law of June 25th, 1881.

ART. 16.—The following articles are exempt from duties on their importation into the Republic, except in amounts as follows:

Gross Weight per 100 kils.

1.—Armament for the States, provided that the exemption be solicited from the Executive of the Union, by the Governors, with the consent of their respective Legislatures.....................

2.—Telegraph wire, the destination of which must be accredited at the Maritime Custom houses, by the respective parties interested..............

3.—Wire, of iron or steel for carding from No 26 upwards...................................... 50

4.—Alabaster in the rough.......................... 50

5.—Animals of all kinds, alive or stuffed for cabinets of Natural History—with the exception of gelded horses................................ 50

6.—Ploughs and ploughshares...................... 50

7.—Masts and anchors for large or small vessels....... 50

8.—Oats, in grain or in the straw................... 50

9.—Quicksilver 50

10.—Sulphur 50

11.—Steel crowbars for mines, cylindrical or octagon, from 4 to 6 centimeters in diameter and from 75 to 175 centimetres in length... 50

12.—Fire engines and *common pumps* of all classes, and materials for irrigation and other purposes. 50

13.—Hoes, "machetes" [common chopping knives for sugar cane] without sheaths, scythes, sickles, rakes, harrows, spades, shovels, picks and pickaxes for agricultural purpose................. 75

Gross Weight
per 100 kils.

14.—Hydraulic lime....................   50

15.—Tubing of all classes, materials and dimensions,
without considering as comprised in this exemption, copper tubes or those of other metals that
do not come soldered or closed with joints or
rivets in their whole length, which shall be
subject to the payment of duties, acording to
the material...   50

16.—Cardclothing of wire, in sheets for machinery
and sheep cards.....................................   50

17·—Wheelbarrows, hand, of one and two wheels,
and hods..   50

18.—Crucibles of all materials and sizes..................   50

19.—Railway cars, coaches and wagons...................

20.—Coal of all kinds.................... ....

21.—Collections, mineralogical and geological, and of
all branches of Natural History....................

22.—Houses, of wood or of iron, complete..............

23.—Whalebone, unmanufactured...........................   50

24.—Designs and models of machinery, buildings,
monuments and ships or vessels..................   50

25.—Staves and heads for barrels...........................   50

26.—Vessels, ships, boats, etc., of all classes and
forms, in their naturalization or for sale, or on
their introduction for navigating the bays,
lakes, canals and rivers of the Republic.........

27.—Iron and steel, manufactured into rails for railways ....

28.—Fruit and vegetables, fresh, with the exception
of those specified in the schedule of duties......   50

29—Guano   50

30.—Ice   50

31.—Hiposulphate of Soda..................................   50

32,—Corn meal, made from maize, and handmills for
grinding it...   50

33.—Instruments, scientific................................... 1 00

34.—Books, printed, bound or unbound.................. 1 00

35.—Firewood..   50

36.—Bricks and clay, refractory...........................   50

37.—Type, letter, gussets, spaces, lines, vignettes and
every kind of printing type......................   50

38.—Box wood...   50

39.—Timber, common, for construction..................   50

40.—Maize, Indian Corn..   50

Gross *Weight*
per 100 *kils.*

41.—Maps and globes.................................... 1 00

42.—Machinery—I. Machines and apparatus of
every kind adapted to industrial purposes, to
agriculture, mining and the arts and sciences,
with their separate and duplicate parts.......... 50

  II. Loose pieces of machinery and apparatus, coming together with or apart therefrom, are included in this exemption, but this exemption does
not comprise the leather or rubber belting that
serves for communicating motion, when it is not
imported at the same time as the machinery to
which it is to be applied............................. 1 00

  III. Those articles of which a separate use can be
made, distinct from the machinery or apparatus, such as pig iron, hoop iron in bars or rods,
stuffs of woollen or other material and tanned
or untanned leather, even when they come
jointly with the machinery shall be subject to
the payment of duties, in accordance with the
rates of the respective Tariff.......................

43.—Steam engines and locomotives, iron or wooden
sleepers, and the other accessories for building railways..

44.—Marble in the rough and in slabs of all dimensions for floors or pavement........................ 50

45.—Fuse and matches for mines...................... 50

46.—Ores of precious metals, in bulk or in powder...

47.—Moulds and patterns for the arts................. 50

48.—Legal coin of silver or gold of all nations...........

49.—Coins,—collections of,—of all classes............. 1 00

50.—Natural History—Specimens of—for museums
and cabinets.. 50

51.—Fodder—dry, in the straw.......................... 50

52.—I. Plants and seeds for the improvements of agriculture exceeding 115 kilograms of each
kind of seed... 50

  II. In order that the seeds be comprised in
this exemption, it must be expressed in the
respective Consular Invoices, that they are imported for the improvement of agriculture.....

53.—Lithographic Stones.................................. 50

54.—Slates for roofing and floors....................... 50

55.—Powder—common, for the use of mines and
dynamite for the same purposes.................... 50

Gross Weight
per 100 kils.

56.—Vaccine matter....................................... 50
57.—Oars for boats and barges......................... 50
58.—Common salt, imported through "Paso del
    Norte.".. 50
59.—Saltpetre... 50
60.—Sulphate of copper................................. 50
61.—Anvils for silver smiths.......................... 50
62.—Printing Ink... 50
63.—Type, wooden, and other materials for litho-
    graphy.. 50
64.—Rays of all kinds for manufacturing powder...... 50
65.—Joists, of iron for roofs, provided no use can be
    made of them for other purposes in which iron
    is employed.. 50
66.—Anvils, Blacksmith's.............................. 50

Article 17th—The Executive of the Union can concede a dispensation of import duties, to the amount of one hundred dollars, on the articles brought in by the States of the Federation, which are intended for the encouragement of material improvements and for the aid of public charities.

Note of the Translator.—Notwithstanding the paragraph No. 42 declares machinery free of duties, iron shoes and dies for mortars and stamping mills are made to pay 6 cents per kilogram, gross weight, and iron stamps for crushing mills the same rate, as per paragraph of the Schedule of duties No. 448.   *George F. Henderson,* Translator.

One small trunk containing necessary wearing apparel, two watches and chains, one hundred cigars, forty small bunches of cigars, one-half a kilogram of snuff, one-half a kilogram of tobacco for pipe, one pair of pistols with their accesories up to 200 cartridges, one rifle, *escopeta* or carbine with accesories up to 200 cartridges, one pair of musical instruments, except pianos and organs.

Formerly the Federal Government of Mexico had four or five additional duties, but these have all been consolidated into the tariff (which is one cause of its high rate), and one other duty paid to the Custom House in Mexico City of two per cent. on the tariff rate when the goods are shipped to Mexico City. There exists also a municipal and State duty on foreign goods, so that when the goods are landed at Vera Cruz they pass through the Custom House and pay the tariff, then another tax is laid upon them by the municipality, when they leave Vera Cruz All foreign goods must be passed regularly through the custom house at Vera Cruz, when consigned to Mexico City by way of Vera Cruz. Upon their arrival in Mexico City the goods have to again go through the custom house in that city, the packages subjected to another opening, the local tax to be paid, and more charges for stamps, stevedores, etc. In spite of all this annoyance, the merchants find the trade very profitable. It may be well to note that there is no bonded warehouse system under the Mexican tariff laws, and hence all goods must pay the duties when imported, one month being the time allowed for adjusting all questions of difference and payment.

Before the goods are shipped: 1st, Consult the Mexican consul at your port on the regulations, and follow his instructions to the letter carefully, obtaining the forms to be filled out from him; 2d, Invoice the goods, procuring the Mexican consul's authentication to the same, or in the absence of a consul or vice-consul, authentication by two responsible merchants; 3d, Manifest the goods with one or the other above specified authentications; 4th, Obtain the Mexican consul's receipt, when it can be obtained, on separate paper, for the fees paid on authentication, invoice and manifest; 5th, Send all documents with the goods to whoever is to conduct the entry of the goods into Mexico; 6th, See that the manifest and invoice is made in triplicate and contain an exact detail of quantity, kind, quality and value of everything in the cargo to be entered. Unless this rule is strictly complied with a heavy fine will be incurred; 7th, In packing the goods put each class as classified by the tariff in separate packages, those calculated by net weight of a certain specified value in one, those by gross weight in another, and those by square metre in another, and those by ad valorem in another, and when different rates are attached to different kinds of merchandise, whether appraised by net or gross weight, or square metre or ad valorem, place the goods with the same tariff rates in their respective packages, classifying the respective goods by values of rates as well as by the manner of appraisement. The classification by value is as necessary as the others from the fact that when different classes of values are packed promiscuously, the appraisement will be made upon the whole package at the rate corresponding to the highest rate of any article contained therein; 8th, In packing goods to be appraised by square metre, every package should contain the same number of yards. This will save the opening of packages, and the calculation can be made much easier for the invoice.

Manner of Acquiring Real Estate.

Land is acquired in Mexico by denouncement, purchase, donation, accession, prescription, adjudication and inheritance. The law relating to public lands limits the acquiring of said lands to 2,500 hectares (about 2½ acres to each hectare) to each denouncer, but this may be increased by Government grant.

The following legal opinion touching the denouncement of vacant lands, by Hon. Judge Carlos F. Galan, one of the magistates of the Supreme tribunal of Sinaloa and Lower California, but now practicing law in this city, is given to the public with the permission of Judge Galan:

"A petition is presented to the District Judge (Federal), describing the lands by metes and bounds. The Judge orders the denouncement to be published in a newspaper for the period of three weeks. If no opposition is made, the Judge orders a survey of the land denounced, to be paid for by the denouncer, but in accordance with certain rules given by the government. That done and presented to the Judge, the expediente is given for examination to the District Attorney, who objects or not, as the case may be. In case of objection, the Judge orders a new survey, or whatever may be needed, in accordance with the District Attorney's opinion. When all is correct, the Judge adjudicates the land to the denouncer; a certified copy of all the proceedings is taken at the expense of the denouncer, and sent to the Governor of the State where the land is situated. He reports favorably or otherwise, and sends the papers, always at the expense of the denouncer, to the Minister of Fomento, in Mexico, and there the papers remain till their turn comes, and the Minister may or may not issue a patent. That issued, it is sent to the District Judge, who gives the judicial possession of the land, (not gratis, however) and the patent is delivered after paying for the land."

The question of the right of foreigners to acquire real estate in the Republic is an extensive one, and we shall content ourselves with the following brief summary and refer our readers to the work entitled "Hamilton's Mexican Law," in which we have elaborately discussed this subject, and quoted all the laws extant relating thereto, together with the Mexican Constitution and decisions of Mexican tribunals.

The law to-day in relation to foreigners may be said to prohibit:

First—Acquisition of private lands within twenty leagues of the boundary line by foreigners without express permission from the Supreme Government.

Second—Denouncement of public lands by natives or naturalized citizens of the adjoining nations in any of the frontier States or Territory.

Third—Acquisition of real estate in any part of the Republic, unless the foreigner is either a resident of Mexico, or admitted to local privileges, or has become a naturalized Mexican citizen.

Mexican Mining Law.

The manner of denouncing mines is briefly as follows: The discoverer presents himself with a written statement before the Mining Deputation of that district, or Prefect, setting forth his name, place of birth, residence, profession or trade, the distinguishing marks of the site, hill or vein of the property. The statement is entered in a book of registry with the hour of discoverer's application, and returned endorsed to the discoverer for his security. Public notice is then posted on the doors of the church, or in other public places, and within ninety days a shaft 1½ varas in diameter at the mouth and 10 varas in depth is sunk. One of the deputies, or the Perito, and a notary then personally inspect the bearings and direction of the vein, its width, inclinations, its hardness or softness, solidity of its walls, nature and indications of the mineral, adding their report to the record with the certificate of possession, which is then given, upon fixing the dimensions of the claim and stakes or boundaries. Official copy of all of which constitute the title to the mine.

Failure to work the mines four consecutive months with four regularly paid miners forfeits the mine, and it may then be denounced by another. Neglect to work the mine in the manner prescribed by law eight months in the year, counting from date of possession, although during said eight months, several days or weeks are interspersed, loses the right to the mine, unless this time is extended, or pestilence, famine or war intervene in the district where the mine is located, or within twenty leagues thereof. The mining ordinance, with all its latest modifications and mining decisions of Mexican tribunals, will be found complete in the work last before mentioned.

The present law originally prohibited foreigners not nat-

uralized or allowed by special license, from acquiring or work·
ing mines.   This provision was repealed by subsequent
laws and circulars, and now foreigners legally may acquire
mines in all parts of the Republic, provided one of the
partners resides within the limits of Mexico.   On this subject
see "Hamilton's Mexican Law," in which is discussed the
right of foreigners to acquire mines within the prohibited
belt, with the laws and circulars quoted therein.   This
right is withheld from foreigners by an unjust interpretation
of the law applicable to foreigners.

Trade with Mexico.

To thoroughly understand the present prospect of trade with Mexico outside of her promise of future development, it will be well to note the following facts:

In 1876, Antonio Garcia Cubas, one of the most reliable of Mexican writers, summed up the population of Mexico at 9,495,157, as the census of 1875, of which 20 per cent. were of the European race and nearest descendants of the Spaniards, or 1,899,031. Of the remaining population 43 per cent. were of the mixed race, or 4,082,918, and 37 per cent. of the native Indian race, or 3,513,208.

Within the last seven years the population has increased considerably, and especially within the last two years, the increase being through colonies and the natural development arising from the unexampled progress made in railroad building. The population of some of the larger cities are as follows: The City of Mexico, 280,000, which is larger than Rome in Italy, which has 244,484, or Lisbon with 253,000, San Luis Potosi 45,000, Puebla 76,817, Leon, in the state of Guanajuato, 100,000, Guanajuato 63,000, Guadalajara 93,875, Toluca 11,376, Colima 31,774, Zacatecas 62,000, Merida, capital of the state of Yucatan, 56,000, Aguas Calientes 35,000, Morelia 25,000, Campeche 26,000, Saltillo 17,000, Chihuahua 18,000, Durango 22,000, Pachuca 15,000, Mazatlan 13,000, Oaxaca 26,708, Queretaro 48,000, and Tlaxcala 36,463. It may be seen from the foregoing that the cities and towns of Mexico will compare favorably with other nations, and that she is almost as thickly settled in proportion to the extent of her territory as the United States, since the latter has only 13.91 inhabitants to the square mile, while Mexico has about 12.21 inhabitants to the square mile.

" There are 146 cities, 372 towns, 4,486 villages, 6 missions, 5,869 haciendas, 14,705 ranches, besides 2,248 collections or groups of houses denominated " congregaciones," " barrios," " rancherias," " cuadrillas," " riberas," and " estancias."

Value of private real estate, rural,...........	$ 773,000,000
Private real estate in cities,..................	2,358,036,000
Live Stock of all kinds belonging to individuals,	123,060,000
Property belonging to the nation,............	340,000,000
Total property, without including other personal property and mines, coasts, ports, lakes, bays, rivers, etc.	$3,794,060,000

267

The annual agricultural production of the Republic reaches to 6,569,524,903 kilograms, valued at $177,451,986. The harvest of corn alone reaches $112,164,424. The products of industrial establishments (manufactories, etc.) are estimated at from $13,000,000 to $14,000,000.

There are 324 mining districts, 23 placers, and 1,694 mines (worked), which produce 2,567,306 cargas (300 lbs. to the carga) of metal per year, reaching the annual value of $29,-713,355; and the number of persons engaged in the mining industry, 102,240.

The exportations from July 1st, 1877, to June 30th, 1878, were $28,777,508.07; and importations, $34,005,299.12.

The above valuable information has been ably compiled by Señor D. Emilliano del Busto, and is recognized as authoritative in Mexico.

The Department of Agriculture and Commerce has published a report upon the wheat yield of Mexico, from which we note the following:

The amount of land cultivated for wheat is officially announced at 6,909,932 hectares (2.48 acres per hectare) in 1880, and in 1879 at 6,876,975 hectares. In 1880 the amount of wheat raised was 68,725,075 metric quintals. From 1871 to 1877, inclusive, the total production of wheat was 701,323,052 hectolitres; and the amount consumed during the same period was 731,341,554 hectolitres, or necessitating an importation of 30,018,502 hectolitres. During the year 1880 the production was 101,081,836 hectolitres, and the amount imported for home consumption was 3,395,529 hectolitres (each hectolitre being 2¾ bushels), or 9,337,704¾ bushels of wheat imported in 1880.

The following table shows that the trade of the United States with Mexico, exports to, and imports from, for the fiscal years 1879, 1880 and 1881, has moved as follows:

	1879.	1880.	1881.
Exports	$ 6,761,284	$ 7,869,864	$11,172,738
Imports	14,047,819	16,325,417	17,454,126
	$20,809,103	$24,195,281	$28,926,864

Exports from the United States to Mexico:

ARTICLES.	1880.	1881.
Cotton	$1,176,067	$1,494,101
Cotton goods	832,000	1,018,600
Machinery	365,200	988,800
Other iron manufactures	390,000	913,000

Quicksilver	377,825	462,159
Indian corn	68,872	240,182
Fire-arms	209,467	224,301
Chemicals, drugs, etc.	142,237	209,053
Builders' lumber	130,506	183,436
Sewing machines	135,823	179,555
Petroleum	155,328	173,155
Gunpowder	49,627	145,397
Edge tools	97,936	138,469
Total	$4,130,888	$6,371,108

The imports into the United States from Mexico of coffee, since 1875, run as follows :

	POUNDS.	
1875	2,691,889	$ 485,489
1876	3,941,229	713,833
1877	6,789,693	1,265,970
1878	6,337,063	1,082,272
1879	8,307,040	1,371,979
1880	9,818,525	1,523,658

According to the Treasury statistics of 1879, the articles now being exported to Mexico are as follows : — Acids, agricultural implements, live animals (principally sheep), beer, ale and porter, billiard tables, blacking, books, pamphlets, brass manufactures, breadstuffs, brooms, brushes, candles, carriages, railway cars, clocks, coffee and spices, coal, combs, copper manufactures, cordage, raw cotton, cotton piece goods, drugs, chemicals, earthen and chinaware, fancy articles, fruit (green and preserved), glass and glassware, hats and caps, hemp manufactures, hides and skins, kips, india-rubber goods, iron manufactures, steel manufactures, lead manufactures, leather manufactures, lime and cement, musical and scientific instruments, matches, naval stores, oil, ordnance stores, paintings, paper and stationery, perfumery, plated ware, printing presses and types, provisions, quicksilver, rice, scales and balances, seeds, sewing machines, soap, spirits, starch, steam fire engines, sugar (refined), candles, tallow, tinware, tobacco, trunks and valises, varnish, watches, wearing apparel, wine, wood manufactures, and some miscellaneous articles. The direction in which large gains are to be made is in the articles which Mexico imports from Europe. The great bulk of the trade which Mexico has with England is in cotton goods. Changes of an economic rather than of a political character are going on, which are destined to enlarge the commercial intercourse of Mexico with foreign nations. The railway era has opened up opportunities for trade and commerce that Mexico has never heretofore known. Besides the goods before mentioned, which Mexico is now importing, she offers inducements to foreign capital in developing her resources, which will increase the demand for foreign articles of every class produced in Europe and the United States. The field is large and is open to British as well as American capitalists. We may take as an instance the establishment of a packery by Mr. L. de Pujal, on the Laguna Madre of Mexico, at Caravajal, Point Jesus Maria, which is canning oysters, red-fish, sea-trout, pompano, mullet, &c., of a very admirable quality, equal in every respect to the products of France and the United States, and which can be sold in the Mexican market at prices that compete with those goods on which no duty is paid ; and, of course, being a product of Mexico, they can be sent to all parts of the Republic free of duty, and sold as reasonably as the same class of goods would be if imported from abroad under a non-protective government duty. Mr. Pujal has started this factory under the unfavourable auspices of being far from routes of travel, and having to bear the expense of production until he was able to introduce his goods, which is just being accomplished, and which will, at an early day, place him in possession of a large and remunerative trade. On the lagoons of the Gulf, and the deep bays of the Pacific, fish, shrimps, and oysters may be had in untold quantities; and with such an inexhaustible supply at hand, the establishment may reach the markets of the rich valleys in the interior, and prove one of the most profitable industries in the country. The enterprise of Mr. Pujal should be the pioneer of many others of a similar class, and with the aid of the Government, which is willing and does foster every industry that is being developed, there is no doubt of the enterprise becoming a profitable one in Mexico.

The region from Lagos northward, and covering a wide belt of country through Jalisco and Aguas Calientes, is called the great granary of Mexico, producing millions of bushels of corn and wheat annually, the crops being certain on account of nearly all cultivation being done under irrigation.

Owing to the primitive methods of threshing and milling, a correspondent of the *Times Democrat* of New Orleans believes that there is a fine field for the introduction of threshers and small horse-power mills and corn-shellers. He goes on to say. "A man with one threshing and cleaning machine, and small mill, could travel through Jalisco and Aguas Calientes, and in three months make what in the United States would be two years' wages. And he could certainly, by thus illustrating the working of his machines, sell to perfectly safe people all he could deliver."

The notion prevailing abroad that the Mexicans are people who will stick indefinitely to antiquated methods is erroneous. They have hitherto held to them simply for the very good reason that they have had no opportunity of acquainting themselves with new ones.

Among other opportunities which Mexico affords to capitalists, the establishment of cotton-seed oil manufacturing may be mentioned. There are extensive cotton-growing regions within the limits of the Republic, but up to the present date the cotton only is utilized, and the seeds, one of the most valuable portions of the product, go to waste. A few years ago there was no thought of utilizing cotton seed, but now there are 275 mills in the United States; and the products of the cotton seed have added many hundreds of thousands of dollars to the annual resources of the Southern States.

The *Chihuahua News* gives an account of efforts making to organize a company to establish a factory in that city, using the cotton seed from the fields of Durango and Coahuila, now brought into easy communication by the Mexican Central. The seed could be bought there cheaply in large quantities, and brought to Chihuahua. The uses of the products of the cotton seed are various. The finest grade of the oil is put up for table use, having a close resemblance to olive oil; it is also largely used for packing sardines. It also produces a lard which for culinary purposes is regarded as superior to the best of hog-lard, on account of its cleanliness and freedom from suspicion of diseases. The lower grades of the oil are used for paints, lubricating, &c.; and the cakes of the crushed seed are in great demand for feeding cattle, especially milch cows. Nothing whatever is lost; the oily seed-hulls supply the fuel for running the whole machinery for manufacture, and even the ashes are of value, as furnishing the finest pearlash and potash, selling in the United States for three times the amount which other ashes bring. The supply for these various products of cotton seed has never yet equalled the demand in the United States. It is evident that in Mexico, where oils and lard are so high in price, the manufacture would be even more profitable than in the United States.

In the neighbourhood of the principal cities, vegetable gardening is a profitable industry, and in many instances the field is as yet unoccupied.

The agricultural wealth of the Republic will be one of its

greatest resources, and if colonies should be established near the lines of the various railroads, their success would be unquestioned.

The raising of cattle on the large grazing estates which exist all over the Republic, if properly managed, will be found to be one of the industries which is always attended with great profit.

To obtain an idea of the various resources of Mexico, let us note the vast increase in its productions.

The tabulated statement of the exports of Mexico for the fiscal year 1881-2, prepared by Mr. José M. Garmendia, chief of the seventh section of the treasury department, is interesting as presenting to the capitalist at a glance the resources of the Republic.

During the year in question, Mexico exported 3,785,565 kilograms of sugar, valued at $266,075.60, of which England took $201,066.87, and the United States, $63,793.63. Of coffee, 10,447,804 kils. were exported, worth $2,414,538.20. The United States bought $2,086,231.36; Germany, $133,221.25; France and Spain came next; while England purchased the least. Of tobacco manufactured, 122,798 kils. were exported, worth $226,952.46, of which England took $104,850.20, while the United States took $95,499.26. Of leaf tobacco, $124,300.70 worth was exported, United States taking $56,709.30, and Germany took $54,794 worth; England, with the other countries, taking small amounts. Horses were exported to the number of 9444, valued at $78,887, mostly going across the Rio Grande to the United States. Beef cattle to the amount of 30,995, value $252,745.50, were exported, the most of which went to the United States. The following articles were also exported :— Indigo, 120,598 kils., value $204,798; rubber or cautchuc, 129,504 kils., value $114,455.92 ; pearl shells, value $71,141.82 (mostly to England and Germany) ; beans, $62,536.20 (mostly to Spain) ; fruit, 1,128,673 kils., value $43,523.19 ; dye-woods, 36,734.74 tons, value $705,269.64 (England took $259,451.56, France, $177,541.29, Germany, $166,835.74, Spain, $57,329.20, United States, $44,111.85) ; honey, 657,889 kils., value $60,911.60 (United States took $45,021.60, Germany, $15,390) ; orchilla, 1582 kils., value $115,617.68 (the United States taking $101,393.06) ; pearls, value $37,500 (to United States) ; tanned skins, value $37,742.70 ; kidskins, value $669,557.77 (to United States) ; raw hides, $69,014.17 (to United States); henequin, 26,182 071 kils., value $2,662,106.72 (mostly to United States) ; ixtle, 4,748,979 kils., value $620,199.24 ($223,696.50 going to United States, $216,581.75 to England, and $150,905.74 to Germany) ; precious woods, value $620,784.90 (England took $326,820.77, United States $262,003.37) ; vanilla, 212,100 kils., value $780,830.47 (United States, $64,5173.07).

The total exportation to the United States was $13,760,161.85, of which $5,451,731.13 was in precious metals, and $8,309,130.73 in regular exports; while England makes a total showing of $10,284,374.85, of which $8,696,379.07 was in precious metals, and $1,587,995.78 in regular exports.

Among the important articles of export which may be mentioned as having shown a remarkable increase in the last five years are henequin, which has risen from $1,078,075.22 to $2,672,106.72; coffee, from $1,242.041.40 to $2,414,538.20; skins, from $997,013.21 to $1,708,554.15; vanilla, from $312,109.46 to $780,830.47; ixtle, $346,196.56 to $620,199.21; tobacco, $86,713.27 to $351,253.17; living animals, from $30,099 to $337,681; indigo, $61,523.60 to $204,798; cautchuc or rubber, $9,055.96 to $114,455 92

The report of the exports of Mexico for the third quarter of the fiscal year 1882-3, states that the total exports for the quarter were $12,083,216.14, of which $8,561,961.97 were precious metals, and $3,521,254.17 of other products. Of this amount, the United States received $4,956,016.61, precious metals included, $2,533,273.88, other products, $2,422,742.73. England received $4,878,212.23 in precious metals; $517,844,53 other products; total, $4,896,056.76.

The crowning statement, however, to show that Mexico has entered upon the flood-tide of prosperity appears in the annual statement of the exports during the fiscal year ending July 31, 1883. The official report, as the others also above are official, shows the sum total to be no less than $41,807,595, against $29,083,293 in the year immediately preceding.

The principal increase has been in the production of precious minerals, of which $29,622,657 of the total amount was in precious metals alone. In the other exports, henequin increased $638,955; woods, $458,326; and live-stock, $296,695. These exports have increased alone to the United States and to England, which shows where the great trade of Mexico is to drift—into the hands of the two most powerful nations of the globe, the future commercial sovereigns of the world.

There are over seventy cotton factories in Mexico to-day, which produce mostly a brown coarse cotton. Besides her own cotton, Mexico purchases from the United States over 21,000 bales annually; although some 4,000,000 pieces of 33 yards each per annum are produced—and nine print works produce 400,000 pieces, and ten woolen mills produce 2,000,000 pieces of cashmere and woolen cloth,—still Mexican manufacturers are unable to supply the home demand, and foreign nations have been consequently benefited by their purchases.

A very large proportion of the wholesale foreign trade

of Mexico is now controlled by German importers and mer-chants, while the balance is in the hands of English, French, Spanish and Mexican merchants. The retail trade is princi-pally controlled by foreigners, for although native Mexican storekeepers are found in every village, town and city, the fin-est and best stocked stores are owned by Spaniards, the ma-jority of whom are not even citizens of the republic. These small dealers are controlled, with an iron hand, by German firms who in turn are held in commercial bondage by the great business houses of Germany, of which the Mexican houses are but branches.

The German merchants wrested this commerce from the English by the means of a system of long credits they extend-ed to the smaller dealers. Once in the clutches of these gen-try the Spanish and Mexican retailers find it difficult to es-cape, and go on, from year to year, the mere commercial slaves of these haughty merchant autocrats.

But within the last two years the influx of foreign capital into Mexico, through the medium of the railroad movement which is now sweeping over the republic, has injured the in-fluence and the commercial power of the Germans. As this foreign capital enters the country and is disbursed by enter-prises that are under American influence, the latter obtain with the masses the credit of bringing this treasure into the republic, and the Mexican people are thus led to look with a more friendly eye on Americans and commercial relations with the United States. The greater part of this foreign money finds its way into the tills of the retail dealers ; by consequence they are enabled to buy on shorter time for less price than formerly, and thereby lessen their interest account with the importers.

The merchants have to pay an exorbitant interest to their creditors. The amount advanced is charged with from 8 to 12 and at times even 18 per cent. per annum, while they have at last come to see that this extravagance more than counter-balances the advantage gained from buying on long time, and are meditating a change of base to a cash system. The time, then, has come for other foreigners to enter this great com-mercial field and compete with the German merchants in the very market they have so long controlled. The same causes which enabled the Germans to capture the commerce from the English and French, will put it in the power of other merchants to displace the Germans in their turn. For the retailers have begun to rebel against the commercial bondage they have so long suffered, and have learned that the long

13

credit system, with the exorbitant interest that attends it, eats away their capital and leaves them at the mercy of their terrible creditors.

As money becomes more plentiful, trade will be correspondingly livelier. New retailers will open stores along the line of the various railroads, and in the vicinity of the newly opened mines that there are now strong hopes of seeing developed. These new merchants will take warning from the experience of those for whom they formerly may have worked, and whose position they are acquainted with, and will be only too glad to eschew long credits, and shun the illusive friendship and offers of the German commercial rulers of Mexico.

A new era has dawned upon awakened and rejuvenated Mexico—an era of material and social improvement. The Mexicans have seen the foreign merchants who make the republic their mere camping-ground; who come to the country to make their fortunes and then leave it, send millions of treasure annually to Germany in payment for goods which, in many cases, can be purchased much cheaper in the United States, and have concluded to change their tactics and buy for themselves in the markets most convenient for them.

They imagine they can find the line of goods they want in this country, and to a great extent they can; thus it depends entirely upon the merchants of this section to send agents to Mexico with samples of goods suitable for that trade during the coming winter, and they will be rewarded for their enterprise by the establishment of a constantly increasing and valuable trade.

How to Secure Mexican Trade.

The "Two Republics," published in Mexico City, in an editorial says: "It would doubtless be a good plan for American manufacturers and merchants to send intelligent agents into Mexico to deal directly with purchasers; indeed, all or nearly all the agents of this character who have come to Mexico have been rewarded with success. However, merchants doing business here complain that the orders sent to the United States or given to American agents here are not always filled with exactitude. Sometimes the articles are not the same as those ordered and at others the quantity sent is in excess of the order. Such recklessness as this is unknown in business here, our merchants do not fancy it, and will not submit to it except as a last resort. The merchant knows when he sends an order to England, France or Germany that exactly what he wants will be sent him, and he runs no risk of having a lot of goods unsuited to the market thrust upon him.

"Merchants in Mexico insist upon having their dry goods sent them in bales; for this they assign various reasons. European shippers comply with this desire, but Americans, with rare exceptions, will use nothing but boxes.

"European shippers make the Mexican tariff and custom-house laws a study; Americans do not consider such small matters worthy of their attention. The goods sent by Europeans pass through the Mexican custom-houses without the slightest trouble; those sent by American manufacturers and merchants are often subject to double or triple duties, on account of irregularities of the manifests, arising from ignorance of the Mexican custom-house laws.

Agents sent by American houses to Mexico should not confine their studies to the market; they should carry their investigations much farther, and completely master the manner of doing business in this country. In order to do this, more time is required than is usually at the disposition of traveling agents, therefore, a permanent agency would be an improvement on the present custom of sending agents into the country periodically, and the establishment of a branch house would doubtless prove more successful in the end than either system."

We take the following extract from a letter written from Mexico to a Boston paper: "There are four methods of seeking the Mexican trade: 1st, Through the medium of commission merchants in the United States, who are intrusted by merchants here with the purchase of such American goods as they require, and who will forward to their correspondents such samples as may be given them for that purpose; 2d, By sending to commission merchants here, samples and catalogues with the idea that they will make such representations as will result in business; 3d, By reaching directly, through the medium of such a publication as yours, the dealers here, and, as I stated in the beginning of this letter, the value of such a medium depends altogether upon carrying out a perfect system of distribution; and if that proposed by you is carried out, the object is attained. The merchants will communicate with the manufacturers or their selling agents—they prefer to do so,—saving thereby the middleman's percentage; *then* the samples, catalogues, and prices can be sent, and if found necessary, the fourth and last method, or final effort, can be made, viz.: sending here the very best representatives to do the business,—men who understand fully the de tail of manufacture, and whose address and bearing will secure such a reception as a gentleman will command. The person sent must expect to spend some time making acquaintances, inspiring respect, and studying the wants and peculiarities of this market. If what he represents possesses excellence, novelty and co-operative cheapness, it will succeed; and the only thing then necessary to drive in the last rivet is by sending out here *just what was sold.*

There is a market for all kinds of hardware, agricultural implements, carriages, harnesses, pianos and organs, fine cotton goods, mill and mining tools and machinery, American flannels, hosiery, woolens for gentlemen's wear, glassware, lamps and gas-fixtures, furniture, fine leather, hats, trunks and valises, surgical and scientific instruments, fire-arms, etc.

In addition to the statements of the commercial traveler, we would call attention to some further important facts: *First,* Under Mexican law it is necessary that an agent should be appointed with two separate powers of attorney, issued in accordance with the formalities of Mexican law, who *is a resident of Mexico,* one with power to transact business, and the other to collect, and if necessary, to bring suit in a Mexican court for the claim that may result from any commercial contracts. Unless this is complied with, no contract made by a foreigner who is not a resident of Mexico, and matriculated, can be enforced in a Mexican court.

Second, No judgment by default obtained in a foreign court will be recognized by Mexican courts, and in every case a trial must either be had in the foreign country, with the defendant, or his representative in court, before the execution can be issued from a Mexican court, or the trial must be held in the Mexican court, the case having been commenced by a representative who is a resident of Mexico and duly authorized by the foreign house, in which case only a judgment by default, or upon trial, can be legally had.

Third, Contracts made by commercial travelers for foreign houses not established in the Republic, or through commission merchants, unless duly authorized agents, can only be legally enforced by placing said claims in the hands of an agent duly authorized, who is a resident of Mexico.

Fourth, Commercial travelers should be matriculated before taking any orders.

Fifth, The safest and quickest manner of collecting claims in Mexico is to communicate with the American consul of the nearest port in Mexico as soon as an order is filled, making inquiry for a reliable person who may act as agent, and send on authority for collection and to commence suit to enforce the claim, if necessary. This should be done as a measure of precaution to save delay.

The American consul in many instances acts as the agent. The formalities required by Mexican law in granting power of attorney may be found, as well as the Mexican commercial and civil law, in "Hamilton's Mexican Law."

Sixth, In filling orders, either upon samples or without, *send only what is ordered*. This is important, for the purchaser, under Mexican law, is obliged to receive only the goods that correspond in kind and quality with the order, and upon his refusal to accept the consignment, delays and expense in recovery of the goods will be costly.

Seventh, Carefully follow the tariff regulations as to invoice, marking, packing, etc., consulting with the Mexican consul upon all questions of doubt.

Importance of Matriculation.

The attention of citizens of the United States residing in Mexico is called to the fact that the laws of Mexico require t at all foreigners shall be matriculated at the Department for Foreign Affairs in order that they may have a recognized foreign nationality.

Application for matriculation papers should be made through the Consulate General at Mexico, and through the consular officials in other parts of the Republic. This is important in the event of any complications between individuals and the government.

Not only is this important in relation to any complications, but it is absolutely necessary in order that a foreigner may have any standing in a court of justice in the Republic.

No act performed prior to the fact of matriculation can be remedied or benefited by subsequent matriculation. Hence the protection awarded by this law must be sought, before any business is transacted by a foreign resident in the Republic. See "Hamilton's Mexican Law," subject: "matriculation."

Importance of Securing Patents for Inventions and Improvements in Mexico.

The present demand for all classes of machinery in Mexico is unexampled in the history of any nation. The slow growth of Mexico heretofore has debarred machinery of all kinds, and inventors and improvers have consequently omitted to secure

patents in the Republic. This state of affairs no longer exists, and if it is desirable that the results of inventive skill in
the United States are to be preserved by those who hold patents, it may be as well to call their attention to this large
field that demands to-day the results of their labors.

Patents may be easily secured in Mexico, and it is sheer
folly to neglect to take the necessary precautions to preserve
the results of years of toil and experiment, that may be utilized in the Republic.

*Mexico must have machinery of all kinds used in the Uni-
ted States or Europe, sooner or later.* Here is the great market, let it be remembered, for years to come, and inventions
or improvements must follow the path of progress. Manufacturers are finding a foothold in Mexico, in the shape of cotton
manufactories, which may be seen by the article upon "The
Trade with Mexico," herein, and machine shops are now
turning out machinery of different kinds in Mexico. Foundries have been established at Durango, Mazatlan, Guaymas
and Puebla, and others will be established in different portions of the Republic. Manufactories of agricultural implements are also being established, one already being in Mexico
City and another in Puebla. This is sufficient to patentees to
show them that Mexico is awake, and with her vast fields of
coal at Laredo, and on the Yaqui river in Sonora, near Cosala
in Sinaloa, and at Santa Rosa and Piedras Negras in Coahuila, Mexico will in the near future be able to establish a
large manufacturing industry. Manufactories and machine
shops may be easily established, and produce, with the aid of
these immense coal fields, all kinds of machinery. The duties
and freights, added to the cost of the articles, that now prevail
offer too strong a temptation to manufacture the various
kinds of machinery, including agricultural implements and various utensils that are to-day needed in Mexico. This suggestion
is sufficient, for the patentee will readily see that unless he se-
cures his patent in Mexico, unscrupulous manufacturers may
maunfacture machinery without the payment of a royalty in
Mexico, and imitate every class of inventions and compete so
successfully with American machinery, that the patentee will
be debarred from the Republic. This becomes the more ob-
vious when it is considered that the Mexican or foreign manufacturer in the Mexican market has no duties to pay, nor
freight for foreign transportation. Hence his advantage over
the foreign manufacturer.

Full and complete protection may be secured under the patent laws of Mexico by any foreigner who has secured a patent

in his own country. The complete patent law applicable to foreigners may be found in "Hamilton's Mexican Law." In addition to which, we herewith give a statement from Mr. D. V. Whiting, a patent solicitor of Chicago, whose experience and ability are unquestioned. The following decision was received by Mr. Whiting from Minister Fernandez:

Department of Public works, Colonization, Manufactories and Commerce.

Section 2, No. 276.—Sr. David Whiting :

Sir:—Your letter of the 5th instant has been received by this department, in which as the attorney for Sr. John S. Adams, you solicit a patent for certain improvements which you say have been introduced into the construction of towers (*torres*) for the electric light, wind-mills, etc., accompanied with their respective drawings and specifications.

In reply to which, and upon consultation with the President of the Republic, it is declared to you that although the law in force only concedes patents for inventions made in the Republic, the Congress has been pleased to concede the same to foreign inventors ; but in future cases it will be necessary that the said inventions be accredited with the patent issued in their own country.

Liberty and the Constitution.

Mexico, July 17, 1882.   M. Fernandez.

In connection with the above we present the following statement of Mr. Whiting :

" The patent laws of Mexico are being so modified that patents for inventions and improvements will be issued for fifteen years upon the payment of a patent fee of $150. Patents will also issue for five or ten years upon the payment of a patent fee of $50 and $100 respectively. They will also be issued for the unexpired term of a foreign patent upon the payment of a patent fee of $10 per annum during the term the foreign patent has to run. Application for a patent from a foreigner must in all cases be accompanied by the patent issued by the government of which he is a citizen. Drawings and specifications must be in the Spanish language, and in duplicate. One copy is returned with the patent, if issued, to the applicant or his attorney, and the other remains on file in the Department of Public Works. Internal revenue stamps to the amount of twenty dollars are to be affixed to the patent when issued. Translations cost about $1.00 per hundred words, and the duplicate Spanish copy about 40c. per 100 words. Attorneys' fees vary from $150 to $500, according to the nature and intricacy of the case.

David V. Whiting,

Attorney and Solicitor of Mexican Patents,

102 Washington St., Chicago, Ill.

Treaties between Mexico and the United States.

The following has been officially published by the Department of Foreign Affairs :

"The treaty of navigation and commerce celebrated between Mexico and the United States of America on April 5th, 1831, was withdrawn from, by the Government of Mexico on the 30th of November, 1880, in accordance with the stipulations of part 1st of article XXXIV. of the said treaty, and of article XVII. of that of February 2, 1848, which ratified the former.

The convention entered into between Mexico and the United States of America on July 10th, 1868, regarding the naturalization and citizenship of parties who emigrate from one country to the other, was withdrawn from by the government of Mexico on the 10th of February, 1881, in accordance with the stipulations of Article V. of the same.

The said treaties ceased to have force, the former on the 31st of November, 1881, and the latter on the 11th of February, 1882.

By order of the Secretary for Foreign Affairs, the present notice is published for the information of the authorities and of the public generally.

Mexico, June 5, 1882.

(Signed) José Fernandez,

Chief Clerk.

An Important Decree.

From the Budget-laws recently passed by Congress and formally promulgated by the President, in the form of a decree, the following is translated :

"From the 1st of November next gold and silver coin, in bars, bullion, ore, or in any other form, shall be free of duty for circulation in the interior or for exportation. In order to compensate the suppression of the duties referred to in this clause, from the above date an increase of two per cent. shall be enforced on the duties now fixed on the importation of foreign goods, but in the meantime the export duties on gold and silver shall be collected in accordance with the laws in force during the present fiscal year."

* * * * * * *

" The following articles are hereby excepted from the payment of package duties (*derecho de bulto,*) imposed by the laws of May 31st and June 25th, 1881:

Plows and plow-points.
Masts, tackle and anchors for shipping.
Quicksilver.
Live animals.
Bricks and tiles of all kinds.
Common timber for building purposes.
Cotton, tobacco, coffee, and sugar-cane seeds.
Slates for roofs.
Vaccine matter.

If Mexico means to profit by foreign enterprise and capital, she must make great reduction in her tariff. She has already gone too far in tempting foreign capital to investment in developing her interior transportation facilities to attempt to recede from the path of progress upon which she has entered. This she cannot do without betraying men who are animated with the liveliest feelings in behalf of her development, and who have not hesitated to pour foreign capital into her bosom and infuse energy throughout her channels of trade. Millions have been invested in her mines and building railroads, and this is but the beginning of continuous development that will lead the emigrant to a land awaiting his coming. Foreigners are aggressive in business affairs, and when once the temptation to investment has met with a response by millions of capital, no attempt by unfriendly legislation will deter or hinder . but temporarily the sweeping changes now being inaugurated. We are satisfied the more intelligent classes of Mexicans are perfectly willing and are even anxious that their country shall keep pace with modern civilization and that they will ultimately remove every obstacle to the commercial and political reciprocity that should bind her with other nations in indissoluble ties of friendship and mutual commerce.

APPENDIX.

COMMERCIAL DIRECTORY

OF THE

PRINCIPAL MERCHANTS OF MEXICO.

FOR PRIVATE USE OF MERCHANTS.

[COPYRIGHT, 1882]

STATE OF AGUAS CALIENTES.—City of Aguas Calientes, capital, 35,000 inhabitants; principal merchants,—Viuda de Chavez é hijos, Davilo Hermanos, Aguilar Hermanos, Severino Martinez, Villanueva y Felgueres, Refugio Güinchard, Francisco Espino, Manuel Asco, Pedro G. Hornedo, Espiridion Gonzalez; lawyers,—Isidro Arteaga and Luis G Lopez; pharmacists,—Luis de la Rosa, Alcibiades Gonzalez, Juan María.

STATE OF CAMPECHE.—City of Campeche, capital, 26,000 inhabitants; merchants,—José Ferrer é hijos, Casselot, Gutierez y Comp., Eduardo Berron Barrett, Manuel Ferrer Itur, Rafael Preciat Estrada, Eduardo Estrada, McGregor y Hermanos, Regil y Comp.; lawyers,—Joaquin Baranda, Francisco Magaña.

STATE OF COAHUILA DE ZARAGOZA.—City of Saltillo, capital, 17,000 inhabitants; merchants,—Juan O'Sullivan, José Negrete, Guillermo Purcell, Damaso Rodriguez, Juan C. Sanchez, N. Sota, Daniel Salas, Carlos Martinez Quiroz, F. Llaguno, Joaquin Zépeda, Zamora Hermanos, Padilla Hermanos, Jesus Montes, Juan Pablo Saucedo, Sabas Ayala, Jose María Ramos, Fermin Villareal, Dionisio Garcia, Romulo Garza, Francisco Flores Martinez, Marcelino Garza, Donato Wolpe, Eusebio Calzado, Jose Juan Rodriguez, Francisco Rodriguez, Hilario de la Peña, Amado Cavazos, Antonio Flores, Sabas Gutierrez, Amado Prado, Jesus Grande, Atanacio Morales; lawyers,—Eugenio Maria Aguirre, Miguel Gomez y Cardenas.

City of Parras de la Fuente, 8,000 inhabitants; merchants,—Evaristo Madero y Co., Guillermo Prince, Fernando Rojo, Redone Lajons; lawyers, —Juan de Dios Argel, Manuel Z. de la Garza.

Monclova, 4236 inhabitants; merchants,—Telesforo Fuentes, Eduardo Hartz, Gregorio Arredondo, Ramon Muzquiz.

San Buenaventura, 3,500 inhabitants; merchants,—Seras Hermanos, Cayetano R. Falcon, Margil Sanchez.

Candela, 3037 inhabitants;—Francisco Rodriguez, Antonio Neira, Montmayor Hermanos.

Zaragoza, 2,600 inhabitants; merchants,—Antonio Urcullo, Eliseo Felan y Antonio Garza.

Piedras Negras, frontier custom-house; 2,500 inhabitants; merchants,— Jesus del Castillo, Santos Coy, Santiago Ridel, Jose Rivera y otros.

Cuatro Cienegas, 3,200 inhabitants;—vineyards,—Anicelo del Castillo, Jesus Carranza y Albino Morales.

STATE OF CHIAPAS.—City of San Cristobal las Casas, 10,295 inhabitants; merchants,—Vicente Ferrera, Wenceslao Panigua, Mariano Avila, Angel de la Vega, M. Armendaris, Mariano Cabrera, Cleofas Dominguez y Rabaza é hijos; lawyers,—J. Antonio Velasco, Clemente J. Robles.

STATE OF CHIHUAHUA.—City of Chihuahua, 18,000 inhabitants; merchants,—Miguel Salas, Felix F. Maceyra, Domingo Leguinazabal, Gonzalez Travino Hermanos, Quetelson y Degetan, Antonio Azunzulo, Benigno Navarro, Refugio Tejada, Gustavo Moye, Stallford Miramontes; commission merchants, lawyers,—Laureano Muñoz, Jose M. Revilla.

STATE OF COLIMA.—City of Colima, 31,774 inhabitants; merchants,—Oetling Hermanos y Comp., Kere Vander Linden y Comp., Alejandro Oetling y Comp., Agustin Schact, Esteban Garcia, Smith y Madrid, Jorge Oldembourg, Manuel Rodriguez, Epifanio Diaz, Gregorio Alvarez, Maximo Vargas, Francisco de la Plaza, Alberto de la Plaza, Antonio de la Calleja, Miguel Barreto, Dolores Güizar y Comp., José Maria Alcaraz, Cenobio Madrid, Salome Gomez, Guillermo Voguez, Enrique Olmayer, Aristeo Gomez; apothecaries,—Augusto Morril, Cosme Suarez, Francisco J. Cueva, Crescencio Orezco, Ignacio Fuentes; lawyers,—Miguel Gonzalez Castro, Juan Rojas Vertiz.

STATE OF DURANGO.—City of Durango, 22,000 inhabitants; merchants,—Garza Hermanos y Comp., Dorman y Comp., Hildebrand y Comp., German Stahlknecht y Comp., Juanbelz Hermanos, Francisco Alvarez y Comp., Salcido Hermanos, C. Rodriguez, Lowree Hermanos, Rios y Comp., Pedro del Rio, Andres Basterra; lawyers,—Francisco G. del Palacio, Ladislao L. Negrete; pharmacists,—Manuel de Avila, Eusebio de Ostolaza.

STATE OF GUANAJUATO.—City of Guanajuato, 63,000 inhabitants; merchants,—Gonzalez y Villaseñor, Caire y Andriffred, Pedro Oscar, Francisco Pedraza, Diego Abascal, Manuel Ajuria, Francisco Castañeda, Juan Romero, Lino Gutierrez, Eulogio Mingo, Palasson, F. Obregon Hermano, Stallforth, Alcazar y Comp.; brokers,—Ramon Fragua. Jesus Fernandez, Francisco P. del Rio, Florentino Manriquez, Feliciano Guzman; lawyers,—Joaquin Chico, J. Ortiz Carcaga.

STATE OF GUERRERO.—City of Chilpancingo, 3,000 inhabitants; merchants,—Gabriel Celis, Pedro Castro; lawyers,—Domingo Catalan, Santiago Cortes.

Acapulco, merchants,—J. M. Indart, Alzuyeta Hermano y Comp., Agustin Dempwolff, Meyerink y Comp.

Chilapa; merchants,—Andraca Hermanos.

STATE OF HIDALGO.—City of Pachuca, 15,000 inhabitants; merchants,—Jose Maquivar y Comp., Francisco Cacho y Comp., Marcial Islas, Juan B. Langier, A. Mercheyer, Nicolas Valdez; lawyers,—Francisco Arciniega, Francisco Hernandez.

Tulancingo; merchants,—Calixto Manuel y Comp., Pontal Castella y Comp., Tomas Urrutia, Juan B. Ortiz, J. Lorenzo Cossio, Jacobo Cortes, Manuel Gonzalez Varona; lawyers,—Francisco Rodriguez Madaringa, Manuel S. Rodriguez.

STATE OF JALISCO.—City of Guadalajara, 93,875 inhabitants; merchants, wholesale,—Palomar Gomez y Comp., Francisco Martinez Negrete y Comp., Teodoro Kunhardt, Alfonso Ayman, Fernandez Somellera Hermanos, Manuel Fernandez del Valle, German Hell y Comp., Oetling y Comp., Justo B. Gutierrez, Agustin Gil, Antonio Alvarez del Castillo; tobacconists,—Enrique de la Peña y Hermano, Heraclio, Farrias y Comp., Sandoval, Franco y Comp.; clothing houses,—Martinez Gallardo y Hermanos, Toofilo Lebre, Juan Muñoz y Comp., Antonio Alcaraz, Canuto Romero, Ramon Ugarte, Manuel Ornelas, Francisco Silva, Jose Garibi y Comp., Julio Rossi, Feliciano Corona, Luciano Gomez y Hermano, Felix Muniz, Juan Bobadilla, Luis Cruz y Comp; hardware,—Julio Yurgensen, Agustin Blume, Agustin Bhartolly, Mauricio Rohd; general merchandise,—Martin Gavira, Ramon Garibay, Donaciano Corona, Miguel Garibi, Celso Cortes, Isabel Cortes, Antonio Romero, Ramon Gomez, Gonzalez Olivarez Hermanos, Lowere y Hermanos, Mardueno y Camarena; druggists,—Lazaro

Perez, Nicolas Puga, Nicolas Tortolero, Vidal Torres; lawyers,—Aurelio Hermoso, Esteban Alatorre.

STATE OF MEXICO.—City of Toluca, 11,376 inhabitants; merchants,—Benito Sanchez, Agustin Hoth, Cortino y Sobrino, Guarduño Trevilla Hermanos, Benigno Rojas, Agustin Ayala; lawyers,—Antonio Inclan, Alberto Garcia.

STATE OF MICHOACAN.—City of Morelia, 25,000 inhabitants; merchants, Gustava Gravenhorst, Ramon Ramirez, Benito Barroso, Luis Infante, Jose Maria Infante, Nemesio Ruiz, Salvador Macouzet, Santiago Ortiz, Loreto Martinez del Campo, Eduardo Iturbide, Placido Guerrero, Vallejo Hermanos, Jose J. Retana, Pablo Torres Arroyo, Gabino y Epifanio Oseguera, Ramon Villareal, Ignacio Solorzano, Audiffred Hermanos, Chazes y Guido, Atanasio Mier, Juan Vallejo, Manuel Montaño Ramiro, Juan Galvan; lawyers,—Bruno Patiño, Jose Trinidad Guido.

STATE OF MORELOS.—City of Cuernavaca, 12,000 inhabitants; merchants,—Francisco Azcarate, Aramburo Hermanos, Juan Pagaza, F rtu y Comp., Santiago Fernandez, Francisco Celis, Felix Vertis, Angel Berguen, Tajonar Hermanos, J. Juan Gonzalez, Agustin Muñoz, J. Rios; lawyers,—Refugio de la Vega, Clemente Castillo.

STATE OF NUEVO LEON.—City of Monterey, 37,000 inhabitants; merchants,—Martinez Cardenas, Zambrano Hermanos y Comp., Hernandez Hermanos Sucesores, Bernardino Garcia, Patricio Milmo, Jose Gutierrez, Jacinto Galindo, Juan B. Gonzalez, Pragedis Garcia, Reynaldo Bernardi, Federico Palacios; lawyers,—Domingo Martinez, Rafael de la Garza.

STATE OF OAXACA.—City of Oaxaca de Juarez, 26,708 inhabitants; merchants,—Allende y Sobrino, Barriga é hijo, Cobo de la Peña, Juan Dominguez, Gabriel Esperon, Ignacio Figueros, Juan Garcia, Luis G. Hinzitres, Carlos y Comp., Quijano y Comp., Stein Gustavo y Comp., Trapaga, Juan S. Wiecher y Comp., Muqueo Hermanos, Jimenez Mariano, Moya Luis, Ramirez Mariano, M. Puyos, Frores Andres, Ibañez Ramon; lawyers,—Marquez Cenobio, Juan Maria Santaella, Justo Benites.

STATE OF PUEBLA.—City of Puebla, 76,818 inhabitants; merchants,—Marroquin y Gauthier, Ramon Laine, M. Toquero, Francisco Traslosheros, Mier y Conde, Manuel Garcia Teruel, Diehl y Comp., J. B. Lyons y Comp., Chaix y Comp., M. Gomez Ligero, Jose Maria Couttolene, Arnau Salles, Jose Diaz Rubin, Jose Caloca, Adolfo Arrioja, Luis Bello, Dionisio Velasco, Luis Garcia Teruel, Francisco Cabrera, Antonio Rossiles, Manuel Conde, Lions y Comp., Felix Perez, Ramon Acho, Florencio Gavito M Hernandez, Hernandez y Comp.; lawyers, Francisco Gomez Daza, Clemente Lopez, Joaquin Ruiz.

STATE OF QUERETARO.—City of Querétaro, 48,000 inhabitants; merchants,—Carlos Rubio, Arnando y Martel, Rivera y MacGregor, Jose Garcia Gonzalez; lawyers,—Juventino Guerra, Prospero Vega.

STATE OF SAN LUIS POTOSI.—City of San Luis Potosi, 45,000 inhabitants; merchants,—Muriedas y Comp., J. H. Bahnsen y Comp., Matias A. Soberon, Aristi y Comp., Herculano M. de Lara Sucesores, A. Guthiel y Comp., Pitman y Co., Caire y Texier, Aguerre Hermanos, Jose Lorenzo Campos, Pons Hermanos, Carlos Danne, Ortolozaga y Comp., Varona y Comp., Jose M. Davalos, Manuel Noriega y Comp., Antonio Delgada Renteria, Balmori y Comp., Larrache Sucesores, Gastinel y Auber, Ignacio Noriega, Juan Jose Ottermin, Macedonio Gomez, Tena, Lavin y Diliz, Juan Equillor, Gedowius y Comp., J. Heredia, J. M. Otahequi, Jose Rodriguez Angelina; lawyers,—Tomas del Hoyo, Ignacio Arriaga.

City of Matehuala, 25,000 inhabitants; merchants,—Soriano y Almanza, Barrenechea Hermanos, Trinidad Avila, Moreno Hermanos.

Ciudad del Maiz; merchants,—Joaquin Barragan, J. Dominguez, Francisco Anaya.

Rio Verde; merchants,—Antonio Castro y Carrion, Testamentaria de Jose Paudo, Antonio Castillo.

STATE OF SINALOA.—City of Mazatlan, 17,000 inhabitants; merchants,—Francisco Echeguren Hermana y Sobrinos, Melchers Sucesores y Comp., Bartning Hermanos y Comp., Hernandez Mendia y Comp., Francisco Telleria y Comp., Federico Koerdell J. de la Quintana y Comp., Somellera, Hermano y Comp., Peña y Comp., Tames Hermanos, Levess y Comp., Canobio Hermanos, Jesus Escobar, Haas y Encinas, Charpentier, Reynaud y Comp., Gustavo Legrot y Comp., Juan Lewels, Hidalgo Carreaga y Comp.; bankers,—Echeguren, Hermanos y Sobrinos, J. Kelli y Co.; brokers and commission merchants,—Francisco Duhagen, Maxemin Hermanos, Manuel Castellanos, Juan C. Farber, Joaquin Santa Cruz, Adolph O'Ryan, Fred Holderness, Ignacio Guerrero; general merchandise,—Angel Podesta, Mateo Magaña, Rafael Vargas Delgado, Tapia y Cevallos, Felton Hermanos, Rogers y Marshall, Mauricio Beltran, Francisco Diaz de Leon, Benjamin Bates, Vicente Ferreira y Co.

STATE OF SONORA.—City of Hermosillo, 12,000 inhabitants; merchants, —Albistegui y Alatorre, Francisco G. Noriega, Agustin A. Pesqueira, Ruix y Mascareñas, Celedonio Ortiz; lawyers,—Jose de Aguilar, N. Rodriguez; brokers,—Florencio Velasco.

Guaymas; merchants,—F. A. Aguilar sucesores, Vicente Ortiz é hijos, Irigoyen y Escobosa, Juan P. Camou, Sandoval y Bulle, Juan de Castro, Müller y Comp.; lawyers,—Jesus M. Gaxiola, Jose Monteverde.

Ures; merchants,—Lauro Morales, Francisco Hernandez, Eduardo Morales, Francisco Sicre, Francisco C. Aguilar.

STATE OF TOBASCO.—City of San Juan Bautista, 8,000 inhabitants; merchants,—Romano Hermanos, Bulnes Hermanos, M. Berreteaga y Comp., Burelo, Mosquera y Comp., Ruiz de la Peña y Hermano, Ramon Lanz Hermanos, Graham y Vidal, Jamet y Sastre, Maldonado é hijos, Oliver Hermanos, Policarpo Valenzuela, Juan C. Fernandez, Ramon Tames; lawyers, —Limbano Correa, Manuel Sanchez Marmol.

STATE OF TAMAULIPAS.—City of Matamoras; merchants,—Jose de la Mora, Adolfo Mak, J. Lira, Jose M. Armendais sucesores, Santiago Belden.

City of Victorio, 6,000 inhabitants; merchants,—Pablo Lavin, Casimiro Lavin, Francisco Cortina, Martin Dosal, Antonio Elguera, Jose Zorrilla, Viuda de Martinez; lawyers,—Juan Garza, Blas Gutierrez.

Tampico, 5,000 inhabitants; merchants,—Lastra y Com., Fuscu Hermanos, Federico J. Schultz, Goldy Herm, Juan J. Viña, Trapaga y Comp., Matienzo y Comp., Prom y Comp.; lawyers,—Modesto Ortiz, Diego Castillo Montero.

STATE OF TLAXCALA.—City of Tlaxcala, 36,463 inhabitants; merchants, —Trinidad Rojas, Emmanuel Trasdefer, Miguel Gomez (p.), Miguel Gomez (h.), Lorenzo Viñas, Juan Vazquez, Felix Diaz, Eulalio Corona, Bernabe Perales, Tiburcio Lopez, Albino Rodriguez; lawyers,—Manuel Tello Covarrubias, Miguel Melgarejo.

STATE OF VERA CRUZ.—City of Vera Cruz; merchants,—Landero, Pasquel y Comp., Bonne, Strucke y Comp., D'Oleire y Comp. sucesores, R. C. Ritter y Comp., Watermeyer, Wieches y Comp., During y Comp., Agustin Gutheil, German Kroncke sucesores, M. C. de Markoe y Comp., Ed. Rongel Junior, Jauffred, Ollivier y Comp., Guillermo Busing y Comp., Cos, Castillo y Comp., Calleja Hermanos y Comp., Villa Hermanos sucesores, C. A. Martinez y Comp., Torre Fischer y Comp., Jorge Bameto, Javier Muñoz, J. Galdinena y Comp., M. Guillacon y Comp. sucesores, Brehem y Comp. sucesores, Wittenez, Villa y Comp., Vendrell, Villenave y Comp., Francisco de Prida y Comp., Jayme Romaice.

STATE OF YUCATAN.—City of Merida, 56,000 inhabitants; merchants,—Milan y Hermanos, Viuda de Regil é hijo, Vernancio Cervera y Comp., Camp y Comp., Crasseman y Comp., Ravensbourg y Comp., Ricardo Gutierrez y Comp., Luis Gutierrez, Fuente y Hermano, Vales y Capetillo, Rodriguez, Atoche y Comp., Alvarez y Comp., Haro y Comp., Celestino Ruiz del Hoyo, Pinelo é hijo, Pedro Cicero, Dario Galero, Rotger y Comp., Manuel Donde Camara, Manual Zapata, Eusebio Escalante é hijo, Carrill

Camara, Ramon Aznar, Jose M. Ponce y Comp., Alfredo Peon, Hoffman y Dominguez, Benito Aznar, Perez y Comp., Pedro Leal, Ibarra y Comp., Palma y Hermano, Jacinto Lizarraga y Comp.; lawyers,—Pastor Esquivel, Olegario Molina.

City of Progreso, 3,200 inhabitants; merchants,—Alejandro Barrera, Ignacio Sabido, Antonio Alonzo, Alberto Morales, Braulio Canton, George Llanes.

STATE OF ZACATECAS.—City of Zacatecas, 62,000 inhabitants; merchants, wholesale,—Oscar Lorense, Kimball, Alverdi y Comp., Pio Arenas, Julien Ibarguen, Ramon C. Ortiz y Comp., Antonio Gomez Gonzalez; clothing merchants,—Jose M. Escobedo, Nava Salvador Tellery, Daniel Escobedo, Jesus Vasquez, Manuel Viadero y Comp., Euteimio Hermanos, Apestegui, Juan Olivie, Fabricas de Francia, Ciudad de Londres, Puerto de Liverpool, Mariano Cuevas, Apolonio Serrano, Jesus Romero, Pedro Dartayer, A. Subriria; general merchandise,—Viuda de Reyna, Gabriel Segura, Manuel Cano, Feliciano Gomez Gonzalez, Ignacio Montes de Oca, Juan Ferran, Cayetano Escobedo, Meade Hermanos, Villanueva Fermin Diaz; hardware,—Carlos Stork, Angel Ramos, Gustavo Shoder, La Palma, Camilo Larras, El Ferrocarril, Jose Flores; brokers,—Domingo Sanchez, Tomas Martinez, Cruz Diaz de Leon, Mariano B. Real, Mariano Ruiz, Luis G. Veyral, Eustaquio Parra, Pascual L. Velarde, Jose M. T. Escalante, Jose Solorzano; jewelers,—Desiderio Lebre, Guillermo Brunert; druggists,—De la Parroquia, del Comercio, de la Caja, del Leon, del Patrocinio, de Tacuba, de Villareal, de Leal; lawyers,—T. G. Cadeno, Alejandro del Hoyo.

TERRITORY OF BAJA CALIFORNIA.—City of La Paz, 4,000 inhabitants; merchants,—Gonzalez y Ruffo, Cota y Palaiz, Pablo Hidalgo y Comp., J. Mendez sucesores, Gregorio Rivera, H. Von Borstel, Lautaro Ramirez, Gilbert Hermanos; lawyers,—Carlos F. Galan, Antonio Canalizo.

El Triunfo, 4,000 inhabitants; merchants,—Aristeo Mendoza, Cota y Pelaiz, Maximo Cota.

San Jose, 2,500 inhabitants; merchants,—Hipps y Comp.

Mulejé, 1,500 inhabitants; merchants,—Moller y Comp., Vicente Gorozavo, Francisco Fierro Mejia, é hijo.

MILITARY CANTON OF TEPIC, INCLUDED IN THE STATE OF JALISCO.—City of Tepic, 23,213 inhabitants; wholesale merchants and manufacturers,—Barron, Forbes y Comp. of sugar,—Juan Antonio de Aguierre, Compania Tepiqueña, Juan A. Tostado, director, of mantas and yarns.—Adolfo Kindt, wholesale dealer, Gustavo Delius; general merchandise,—Menchaca Hermanos, Ernesto Stegemann, Nicolas Perez Gomez, Sara Garcia, Viuda de Leal, Dolores Escudero, Viuda de Muñoz, Trinidad Hernandez, Vicente Castillo, Prudencio Robles; clothing,—Francisco Anaya é hijo, Manuel Pacheco, Jose M. Muñoz Ruiz, Julio Fuentes, Alejandro Santa Maria; Mexican goods,—Juan Mardueño, Marismo Perez Torres; hardware, notions, etc.,—Federico Nolte, Joaquin Perez Gomez; general merchandise and cigar manufacturer, Jose Corona; cigar manufacturer, Amado Fletes; druggists,—Geronimo, G. Gonzalez, Francisco Gomez Virgen, hijo, Antonio Ibarra.

San Blas; merchants, general merchandise and cigar manufacturer and commission,—Juan Lanzagorta; general merchandise and commission, Manuel Carpena, Natividad Rivera; general merchandise, Abel Villaseñor, Felix Uribe; druggist, Antonio Castilla; commission, Edmundo Weber.

Santiago; merchants, manuf'r of mantas, Joaquin Perez Gomez; clothing, Federico Beyer.

Ahuacatlan; merchants, clothing and general mdse.,—Emigdio Ulloa, Flavio Partida, Flaminio Ulloa.

Compostela; merchants, clothing and general mdse.,—Jose M. Perez Sandi, Vicenti Pintado.

Ixtlan; merchants, clothing and general mdse.,—Enrique Menchaca, Jose M. Partida, Emilio Cosio.

Federal District, City of Mexico.

PRINCIPAL MERCHANTS.

Commission. — Best Ricardo, calle del Puente del Espiritu Santo número 7; Esteinon José P., calle de Cadena número 4; Revueltas Valentin, calle de San Agustin número 11; Argüelles Eduardo, calle de Capuchinas número 16; Gonsalez Guerra Antonio, calle de Capuchinas número 14; Horn Agustin, calle de Capuchinas número 9; Prueba R. de, calle de Cadena número 14; Gandolf Clemente, 1ª calle de la Monterilla número 6; Gutierrez M., calle de Capuchinas número 15; Claussen Sucesores, 2ª calle de la Monterilla número 6; Peredo y comp. Eduardo, calle de Tiburcio número 20; García L. C., calle de la Independencia número 3; Espejel M., calle del Espiritu Santo número 3; Beigne R. N., calle de Tiburcio número 7; Daza y Merodio, calle de Don Juan Manuel número 1; Santiago Agustin de, calle de Don Juan Manuel número 13; Valle Ramon del, 1ª calle de San Ramon número 2; Prado y comp. C., Bajos Porta Cœli número 1; Pelaez Santos, calle de Meleros número 1; Torre Rodolfo, calle de Don Juan Manuel número 11; Sttüer y Aguilar, calle de Don Juan Manuel número 20; Carrera Rafael I., calle de San Bernardo número 2½; Reyes, Vazquez y comp., calle de Don Juan Manuel número 9; Rivero y Lazo, calle de San Bernardo número 10; Borbolla J., calle de Tacuba número 14; Delgado Eusebio, 1ª calle del 5 de Mayo; Goy Juan, calle de Donceles número 22; Buenrostro é hijos, calle de las Esculerillas número 13; Luviaur y Lara, calle de Cocheras número 22; Legrand Manuel, 2ª calle del 5 de Mayo número 13; Cárdenas y comp., calle de Mecateros número 4.

Note Brokers. — Best Fernando, calle del Espiritu Santo letra G.; Honig Bernardo, calle de San Andrés número 17; Lartundo Juan, calle de Manrique número 6; Arellano José, 2ª calle de la Aduana Vieja número 6; Pinzon Cleofas, calle de las Inditas número 5; Gutierrez Manuel, Puente de San Pedro y San Pablo número 9; Hernandez Amado, calle del Cuadrante de Santa Catarina número 14; Serrano Nicolás, calle del Empedradillo; España N., callejon de Santa Inés número 7½; Quiroga y comp., calle de Cardobanes número 4; Dueñas Juan, 2ª calle del 5 de Mayo número 4; Salgado Refugio, Portal de Santo Domingo numero 5.

Custom House Brokers. — Peredo y comp. Eduardo, calle de Tiburcio número 20; Aranzubia Manuel, calle de Tiburcio número 20; Legrand Manuel, 2ª calle del 5 de Mayo número 7; Arellano Jesus G., calle de D. Juan Manuel número 11; Enciso y Cardeño, calle de Capuchinas número 6; Turlong y comp., calle de Zuleta número 22; García Mora E., calle de D. Juan Manuel número 21; Guerrero J. M., Juan Manuel número 24; Kern Santiago, Tercer Orden de San Augustin número 4; Marchand A. N., calle de Cadena número 24; Romero Pedro M., 2ª calle de la Monterilla número 8; Vazquez Cirilo, calle de D. Juan Manuel número 9; Sanroman Telésforo, calle de San Agustin número 17.

Wholesale, in Mexican and Foreign Goods.—Santo Mañúzuri y comp. calle de Tacuba y 1ª de Santo Domingo; Huerta Manuel, calle del Empedradillo número 11; Messer Agustin, 2ª calle de San Francisco número 4; Baxas Justino, 2ª calle de San Francisco número 4; Viuda Genin, 2ª calle de Plateros número 3; Villegas Emilio, calle Ancha y callejon de San Antonio; Gutierrez y comp., Quintin, Seminario esquina; Torro Isidoro de la, 1ª calle del Reloj número 8; Dupeyron Alejandro, calle del Coliseo Viejo número 20; Zepeda Francisco, 2ª calle de San Francisco y Coliseo; Noriega Ignacio de, calle del Angel número 5; Noriega Remigio, calle de Capuchinas número 12; Clare y Hellion, calle del Coliseo Viejo número 23; Cortina Mendoza M., calle de Tiburcio número 1; Payro Leandro, calle de Don Juan Manuel número 18; Guerra José T., calle de Jesus Nazareno número 2; Lavié y comp., calle de Don Juan Manuel número 7; Rovalo A., calle del Puente de Jesus número 9; Ponton hermano, calle de las Rejás de Balvanera número 3; Ubink y comp., calle de Don Juan Manuel número 22; Vidal Manuel, esquina de la Joya y Jesus; Abascal y Perez, calle del Puente del Correo Mayor número 6.

Wholesale, Mexican Merchandise.—Sevilla y Roa, 1ª calle de Plateros número 3; Rodriguez Feliciano, calle del Puente de Palacio número 10; Nosti Cárlos, calle de San Bernardo número 9; Arenas Alejandro, Rejas de Balvanera número 1; Pelaez Pedro, calle de Cadena número 16; Portilla é hijos, calle de Capuchinas número 13; Teresa é hijos, calle de Lerdo número 6; Arzamendi F., calle del Tercer Orden de San Agustin 2; Suinaga hermano, calle de Cadena número 20; Martinez y Compañia, calle del Angel número 2; Escandon hermanos, calle de Capuchinas número 11; Teresa Nicolás de, calle de Lerdo número 4.

Wholesale, Foreign Merchandise.—Wexel y De Gress, 1ª calle de Plateros número 5; Delarue E., 2ª calle de Plateros número 4; Jacott Alfredo, 1ª calle de Plateros número 4; Weil y Simon, 1ª calle de Plateros número 1; Richaud y André, calle del Empedradillo número 12; Fortuño Leandro, calle de Tacuba número 22; Jauretche y Cª, calle de Capuchinas número 2; Córdova Pedro, calle del Espiritu Santo número 7; Rio José Maria del, calle de la Palma número 6; Bocker y Cª Roberto, Puente del Espiritu Santo 4; Jacott A., calle del Refugio número 19; Gutheil y Cª, calle de la Palma número 13; Lohse y Cª, calle de la Palma números 9, 10 y 11; Peñaña Marcial, calle del Refugio número 19; Breheun y Cª, 2ª calle de la Monterilla número 3; Shemidt y Borjian, calle de Capuchinas número 4; Wissel y Cª, calle de San Agustin número 6; Bonne Struck y Cª, calle de San Agustin número 10; Bermejillo hermanos, calle de Capuchinas número 10; Waston Paillips y Cª, Don Juan Manuel número 10; Wattemayer y Wincher, calle de San Agustin número 15; Guerin y Cª, calle de Espiritu Santo número 9; Jauffred Ollivier y Cª, 1ª calle de la Monterilla números 5 y 6; Faudon Argentin y Cª, 1ª calle de la Monterilla 2; Fourcade y Gouppil, 1ª calle de Plateros números 7 y 8; Albert Julio, 1ª de la Monterilla número 4; Hubvershon y Cª, Esquina de la Monterilla y Capuchinas; Sengstack y Cª, calle de San Augustin número 7; Moreno y Rover, Monterilla y Capuchinas; Gassier y Reynaud, Portal de las Flores y Callejuela; Kienast y Cª, 2ª calle de la Monterilla número 12; Ebrard y Cª, esquina de San Bernardo y Callejuela; Shults y Cª, 2ª de la Monterilla número 9; Levy y Marsau, calle de Don Juan Manuel número 23; Aubert y Cª, Portal de las Flores números 3 y 4; Lohse Santiago, calle de Don Juan Manuel números 6; J. M. de Prída, calle de San Bernardo número 3; Benecke sucesores, calle de Capuchinas número 7.

Wholesale Druggists.—Wandlen Wingaert, calle del Puente del Espiritu Santo; Mäyers, Fribolin y Cª, calla de la Palma; Labadi y Pinsau, 3ª calle de San Francisco número 5; Lozano y Cª, 3ª calle de San Francisco número 4; Farine Sauders y Cª, esquina de las calles del Refugio y Lerdo; Vargas y Cª, calle del Espiritu Santo número 3; Andrade y

Soriano, calle de la Joya número 10; Bustillos J. E., calle de Tacubo número 8; Llauo J. M. P., calle de Manrique número 5; Urhlein y C^a, calle del Coliseo número 3.

Firearms.—Morel y C^a, calle del Refugio número 11; Roche A., calle del Espiritu Santo número 1½; Wexel y De Gress, 1ª calle de Plateros número 5; Sanchez D., calle de Balvanera; Pagliari Fernando, calle del Coliseo numero 14.

Banks.—Banco de Lóndres, México y Sud-América, calle de Capuchinas; Bermejillo Hermanos, calle de Capuchinas numero 10; Martin Pedro, calle de Cadena número 21; Banco Franco—Egipcio; Banco Commercial.

Druggists.—Gonzalez Julian, 3ª calle del 5 de Mayo número 3; Kaska Francisco, calle del Espiritu Santo número 1½; Tinoco Francisco, calle de Guadalupe número 9; Bernal Francisco, calle de San Hipólita número 7; Altamirano Fernando, calle de Don Toribio número 9; El mismo, calle de la Aduana Vieja número 4; Loaria Menores, 1ª calle de San Juan número 10; Arteaga Ramon, 2ª calle Ancha número 7; Santoyo Ramon, calle de la Joya número 10; Arteaga Ramon, calle del Sapo número 18; Urbina Manuel, 3ª calla de San Juan número 1; Lares Manuel, calle de la Mariscala número 1; Vértiz Ricardo, 2ª calle de las Damas número 5; Oropeza Marcial, calle de Hidalgo y Lerdo; M. Rio de la Loza, Hospital Real; El mismo, 1ª calle de Santa Catarina número 4; El mismo, calle de la Merced número 21; El mismo, Puente del Fierro y Chaneque; Perez Severiano, 1ª calle de la Rivere de San Cosme número 7¼; Aranjo Jesus, calle de Manzanares; Aveleyra Ramon, Puente de Jesus número 8; Lelo de Larrea N., 1ª calle del Reloj número 1; Bustillos J. E., colle de Tacuba aumero 7; El mismo, calle del Tompeate número 5½; El mismo, calle de Manrique y Canoa; Lazo de la Vega J. M., 3ª calle del Reloj número 12; Patiño y comp., Hospital de San Andrés; Coronado Agustin, calle de Olmedo número 1; Gaona Juan B., Rejas de la Concepcion número 6; Carmona y Valle, 2ª calle de Santo Domingo número 4; Garaycoechea Angel, Puente del Espiritu Santo número 10; Cervantes Silva A., 1ª calle de Santo Domingo número 4; El mismo, calle de las Rejas de Balvanera número 5; El mismo, calle de Leon número 9; Esnaurizar M., calle de la Mariscala número 1; Gonzalez Francisco, Bajos de Porti Cœli; Iriarte M., Puente de Santa Catarina; Muycelo José, calle de San Hipólite número 17; Montes de Oca Francisco, calle del Niño Perdido 5½; Patiño Pomposo, Plazuela de Villamil; El mismo, 3ª calle del Rastro número 7; Vallejo Testamentaria de, calle de Roldan; Pauer L., 1ª calle del 5 de Mayo y San José el Real; Guerrero Agustin, San Cosme; Rio de la Loza M., calle de Santa Catarina número 1; El mismos, Sepulcros de Santo Domingo número 10; Rio de la Loza Francisco, 2ª calle de Vanegas; Tinoco Cárlos, 1ª calle de San Francisco número 13; Urueta Bernardo, 2ª calle de San Francisco número 5; Noriega Tomás, calle de la Alhondiga número 5; Gutierrez Miguel, Puente de la Misericordia; Ramoa Manuel, calle de Santa Ana número 7.

Glassware.—Rigal y Masson, Portal de Agustinos número 1; Gómez de la Vega J., 1^a de Santo Domingo; Hildebrand y comp., 1.ª calle de Plateros número 1; El mismo, calle del Empedradillo número 4; Serrano y comp., calle del Empedradillo; Pino Tomás del, Portal de Agustinos número 5; Jiminez Miguel, 1.ª calle de la Merced número 28; Martinez y comp., Bajos de Porta Cœli número 11.

Furnishing Goods.—Coblentz Benito, 2^a de Plateros y Palma; Tousaint Clara, calle del Espiritu Santo número 4; Coblentz B. y S., calle de la Palma número 11; Sabás Lorenzo, calle de la Palma número 1; Carballeda Manuel, calle del Coliseo número 11; Andrés Julian, calle de la Palma número 13; Iglesias Francisco, 2.ª de San Francisco número 9; Mangard Fernando, 1.ª calle de Santo Domingo; Manterola Angela, 2.ª de San Francisco número 7; Ouvrard viuda de, calle de la Palma número 2; Sales L., calle de la Palma número 1; Nieto de Parra M., calle de Tacuba número 11; M. Chauvet, 1.ᵃ de la Monterilla y San Bernardo; Rubio Felipe C., Portal de la Aguila de Oro; Bardet y comp., calle del Coliseo número 25; Pastor Concepcion, 2.ᵃ calle de San Francisco número 13.

Clothing.—Ollivier y comp., 1.ᵃ calle de la Monterilla números 5 y 6; Jandon Argentin y comp., 1.ᵃ calle de la Monterilla número 2; Fourcade y Goupil, 1.ᵃ calle de Plateros números 7 y 8; Gassier y Reynaud, Portal de las Flores y Callejuela; Evrard y comp., San Bernardo y Callejuela; El mismo, 1.ᵃ de Monterilla y Refugio; Aubert y comp., Portal de las Flores números 3 y 4; Palacio y hermanos, Diputacion y Callejuela; Signoret hermanos, 1.ᵃ de la Monterilla número 8; Fourdant y com., 1.ᵃ de la Monterilla número 8; Barreda y comp., sucesores, San Bernardo número 18; Gómez y comp., Portal de las Flores número 9; Fernandez y Mijarez, calle de Flamencos número 5; Llacuri y Arrechedera y comp., Portal de las Flores número 5; Valdés Antonio, Portal de las Flores número 2; Arróyave Genoveva, 2.ᵃ calle de Santa Catarina número 11.

Foreign Exchange Brokers.—Barron, Forbes y comp., 1.ᵃ de San Francisco número 9; I. R. Cardeña y comp., sucesores, callejon de Betlemitas número 12; Ortiz de la Huerta R., calle del Empedradillo número 11; Gutheil y comp. A., calle de Ocampo número 1; Watson, Phillips y comp., calle de Don Juan Manuel número 10; J. M. De Prida, calle de San Bernardo número 3; Martinez, J. L., compañia del Ferrocaril de México á Veracruz; Benecke sucesores, calle de Capuchinas número 7; Martin P., calle de Cadena número 21; Bermejillo Hermanos, calle de Capuchinas número 10; Bonne, Struck y comp., calle de San Agustin número 10; Teresa Nicolás de, calle del Lerdo número 4; Ibañez Manuel, calle de Capuchinas número 2½; Lascurain A., Tercer Orden de San Agustin número 5.

Petroleum and Oils.—Arcila M., calle de Zuleta número 8; Aguirre José M., calle de la Merced número 19; Diaz Guadalupe, Puerta Falsa de Santo Domingo número 7; Marenco Miguel, 3.ᵃ calle del Relox número 6; Muñoz Riva I. de, 2.ᵃ calle del Rastro número 3; Aguirre y hermanos, Puente del Correo Mayor números 10 y 11; Bocanegra Juan, Zaragoza número 26; Rivera Manuel, Portillo de San Diego número 8; Campa N., calle de Santa Clara número 10; Robelo Maria, calle del Puente Quebrado número 11.

Sewing Machines.—G. Lohse y comp., calle del Refugio número 8; Bocker y comp., Puente del Espiritu Santo; Adams Francisco, 1.ᵃ del 5 de Mayo número 4; Gutheil y comp., calle del Refugio número 10.

Book Binders.—Vargas Machuca C., 2.ᵃ calle del Relox número 3; Vanegas Antonio, calle de la Encarnacion número 9; Arroyo de Venegas A., calle de la Perpétua número 8½; Calvillo Jesus, calle del Esclavo número 1; Tornel M., 1.ᵃ calle de San Lorenzo número 6; Sainz Ricardo, calle de las Escallerillas número 13; Castillo Andrés, calle de San José el Real número 21; Figueroa Francisco, calle de San Agustin letra G.; Marcué Alejandro, calle de Tiburcio número 18; Machuca Jesus, calle de Medinas número 21; Freire Alejandro, calle de la Moneda número 8; Galves Mariano, 2.ᵃ calle de San Lorenzo número 11; Guerra Mariano, 1.ᵃ calle del 5 de Mayo número 4; Guerra Manuel, callejon de Santa Clara número 10; Jara Celso, calle de Zuleta número 15.

Piano Manufacturers and Dealers.—Wagner y Levien, calle de Zuleta número 14; Nagel sucesores, calle de la Palma número 5; Bardet y comp., calle de Cadena número 24; Wisseman Cárlos, calle de las Escalerillas número 6.

Metal Foundries.—Finamori y comp., calle de Tiburcio número 4; Pasquali J. M., calle de Ortega número 11; Fusco Antonio, calle de Ortega número 24; Brandi J., calle de Ortega número 17; Dantan Luis, calle de Zuleta número 7.

Manufacturers of Brass Bedsteads.—Linet Luis, callejon del Espiritu Santo número 14; López Antonio, calle de Ortega número 11; Zapata Eutimio, Puente del Correo Mayor número 5.

Jewelers.—Dietrich J., calle del Empedradillo número 4; Lagarrigue L., Empedradillo y Plateros; Dicimer R., calle 1.ª de Plateros número 1; Schreiberg y comp., 2.ª de San Francisco número 3; Ducommun hijo A., 2.ª calle de Plateros número 4; Garcia E., 2.ª calle de Plateros número 2; Llop Francisco, calle Santa Clara número 7; Muiron y comp., 2.ª calle de Plateros número 11; Sommer y comp., 1.ª calle de Plateros número 11; Lazo German, 2.ª calle de la Plateros número 9; Hartman y comp., 1.ª calle de Plateros número 14; Jehoffer Martin, 1.ª calle de Plateros número 11; Bittroff, 2.ª calle de Plateros número 9; Zivy hermanos y Hauser, 2.ª de Plateros número 10; Rotracker Alfonso, 1.ª de Plateros número 14; Aldana Ramon, calle del Coliseo Viejo número 3; Sobrado Pedro, calle del Coliseo Viejo número 25; Quintana hermano, calle del Coliseo Viejo número 17; Saesy y Callado, calle del Coliseo Viejo; Spaulding, calle de Cadena número 4; Diaz Florencio, 2.ª calle de la Monterilla número 10; Hernandez Tomás, 3.ª calle de San Francisco número 6.

Fancy Goods, Notions, etc.—Echeverria Delorez, Alcaiceria número 22; Pivardierre A., 2.ª calle de Plateros número 5; Rivero Luis, calle de San José el Real número 14; Reynaud E., calle del Espiritu Santo número 10; Deverdun H., Puente del Espiritu Santo; Perezcano L. G., Portal del Aguila de Oro.

Booksellers.—Terrova Ramon, calle de Flamencos números 18 y 19; Andrade y Morales, Portal de Agustinos número 13; Buxó Juan, calle del Coliseo Viejo número 25; Murguia Eduardo, calle del Coliseo Viejo número 2; Vincourt Cárlos, calle del Espiritu Santo número 5; Bouret y comp., calle del Refugio y Puente del Espiritu Santo; Nicolaye, calle de Gante y San Francisco; Chavez Nabor, Portal del Aguila de Oro; Jeno J. Federico, calle de San José el Real número 22; Dublan y comp., 2.ª calle de Plateros número 4; Bouret y comp., calle de San José el Real 18; Cudin A., 2.ª calle de San Francisco número 2; Cueva Ramon, calle del Seminario número 3; Abadiano Francisco, calle de las Escalerillas número 7; Aguilar é Hijos, J. M., 1.ª calle de Santo Domingo número 5; Ballescá y comp., calle del Amor de Dios número 4.

Lumber.—Galindez Diego, calle de los Misterios de San Lázaro número 2; Garcia y Vega, calle de Guatimotzin número 4; Landa Juan A., calle de la Escobillería número 4; Palacios y comp., calle de la Providencia; Sanchez Cárlos, Plazuela de Juan Carbonero; Bueno J. M., 2.ª calle del Salto del Agua número 9; Valle de G. M., 1.ª calle de Necatitlan número 1; Valdés Manuel, Plazuela de Juan Carbonero número 6; Sanchez Barquera E., Plazuela de Villamil número 2; Tellez Antonio, 3.ª calle de Revillagigedo; Huerta y comp., calle del Matadero número 20; Hernandez y Arauzabal, calle del Cacahuatal número 12; Guerrero Manuel, calle del Matadero número 7; Guerrero Gerónimo, calle de Guatimotzin número 16; Romero Francisco, calle de Chaneque número 2¼; Rio y Cantero, calle del Matedero número 11; Fonseca de G. Victoriano, Plazuela de la Concepcion número 5; Meza Nicolás, calle de Cadena número 1.

Fine Hardware and Tools.—Del Rio José Maria, calle de la Palma; Fabre Julio, 1.ª calle de San Francisco; Gagne y comp., calle del Refugio número 9; Garcia Eduardo, 1.ª calle de Santo Domingo número 9; Tellez y comp., 1.ª calle de Plateros número 17; Bocker y comp., Puente del Espiritu Santo número 4; Gutierrez Miguel, Puente del Palacio, número 4; El mismo, calle de Flamencos y Portacœli; Lefebre A., calle de la Palma y Refugio; El mismo, 2.ª calle de la Monterilla y San Bernardo; Jacot A., calle de Tlapaleros número 19; Gutheil y comp., calle de la Palma número 13; El mismo, calle de Ocampo número 1; El mismo, calle de Flamencos números 22 y 24; Lohse y comp., sucesores, calle de la Palma números 9, 10 y 11; Rivero Luis, calle de San José el número 14; Carazo Luis C., 2.ª calle de Plateros número 2; Pivardierre A., 2.ª calle de Plateros número 4; Uriarte y comp., calle del Empedradillo número 10; Calpini y comp., 3.ª de San Francisco número 5; Joransson C., 3.ª de

San Francisco número 4; Boneruó Pablo, calle del Refugio número 9; Zivy David, 1.ª calle de Plateros número 11; Jougla y comp., calle de Lerdo y Refugio; Troncoso y Silvetti, calle del Refugio número 7; Bizet y comp., calle de Capuchinas y Angel; Mondragon Rafael, calle de Flamencos número 4; Diehl y comp., calle de Flamencos número 4; Izquierdo y Garibay, calle de Meleros números 101 y 4, Villanueva Rafael, calle de Flamencos número 5; Phillips y comp., calle del Empedradillo; El mismo, calle de San Bernardo y Flamencos; Munguía ó hijos, calle de la Merced número 7.

Silversmiths.—Villaseñor Joaquin, calle de San José el Real; Aranda Francisco, calle de la Alcaicería número 17; Velarde Apolonio, calle de San Felipe Neri número 1; Cañas Pedro, 1.ª calle de Plateros número 8; Carrillo Guadalupe, calle de Ortega número 9; Carrillo Jesus, calle del Puente Quebrado número 30; Saldívar Sóstenes, calle de Balvanera número 18; Ponton Antonio, calle de Donceles número 2; Nieva J., calle de la Alcaicería número 13; Llop J., calle de Santa Clara número 7; Cosio Alejandro, calle del Hospicio San Nicolás número 1; Cherlin Jesus, 1.ª calle de la Independencia número 3.

Saloons.—Iturbe Manuel, esquina de Mesones y Tompeate; El mismo, 1.ª calle de Factor y Sta. Clara; El mismo, 1.ª calle de Santo Domingo; El mismo, Bajos de Porta Cœli; El mismo, calle de San Bernardo número 10; El mismo, calle del Factor número 4; Torres Adalid I. 2.ª calle de Santo Domingo número 2; El mismo, 1.ª calle de la Independencia número 3; El mismo, esquina de la calle de Leon y Dolores; El mismo, calle de Leon; El mismo, esquina de San Juan de Letran ó Independencia; El mismo, 2.ª calle de las Damas; El mismo, calle de Santa Clara número 18; El mismo, calle de Jesus número 18; Saenz Patricio, Ex-colegio del Seminario; El mismo, calle de San Bernardo número 1; El mismo, calle de Tacuba; El mismo, callejon del Espíritu Santo; El mismo, 1.ª calle de las Damas; Campero Manuel, calle del Coliseo número 4; El mismo, Bajos de Porta Cœli; Castillo Manuel J., Bajos de Porta Cœli; El mismo, calle del Indio Triste; Garnica Ramon, calle de la Alcaicería; El mismo, esquina de San Andrés y Factor; Guadarrama M., callejon de las Delicias y calle Ancha; Zamudio J., calle de la Aduana Vieja y Corchero; El mismo, esquina de la Puerta Falsa y Sepulcros de Santo Domingo.

General Merchandise.—Huerta A., Plazuela de Villamil número 2; Oropeza Demetrio, esquina de Santa Catarina y Estanco de Hombres; Almiraill F., esquina de Medinas y Santo Domingo; Atucha Casiano, esquina de Santa Clara y Vergara; Sordo Noriega A., esquina de San Lorenzo y Leon; Casprina Wenceslao, esquina de la Pila Seca y Cerca de Santo Domingo; Yarto y Trueba, 2.ª calle del Factor número 6; Márquez Isidoro, esquina de la 2.ª calle de la Amargura y Gachupines; Perez Antonio, esquina de Tacuba y Manrique; Espinosa y comp., esquina de Tacuba y Alcaicería; Loidi hermano, esquina del Aguila y Leon; Sordo Vicente, esquina del Jardin y Verdeja; Briz German, Espalda de San Lorenzo y Misericordia; Llano Cayetano, esquina de las Papas y Estanco de Hombres; Barquin Vidal, Puente de Santo Domingo número 5; Llano Pedro, esquina de Santa Catarina y Rinconada; Perez Francisco S., esquina de Santa Catarina y Estanco de Hombres; Posada y Fernandez, calle de Mecateros número 16; Gavito Manuel, esquina de Tacuba y San José el Real; García Benito, calle de la Alcaicería número 3; García Amado, calle de Santa Ana letra A.; El mismo, calle de Santa Ana número 5; Lecanda Juan, esquina de San Andrés y Mariscala; Gutierrez y García A., calle de Leon número 11; Zaballa Ignacio, 1.ª calle del Factor número 6; Hermosillo Eduardo, esquina de la Cazuela y Arquillo; Rozada M., calle de Verdeja; Posada y Fernandez, Alcaicería número 5; Martin Francisco S., San Diego y San Hipólito; El mismo, Portillo de San Diego; Mijares y Urrutia, Portillo de San Diego; Mijares Ramon, esquina de Peredo y

San Juan; Gutierrez Federico, Plazuela de San Juan número 2; Gutierrez Patricio, San Cosme y Santa Maria de la Rivera; López Mariano, esquina de Nueva México y Guadalupe; Yarto Ignacio, esquina de la Mariscala y Gallos; Herrero Manuel, calle del Niño Perdido número 6½; Balmori R., esquina del Santisimo y Rebeldes; Herrero Cristóbal, calle del Niño Perdido; Herrera Agustin, Plazuela de San Juan número 4; Caso Ramon, esquina del Sapo y Santisimo; Ruiz Antonio, calle del Sapo número 18; Moreno Hermenegildo, calle del Jardin número 9; Fernandez Santiago, esquina de la Estampa de San Lorenzo y Misericordia; Quesada Dolores, Plazuela del Jardin número 5; Arias Agustin, callejon de Dolores número 11; Benet José, 2.ª calle del Factor número 3; Montes de Oca D., Estanco de Hombres número 10; Noriega Remigio, esquina de Plateros y Alcaicería; Gavito Domingo, plazuela de Juan Carbonero número 4; Helguera Vidal, esquina del Puente de San Francisco y López; Guazo Angel, plazuela de Zaragoza (Angeles); Noriega y comp., esquina de la Magnolia y Lerdo; Ibarra y comp., Humboldt número 3; Helguera J. M., esquina de las calles Ancha y Artes; Gomez B., esquina de Santa Isabel y Puente de San Francisco; Abascal M., esquina de la plazuela de Madrid y San Juan de Dios; Ponton hermanos, Camarones número 18; Perez y Fernandez, Hoacalco y Pelota; Mendez y Antonio, esquina de las calles Ancha y Delicias; Roqueña Adrian, callejon de Dolores número 14; Aldama Victor, calle de Alvarado número 1; Pesac Angela, callejon de Dolores número 4; Crespo y Gandarillas, calle de Lerdo I.; Robina y comp., San Bernardo y Callejuela; Sotres y Noriega, Portal de las Flores número 8; Ortiz hermano, Hospital de Jesus, esquina; Marroquin Federico, esquina del Puente de Jesus y San Felipe de Jesus; Gonzalez y Gonzalez, esquina de las calles 3.ª del Rastro y Cuadrante de San Miguel; Ortiz y comp., San Felipe de Jesus y 2.ª de la Aduana; Sordo y comp., 2.ª de la Aduana Vieja y Cuadrante de San Miguel; Noriega Alonso, Puente de Jesus Maria número 7; Solorio Benito, calle del Consuelo, esquina; Enriquez hermano, Puente del Fierro número 12; Sanchez Rivero, Mercado Principal 13 y 15; Valdéz Gabino, 3.ª calle de Santo Tomás y Plazuela de la Palma; Baranda y comp., Bajos de Porta Cœli, esquina; Villalobos Agustin, 2.ª de Manzanares número 8; Pandal hermanos, Meleros 1; Crespo Baltazar, calle de Flamencos 6; Noriega y Santos, 2.ª calle de Manzanares 12; Mijares Manuel, Manzanares y Susanillo; Fuentes y Gutierrez, 1.ª calle de Manzanares, esquina; El mismo, 1.ª de Manzanares 17; Ortiz hermano, Ratas y Portal de Tejada; Pujon Juan, Colegio de niñas y Coliseo; Vega José, calle de Don Toribio 6; Somoano Remigio, esquina de la Polilla y San Juan; Bárcena José, calle de Don Toribio número 10; López Bernardo, 2.ª de Regina y Salto del Agua; Valle y Gutierrez, esquina de la Independencia y Coliseo; Posada y Ruiz de Noriega, esquina del Espiritu Santo y Refugio; Hidalgo José, calle de Alfaro número 11; Gonzalez José, calle del Puente Quebrado 5; Gutierrez y Abascal, calle del Coliseo Viejo 7; Segura Guillermo, esquina del Coliseo y Espiritu Santo; Alva Celedonio, esquina de Gante y San Francisco; Busto y Ortis, 1.ª calle de San Francisco número 14; Aparicio Juan, 3.ª calle de San Juan y Vizcainas; Gonzalez y C.ª 3.ª calle de San Juan y Plazuela de las Vizcainas; Lecunda Juan, esquina de Ortega y San Juan; Sordo y Márcos, 1.ª calle de la Aduana Vieja; Casso Manuel, calle de la Palma número 5; Crespo y Abascal, esquina de los portales de Mercaderes y Agustinos; Castillo José O., esquina de las calles de Alfaro y Mesones; S. Juan Mariano, esquina de las calles del Angel y Cadena; Perez Facundo, 1.ª de las Damas y Tiburcio; Sordo Juan, esquina de la 1.ª calle de Mesones y Regina; Perez y Pacheco, Puente de Monzon y San Gerónimo, esquina; Sordo Noriega M., esquina de Don Toribio y Monserrate; Carreras Evaristo, esquina de Zuleta y Hospital Real; Portillo hermanos, esquina de la 2.ª de las Damas y Puente Quebrado; El mismo, esquina de la 1.ª de San Juan y Puente Quebrado; Robina y Arenas, calle de Zaragoza número 1; Noriega Fernando, esquina

de la Merced y Puente de Jesus Maria; Noriega Manuel S., esquina de la
Universidad y Meleros; Sanchez y Fernandez, Mercado Principal 62 y
64; Sanchez y Martinez, calle de Flamencos 10 y 12; Salcedo y Fernandez,
calle de Porta Cœli 36 y 38; Fernandez y comp., calle de Porta Cœli 39 y
41; Ponton Ramon, calle de Porta Cœli 1; Oraris José, 2.ª calle de la
Merced 15; Mijares Juan, esquina de la calles de Jesus y Parque del
Conde; Flores Agustin, Nahuatatlo, esquina; Mijares Antonio, Estampa de
Jesus, esquina; Cabrales José, San José de Gracia, esquina; Noriega
Santos, calle de las Gallas, esquina; Isla y comp., calle de las Gallas,
esquina; Aceves Victoriano, Puente de la Leña, esquina; Ortiz Juan O.,
1.ª calle del Reloj y Escalerillas; Noriega y comp., 2ª calle del Indio
Triste y Hospicio de San Nicolás; Fernandez Manuel, esquina de Celaya
y Puente de Santo Domingo; Hermosa Estanislao, esquina de la Plaza
de la Santisima y Maravillas; Gonzalez Gaspar, esquina de San Ildefonso
y San Pedro y San Pablo; Gonzalez Cándido, esquina del Relox y Mon-
tealegre; Vadlés Juan, esquina de la 6ª del Relox y Golosas.

Lawyers.—Aguilar Jesus Maria, Acequia 23; Azpiroz Manuel, Escale-
rillas 1; Barros José Maria, 3ª del Reloj 5; Becerra Cárlos, San Hipólito
5; Calva Estévan, Alcaiceria 5; Castañeda y Nájera Vidal, Cordobanes 15;
Diaz Barreiro P., Monzon 7; Doudé Rafael, 1ª del Factor 3; Enriquez
Gunnesindo, Alcaiceria 17; Escoto Joaquin, Medinas 10; Hammeken y
Mexia J., 1ª de la Independencia 12; Hidalgo y Teran M., Seminario 8,
Frederic Hall; Islas Gabriel, Zuleta 16; Islas y Bustamante Nicolás, calle-
jon de Santa Inés 5; Martinez del Rio P., Seminario 5; Mendez Luis,
Hospicio de San Nicolás 4; Palacio Antonio del, 2ª de las Damas 2;
Palacios Rafael, 2ª de las Damas 6; Salazar y Murphy Joaquin M.,
Puente del Correo Mayor 5; Sanchez Ramon, Santa Teresa 8; Tápia
Joaquin C., Plazuela de la Santísima 1; Vallarta Ignacio, San Agustin 9;
Velazco Ignacio, Manrique 5.

Hotels.—Guillow San José el Real; Nacional, 3ª calle de San Francisco;
Vergara, calle de Vegara; Comonfort, calle de Cinco de Mayo; Bazar, calle
del Espíritu Santo; Bella Union, calle de la Palma y Refugio; Europa,
calle del Coliseo; Gran Sociedad, calle del Espíritu Santo y Coliseo;
Universal, calle del Puente del Espíritu Santo y Coliseo; Havre, 1ª calle
de la Independencia; Iturbide, 2ª calle de San Francisco; Refugio, calle
del Refugio; San Agustin, calle de San Agustin; San Cárlos, calle del
Coliseo Viejo; Tlapaleros, calle del Refugio; Turco, calle del Coliseo;
Cuatro Naciones, calle de Tacuba; Guadalupe, calle del Parque del Conde;
La Estrella, calle de Tlapaleros; Ortega, calle del Ortega; Cordobanes,
calle de Cordobanes; Escalerillas, calle de las Escalerillas.